THE BRONZE LIE

At this time, however, since the phalanx of Epaminondas bore down upon them alone and neglected the rest of their force, and since Pelopidas engaged them with incredible speed and boldness, their courage and skill were so confounded that there was a flight and slaughter of the Spartan Peers such as had never before been seen.

PLUTARCH, *LIFE OF PELOPIDAS*

THE BRONZE LIE

SHATTERING THE MYTH OF SPARTAN WARRIOR SUPREMACY

MYKE COLE

OSPREY PUBLISHING
Bloomsbury Publishing Plc
Kemp House, Chawley Park, Cumnor Hill, Oxford OX2 9PH, UK
29 Earlsfort Terrace, Dublin 2, Ireland
1385 Broadway, 5th Floor, New York, NY 10018, USA
E-mail: info@ospreypublishing.com
www.ospreypublishing.com

OSPREY is a trademark of Osprey Publishing Ltd

First published in Great Britain in 2021

Artwork in the plate section previously published in the following Osprey titles: CAM 188:
Thermopylae 480 BC (pp. 6 (top) and 7 (bottom)); CAM 195: *Syracuse 415–413 BC* (p. 16
(both images)); CAM 222: *Salamis 480 BC* (pp. 8 (both images) and 9 (top)); CAM 239:
Plataea 479 BC (p. 10 (bottom)); CAM 261: *Pylos and Sphacteria 425 BC* (pp. 12 (bottom),
13 (both images), and 14 (top)); ELI 7: *The Ancient Greeks* (pp. 5 (bottom), 11 (bottom),
17, and 22 (top left)); ELI 66: *The Spartan Army* (pp. 2 (bottom), 4 (top right and bottom),
5 (top), 7 (top), 10 (top), 11 (top), 15, 18, 19 (top two), and 21); WAR 27: *Greek Hoplite
480–323 BC* (pp. 1 (top) and 19 (bottom)); WAR 163: *Spartan Warrior 735–331 BC*
(pp. 1 (bottom), 2 (top), 4 (top left), 9 (bottom), 14 (bottom), 20 (top), 22 (top right));
WAR 180: *Early Iron Age Greek Warrior 1100–700 BC* (p. 3).

A catalog record for this book is available from the British Library.

ISBN: HB 978 1 4728 4375 3; PB 978 1 4728 4376 0; eBook 978 1 4728 4374 6;
ePDF 978 1 4728 4373 9; XML 978 1 4728 4377 7

21 22 23 24 25   10 9 8 7 6 5 4 3 2 1

Maps by www.bounford.com
Chapter opener image: Iron machaira, 5th–4th century BC. (The Metropolitan Museum of
Art, New York, Rogers Fund, 2001, CC0)
Index by Zoe Ross
Typeset by Deanta Global Publishing Services, Chennai, India
Printed and bound in Great Britain by CPI (Group) UK Ltd, Croydon CR0 4YY

Osprey Publishing supports the Woodland Trust, the UK's leading woodland
conservation charity.

To find out more about our authors and books visit **www.ospreypublishing.com**.
Here you will find extracts, author interviews, details of forthcoming events
and the option to sign up for our newsletter.

CONTENTS

PART III
TANGLING MYTH AND REALITY

PREFACE

To say I'm both thrilled and surprised to be writing my second history book is an understatement. The truth is that I never expected to write my first one, much less to have it well received. What began as an obsession with wargaming and a desire to fill a gap I saw in the literature is now maturing into a desire to contribute to the field of military history – a field that, despite its immense popularity, still has so many untold stories and unexamined questions.

As I mature as an historian, I'm delighted to discover that so many of the skills I built as an intelligence and law enforcement officer, as a manhunter on TV, as a counterterrorism "targeter" and as a criminal investigator translate perfectly. History is, in the end, detective work – sifting through facts, digging up evidence, trying to claw truth from tangled memory in witness accounts, battling your own biases in an effort to come up with cogent analysis that rests on the available data.

But while these skills translate, they do *not* make me a full-time professional. My only qualification is that I really, *really* like this stuff and I want to see the widest possible audience falling in love with the topic as much as I have.

I feel that one of the successes of *Legion Versus Phalanx* was its accessibility. I don't come from academia, so I never really learned to write in an academic style. I'm not knocking those who do (I hungrily consume work coming out of academia) but writing *Legion Versus Phalanx* cemented my belief that it's possible to write history that rests on a foundation of rock-solid scholarship and reads like a conversation in a bar with your nerdy friend.

I'm writing for those nerdy barflies – lovers of games like *Rome: Total War II* and *Seven Wonders*, fans of the shows *Rome* and *Spartacus*, tabletop wargamers, sword-and-sandal movie dorks, the wide world of folks who've never taken a graduate-level history class in their lives. I'd be honored if the scholars out there would read me too, but I must beg their patience as I loosen my tie a bit, so to speak.

Keeping this in mind, you'll notice that I sometimes use Greek words only once before switching to their rough English equivalents. Again, my goal here is to make this tent as big as possible, and I don't want to lose readers who don't read classical languages. Sometimes I will not define a word on first use, but only if I think the definition is clear from the context. Hang with me, a definition will surely be coming shortly. A glossary is included in the back of the book for your reference.

I will also try to stick to anglicized versions of Greek names. Lycurgus instead of Lykourgos. Lacedaemon instead of Lakedaimon. Herodotus instead of Herodotos. Again, my goal here is to use terms that are more likely to be recognized, and thus comfortable, for the uninitiated reader.

When I quote historical figures, I will put their words in italics when I am directly quoting from the sources and just in plain quotes when I am paraphrasing for purposes of clarity. Direct quotes from modern figures are also in italics.

While I bring a warfighter's lens to this work, I don't want to exclude those who haven't served. I have often said that nobody owns the military experience. All society is plagued by war at all times, and so military experience is a thing *all* people, service member and civilian alike, share. My experience having fought in Iraq is no more authentic than that of a civilian who has had to go through their life watching that same war unfold on TV, reading about it on Twitter, having it impact their pop culture, politics and interpersonal relationships. These are *both* genuine military experiences, only differing in perspective. Neither is more authentic than the other. Anyone making even a cursory study of warfare knows that organized violence impacts civilians far more significantly than it does combatants.

As with *Legion Versus Phalanx*, I am sticking with BC and AD for dating. My argument remains the same – changing letters without changing the system is just papering over the issue. We all know BCE and CE still means BC and AD, and intent matters. If we're not going to come up with an

PREFACE

entirely new dating system, then we can also simply use the same letters and accept that, in this case, my intent is *not* to convey religious connotations but rather to use terms with which the widest possible audience will be familiar. If this ruffles feathers, I hope you will accept my apology in advance. Insult is absolutely not my intent.

You'll also notice that while this book is about the military history of Sparta, I will be tackling a wide array of topics that seem to have nothing to do with warfare – the personalities of commanders, economics and the love of wealth, poetry and codes of law, social status and personal interactions. I hope the reason for this is clear – one thing that was *not* mythical about ancient Sparta was the important role that war played in Spartan society. The ancient world was violent, and the use of violence was a fundamental part of life to the point where considering it in a vacuum would be counterproductive. To understand how the Spartans fought, we also need to understand how they lived apart from fighting.

While Plutarch tells us that Spartans were the only men in the world for whom fighting a war was a welcome break from training to fight a war, the reality is that they fought no more than other ancient Greek city-states, and less than other ancient powers. But this is still a military history, and one of the best ways to break up Sparta's history into understandable epochs is to use its many wars and to see how each one shaped Spartan life – the fumbling toward the famous Lycurgan social model in the Messenian Wars. The foundation of their legend in the Greco-Persian War. Their eventual mastery of Greece in the Peloponnesian War (or wars, depending on how you reckon them). Their overreach and the eventual snapping of Sparta's spine in the Corinthian and Boeotian Wars. Since my goal in writing this book is to compare Sparta's actual battlefield record with the legend of its military superiority, I will try to be as comprehensive as possible, touching on (very briefly some of the time) most (but not all) of Sparta's many battles, skirmishes, military expeditions and other acts of organized violence. You'll notice that I have opted to select a single representative battle from each overarching war (with the exception of the Messenian Wars and the Corinthian War, for which we don't have enough detailed accounts to really dial in) that marked the epochs of Sparta's history.

I've chosen battles that I feel best serve the goal of comparing Sparta's actual military record to the legend of its prowess, both the standard to which modern people hold Sparta, and the standard (as we know it from the poetry of Tyrtaeus, and from writers such as Xenophon) to which Spartans purportedly held themselves. I will certainly cover many battles. It would be impossible to properly reckon Sparta's truly fascinating military record if I didn't! But I will dive deep on only four.

There's a secondary motive for this – I mentioned before that I write history to emphasize narrative drama without sacrificing scholarship. The action and excitement of warfare, the gripping drama, the heart-rending tragedy, only truly comes to life at the "deck plate level" as we say in the Coast Guard. It is through the point of view of commanders and officers, in the description of the trials and hopes of the rank and file, the suffering of the wounded and dying, that we truly experience a battle narrative. It's at the *tactical* level that we are moved by war's harrowing story.

That said, I do not cover *every* violent conflict Sparta engaged in. There are many skirmishes, raids and even battles throughout the city-state's history that are so poorly documented that little more than a sentence or two can be written about them, and I won't waste your time with that. I am interested in those fights that are well-sourced enough to be analyzed at least to some minor degree, and that can paint an overall picture of Sparta's real battlefield performance that can be compared to their legend.

I have included a color-coded scorecard at the end of the color plates in the center of the book to give you an at-a-glance view of Sparta's military record – when it won, when it lost, when it fought to a draw. In the notes section I indicate things that are relevant in terms of the Bronze Lie we're seeking to dispel (e.g. the death or flight of a commander, the use of trickery to win). I have tried to be as expansive as possible in generating the scorecard. This certainly isn't *all* the fights Sparta got into, but I feel confident it's most of them.

My criteria for selection are necessarily loose. I want the reader to consider Sparta in *every* kind of military engagement – skirmishes and sieges, on land and sea, Spartan leaders in command of non-Spartan troops, set-piece battles between phalanxes, running fights on bad terrain. If you're looking for an exact taxonomy for my selection I will honestly shrug my shoulders and say I aimed for a large enough sample to give us a fairly (but not entirely) complete picture of how Sparta did when it decided to use violence.

PREFACE

In *Legion Versus Phalanx*, I included sections on historiography and the fundamentals of ancient battle up front. My goal there was to make sure that people coming to the topic with absolutely no general historical or specific ancient warfare knowledge would have the basics they needed to understand what was coming later in the book. Since many of my readers turned out to already know these basics, I have included both sections (adapted a bit to match this book) as appendixes A and B in the back this time. If you are new to either the study of history (and the use of primary sources) or to ancient warfare, please go read both of those appendixes before starting the book. I did my best to keep them short and entertaining, and they will get you rapidly up to speed to tackle the rest of the book (and make you a great conversationalist at parties). I am writing to inform. I am writing to make a point. But I also freely admit that I am writing to entertain. And I need the space to give the truly epic battles I will cover in this book their due.

This book, and my career as a historian, would not be possible without the generous help of a veritable army of people who graciously donated their time and counsel. First and foremost among these will always be Professor Michael Livingston at the Citadel, who quickly moved from a mentor to a dear friend and counselor, and who has kept me on track personally and professionally. Mike also co-starred with me on my last TV show, which made the whole experience an absolute blast. Next up is Professor Stephen Hodkinson of the University of Nottingham and the internationally acknowledged authority on Sparta. Having his input is a bit like a novice guitar player getting pointers from Jimi Hendrix, and I am beyond grateful for his time, attention and encouragement. Others who have supported my work include Professor Joel Christensen of Brandeis, Dr Stephanie Craven, Professor Matt Simonton of Arizona State University, Professor John Ma of Columbia University and Professor Sarah Bond of the University of Iowa. Some of these people have met with me personally, exchanged emails, and even reviewed my writing. Others have inspired me with their Twitter activism and incredible published work.

I also want to thank my publisher Osprey and my editor Marcus Cowper, and Mr Richard Sullivan, who believed in me and championed my work. I am sure I am forgetting some people, and beg their forgiveness in advance.

Lastly this – the story of Sparta is a warrior's story and I am, for better or worse, a warrior. This is my story to tell. An old friend once told me, "if you don't tell your story, someone else will, and I promise you, they'll get it wrong."

For too long, we've been getting Sparta's warrior story wrong. It's my fervent hope that this book can contribute to the hard work of getting it right.

Myke Cole
Hudson Valley, NY 2021

LIST OF MAPS

The Persian Empire

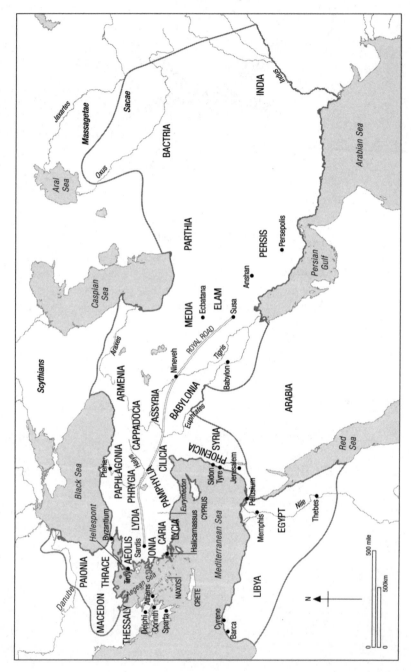

Greece, the Aegean and Western Asia

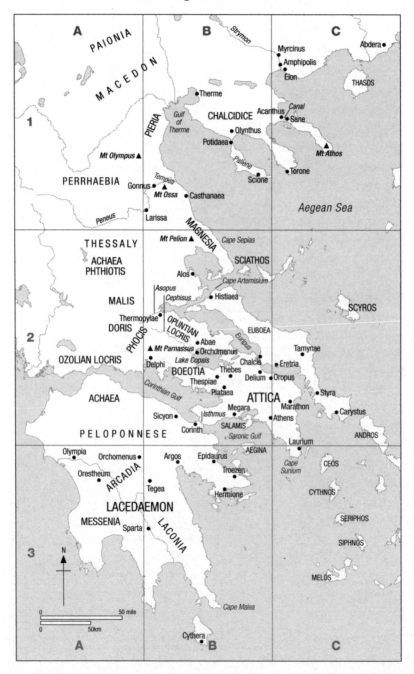

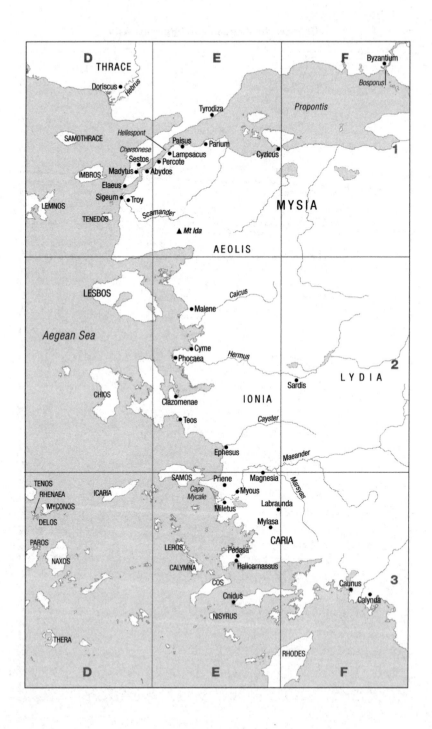

PART I

THE MYTH OF SPARTA

INTRODUCTION

While this is a military history, it's a work that cannot help but be culturally, politically and socially charged. In the course of researching this book, I have come to fully understand how invested people are in what the pioneering early 20th century Sparta scholar François Ollier called *Le Mirage Spartiate* – "The Spartan Mirage." It is truly breathtaking how committed people are to the legend of the Spartans as history's greatest warriors.

I published three short pieces questioning Spartan superiority while preparing for this book, one in *Military History Now*, one in *The Daily Beast* and a third in *The New Republic*. The first got me angry comments like "You're just jealous." The other two got me death threats. In reading these, I began to truly appreciate how much the Spartans mean to so many people, even 2,500 years after the battle that set the foundation stone for their legend.

Laconophilia – a love of all things Spartan – is a very real thing even in 2021. The Spartan legend is so pervasive in American, British and European culture that we marinade in it. So it's not surprising to find it coloring even the work of professional historians. There is far, far, *far* too much material on the Spartans that doesn't do the simple work of reckoning their documented military record against the myth of their might, with the end goal of seeing them for who they actually were.

Under normal circumstances, I'd be content to let this lie. Lord knows there are plenty of historical misconceptions enshrined in popular culture. Loose lips, in fact, never sank a single ship. Vikings actually didn't have horns on their helmets. Napoleon wasn't any shorter than the average Frenchman.

But the misconception of Spartan military supremacy has been put to work in service to darker forces, a development that cries out for someone to set the record, loudly and publicly, straight.

We live in an age where the term "toxic masculinity" is repeated by a world grappling with an epidemic of violence, xenophobia and a resurgence of political extremism that has severely darkened our horizons. This term is an effort by intellectuals to dial in on what's going on. At the heart of what can make masculinity toxic, we see the Spartan myth at work – adopted as a sacred cow by right-wing extremists worldwide, held aloft as a symbol of beleaguered nativists standing, as they believe the Spartans did at Thermopylae in 480 BC, against a tide of immigration, globalism and erosion of native identity. Zack Snyder's famous film *300*, an extremely faithful adaption of the Frank Miller comic of the same name, is absolutely transparent in its portrayal of the popular impression of the Spartans – white men who stand for freedom against dark-skinned foreigners seeking to invade and subvert the purity of European culture. That Miller and Snyder's view is so widely shared serves only to make it more disgusting, and the task of tearing it down more urgent.

Orwell's famous quote bears repeating here: "He who controls the past, controls the future." We have an obligation now, more than ever, to poke holes in legends, to dispel myths. As public trust in media erodes, as psychological operations upset elections, as "alternative facts" become the order of the day, commitment to the truth is critical. In the current crisis, worsening daily, truth is perhaps the greatest weapon we have. And it's a weapon I will gladly use. Because the people sending me those death threats were so upset by my writing about warriors, that they forgot they were addressing one.

In an age that is seeing the rise of totalitarian, nationalist, "blood and soil" style hard-right conservatism, it is more vital than ever to present the historical record accurately. I cannot stop the hard right from taking inspiration in the purported deeds of Spartan warriors, but I *can* examine their record honestly, and try to shed light on the reality of their limits as fighting men.

Note the word *truth*. I am writing this book to dispel a bronze lie, not to replace it with a paper one. I am not here to savage the Spartans. I am here to *see* them, to treat them not as the gods of war they have been made out to be, but as the human beings I know they were. Not to blame them, but to treat them fairly. This is a mistake we make with all warrior elites – Samurai, medieval European knights, modern-day US Navy SEALs or British SAS operators. There is an unfortunate tendency to assume that military elites are infallible, and, worse, to assume that being a great fighter makes someone a great *person*, that military might somehow equals moral superiority.

Nothing could be further from the truth, of course. I once tweeted "Human beings are human beings at all times. Show me an elite warrior cult revered for their stoic self-deprivation, and I'll show you examples of them succumbing to bribes, running from fights, seeking personal advantage, and making poor tactical decisions." This is true of Vikings, Gurkhas and Air Force Pararescuemen. It is true of the Spartans, too.

Researching this book, I found myself inspired by the *humanity* of the Spartans – people just as flawed as I am, just as striving and ambitious as I am, just as prone to error as I am. When we strip away the myth and see the people, we can finally connect to and be moved by them. Because the Spartans *were* extraordinary and they *did* do amazing things. And if they did, well, maybe we can too.

My feelings about *300* are actually more mixed than you might think. The film, which depicts the supposedly glorious stand of the 300 Spartan hoplites at Thermopylae in 480 BC, outnumbered perhaps 20-to-1 by the Achaemenid Persian army of Xerxes I, is rife with all the racist stereotypes I despise. But the film is also probably the single greatest catalyst for public interest in ancient military history. That said, it is *also* the single greatest engine for the perpetuation of the toxic myth of Spartan military superiority.

But we can't just blame *300*. Even before the film came out, "Spartan" was one of those words grown far beyond its denotation. It's a synonym for bare and simple living, for prioritizing the state over the individual, for "laconic" brevity (from "Laconia" – the land Spartans hailed from), and most of all for unrivaled military excellence. Before *300* high schools across the country already named their sports teams "the Spartans" in the hopes of invoking warrior primacy. The word "Spartan" means the ability to endure any hardship without complaint, to suffer endlessly without expressing emotion. In Plutarch's *Life of Lycurgus*, there's an impressive story about a Spartan boy who stole a fox and hid it under his cloak. He kept it hidden there without showing any hint of pain or guilt, presumably as he tried to carry the animal someplace he could kill and eat it (Spartan youths were famously half-starved and encouraged to steal their food) until he suddenly collapsed, dead. The fox had been gnawing at his insides under the cloak. The boy refused to show pain or to admit that he had stolen the fox, preferring slow death.

Even before *300*, such was the popular reputation of the Spartans.

300 kicked this myth into overdrive. Since the film, triathletes and "mud run" enthusiasts don sports gear blazoned with the word. The famous firearms manufacturer Sig Sauer offers a "Spartan" variant of its 1911 pattern handgun. Spartan Arms is one of the busier gun sellers in Las Vegas. The stylized Corinthian helmet worn by the Spartan king Leonidas in *300* is seen everywhere, from pistol handles to patches to t-shirts, as a shorthand for military might, for endurance against the odds, persevering through to the ultimate victory. Thanks to *300*, the Spartans have been seared on the public consciousness as masters of war.

But there's one small problem.

They weren't.

In fact, even a cursory examination of the historical record reveals that the Spartans lost again and again. The literary sources show us Spartan kings running from fights, failing in the heat of battle, outsmarted and outmaneuvered and just plain outfought. Spartans floundered and died in the waters off the coast of Naxos, outsailed by the Athenians they'd so recently beaten in the Peloponnesian Wars (404 BC). At Leuctra in 371 BC, their greatest warriors were run down and killed by another 300 – the Sacred Band of Thebes (which disputed legend has as 150 pairs of homosexual lovers) – who not only crushed the Spartans, but killed their king in a battle so decisive that a Spartan relief army opted to retreat rather than take vengeance. Even Thermopylae in 480 BC, the battle that made the Spartans' reputation, while certainly a propaganda victory, was little more than a speed bump beneath the wheel of the Achaemenid war machine that went on to rampage across Greece unopposed, burning Athens to the ground.

This is not to say the Spartans were not great warriors at all. They absolutely were. For a time, they did produce the finest heavy infantry in Greece, a fighting force that propelled them (with help from incompetent enemies and plenty of Persian gold) to a brief hegemony over the entire land. The Spartans enjoyed some truly glorious victories, at Mycale and First Mantinea, at the Nemea and Aegospotami, but these are equaled by truly disastrous defeats.

All of this of course raises the question of the Spartans' military legacy – "Just how good were they really?" That's what I will seek to do with this book – to review the material and literary record and examine how the Spartans fought, how they carried themselves in victory and defeat, when they were brave and when they were not; and to shed light on how well the history supports the legend. I will track most of the battles that Sparta fought, keeping score, and present to the reader a color-coded scorecard at the end of the color plates in the center of the book, which will allow you to see at a glance Sparta's nearly full record – how it did in fight after fight, throughout its entire history – from its first known battles in the Messenian Wars, to its final collapse and subsumption by the Achaean League, which ended its run as an independent power. This scorecard isn't comprehensive, but I do feel confident that I've at least covered the majority of Sparta's military actions, more than enough to give you a real overall view of how it performed on the battlefield.

The "Bronze Lie" I am seeking to refute in this book is simply this – that the Spartans were history's greatest warriors. But this falsehood is a pediment supported by many pillars. Those pillars are additional lies that also have to be knocked down if we want to make the pediment fall. So, I include the following falsehoods as part of the Bronze Lie this book will dispel:

- The Spartans never surrendered and never ran from a fight. They always preferred death to dishonor. They feared no enemy.
- The Spartans hated wealth and luxury and refused to use money. They only ever wore simple clothing and ate simple food. They neither gave nor received bribes.
- The Spartans held the good of the city-state above the individual. They did not seek individual fame or glory.
- The Spartans were the ultimate xenophobes. They hated foreigners, especially the Persians, and kept Greece "free" (from foreign influence) and "for the Greeks."
- The Spartans loved liberty, and opposed tyranny.

I will work to dismantle each of these pillars using examples from Sparta's history, until the whole Bronze Lie comes crashing down.

In this introduction, I've established the popular myth of who the ancient Spartans were. In the chapters that follow, I will show the reality. Finally, I will show what happens when the myth and the reality get tangled and examine the far right's perversion of the Spartans to meet its political objectives, and the long history of this misuse.

Getting at the truth of ancient history is tough. Few sources survive and those that do were written by humans with agendas of their own. We can't be angry at the ancient writers for their biases. We are all, as humans, bound to our own world view. This is as true for you reading this book as it was for the ancients. It's true for me, too. The historian's greatest challenge is to cut through the biases of the sources, even as we examine our own biases – and in the end to reach something akin to truth.

In this book, you will see that I have strong opinions about the Spartans, opinions that are not always kind.

But they are, to the best that I can make them, fair.

I will be guided by the *evidence* – singing the Spartans' praises when the evidence shows them worthy of praise, and calling them out when the evidence shows them worthy of condemnation.

And in the end, I'll lean on the turn of the 5th century BC philosopher Xenophanes of Colophon: "*There never was nor will be a man who can be sure of the gods and about all the things I speak of. Even if he should by chance speak the truth, he would not know he had done so.*"

I'll do my best, and leave the rest to the gods.

PART II

THE REALITY OF SPARTA

I

CUCKOLD KINGS AND WOLVES' WORK: BEHIND THE SPARTAN MIRAGE

Some say that a Sybarite who traveled to Sparta and was entertained in their public mess said: "It is no wonder that Spartans are the bravest men in the world; for anyone in his right mind would prefer to die ten thousand times rather than live so poorly."

Athenaeus, *Dinner Table Philosophers*

We know the Spartans are famous for their myth, which of course begs the question, what was their reality?

Here we come up against Ollier's Spartan Mirage – of all the ancient Greeks, the secretive Spartans are the hardest to understand. If we're going to properly consider the battles that follow, we need to examine the society that underpinned the Spartan military machine. We also need to understand how the Greeks waged war in the period of Sparta's legend. In all cases, we need to contrast the myth with the reality – for in almost every specific instance of Sparta's legend there are exceptions and contradictions.

The Impenetrable Mists of Sparta's Mythic Past

It's perhaps not surprising that we first meet the Spartans in a tangled tale of jumbled myth and fact – Homer's *Iliad*, which tells the story of the Spartan king Menelaus and his beautiful wife Helen, romanced out of his grasp (depending on which version of the story you believe) by Paris to far-flung Troy in what is now western Turkey, sparking one of the greatest amphibious assaults in history.

It's interesting that Sparta's first tangled myth-fact revolves around a cuckold king. Spartan women enjoyed considerable freedom and dignity (at least by the epically misogynistic standards of ancient Greece). Nor was Menelaus the last Spartan king with a publicly unfaithful wife. Timaea, the wife of the Spartan king Agis II, was widely believed to have had an affair with the Athenian celebrity general Alcibiades, greatly influencing both his future and the outcome of the Decelean phase of the Peloponnesian Wars (413–404 BC). Unmarried Spartan girls engaged in regular public exercise (purportedly in the nude, though this is disputed), trained in running and wrestling, could own and inherit property, and enjoyed enough freedom to provoke the famous 4th century BC philosopher Aristotle to complain that the Spartans were "ruled by their women."

The Roman city of Tarentum (modern-day Taranto) was founded as Taras – a Spartan colony initially built by the *partheniai* – the "sons of virgins." These men were, according to one story, the bastard children of unfaithful Spartan wives who took lovers while their husbands were away during the First Messenian War (probably in the mid-8th century BC). Rather than accept these children, the Spartans expelled them, sending them abroad to found the new city. There are other explanations that allow the Spartan men to avoid being cuckolded, but the logic of all the tales of the *partheniai* is tortured, and the sexual freedom of the Spartan women makes as much sense as any other.

Menelaus' kingdom likely belonged to the civilization lost during the turn of the 12th century BC as a result of an unknown cataclysm. Some scholars attributed this cataclysm to a migration that saw the settlement of the Peloponnese (Greece's southern peninsula) by the Dorians, the progenitors of classical Sparta. Even this early foundation tale is a tangled mass of fact and myth. There are good reasons both to believe and to disbelieve that a Dorian migration occurred, but 19th century AD historians tried to attach it to the myth of the "Return of the Heraclids" – in which the Dorians aided the sons of the demigod and hero Heracles, taking rightful possession of their lost lands. This was, of course, a myth that the Spartans eagerly exploited. Having your kings descended from one of the most famous demigod warriors, one known first and foremost for his great strength, certainly had propaganda value.

The "wolf's work" of founding the city

Part of the problem with understanding the Spartans is that the main document that modern people accept as fact is Plutarch's biography *Life of Lycurgus*. But Plutarch was writing at the turn of the 2nd century AD, around a thousand years after the events he was describing. Most modern historians agree that *Life of Lycurgus* is little more than a catalog of all the common myths about Sparta, the vast majority of them false. But there are kernels of truth in there, or at least guideposts to how these distortions came to be accepted as fact, so we can't dismiss Plutarch's account altogether. However we have to treat it very, very carefully as we examine what is very likely a mostly mythic account of Sparta's foundation.

The Spartans had as their founding father the almost certainly mythical Lycurgus – which roughly translates to "wolf's work" or "wolf's deeds." Even Plutarch admits that "*the history of these times is a labyrinth*" and "*Of Lycurgus the Lawgiver, nothing can be said which is not contested.*" As with all other things Spartan, fact and myth are hopelessly tangled, and we have to reckon with legends to have any chance of even glimpsing the truth. We also have to be willing to admit the likelihood that Lycurgus is entirely made up – and that much of his story is a fiction created by much later Spartans (and in particular the reformer Spartan kings of the Hellenistic era (323–31 BC), Agis IV and Cleomenes III, both of whom we'll meet later) in an effort to justify their coups and later efforts to change the Spartan government.

Here is what we are told in Plutarch – Lycurgus voluntarily went abroad to silence rumors that he sought to steal the Spartan throne from his ward

Charilaus (the son of Lycurgus' dead brother Polydectes). His travels took him to Crete and Egypt as well as Ionia (modern Turkey's west coast) and North Africa, where he learned both what was good in government (Crete), and what was decadent (Ionia). He then returned to Sparta, intent on reforming the government.

Knowing that this effort would require divine sanction, he traveled to Delphi to consult the famous oracle – a woman who supposedly could channel the voice of the god Apollo. The Pythia (another name for the oracle) gave Lycurgus a divinely inspired constitution that promised, according to Plutarch, to be the best in the world. Lycurgus returned with this "Great Rhetra" (and apparently numerous less great rhetras) which formed the whole of Sparta's new system of government. It was entirely oral (presumably Lycurgus got it directly from the Pythia in verse). Indeed Lycurgus forbade writing down Sparta's laws to ensure that all citizens would get to know them by heart.

Lycurgus was now ready to persuade his fellow Spartans to accept his reforms. Plutarch tells us he *"ordered thirty of the best men to go armed into the marketplace at dawn, to strike worry and terror into those who opposed him."* Few scholars remark on what seems to be a story of a Spartan regent sent into exile, who then returned and pulled off a military coup. To hear Plutarch tell it, the wisdom of Lycurgus' reforms and his good and wise nature brought everyone over to his side to live happily under his new and, as we'll see, extremely draconian regime, rather than the fact that he had 30 goons in the market ready to break the legs of anyone who had different ideas. We can never know the absolute truth, but he remains known to history as Lycurgus "the Lawgiver" and not Lycurgus "the Dictator."

Herodotus, the 5th century BC Greek historian known as "the father of history," cast doubt on the oracle's role in the story, saying the Spartans themselves said that Lycurgus instituted his reforms while he was regent, modeling them on the Cretan system of government. Lycurgus at least maintained Sparta's unique dual system of kingship – a traditional monarchy with co-rulers handing down power from father to son through two royal houses, the Agiads and Eurypontids.

Lycurgus supposedly instituted many reforms, which we know from other ancient sources formed the governing structure for Sparta throughout almost its entire ancient history. These included the establishment of the *gerousia* or council of elders, which consisted of 28 men over the age of 60, each elected to the office for life. The council was padded out to 30 by the two co-kings (indeed the one written Spartan law that survives confirms this). The elders decided what issues would be voted on by the citizen assembly and also acted as the Spartan court of last resort, with the right to try even the kings.

If you believe Herodotus, Lycurgus also established the ephorate, five Spartans elected for a single year and forbidden to hold the office more than once (Plutarch claims that the ephorate wasn't established until 130 years after Lycurgus' death). These ephors (the word means "guardians") served as chief executives of the state, with powers that seemed tailored to acting as a check on the dual kings, including sending two ephors to accompany the kings on military campaigns to keep an eye on them (following a disastrous disagreement between the two ruling co-kings attempting to invade Athens in 506 BC) and having the power to indict the kings if their conduct ran counter to Spartan law. At least later in Sparta's history, one of the kings led the army in the field, while the other remained at Sparta to oversee the day-to-day administration of the city-state. Aristotle, who more than once stuck a pin in the balloon of the Spartan legend, reminds us that the ephors' power was excessive and that they used their authority to break the law and take delight in sensual pleasures (presumably food, luxury goods and the hoarding of wealth) that were denied to other Spartans.

Aristotle also points out the frankly hilarious method of electing the ephors. The candidate names were read out to the assembly, who yelled to express support for their preferred candidate. Those for whom the assembly yelled the loudest were chosen. Aristotle notes that this system was easy to abuse and it's hard to disagree with him.

Lycurgus' arguably most significant reform was the creation of the requirements for Spartan citizens. A fully fledged Spartan citizen was known as a Spartiate (they referred to one another as *homoioi*, which roughly translates to "peers" or "similars"), and the following was demanded of them: membership in the communal dining mess or *syssition*; maintenance of their *klēros* or portion of land (part of a land redistribution program that Lycurgus purportedly undertook to eliminate wealth inequality. Historians have proven this redistribution did not actually take place); and graduation from the *agōgē* (Spartan boys were stripped from their families and enrolled in this rigorous military education at the age of seven). Failure to be selected to one of the 15 (or so)-man communal messes, or to pay one's mess bill (Plutarch states each member had to make a monthly contribution of a bushel of barley, 8 gallons of wine, 5 pounds of cheese, 2½ pounds of figs and some money to buy meat and fish. A portion of the proceeds from all hunting expeditions was also sent to the mess), or to graduate the *agōgē* could resign a Spartan to lifelong status as one of *hypomeiones* or "Inferiors," a quasi-citizen status that isn't well understood, but likely still allowed the Spartan to fight as part of the army.

Apart from the full Spartiate citizen Peers, Spartan society was composed of *perioikoi* or "people who live around," presumably because they lived in the hills and along the coasts of Laconia outside the core Spartan villages. These *perioikoi* were free, living in their own communities, but firmly under the Spartan thumb and with no voting rights in the Spartan assembly. They owned land, which was necessary to support them as warriors, as they formed a significant portion of the Spartan army.

Lycurgus' laws forbade the Peers from engaging in *any* work other than training for war, and so the *perioikoi* served as Sparta's artisans, manufacturers and craftsmen, making arms and armor, pots and metalwork, and conducting whatever trade the Spartan state required.

However, Lycurgus' prohibition of all work for Peers is another pillar of the Bronze Lie – the notion that the Spartan's superwarrior status came from a single-minded focus on military training. The reality was far more expansive. Forbidden to work, Spartan Peers instead lived lives of leisure. Sure, they trained for war, but they also socialized, engaged in non-military exercises, sang and danced, hunted and managed their agricultural estates. A Spartan Peer's life was far more that of the aristocrat dandy than the hard-bitten single-minded warrior.

Agricultural labor was carried out by another class of Spartan, the *helots*. The helots were Sparta's slave class. Legend has it they were directly tied to the land redistributed under Lycurgus' reforms, not owned by individuals, and thus technically state property. However, more recent research shows the helots were privately owned by individual Peers, but that their use of helot labor was subject to intensive state oversight.

The keeping of slaves was hardly unique to Sparta, but helotage shocked other Greeks as the helots were neither foreigners, nor debt-slaves, nor captured barbarians. They were the Spartans' neighbors, speaking the same language, sharing the same culture, subjugated methodically and held down in bondage as a social class for centuries.

Helots shaped Spartan society more than any other population. This is because the helots outnumbered the Spartan citizenry by a huge number. Xenophon said that the helots, along with the Inferiors and the *perioikoi*, would be more than happy to "*eat the Peers raw.*" He was referring to a specific 4th century BC plot to overthrow the Spartan state, but many scholars believe that the danger of a helot revolt against the vastly outnumbered Peers was constant, prompting them to note that Sparta's commitment to military excellence was less about dominating the rest of Greece and more about protecting the tiny minority of Peers from being chewed to pieces by their slaves.

Helots attended their masters at war, carrying gear, performing camp labor, and often fighting as light infantry. Later in Sparta's history, the *oliganthrōpia* or shortage of full Peers forced Sparta to free helots and grant them the status of *neodamōdeis* or "New People" so they could fight in the army as heavy infantry, but we also have disputed evidence (in Pausanias and Herodotus) of helots fighting alongside their oppressors in much earlier battles. Helots also provided domestic services for Spartan women.

By all accounts, the helots were treated brutally and routinely humiliated (Plutarch tells us they were forced to get drunk so that older Peers could demonstrate to their younger charges the dangers of consuming too much wine). The ephors annually declared war on the helots so no ritual pollution would accrue from their murder (the ephors also charged the Peers with shaving their mustaches and obeying the laws – supposedly to get them used to obeying even trifling rules).

The most promising Spartans on the cusp of adulthood (around 28 years old) were enrolled in the crypteia or "Secret Squad" and sent out among the helots with nothing but knives and basic supplies. They would hide by day and by night murder either every helot they could find, or just those helots who appeared most likely to emerge as leaders of a revolt (depending on whose story you believe), with the goal of generally spreading terror among the helots and reminding them that the Peers could reach out and touch them whenever and wherever they wanted.

Another key pillar of the Bronze Lie is Lycurgus' supposed banning of the use of gold and silver coins, replacing them with iron that was too large and heavy to store and transport easily. But this myth is shot full of questions and contradictions.

Firstly, depending on when Lycurgus' reforms were introduced, they may have predated the use of any coinage in ancient Greece. Further, there is some evidence to indicate that Spartans used the gold and silver coinage of other Greek city-states. You see above where Plutarch talks about money necessary to buy meat and fish as part of a Spartan's mess dues. The late 4th century BC Greek writer Dicaearchus clarifies that the money required was "*ten Aeginetan obols*" but it's not clear what he means by this. An obol (*obolos*) could refer to a weight, or it could refer to a coin. Dicaearchus could be referring to the Spartan iron equivalent of an obol in Lycurgus' iron money, but it is far more likely that he is referring to gold or silver money being used according to the Aeginetan standard, one of two standards for currency in mainland Greece at the time (the other standard being the Attic). The indication of a silver currency standard strongly indicates that the Spartans were indeed using normal money.

Further evidence comes from a song attributed to the famous Spartan ephor Chilon in the 6th century BC by the 3rd century AD biographer Diogenes Laertius: "*A hard whetstone is the best test for gold, a sure proof of purity, and for us to know their purity of mind, gold itself is the best test of men.*" If this song is correctly dated and attributed, it shows an influential Spartan leader very concerned about the corrupting influence of money. It's possible that Chilon is referring to other Greeks or even "barbarians" (non-Greeks, from the Greek *barbaros*, meaning "they don't speak Greek. Everything they say just sounds like 'bar bar bar'"), but in closed and xenophobic Sparta, it's just as likely he's talking about his own people. Some modern scholars believe that Peers routinely owned and used non-iron money and in particular Aeginetan currency.

The 7th century BC poet Alcaeus notes a supposed Spartan saying "Aristodemus, they say, once put it very effectively in Sparta: 'A man is what he owns, and not a single poor man is noble or respected.'" It would be surprising if this saying evolved in a Spartan society where money was forbidden and all wealth was equal. A supposed oracle from Delphi ran: "*Love of money will destroy Sparta, but nothing else.*" More holes in the Bronze Lie of Sparta's supposed hatred for wealth.

In Plutarch's *Life of Lysander* he describes the theft of public money by the Spartan commander Gylippus, and a protracted effort to outlaw the use of gold and silver within the city – an act that wouldn't have been necessary unless that money was being used in the first place. Further, Plutarch is clear that the effort to ban precious metal currency was defeated by the rich and powerful.

Lycurgus' reforms purportedly also set up a system in which all wealth was distributed equally and rules were put in place governing everything from building one's home to owning property, which ensured that everyone had only what they needed and no more. But this legend doesn't match up to the evidence, and it's pretty clear that Spartan society had both rich and poor. Our sources are rife with stories of Spartans taking and offering bribes, swindling and tricking people out of money, and generally seeking personal wealth. The notion that Spartans hated wealth and embraced a "Spartan" lifestyle devoid of all luxury, one of the pillars of the Bronze Lie, is straight up false.

While Lycurgus' reforms paint a picture of a truly extraordinary society, they also show us a system geared entirely around the welfare of a tiny minority of Peers at the top of the social ladder. At the time of the Battle of Thermopylae in 480 BC, Sparta could field just 8,000 of these Peers (they sent only 300 not counting their king). To give you a sense of the scale of the Spartan apartheid system, at the Battle of Plataea the following year, the 5,000 Spartan Peers were accompanied by 35,000 helots – seven for each citizen (though this mobilization was exceptional, it still shows the disparity in population between Peers and their inferiors). The vast majority of Spartan society lived either as slaves or as other second-class citizens, while a tiny minority enjoyed complete freedom from labor of any kind.

But this tiny minority at the top had a hard time staying there. Contrary to the myth of equal land distribution in Plutarch, inequality in land ownership meant that Spartan Peers often lost their position in their communal messes due to inability to pay the mess dues, which in turn meant they lost their status as Peers and became Inferiors. This steady shrinking of the number of Peers would eventually become a crisis for Sparta, as we'll see.

One last thing to note about the Lycurgan reforms – they were clearly revolutionary, sweeping and dramatic. I find it highly unlikely that any society could undergo such sweeping changes suddenly, even as a result of a military coup. Big changes like these usually come gradually. It makes far more sense to me that the Lycurgan model of Spartan society, to the extent that it was true at all, was arrived at over decades if not centuries of trial and error, and that a backstory of the mythical Lycurgus was added later.

But if you accept Lycurgus' existence and Plutarch's story of his life at face value (and unfortunately, many people do), its end has a truly mythic resonance. Lycurgus extracted an oath from the Spartan kings, elders and people that they would make no changes to his laws until he returned from a trip to the oracle at Delphi. The oracle supposedly told Lycurgus that the laws he had established were good and that Sparta would prosper as long as it held to them. Lycurgus then starved himself to death, for if he never returned to Sparta, the Spartans would have to keep their oath and uphold his laws forever.

Hoplite Warfare in Classical Greece – Arms, Armor and Tactics

We have to depart from Sparta for a moment to talk more generally about how the Greeks fought in the classical period (roughly the 5th to 4th centuries BC) and then examine how the Spartans specifically organized, armed and fought. This will give you the information you need to understand the battles we'll be examining in the later chapters.

The classical Greek battlefield was dominated by the hoplite (in Greek *hoplitēs*, pronounced in Greek as "hoplee-tays" but anglicized as hoplite, pronounced "hop-light"). *Hoplitēs* comes from the Greek word *hopla*, meaning "panoply," or "war gear." The hoplite therefore was "the guy with all the gear." It was a fitting title, because the hoplite was the most heavily armored infantryman of his day. He wore a bronze helmet and greaves (a pair of combination shin and knee guards that were form fitted to the calf and shin, often embossed to show the contours of the muscle and using the metal's natural flexibility to "clip on" to the leg), and a bronze cuirass (body armor).

Prior to the 6th century BC, there's evidence of more complete armor, including vambraces (forearm protection), rerebraces (upper arm protection), ankle guards, cuisses (thigh armor) and even sabatons (foot armor), but all of this extra protection seems to have been discarded by the height of the classical period.

Indeed, lightening of armor is a trend we see beginning to accelerate in the 6th century BC, as bronze body armor began to be replaced with cuirasses made of layers of glued linen (*linothorax*), or leather (*spolas*), which were lighter, breathable and more flexible. The linen or leather body armor would often be fitted with a kilt made of two layers of linen or leather flaps called *pteryges* ("feathers") that provided protection for the groin, buttocks and upper thighs. This new body armor possibly came into fashion as a reaction to the Greek experience of fighting Persian archers, which highlighted the need to close with the enemy quickly to limit the number of shots he could get off. It's interesting to note that during this period, the first armored foot race (*hoplitodromos*) was introduced in the Olympic Games, possibly as the Greeks strove to increase their ability to run in armor so that they could close with enemy archers.

A brief aside to note that some scholars dispute whether linen cuirasses were ever used and insist instead that the leather *spolas* body armor was commonly worn. It's an ongoing debate that I won't take a side in, and both camps present compelling evidence.

The bronze cuirass began with a distinctive bell shape in two pieces (breastplate and backplate), including a flaring lip over the hips. In the early 5th century BC, this was replaced with a two-piece bronze cuirass that got rid of the flaring lip, and included cutaways over the hips to allow for more freedom of movement. These new cuirasses were frequently embossed to mimic the muscles of a fit man.

This full armor began to disappear at the turn of the 5th century BC until most hoplites, Spartans included, got rid of both body armor and greaves and relied entirely on their shield and helmet for protection. This was probably a decision to increase mobility and prevent overheating as increasing missile combat (by "missiles," I mean anything launched or

THE BRONZE LIE

thrown – rocks, javelins, arrows, sling bullets) made closing with the enemy more and more important. Body armor and greaves came back into use once the Greeks came into conflict with neighboring Macedon under Philip II and his son Alexander the Great in the 4th century BC, and hoplites were replaced with *pezhetairoi* or "foot companions," who fought in much closer ranks using a very long (around 21-foot) pike which severely limited mobility. Without the ability to maneuver or close with an enemy quickly, the Macedonian heavy infantryman was forced to rely on heavy armor. The Greeks, in turn, were now facing a less mobile enemy who relied far less on missile combat, and so began to increase their own reliance on armor to counter this new threat.

The hoplite's helmet from around the 7th century BC was the "Corinthian" pattern (named because it appears on Corinthian pottery, and also because Herodotus straight up calls it a Corinthian helmet) that protected the head, neck and face, leaving a kind of Y-shaped opening for seeing and breathing. This helmet, made from a single sheet of bronze, offered great protection, but limited vision and hearing and could also make the wearer overheat. In the same period that body armor began disappearing, hoplites also replaced the Corinthian helmet with other patterns, most notably the simple, conical *pilos* style which was little more than a bronze (and later felt or leather) cap covering the back and top of the head.

The hoplite's helmet usually had a stiff and highly decorated horsehair crest. Apart from decoration, this crest was meant to make the hoplite appear taller and more intimidating. These crests almost always ran from front to back, but Spartan officers and kings may have worn transverse (side-to-side) crests. The later Roman centurion (an officer in command of approximately 60–100 Roman legionaries) definitely wore a transverse crest, possibly an outgrowth of this tradition.

The hoplite's principal piece of equipment was his *aspis*, a round, bronze-faced, wooden shield nearly 3 feet in diameter. The shield's grip was revolutionary for its time – instead of a central handle inside the shield's protruding center or "boss," the *aspis* used an "Argive" grip (named for the ancient Greek city-state of Argos). This grip consisted of a bronze loop (the *porpax*) through which the warrior passed his arm up to the elbow. He then grasped the *antilabē*, a handle of leather or cord attached to the inside of the shield's right rim. This created tension between the elbow and hand, providing greater stability to, and control over, the shield. These shields were heavy, at least 16 pounds for lighter versions, but they were deeply convex, allowing the warrior to rest the upper lip on his shoulder so that his skeleton could take the weight.

The Spartans in particular attached great significance to the shield and regarded its loss as a signal dishonor and sign of cowardice, but as with all Spartan legends, there are glaring contradictions. Thucydides describes the great Spartan hero Brasidas clearly losing his shield at the Battle of Sphacteria in 425 BC and makes no mention of the man being shamed for it. Plutarch gives us probably the most famous anecdote about Spartan shields – a Spartan mother handing her son his shield as he prepares to head out for battle. "*Return with this or on this*," she says – meaning that he should bring the shield home victorious, or be carried on it as a corpse. However, there's plenty of evidence to show that Spartans didn't carry their war dead home, but instead buried them in communal tombs (*polyandria*) in the closest allied territory to the battlefield. In the 1930s, the Deutsches Archäologisches Institut excavated a tomb in Athens that housed 23 Spartan skeletons, all showing battle wounds. Pottery of the period depicts Spartan warriors carrying their dead on their shoulders, as do numerous depictions of the Homeric hero Ajax carrying the body of Achilles. It's possible these depict the practice of carrying Spartan dead to the communal tombs. It's also possible that the Spartan mother Plutarch describes was referencing a truly ancient practice that went out of style before ancient writers began chronicling it or that it was an expression of some other custom (I've heard the suggestion that it might mean the dead warrior's name was inscribed on the inside of his shield, which would be brought home by a comrade). In the end, we can't know the truth, but it's another example of the Spartan myth and the reality of the sources conflicting.

A less dramatic and more important saying comes also from Plutarch, who quotes the Spartan king Demaratus (later a Persian lackey and advisor) answering a question about why Spartans held those who threw away their shields in contempt, but not those who threw away their helmets or body armor: "*Because these* [helmets and cuirasses] *they wear for themselves, but the shield they carry to protect the whole line.*"

Demaratus wasn't kidding. The hoplite's shield protected not only him but, by overlapping with the man beside him, his comrade-in-arms, too. So critical was your comrade's shield for protecting your right side that Thucydides reports that entire battle lines slid to the right as they advanced, owing to each warrior trying to take cover behind his comrade's shield. At the First Battle of Mantinea in 418 BC (a major Spartan victory), this rightward drift had a serious effect on the outcome. Because of this, many ancient armies (not just the Greeks) stationed their most elite units on the right of the battle line to anchor it and prevent rightward drift (as they would have been the steadiest in the army). The right side of the battle line was considered the position of honor in the ancient Greek world.

The hoplite's shield wasn't significantly updated during the classical period, save that an apron of leather or cloth was sometimes added to the bottom, starting around the late 5th century BC; it was probably as added protection against missiles, or as basic missile protection for men who didn't want to wear the heavy, hot, bronze greaves.

Each hoplite was armed with the *doru* or *dory*, an ash-hafted, iron-tipped thrusting spear that ranged from 6 to 9 feet long. It was backed by a bronze butt-spike called a *saurōtēr* or "lizard killer," presumably because it was used to spear lizards that strayed too close to the hoplite's foot as he stood waiting for orders. In reality, it probably saw more service killing people than lizards, usually as they lay wounded on the battlefield. It also served as a backup point in case the spearhead broke off. The hoplite was also armed with a sword, usually either a straight, leaf-bladed *xiphos* that was sharp on both sides, or a curved, cleaver-like *kopis* that was sharp only on one, each approximately 1–2 feet long.

The Spartans began using shorter swords by the mid-5th century BC, to the point where they were little more than long knives. Plutarch tells us that an Athenian teased the Spartan Eurypontid king Agis III that Spartan swords were so short a juggler could swallow them. Agis gave the badass reply, "even so, we can reach our enemies with them." Plutarch has another Eurypontid king, Agesilaus II, saying that Spartans preferred shorter swords because they fought up close. Like the "come back with your shield or on it" maxim, he has yet another Spartan mother admonishing her son to "add a step" to his strike when he complains that his sword is so short.

Spartans probably preferred shorter swords for easy handling in close fighting. The 4th century AD Roman writer (and likely soldier) Vegetius notes that the Romans preferred to thrust with their short swords rather than slash:

> *For the Romans not only made a joke of those who fought with the edge of that weapon, but beat them easily. A stroke with the edges, though made with great force, rarely kills, as the vitals are protected both by the bones and armor. On the contrary, a stab, though it penetrates but two inches, is generally fatal. Besides in the attitude of striking, it is impossible to avoid exposing the right arm and side; but on the other hand, the body is covered while a thrust is given, and the adversary receives the point before he sees the sword.*

This makes good sense and may have been behind Spartan thinking as well, prompting the use of a shorter, thrusting-oriented weapon. Either way, it's important to note that the hoplite was first and foremost a spearman and that the sword was a backup weapon. Unlike the Roman legionary, the Greek hoplite was not a skilled individual fencer and unit cohesion was paramount in warfare of the period.

Each hoplite stood sideways behind his shield, his left shoulder forward and his right bladed back. His shield overlapped with the man to his left and right providing an unbroken wall of wood and bronze. If you were facing a line of hoplites head on, you wouldn't be able to see a single unprotected opening. The shield would cover each man from chin to knee. Above the chin, the bronze helmet would cover everything. From the knee down, the bronze greaves provided protection. The hoplite likely held his spear sometimes high, to stab down over the top of his shield and sometimes low, to thrust from underneath.

Some scholars dispute that the hoplite would thrust from below his shield, arguing that this would cause him to stab the man behind him with the butt-spike as he drew his arm back for a thrust. Stabbing down from overhead keeps the butt-spike in the air, where it isn't a threat. My experience in reenactment combat makes me doubt this. Frequently I found myself stabbing "down" at targets that were straight across from me, which meant that my spear was pretty much level and I was driving my spear-butt into the face of the people behind me. I also found that I didn't put nearly as much force into pulling my arm back as I did driving it forward. This allowed the butt-spike to slide fairly gently off the armor of people behind me in the relatively rare cases where I hit them. Ancient Greek vase painting depicts hoplites wielding their spears in *both* positions.

This battle line stacked back usually eight ranks deep to form a long block of men. This block of men was known as a phalanx, and it was the standard classical Greek heavy infantry formation from roughly the 7th century BC until the Macedonian innovations reformed it around four centuries later, replacing the hoplite with the foot companions in a similar formation that used smaller shields and longer pikes held in both hands.

The classical phalanx was designed to fight other classical phalanxes on flat, even ground. It was designed to fight in one direction – straight ahead. It was intensely vulnerable on its sides (flanks) and to attacks from the rear. Only the first two ranks could stab effectively with their spears, leaving the remaining ranks the job of leaning into their shields and pushing the men in front of them.

The two phalanxes would move quickly to shield-to-shield contact and then engage in a mass shoving match, with the first two ranks stabbing at one another, called the *ōthismos*. The shoving and stabbing would continue, with the rear-rankers stepping forward if the men in front of them fell, until one side broke and the rout and pursuit began.

As with all ancient warfare, the vast majority of the casualties occurred during the rout and pursuit and not during the actual fighting. *Ōthismos* is hotly disputed, with some scholars advocating the "figurative" or "heretical" model, where the phalanxes stand off and fence with their spears, as opposed to the "literal" model, which advocates that the phalanxes actually went toe to toe and shield to shield, engaging in a real shoving match. The evidence strongly supports the literal model and this book will proceed with it taken as fact.

The Spartan "Upbringing" – Myth and Reality

It was at this form of warfare – the *ōthismos* of the hoplite phalanx – that the Spartans reputedly excelled. But how much they excelled and why is, as with everything else about the Spartans, a tangled mess of myth and fact. In order to untangle fact from fantasy, we have to first be willing to admit that in many cases (even in most), the source material simply doesn't exist for us to be completely sure what is true. The best historians are the ones willing to admit that "this is my best guess" instead of pretending a certainty they can't possibly have.

We'll look first at the *agōgē* or "Upbringing" supposedly put in place by Lycurgus and specifically designed to breed the tiny minority of Spartan Peers for war from their youngest days. Even the term *agōgē* is disputed. Xenophon, who unlike Plutarch was a contemporary of the classical Spartans, called it the *paideia* (education).

First, there is the story Plutarch tells that at birth (presumably to a Spartan citizen only), the mother would bathe the child in wine instead of water, as the Spartans believed that a weak child would react badly, and a strong child would be "tempered." Spartan elders would then examine the infant, and if it was weak, sickly or deformed, "*they sent it to the Apothetae, a chasm at the foot of Mount Taygetus, in the belief that the life that nature had not well equipped at the very beginning for health and strength, would not help either itself or the state.*"

As horrific as this story is, it's not surprising or outlandish. There is plenty of evidence, both literary and archaeological, that many ancient Greeks (and many ancient peoples in general) practiced infanticide.

But the notion that Spartan eugenics, a practice that Hitler publicly admired, was uniformly practiced to ensure that Sparta produced the best warriors from the healthiest stock has glaring holes in it, and very likely isn't true.

The first striking contradiction is the famous and highly successful Spartan Eurypontid king Agesilaus II, who reigned from 398 to 360 BC. Agesilaus was so successful that he is one of only five Spartans to receive full biographies in Plutarch's most famous work *Parallel Lives*. Agesilaus' father Archidamus II already had an elder son, Agis II. Agis II, in turn, also already had a son, Leotychides. With the line of succession already in place, Agesilaus was not expected to become king and therefore was enrolled in the Upbringing for training. This was unusual – Spartan kings were exempt from the brutal Upbringing ... which is yet another departure from the Spartan warrior myth – that *all* Spartan warriors graduated the Upbringing. Kings (and Spartan kings nearly always led Spartan armies) got a pass.

But Agesilaus had another problem: he was born lame, probably with a clubfoot. By the laws of Lycurgus the way Plutarch describes them, he should have been thrown into the chasm to die. But clearly he wasn't, as not only was he kept alive despite a clear and visible disability, but he was also enrolled in the Upbringing and performed exceptionally well. Plutarch even points out how Agesilaus cheerfully dealt with the setback, how his youthful good looks compensated for it, and that *"his lameness brought his ambition into clearer light, since it led him to decline no hardship and no enterprise whatever."*

Another hole in the Bronze Lie of Spartan eugenics comes from Plutarch's quoting of an anonymous Spartan mother accompanying her lame son on his way to the battlefield, *"At each step, my child, remember your valor."* Here, language comes into play. In describing the crippled leg of the Spartan Androcleidas, Plutarch uses the Greek *pērōtheis* or "maimed." Plutarch clearly identifies that Androcleidas is crippled by a wound. But in describing this unnamed Spartan, Plutarch uses the generic *chōlon* or "lame." Why did Plutarch choose this word? Could it be because the unnamed Spartan's condition was from something other than a wound? Could he have been born with it? If he was, then he clearly escaped the infanticide the Lycurgan laws should have demanded.

In the cases of both Agesilaus and this unnamed Spartan campaigner, it is possible that they came by their "lameness" due to an accident or a wound after passing inspection as infants. But it is also possible that the Spartans didn't practice infanticide as rigorously as Plutarch says, that there were exceptions for, say, the child of the Eurypontid royal house, or someone rich enough, connected enough or loved enough to escape the elders' scrutiny.

Plutarch is our only ancient source for this supposed practice of killing weak or deformed children and he was writing in the 2nd century AD, somewhere in the neighborhood of 500–600 years after Sparta in the classical era. It is possible that Plutarch was passing along a folktale with little to no basis in truth. It's also possible that Plutarch was in the grip of the same laconophilia we discussed in the introduction, and passing it along to an audience he knew would be eager for it.

Spartan boys were taken from their families at the age of seven (if you believe Plutarch) or five (if you interpret the turn of the 3rd century AD Greek writer Athenaeus' statement that all Spartans from the age of five learned the "Pyrrhic" war-dance to mean that boys of five were starting the Upbringing) and enrolled in the Upbringing as a *pais* (boy).

These boys were supposedly placed under the supervision of a high-ranking, mature Spartan citizen *paidonomos* ("boy herder") and organized into "packs" (*agelai*) led by the pack member who proved to be the toughest fighter. They were immediately pitted against other packs and each other in a relentless struggle to be the best at literally everything. The majority of this consisted of fighting and rough-and-tumble play, often under the supervision of adults who encouraged competition and kept an eye on the proceedings.

The Spartans believed that a boy would be faster and more agile barefoot, and so they were forbidden to wear shoes, toughening their feet in expectation of hard marches to come. The boys were permitted only a single cloak that had to be worn year round.

Theoretically, every Spartan adult was to take an interest in the boys' education. To emphasize that the boys were the collective wards of the state, they were instructed to call every adult male Spartan "father." Aristotle criticized this system, because if everyone was responsible for the education of the boys, then no one was. "*Each boy had a thousand fathers,*" the famous philosopher wrote, "*as he was everyone's responsibility, so he was neglected by all.*" Indeed, Aristotle was highly critical of the Upbringing as a whole, saying that it produced "*brave little beasts.*" The Bronze Lie holds up the education of Spartan youth in the Upbringing as an absolute good, but Aristotle's commentary casts doubt on how well it worked in practice.

At around 14, the boy became a *paidiskos*. These older boys lived in the barracks in their packs, sleeping on beds of reeds which they hand-picked from the banks of the Eurotas river (Laconia's main river). In the winter, the older boys were allowed to add thistledown to the bed or reeds for warmth. Their *eirēn* (prefect), a young man of around 20 years old who served as a combination of residential supervisor and military instructor, would now begin tasking the youths with things like stealing food or gathering firewood. The older boys waited on him at meals, during which they would be incessantly tested, made to sing, or quizzed on the character of Spartan citizens and punished when they either gave unsatisfactory answers or were too timid to answer quickly or boldly enough.

But the critical development for Spartan older boys was their entry into the system of institutionalized pederasty. Older males would now select the older boys as lovers. While this relationship was possibly (or even likely, depending on which scholars you believe) sexual, there was also an important mentorship aspect.

Scholars debate the exact nature of these relationships, citing Xenophon's writing that the relationships were considered "abominations" if they were solely sexual (he also added "*I am not surprised, however, that people refuse to believe this*"). The turn of the 3rd century AD Roman writer Aelian also wrote of the mentorship and instructional responsibilities of the older man to his youthful lover. But multiple sources strongly suggest that this was a sexual relationship, and I believe much of the debate stems from modern scholars made uncomfortable by having to stare pederasty in the face. That homosexuality was a key component of Spartan life is underscored by the Spartan marriage custom of cutting the bride's hair short and dressing her in a man's military cloak. In short, making her as mannish as possible in an effort to ease the Spartan man into his new role as a heterosexual husband.

This isn't to say that the instructional/mentoring aspect wasn't important in homosexual relationships. It absolutely was. The older lover (*erastēs*) was responsible for educating his younger partner (*erōmenos*), not only instructing him, but looking out for him politically, making connections and advocating for him. The *erastēs* even helped his *erōmenos* get items from the market, which the young *erōmenos* was forbidden to enter.

The same King Agesilaus whom we just discussed was the *erōmenos* of the famous Spartan Lysander, whom we'll meet again in later chapters. The relationship was clearly not only romantic, but political, and gave both partners a critical boost to their career prospects. That the *erastēs* had real responsibilities to his *erōmenos* is underscored by the famous story of the Spartan *erastēs* who was punished in the place of his *erōmenos*, who cried out in pain while fighting. The belief was that the older man was responsible for not educating his younger lover correctly.

Older boys were deliberately underfed and encouraged to steal to supplement their diet. Plutarch implies that the idea was to train them to be crafty and stealthy for their future careers as warriors. For purportedly the same reason, Spartans were forbidden to carry a light when coming from or going to the communal mess for their evening meal. Even though stealing was encouraged, getting caught was not, and the punishment for getting found out was dire (hence the story of the fox in the introduction).

At 18 (or 20, depending on whom you believe), the Spartan became a *hēbōn* and spent his first year training older boys. The *hēbōn* wouldn't be permitted to enter the market, nor to live at home with his wife, until he was 30. Though they lived apart, Plutarch points out that Spartan couples had sex secretly, again with the man at great pains not to get caught. Plutarch doesn't mention that this custom was intended to train the Spartan warrior for stealth, but the implication is definitely there.

As he approached the age of 20, the Spartan adult applied to join one of the communal messes. Plutarch tells us that each of the members voted by casting a piece of bread into a bowl. If the bread was squeezed (showing the imprints of the fingers), then the vote was "no." A single no-vote was enough to deny membership. A Spartan who failed to be accepted to a communal mess could not be a full Peer and became some kind of Inferior, though the exact status isn't known. The same fate awaited any member who could no longer afford to contribute the required items to maintain membership in the mess, which prompted Aristotle to complain that the system excluded the poor – our first clue to the role of wealth in what would eventually become the manpower crisis that saw Spartan armies first shrinking, then diversifying, and finally collapsing.

These young men were responsible for their own exercise but still subject to inspection, and had duties serving as prefects or assisting the boy-herder. One of the greatest honors that could be earned by a *hēbōn* was being selected for the *hippeis* (literally cavalry – but the word is probably a holdover from an earlier period. These *hippeis* served as infantry), the royal bodyguard of the two Spartan kings. The royal bodyguard was selected in 100-man lots by three *hippagretai* ("the ones who select the *hippeis*") appointed by the ephors.

At some point (we don't know precisely when), the most promising Spartans would be selected into the crypteia I described above.

The graduates of this long, complex system became the Peers, bound together by the same shared hardship. If the picture Plutarch paints is true, all had entered the same crucible, suffered equally, and emerged tempered by it and prepared for a life at war. I know this feeling well. Military training is the great leveler. Done correctly, all candidates experience the same trials, are broken down together, built back up together, and graduate together feeling a common bond that is born of shared hardship. To this day the first word that enters my mind at the sight of a military uniform is "family." Whatever the truth of the Spartan Upbringing, I recognize in the story of it that same harrowing, construction and rebirth that results in a bond that is deep and unshakeable. Of such stuff, great warriors are certainly made.

The Spartan Upbringing wasn't precisely military training (it was clearly physical, but there is no mention of weapons training, drilling in formation or even practicing marching; there are also some hints that the youths were trained in reading, writing and music). However, it clearly was intended to produce a similar effect. The Upbringing very likely cultivated that same sense of family-like bonds.

Spartan Warrior Values – Clues from Tyrtaeus

In trying to understand Spartan military values (or rather, their lack of them) and how they organized to fight, we get our best glimpse from the Spartan lyric poet Tyrtaeus, who (if you believe what entirely non-Spartan writers said of him) was a cornerstone of Spartan military culture.

Athenaeus (citing the 4th century BC Athenian historian Philochorus) tells us the Spartans "*in their wars march in time to the poems of Tyrtaeus which they recite from memory*" and "*they established the custom in their campaigns that, after dinner and the hymn of thanksgiving, each sing in turn the poems of Tyrtaeus, their commander acts as judge and gives a prize of meat to the winner.*" The 4th century BC Athenian orator Lycurgus (not the mythical Lycurgus who established Sparta's system of government) noted that since the Spartans were "*a people who take no account of poets,*" it was doubly amazing that they "*made so much of Tyrtaeus as to pass a law that whenever they take the field under arms they would all be summoned to the king's tent to hear his poems, in the belief that this will make them most willing to die for their country.*" These are just two examples of ancient writers indicating that Tyrtaeus' poetry was a major force in establishing Sparta's military ethic.

And just as with everything else in the history of Sparta, there are questions and contradictions. The biggest one is the question of where Tyrtaeus came from. Multiple sources raise the possibility that this important poet, a foundation stone of Sparta's military culture ... was from Athens.

Tyrtaeus' origins are hotly disputed, with some scholars saying the idea that he was Athenian was Athenian propaganda, but we can't ignore the fact that writers from the unknown authors of the 10th century AD Byzantine encyclopedia, the *Suda*, to Plato, to Pausanias, to Diogenes Laertius, to the possibly 2nd century AD Roman writer Justin all either flat-out state or at least strongly imply that Tyrtaeus was an Athenian. The stories of his origins vary – that he was a lame schoolmaster (again, lameness in a major figure of a society that supposedly killed lame children), that he was a general, that he was missing an eye, that he was deranged, that he was sent by Athens to Sparta as an insult, that the oracle at Delphi instructed the Spartans to take him as a general. The truth can never be known, and Tyrtaeus' origins are every bit as murky as Lycurgus'.

But the impact of his poetry is clear, and in examining the few fragments that survive, we can barely sketch the outline of Spartan warrior values. However, as we examine Tyrtaeus' poetry, we have to note that he is writing exhortations – he is trying to influence the Spartans to behave in a certain way. And if he's having to do that, that means that either some or even most Spartans were *not* behaving in the manner Tyrtaeus recommends. In examining the values Tyrtaeus encourages, we see glimmers of the Bronze Lie – clues that the Spartans were falling short of the warrior reputation they would later enjoy.

According to Tyrtaeus, Spartans should do the following (which likely means many of them didn't behave this way):

- Fight using the literal *ōthismos* model I described above. There is no standing off and dueling with spears in Tyrtaeus' poetry. He is crystal clear that a Spartan was to fight *"foot beside foot, resting shield against shield, crest beside crest, helm beside helm, fight his man chest to chest."*
- Obey their kings as if they were gods.
- Prize order above all else.
- View love of money as a threat to Sparta.

- Love Sparta more than any individual.
- Believe that it was good to die in service to Sparta, preferably in battle.
- Believe that poverty and want were shameful, and that begging was the lowest level to which a person can sink (an odd thing to specify if all wealth is distributed equally and everyone has just what they need. Here is another example of the Bronze Lie).
- Not prize their own lives, laying them down willingly for the land or their children.
- Not give in to fear, which they found shameful. Fleeing from a fight was the height of shame.
- Fight shoulder to shoulder with other Spartans. Wounds in the front of the body were honorable. Wounds to the rear of the body were dishonorable.
- Not keep outside missile range. To do so showed fear, and was therefore dishonorable.
- Believe that the young should fight before the old, and find it shameful for an older man to die in battle when a younger man could have stood before him.
- Aspire to be as close to the front of the phalanx as possible.
- Carry a shield that covered them from mid-thigh to shoulders (this matches the *aspis* I described earlier).
- Carry a spear in their right hand, use swords and wear crests.
- Spartan light-armed troops should take shelter behind the shields and armored bodies of heavier-armed Spartans. They should throw stones and javelins.
- Believe that being a warrior was the most important life goal. Being great at war exceeded greatness in athletics, beauty, wealth, leadership or persuasiveness.
- Believe that prowess in war was a common good – the great warrior benefits Sparta.
- Believe that a Spartan falling in battle (with wounds to the front of his body) would be mourned by the entire city, and remembered. His legacy would reflect positively on his children. If that same warrior lived via being repeatedly victorious in battle, he would be revered and well treated all his life.

Looking at these values, we see a lot of overlap between Plutarch and Xenophon's description of the Lycurgan model of what was expected from a Spartan warrior, and what the Spartans expected of themselves. This lends credence to the idea that the fearless, selfless, devoted-unto-death Spartan warrior was at least an *ideal* toward which Spartans strove. However, we should also remember that Tyrtaeus' poems were intended to guide and inspire Spartans who were engaging in behavior opposite to the values listed above. In his poetry, we see a glimmer of the Spartans' humanity, warriors who felt fear and ran from fights, who wanted to be at the rear of the phalanx where they'd be least likely to be harmed, who would prefer that the older men of the community took wounds if it meant they'd be spared, who loved money and were sometimes bad at managing it.

The question remains how well Tyrtaeus' poems worked in encouraging the Spartans to live by his ideals. We'll dig into the gap between those ideals and the reality in the chapters that follow.

The Spartan Army

The organization of the Spartan army is not well understood and our only real source tackling the subject direct is Xenophon. We know that Spartans began serving before they were considered full adult citizens at the age of 30, as we see *hēbontes* being selected to form the royal bodyguard from the age of probably 21, after they completed a year of training younger boys. Military service continued until the age of 60, when a Spartan became a *gerōn* (elder), eligible for election into the *gerousia*. Elders were, after a lifetime at war, finally permitted to set their burdens down.

The army's numbers – land and Sparta's manpower crisis

We have some idea of the number of full Spartan citizens available to serve in the phalanx. Plutarch tells us that Lycurgus, "*in order that every vestige of unevenness and inequality might be removed,*" redistributed all land (and all other property as well) in equal plots (*klēroi*). These plots were "*large enough to produce annually seventy bushels of barley for a man and twelve for his wife, with a proportionate amount of wine and oil. Lycurgus thought that a lot of this size would be enough for them, since they needed sustenance enough to promote vigor and health of body, and nothing else."*

However, this idea of land redistribution has been severely attacked in the scholarly community and largely disproven. Also hidden in Plutarch's text is that these plots (however the Peers acquired them) would allow the citizens to pay their communal mess dues and maintain their membership. This made Spartan citizens vulnerable to losing their place in the mess (and so losing their status as Peers) if they lost their land, or part of their land, for any reason. Keep this in mind as we see the Spartan manpower crisis grow over time in the chapters that follow.

Aristotle seems to buy the notion of land redistribution, but notes that it didn't last:

> *It has come about that some of the Spartans own too much property and some very little; owing to which the land has fallen into few hands, and this has also been badly regulated by the laws; for the lawgiver [Lycurgus] made it dishonorable to sell a family's existing estate, and did so rightly, but he granted freedom to give land at will by gift or bequest; yet the result that has happened was bound to follow in the one case as well as in the other. And also nearly two-fifths of the whole area of the country is owned by women, because of the number of women who inherit estates and the practice of giving large dowries; yet it would have been better if dowries had been prohibited by law or limited to a small or moderate amount. But as it is he is allowed to give an heiress in marriage to whomever he likes; and if he dies without having made directions as to this by will, whoever he leaves as his executor bestows her upon whom he chooses.*

You have to take Aristotle's comments on women with a grain of salt. His writings show him to be an epic misogynist, but his point about the unequal distribution of land, with the inevitable result of fewer and fewer full Spartan citizens (as the poorer ones would have been unable to pay their mess dues) is important.

One thing that is borne out by all the sources is that the Spartans simply refused throughout most of their history to expand the citizenship franchise. They took no real action to make sure there were more Peers. This conservative cleaving to the notion of elite status had the ironic effect of seeing that elite status completely undone.

And here we also see another hole in the Bronze Lie – additional proof that the idea that the Spartans hated wealth and personal gain isn't true. The people with the power to change land inheritance and distribution law were the Peers themselves – the ephors and the council of elders. In other words, the rich landholders who had every incentive to perpetuate the current system because it made them richer.

Still, Herodotus quotes the exiled Spartan king Demaratus (acting as an advisor to the Persian king Xerxes as he invaded Greece – Demaratus' role is noticeably absent from films like *300*) that Sparta fielded an army of 8,000 men at the time of Xerxes' invasion in 480 BC. At least at the beginning of the 5th century BC, Sparta could field a solid number of Peers.

Army organization

The organization of the army made up of the Peers is, to put it mildly, not well understood. We know Spartans were called up by age groups (starting from around 20 years old, when the still technically not full adult citizens could be chosen for the royal bodyguard) as Xenophon writes of call-ups by a number of years "from youth." For example, when Xenophon writes of a call-up of those who are "40 from youth," he means every available Spartan from age 20 to 60 (at which point as elders they were exempt).

There's some hint that the communal messes played a role in how Spartan units were organized. Xenophon describes them using a different Greek word – *syskēnia* or "tent group," which implies men camping together on the march. We know the communal messes were a mix of different ages, which meant that, whatever age groups were called, all the units would have a roughly equal number of men with even distribution of ages.

Tyrtaeus gives us our first clue into Spartan organization, stating that the army deployed in three "tribes," the Pamphyloi, Hylleis and Dymanes (could the 300 members of the royal bodyguard be 100 from each tribe?).

It was the 7th century BC Spartan poet Alcman who first noted that the Spartan army formed as five *obai* (villages). The turn of the 4th century BC Athenian comic playwright Aristophanes wrote the famous play *Lysistrata* about the women of Greece going on a sex-strike to convince their men to end the

Peloponnesian Wars. That it's a fantastic play is proven by the fact that it's still performed today, but it also gives us an important clue about the organization of the Spartan army. In the play, Aristophanes refers to four *lochoi* (the word literally translates to "ambushes"). Some scholars believe the comic playwright was poking fun at the Spartans, and this is backed up by the much later (turn of the 6th century AD) Roman writer Hesychius, who cites a now lost work by Aristotle correcting Aristophanes. Hesychius confirms that the *lochoi* are indeed referencing Sparta, and that there were actually five – the same number of villages we have from Alcman. This has led some scholars to guess that the early Spartan army was organized into five units (*lochoi*) – one from each village.

Herodotus possibly names one of these – the Lochos Pitanates (the Pitanate Unit; Pitana was one of Sparta's original five villages) – in his description of the Battle of Plataea in 479 BC. But Thucydides flat-out says the Pitanate Unit didn't exist, that it was an "unfounded notion popular with the Greeks." Here again is the Spartan Mirage – as soon as we have what seems like a clear description of who the Spartans were, it is instantly contradicted.

For anything approaching a complete description of the Spartan army, we have to rely almost entirely on two sources – Thucydides and Xenophon. Both of them describe the Spartan army fairly late in its evolution (in the late 5th century BC for Thucydides, and just at the turn of the 4th century BC for Xenophon). But even though the armies they describe are very close together in period, the descriptions are confusingly different.

Thucydides lays out the following deployment:

> *There were seven lochoi in the field without counting the Sciritae, who numbered six hundred men: in each lochos there were four pentēkostyes, and in the pentēkostyes four enōmotiai. The first rank of the enōmotia was composed of four soldiers: as to the depth, although they had not been all drawn up alike, but as each captain chose, they were generally ranged eight deep; the first rank along the whole line, exclusive of the Sciritae, consisted of four hundred and forty-eight men.*

First, let's untangle the Greek words. We already said the *lochos* means "ambushes" – presumably an ancient group of warriors preparing for a raid or ambush. *Pentēkosty* implies "band of 50," and *enōmotiai* "sworn bands" or "oath-bound bands" (Herodotus also confirms that the sworn band was the unit of maneuver in the Spartan army).

The Sciritae were a special class of Spartan subject who lived in the Sciritis, a mountainous region to the north of Sparta. Near as we can tell, the Sciritae occupied a status like the *perioikoi*, save that they had a special military role. Per Thucydides, the Sciritae fought on the left wing of the Spartan line and acted as a rearguard when the army was on the march, an important duty that would have been given only to trusted troops. Xenophon described them as scouts for the kings. Scholars debate how the Sciritae were armed, with some saying they were light-armed and others arguing that if they were on the left wing of the phalanx, they would have to have been equipped as hoplites.

If we do the math based on Thucydides' description of the sworn band as eight ranks deep and four files wide (four men in the front rank), we get a sworn band of 32 warriors, about the size of a middling modern platoon. That would mean that the band of 50 wouldn't match its name at all, numbering 128 hoplites (about the size of a small modern company). This means that the "ambushes" (*lochoi*) were each composed of 512 hoplites (about the size of a small modern battalion) – for a grand total of just over 3,500 men in the phalanx (roughly the size of a modern brigade). This doesn't count cavalry, light troops or the royal bodyguard of 300 men. Scholars also dispute whether or not this number includes the New People (freed helots) that I mentioned above.

Xenophon describes a very different army made up of six *morai* (divisions, and not in the military sense of the word "division." A *mora* is simply a portion that has been divided from a larger whole). Keep in mind that Xenophon and Thucydides are describing the same army approximately 15 years apart. Had the Spartan army changed so much that an entire new unit type had been introduced? Or was Xenophon using the word *mora* in place of *lochos*? This would make sense if you agree with those scholars who say that one of the seven *lochoi* described by Thucydides was composed of freed slaves. That would leave six, which would match the six *morai* described by Xenophon. But the Spartan Mirage rears its ugly head again, for Xenophon *also* mentions *lochoi* in his description. Xenophon breaks the Spartan army down into two (not four) sworn bands of 36 hoplites each, forming a "band of 50" of 76 men. Two of these "fifties" form a *lochos* of 144 men, and four of these make up the *mora* of 576 hoplites.

These accountings are similar enough to be tantalizing, but different enough to be confusing, and have resulted in a fierce debate about which is correct. The majority of modern scholars dismiss Thucydides (an Athenian who fought against Sparta in the Peloponnesian Wars), and prefer Xenophon (also an Athenian, but enormously pro-Spartan, with strong ties to the city-state. He sent his son to be educated there and was a companion to Agesilaus II, writing his biography. He also campaigned with the Spartan Clearchus when both were hired as mercenaries by the Persian prince Cyrus the Younger in his unsuccessful bid to take the Persian throne).

The strongest argument I've heard is that the *mora* was created around 413 BC when Sparta needed for the first time to have units serving abroad (to garrison Decelea in the Decelean phase of the Peloponnesian Wars, which we'll examine later). As these units needed to be able to operate and fight independently, they contained both infantry and cavalry. The need for these units increased during later wars when Sparta fought abroad around Corinth and Boeotia.

The truth is we can't be sure how the Spartan army was organized and how it deployed, but we *can* be sure that it was organized.

Whether Thucydides' or Xenophon's descriptions are accurate, they show a military organization that's instantly familiar to modern service members. Modern militaries break down forces into similar structures because it provides proper "span of control" – the ability for officers at each level of the hierarchy to exercise command over the troops underneath them effectively.

Thucydides describes a clear chain of command that takes full advantage of proper span of control – with the king giving orders to his generals (*polemarchoi*, literally "war leaders"), the generals relaying orders to the *lochagoi* (the officers in charge of the *lochos*), the *lochagoi* relaying orders to the *pentēkonteres* (the leaders of 50), and the *pentēkonteres* to the *enōmotarchoi* (leaders of the sworn bands), who in turn relay the orders to each individual warrior. As with modern commands, centralized control is exercised over the whole of the army through a clear chain of officers all the way down to the smallest units in the force. That we see a clear understanding of this critical military concept, so crucial in AD 2021, in the Spartan army of the 4th century BC is an indicator of their strong discipline and organization.

Disciplined, organized warfighters

I use the words "disciplined" and "organized" deliberately. Many scholars refer to the Spartans as the only truly professional warriors in ancient Greece.

But this is just another element of the Bronze Lie. The Spartan Peers were certainly far more disciplined and organized than their contemporaries, but they were *not* full-time warriors in the modern sense of the word "professional." Rather, as we have seen, they were full-time aristocrats enjoying lives of leisure, a portion of which was spent in training for war.

Hoplite warfare in classical Greece was an entirely amateur affair. You'll note that the formation of the phalanx and the tactics of *ōthismos* are incredibly simple. Literally anyone could, with minimal training, stand in a block of men, face forward, and push. Simplicity was necessary, because Greek hoplites were necessarily amateurs. The majority of them were farmers, only picking up spear and shield when called to do so on behalf of their *polis* (city-state).

While the *perioikoi* had crafts and duties to attend to, the Spartan citizens were forbidden all work. They alone of all Greeks had the time, resources and capacity to truly devote themselves to something approximating what we in 2021 would consider military training. Aristotle notes that the Spartans "*used not to excel because they exercised their young men in this fashion but only because they trained and their enemies did not.*"

While Aristotle is specifically referring to physical exercise here, his point certainly applies to Spartan military training as well. In other words, the Spartans weren't better than their opponents because they trained hard, but because they trained *at all*.

Thucydides attests to the discipline and organization of the Spartan army, noting that they marched "*slowly and with many flutes, according to their military discipline, not as a point of religion, but that, marching evenly and by measure, their ranks might not be distracted ...*" Keeping in step to music was just one distinctive mark. The Spartans also sang either a battle hymn or a war cry known as the *paean*, which the Athenian tragic playwright Aeschylus described as "*the sacred cry of joy and goodwill, our shout of tribute, that brings courage to our friends and dissolves fear of the enemy.*" They also possibly garlanded their helmets with wreaths of flowers or other plants, though this may have been only during the pre-battle blood sacrifice and taking of omens, and not during the fight itself.

Herodotus' tale of Demaratus' interview with Xerxes also gives us a clue regarding Spartan military discipline. When the Persian king asks the Spartan exile how good the Spartans are in a fight, Demaratus tells him that man-for-man, the Spartans are no tougher than anyone else, but when they fight *together* they are the best warriors of all. That's a clear indication that it was the Spartans' discipline and high level of organization that gave them their supposed edge, an edge that, as Aristotle notes, seems to have come just as much from the *lack* of training among Sparta's opponents as it did from anything the Spartans did themselves.

There's a famous scene in the film *300* where Leonidas is chided by other Greeks for bringing so few warriors with him to the fight. Leonidas responds by asking other Greeks in the defending force their profession. Each gives the answer – a non-military job such as potter or blacksmith. Leonidas then turns to the Spartans and bellows "Spartans! What is your profession?" The assembled Peers pump their fists, holding their spears aloft (and making a dog-barking noise that I suspect would have made actual Spartans laugh), showing that while they are few in number, only they are professional soldiers.

The scene is based on a story by Plutarch from his *Life of Agesilaus*, chronicling the actions of a Eurypontid king (Leonidas was an Agiad) who wasn't even born until over 30 years after Leonidas was killed. Plutarch's story goes like this:

> ... *wishing to refute their argument from numbers,* [the king] *devised the following scheme. He ordered all the allies to sit down by themselves, the Spartans sitting apart. Then his herald called upon the potters to stand up first, and after them the smiths, the carpenters next, and the builders, and so on through all the handicrafts. In response, almost all the allies rose up, but not a man of the Spartans; for they were forbidden to learn or practice a manual art. Then Agesilaus said with a laugh: "You see, O men, how many more soldiers than you we are sending out."*

This fun story was probably false and, like every other aspect of the Bronze Lie, easily shot full of holes. None of the men speaking lists his occupation as "farmer" although that was the occupation of most hoplites. Also, the Spartan contingent would have consisted not only of Peers, but of *perioikoi*, which means that Agesilaus would have had plenty of smiths and carpenters of his own. But this doesn't change the fact that among all the Greeks, the Spartans were the only truly disciplined and organized army. That this was made possible by their oppressive, apartheid system of course goes unmentioned.

Xenophon describes Spartan organization in the field:

> *Most think the Spartan infantry formation is very complicated. But that is the very opposite of the truth. In the Spartan formation the front rank men are all officers, and each file has all that it requires to make it efficient. The formation is so easy to understand that no one who knows man from man can possibly go wrong. For some have the privilege of leading; and the rest are under orders to follow. Orders to wheel from column into line of battle are given verbally by the leader of the sworn band acting as his own herald, and the line is formed either thin or deep, by wheeling. Nothing whatever in these movements is difficult to understand.*

We can see clearly here that the sworn bands were the tactical units of maneuver, with their leaders acting more or less in the capacity of a modern second lieutenant (in terms of span of control). Xenophon was clear that being drilled "under the laws of Lycurgus" enabled Spartan warriors to keep formation even in the confusion of battle.

This was a critical factor for ancient armies. When fighting in the hoplite style, unit cohesion was everything. So long as the hoplites kept their shields overlapping, there were precious few openings for an enemy to exploit. But once gaps appeared, an enemy might get a spear thrust in at an exposed thigh or neck. Without his comrades, a hoplite might be flanked and attacked from multiple sides, forced to pick which enemy he could defend against with his large, heavy shield, leaving himself vulnerable to the other.

I mentioned before that most casualties in ancient battles happened during the rout and pursuit. This is largely because in a rout, unit cohesion dissolves entirely, as every man runs for his life.

There are no overlapping shields then.

Xenophon even gives us some details of precisely what the Spartan army could do, and while these maneuvers may seem simple to a reader who is thinking of a modern military, by ancient standards (and especially by classical Greek standards), this was nothing short of spectacular.

Xenophon describes the Spartan army marching in columns, with each sworn band in its correct order, one behind the other. That way, when contact was made with the enemy, each sworn band could simply deploy from column into line to the left of the unit it was marching behind. This could be done quickly and efficiently, even if the enemy made a sudden surprise appearance at the front of the column.

Xenophon also points out that the Spartans had mastered the "wheel" and "countermarch" familiar to anyone who has learned to march in a modern military, which allowed them to quickly change the facing of the entire battle line in case they were surprised by the enemy behind them (keep in mind that, if what we know of the Sciritae is true, then surprising a Spartan army from the rear would be difficult, as you would have light troops used to moving through rough terrain whose specific job was to prevent that from happening while the army was on the march).

Xenophon is careful to point out that Spartan armies countermarched to the rear; they did not simply about-face (which would put the warriors in the last rank suddenly in the front rank). Xenophon claims this was to put the best warriors always in the front. That's another valuable clue – that the Spartans put their best fighters in the front rank.

Since the officers of each sworn band would have occupied the honored position on the right of the front rank, and the overall leader (probably the *lochagos*) would have occupied the right-most position in the whole line, this countermarch would have put the most senior officer on the left of the line. But Xenophon tells us the Spartans weren't worried about that:

> *True, the leader is then on the left, but instead of thinking this a disadvantage, they regard it as a positive advantage at times. For should the enemy attempt a flanking movement he would try to encircle them, not on the exposed but on the protected side. If, however, it seems better for any reason that the leader should be on the right wing, the left wing wheels, and the army countermarches by ranks until the leader is on the right, and the rear of the column on the left.*

The critical thing to remember is that even simple maneuvers like wheeling and countermarching are incredibly difficult for untrained troops. They require constant drill even in a modern military, and the Spartans didn't have the benefit of radios or loudspeakers. Thousands of men moving together kick up a tremendous amount of dust, and helmets before the Peloponnesian Wars would have very likely covered the ears. If you're in the center of a column of 5,000 men, it's incredibly difficult to suddenly stop and change facing, all while keeping the critical cohesion that will allow you to ensure that your shields are overlapping and there are no gaps in the line for the enemy to exploit.

Remember that most ancient Greek hoplites were amateurs, full-time farmers and only part-time warriors. Xenophon's point is clear: "*if you watched them, you would think all other men mere improvisers in soldiering and the Spartans the only artists in warfare.*"

Clearly, Sparta's apartheid system allowed its elite Peers to train full-time for war, and thus made them some of the most disciplined heavy infantry in the ancient world. But we shouldn't oversell the idea that the Spartan Peers lived a life of endless disciplined training. Given the relatively amateur status of their enemies, it's far more likely that the Spartans trained *somewhat*, and that this alone gave them an edge over the other Greeks.

But this sporadic training still afforded the Peers a life with plenty of leisure time, and meant that the life of a Peer was pretty relaxed and easy by the standards of ancient Greece. Even when you take Spartan training into account, the flawed nature of humanity has a way of asserting itself. People aren't machines, no matter how much we might try to make them so. In Sparta's performance on the battlefield, we will see both their incredible effectiveness, and their all-too-human nature.

II

ARCHAIC SPARTA AT WAR: EARLY LOSSES, FOREIGN ROOTS

It was the view of Aristomenes that any man would be ready to die in battle if he had first done deeds worthy of record, but that it was his own special task at the very beginning of the war to prove that he had struck terror into the Spartans and that he would be more terrible to them for the future. With this purpose he came by night to Sparta and fixed on the temple of Athena of the Brazen House a shield inscribed "The Gift of Aristomenes to the Goddess, taken from Spartans."

Pausanias, *Description of Greece*

This book is chiefly concerned with Sparta at its height during the classical period. But in order to understand Sparta's military roots, it's necessary for us to go all the way back into the archaic period (roughly 800–490 BC). We're not certain when the supposed Lycurgan reforms that shaped Sparta's extraordinary society were laid down. Some scholars estimate that Lycurgus lived (if he existed at all) as early as the 10th century BC, and others as late as the 6th century BC. I believe the truth is somewhere in the middle, and that the Lycurgan reforms, to the extent they existed at all, were arrived at gradually, but may have been accelerated partly as a reaction to the stalemate of the First Messenian War.

In the classical period, Greek society centered on the *polis* or city-state. These city-states had this in common – the military formation of the phalanx was the standard mode for conducting warfare. As we've seen, phalanxes relied on unit cohesion and synchronized movement. Shields had to stay overlapping to prevent fatal gaps in the line from appearing. Hoplites had to move and strike together if their defenses were to hold. The round *aspis* shield was designed to protect not only the individual warrior, but the man to his left, even at the expense of exposing the right side of the warrior holding the shield. This style of fighting demands a degree of social equality. You can't have heroes or kings breaking ranks to engage in acts of glory. In phalanx warfare, the opposite is required – fighters must keep ranks and not create fatal gaps by breaking away.

Scholars debate whether the city-state arose as a result of the equality demanded by phalanx warfare, or if the phalanx was made possible by politico-cultural changes emphasizing equality. We will likely never know the truth, but we are reasonably sure that before the city-state, the Greeks in the archaic period were organized around the *oikos* (household) led by an aristocratic warlord. These warlords held their positions by merit, and that merit was measured largely by their strength and courage in battle. Reading the poet (or many poets) known as Homer, we see the use of the word *promachoi* (the fighters out front). In the classical period, this refers to the first hoplite in the file of a phalanx (recall that Xenophon points out that the Spartans put their best warriors in the front of the phalanx). But in the archaic period, the *promachoi* were the warriors who fought out in front of the army, possibly in individual duels against other warriors of high social status, whose defeat would bring great glory. The picture that emerges here in archaic Greek battles is of loosely organized warbands, with their warlords and other heroes dashing out to engage in hit-and-run strikes either on other heroes or on the enemy army, before retiring to their own side to rest.

Weapons and armor differed, too. Most critically, the *aspis* with its Argive grip that provided the stability and control necessary to make the phalanx possible hadn't yet become standard. We can't date the evolution of this shield exactly, but it probably came into common use around 700 BC or a bit earlier. Round shields of the correct size are depicted on 8th century BC pottery, but they're shown from the outside, so it's impossible for us to see whether they had central, single-handle grips or the new Argive grip. Art from the period indicates that some warriors may have used rectangular shields, and some "dipylon" shields (named after the cemetery where pottery depicting them was found) – round shields with two C-shaped cutaways in the left and right sides, which would allow a warrior to deploy a spear or sword thrust without having to expose himself from behind his shield.

It's important not to get caught up in the idea that some scholars have put forward of a "hoplite revolution." I don't like this term, because it implies that Greeks were fighting in the archaic warband style I just described and then suddenly there's a revolution and we get the hoplite phalanx overnight. That is never how any military development happens, and it certainly didn't happen that way here. By the best estimates, the transition from archaic styles of warfare began around 750 BC and were complete by around 650 BC.

Our best evidence here is the famous Chigi vase (currently in the National Etruscan Museum in Rome). This vase dates from around 650 BC and is possibly the first known artistic depiction of what are clearly hoplites fighting in phalanx formation (ordered rows, multiple ranks). Even here we see some holdovers from the archaic period. Each hoplite is depicted wielding *two* spears and neither has a butt-spike, implying that at least one of them was intended to be thrown. Another fascinating detail of the Chigi vase is the appearance of an *aulos* (a dual-piped oboe-like instrument) player in between the hoplite ranks. Only Spartans are mentioned as using "pipers" to keep in step, so this could mean that the Chigi vase depicts the Spartans marching to battle. If this is the case, the Chigi vase almost certainly depicts a battle from the Second Messenian War (*c.* 684–669 BC).

Both grave finds and art also show that greater amounts of armor were worn during the archaic period, including protection for the upper arms, thighs, groin, ankles and even the feet. This extra protection was shed over time, and we can look at the evolution of the hoplite as a constant process of shedding armor, until you get to the bare minimums of *pilos* helmet, shield and nothing else during the Peloponnesian Wars.

So Sparta's earliest known wars occurred in a period of transition and it is possible that the Lycurgan coup and subsequent reforms were meant to hasten that transition from an archaic-style army locked in a stalemate to a *polis*-style one that was able to employ the phalanx to achieve ultimate victory. It's easy to picture aristocrats entrenched in power refusing to go along with reforms until ... encouraged by Lycurgus (or whatever party the mythical figure of Lycurgus was created to represent). It's no coincidence that smack in the middle of this transitional period, the poetry of Tyrtaeus appears, specifically encouraging Spartans to practice what is clearly the organized, disciplined style of phalanx warfare. The *promachos* was no longer to be the single hero running out ahead of the army: he was the disciplined, committed first man in the file, a steadying presence to everyone behind him, keeping the formation tight.

The First Messenian War – A Twenty-year Slog to Victory

The First Messenian War is Sparta's first documented war and we have but one literary source for it, the writings of Pausanias. Unfortunately, Pausanias is unreliable and his account hotly disputed by modern scholars. He wrote in the 2nd century AD, more than 800 years after the events he describes. Worse, he cites as his two main sources unreliable Hellenistic writers, the likely 3rd century BC historian Myron and the 3rd century BC Cretan poet Rhianus – both of these writers are also centuries removed from the events. Scholars dispute the exact dates, but most set the First Messenian War as starting around 735 BC and ending around 715 BC (Pausanias gives the exact start date as 743 BC – based on the Olympic Games of the time).

It's important to point out that some scholars believe that Pausanias is not to be taken seriously at all and should be discarded altogether. I disagree with this, and believe he should be considered *very carefully* (after all, we consider Plutarch). He may have been working from other sources he doesn't specifically mention, and he provides one of our few windows onto this early period of Sparta's military record. My view? Take him with a giant grain of salt, but take him.

One interesting piece of evidence is that following 736 BC, no Messenian victors are listed at the Olympic Games, a strong indicator that they had their hands full dealing with Sparta. Other dates are given, based on the archaeological find of a destroyed layer of a coastal Argolid town called Asine (Argos, allied with the Messenians, supposedly burned the town as punishment for the Asineans allying with Sparta), but these are all within a decade or so of the dates above. We're reasonably sure the war was fought at the end of the 8th century BC and that it lasted 20 years. The comparatively long slog of the war may have been partly due to the nature of warfare in the archaic period – hit-and-run raids and individual combats between heroes are a far cry from decisive battles where armies are smashed. The Bronze Age Trojan War (if you believe it was not just a legend, as some scholars do) lasted around ten years and the archaic period Lelantine War between the Greek city-states of Chalcis and Eretria may have lasted as long as 60 years. Wars in the classical period did not last even close to this long, the great exception being the Peloponnesian "War," which is debatable as it can be divided into several shorter wars with significant periods of tense peace between them.

So, what do we know? We know that Mycenaean "palatial" society underwent some kind of cataclysm that saw it destroyed. We know that Doric peoples settled in and around what is now Sparta along the Eurotas river around the end of the 11th century BC. We also know these peoples systematically conquered the region of Laconia and set themselves up as lords over the *perioikoi*, probably the original inhabitants of the other towns and villages they conquered. Some scholars argue the helots were the descendants of the Achaean (non-Dorian) peoples who originally inhabited the area when the Dorians showed up, and others that they were the inhabitants of the southern Laconian region of Helos (Pausanias seems to think this is true). However, scholars dispute this, saying the word comes from the root for "to be captured," making helot literally mean "prisoner of war." We'll likely never know what the original population was, but around 750 BC we are reasonably sure the Spartans were masters of Laconia, possibly with the Lycurgan reforms slowly taking root.

This would make sense, because the Lycurgan model for producing superwarriors purpose-built to die for the state doesn't seem to have helped Sparta a whole lot in its first major war, a two-decade-long slog that saw it defeated again and again, with the cause of final victory totally unclear and steeped in myth, hidden firmly behind the frustrating cloak of the Spartan Mirage.

One interesting quote from Aristotle gives a clue that the Lycurgan system didn't come into full force until after the First Messenian War. The famous philosopher writes:

> ... *during the wars of the Spartans, first against the Argives and Messenians, the men were away from home for a long time. The discipline of military service prepared them to give themselves over to those making the laws and on the return of peace they submitted to this legislation.*

It's also interesting to note that Aristotle specifically calls out the Argives as a people against whom Sparta made war (as opposed to merely allies of the Messenians).

This is another clue that Sparta engaged in a war against Argos during a pause in the First Messenian War (which we will examine later in this chapter).

The Messenians were Achaeans ruled over by a Doric people, ethnically and linguistically linked to the Spartans. Their fertile lands were separated by the Taygetus mountain range, bordering Laconia on the West and Messenia on the East. The causes of the war are again a tangle of myth and history, but one thing is certain – other Greek city-states dealt with population pressures by sending out colonies to found new cities. Sparta clearly chose conquering its neighbors as an alternative. Some scholars have speculated this may have been due to Sparta's odd dual kingship. We know that in the archaic period, leaders maintained power by constantly displaying skill and valor in war. The moment a leader was perceived as weak or stagnant, that power was in question. With two royal houses constantly vying to ensure they were perceived as the "bravest and the best" (I'm paraphrasing from Homer), it makes sense that Sparta would be a city-state in a constant state of war with its neighbors. Further, Sparta was not coastal, so piracy wasn't a good option, nor was sea trade. Sparta's neighbors Argos and Corinth were strong and enriched by active trading. Sparta would try its hand against both eventually, but was probably not willing to take them on just yet. Messenia had fertile farmlands and was not united around a comparatively strong central government, as Sparta was in the period. So, whatever the specific causes may have been, the real one appears to have been simple hunger for rich farmland, slave labor and plunder – a stronger neighbor picking on a weaker one.

Pausanias, however, gives two specific causes for the war.

The First Messenian War begins

The first cause Pausanias gives has two sides: The Spartan side is that the Messenians raped Spartan "maidens" while they were worshipping at the temple of Artemis Limnatis ("Artemis of the fast waters." Artemis was the Greek goddess of hunting, the wilderness, and the animals that lived in the wild). The Spartan Agiad king Teleclus was reportedly killed trying to defend their honor. Pausanias then tells the same story from the Messenian side. The Messenians claimed that Teleclus disguised Spartan beardless youths as women and then sent them among the Messenians to assassinate them. The Messenians, discovering this trick, killed the youths and Teleclus himself. Pausanias then throws up his hands, saying, *"These are the stories given by the two sides; one may believe them according to one's feelings towards either side."*

Pausanias goes on to add the Messenian claim that the Spartans didn't seek justice for Teleclus' death, since they knew they were in the wrong. This doesn't sound right to me. The Spartans were famous for their supposed intense religiousness and concerns about ritual pollution, but the truth is they violated religious norms whenever it suited them, as we'll see time and again throughout this book. It's also interesting to note that Pausanias' narrative matches up with trends in Herodotus – stories of wars beginning with the abduction of women. This is a trend throughout a lot of ancient literature, which doesn't cast Pausanias' story in a particularly believable light. It's impossible to tell which story is true, but we must accept one thing if we're not to throw out Pausanias' account entirely – that the opening salvo of Sparta's first recorded war began with a clear Spartan defeat.

Whoever was at fault, the death of Teleclus and the rape of the Spartan maidens (who later committed suicide) didn't start an open war. Hatred and mistrust over the incident simmered for an entire generation until the reign of Teleclus' son Alcamenes as the Agiad Spartan king. His Eurypontid counterpart was Theopompus, the great-grandson of Lycurgus' brother Polydectes (if you believe Plutarch). So, if we believe Plutarch's story about the life of Lycurgus, that would mean that Sparta was already operating under the Lycurgan reforms. Plutarch gives Theopompus a great quote that would seem to argue in favor of a people living under Lycurgan law. When told that Sparta was secure because its kings knew how to command, Theopompus reportedly replied, "No, it is because its people know how to obey."

Pausanias is careful to point out that the Spartans had nursed their hatred over the incident at the temple of Artemis and were eager for any spark that might ignite the flames of war. That spark came in the form of a livestock dispute.

Keep in mind once again that Pausanias is not a very reliable source, and his description of the causes of wars seems especially mythic. So, while we take what follows with a big grain of salt, I will narrate it more or less as Pausanias does.

There was a Messenian named Polychares, famous for winning the foot race in the fourth Olympics. He owned a herd of cattle, but lacked the land to graze them on.

Polychares cut a deal with the Spartan Euaephnus – Polychares' cattle could graze on Euaephnus' land in exchange for a portion of the produce (I assume milk and meat). A note here – if we are assuming this deal was cut after the Lycurgan reforms, then each Spartan would supposedly have only the minimal equal plot of land he needed per the redistribution. But Euaephnus clearly had enough not only to meet his own needs, but to host an entire extra herd of cattle. This again raises questions about the truth of the Lycurgan reforms. Euaephnus could have somehow acquired more land than other Spartans, either through inheritance or purchase. It's not proof-positive of early wealth inequality among ancient Spartans, but it is a point of evidence.

Another point of evidence against the myth that Spartans hated wealth is the next twist in Pausanias' story – Euaephnus then *sold* Polychares' cattle and lied to the Messenian, saying the herd had been stolen by pirates. He probably would have gotten away with it too, except that one of the herdsmen (presumably a slave who was sold along with the cattle) escaped the buyers and returned to Polychares, telling him the truth of what Euaephnus had done.

Polychares promptly confronted the Spartan, who apologized and said he would make everything right. Polychares should send his son, and Euaephnus would turn over all of the money he'd been paid in the sale of Polychares' herd. Polychares sent his son (we never learn his name) and Euaephnus promptly murdered him.

When Polychares found out his son had been murdered, he appealed to the Spartan kings and ephors for justice, and despite continual complaints, was ignored. At last, out of his mind with rage, Polychares began murdering every Spartan he could lay his hands on to try to right the wrong.

One more reminder: This is mythic story told by an unreliable narrator. I cannot vouch for its truth. I am, however, unwilling to dismiss it entirely. It is possible that Pausanias is mythologizing disputes over borders and grazing land for livestock as the cause of the war, but we cannot know for sure. Again: Many scholars dismiss Pausanias entirely, but I believe we are much better off considering him carefully than not considering him at all.

Sparta invades and establishes a foothold at Ampheia

Here again, Pausanias refuses to takes sides. He is clear that this sequence of events started the war – the Spartans claiming that Polychares' killing spree and the murder of Teleclus were the causes. The Messenians claimed that they offered to submit the matter to the arbitration of neighboring Argos or of Athens. The Spartans ignored this and secretly made plans to invade. They then swore an oath that nothing would stop them until they had taken Messenia by the sword. A few months later, they invaded, with Alcamenes personally leading the Spartan force that took the Messenian hilltop town of Ampheia in a night attack. Ampheia had no garrison and the inhabitants were taken completely by surprise (Pausanias says the gates were open). The Spartans massacred the inhabitants, many still in bed. Pausanias notes morbidly that "*few escaped.*"

Not only was Ampheia a hilltop fort, but it had natural springs to provide water and was close enough to the Spartan border to be easily resupplied. The Spartans moved in and used it as a forward operating base for the remainder of the war. Pausanias gives a date for this attack (based on the coinciding Olympic Games) of 743 BC, though some scholars argue it must have occurred slightly later. But whatever the date, one thing was clear, first blood had been drawn, not in a pitched field battle, but in a lopsided surprise night attack, in Sparta's first major recorded war.

Pausanias reports that the Messenians reacted by mustering at the town of Stenyclerus to the southwest of Ampheia. There, their king Euphaes worked hard to revive flagging hearts. Pausanias implies that the Spartans already had a fearsome reputation as warriors even this early on and that it took some work by Euphaes to remind his people that they could beat the enemy back. They were clearly not ready to respond, for they did not immediately march out to retake Ampheia, but rather Euphaes dismissed the Messenians back to their homes with strict orders to keep *"all the Messenians under arms, compelling the untrained to learn the art of war and the trained men to undergo a more rigorous discipline than before."* The Messenians apparently needed time to get on a war footing if they were to match the Spartans. This is possible evidence that some degree of the military aspect of the reforms attributed to Lycurgus was already in place and that Sparta had something approaching a professional army. In the meantime, the Spartans conducted hit-and-run raids throughout the country, plundering crops and driving off herds, but Pausanias notes they did not *ravage* the countryside (burning structures and fields) as they expected to be owners of it soon enough.

If this sounds spectacularly ineffective, it was. The Spartans may have had stronger infantry (Pausanias notes that they were more experienced, and we can also see this in Euphaes' reaction – that his people needed more training), but they lacked any ability to take fortifications. Remember that Ampheia was taken utterly by surprise. The Messenian towns were now forewarned and presumably set watches and made sure their gates were shut. The Spartans attacked the Messenian towns, but were unable to take a single one and eventually gave up. Meanwhile, the Messenians raided Spartan farms in the foothills of Mount Taygetus and on the Laconian coastline.

Apart from the capture of Ampheia, the war was not off to a promising start for Sparta. Even more interesting, the stalemate dragged on for three years with the Spartans still unable to take any Messenian fortified positions. There is absolutely no indication that, faced with the need to learn more effective methods of siege warfare, the Spartans adapted. They appear not to have learned a thing. After three years Euphaes judged that his people had trained enough and were ready to take the Spartans on in a pitched battle – the first of five that made up the war. This battle doesn't have a formal name, but I call it "The Battle of the Ravine."

The Battle of the Ravine

We do not know exactly where this first battle was fought, but Pausanias notes that it included some kind of ravine that kept the two armies apart. He also mentions that Euphaes deployed his army with supplies necessary for building fortifications. The Spartans were probably thrilled to finally have a chance at a field battle given their previous three years of failing to take a single Messenian town. They left the safety of Ampheia and headed out to meet Euphaes.

We don't have specific details on either army. It's far too early for this to have been a battle between hoplite phalanxes and was likely a meeting of warbands under their respective warlords. We do know that the Messenians fielded fewer than 500 combined cavalry and *"light-armed"* troops (light infantry – fighting in loose formation, either unarmored or very lightly armored and using missile weapons like slings, javelins or bows). We have no description of the Spartan forces at all. We also get some additional names here on the Messenian side – Cleonnis, Euphaes' chosen general, and Pytharatus and Antander, commanders of the cavalry and light infantry (we don't know who commanded which units, or if they shared command of both).

The ravine kept the heavy infantry (the main body of the warband, probably a loosely organized cluster of men with bronze helmets, greaves, textile or bronze cuirasses and shields, and armed with swords and spears) apart, and the light infantry and cavalry on both sides were able to skirmish either around it, or possibly across it using missiles.

Meanwhile, Euphaes ordered his slaves to construct fortifications, eventually enclosing his army's position, completing the last wall overnight after the fighting had broken off. When the Spartans awoke the next morning to see the enemy had fortifications they couldn't hope to breach (remember their three-year-long failure to take a single fortified town), the Spartans gave up and marched off.

Most scholars declare this battle a stalemate, which boggles my mind and smacks of laconophilia. Keep the facts we have in mind – the Messenians were taken completely by surprise, losing a fortified town. Aware they were outmatched by the invader, the Messenians persevered, dug in and trained. They managed to keep the Spartans from doing anything more than ineffectually raiding for three years, all the while counterraiding into Spartan territory. When they judged themselves ready, and on ground of their choosing, they offered battle to the Spartans. They then held the Spartans at bay, built fortifications the Spartans could not overcome, and forced them to quit the field.

That is, by any measure, a Messenian victory. Certainly not a decisive one, and not a tactical one (they didn't defeat the Spartans in combat) but a strategic victory nonetheless. We have here the first real pitched battle of the Spartans' record, and it is a loss. It's also a clue to a Spartan shortcoming that would dog them throughout their entire military history – a rigid social conservatism that prevented them from innovating with the speed and creativity necessary to keep pace with not only their enemies, but also the changing nature of warfare in the ancient world. The Spartans were both slow and reluctant to embrace cavalry, missile capability and – as we are seeing here – siege warfare. Despite three years in the field against the Messenians, at the Battle of the Ravine they were every bit as helpless in the face of fortifications as they had been on the day they marched through Ampheia's open gates.

That the Battle of the Ravine was a loss is made clear by the fact that the Spartans "*went home*" (I assume this means returned to Ampheia, which they would not have abandoned) and made no further expeditions against the Messenians (I also assume the raiding continued) for an entire year, and only then when they were cursed and accused of cowardice by the Spartan elders for failing to fulfill their oath to take Messenia by the sword. I can picture some time to regroup after a stalemate, but certainly not an entire year. The loss clearly had such an impact on Spartan morale that they had to be shamed into taking the field again.

The Battle of the Kings

The second battle of the First Messenian War also goes unnamed. I call it "The Battle of the Kings" for reasons that will become clear as you read on. This second battle is a bit better documented. We know that by this point Alcamenes had died and been succeeded by his son Polydorus as the Agiad king. Theopompus still reigned for the Eurypontid royal house. The two kings took the field together and offered battle, which the Messenians accepted.

For this second battle, we again have neither troop numbers (we do know that the Spartans outnumbered the Messenians) nor a location, but we do have a very vague order of battle (a description of troop deployment). We know that Polydorus commanded the Spartan left and Theopompus the right (which in later years was considered the position of honor. It is not clear if this was the case during the 8th century BC). If the right was the position of honor in this early period, it does make sense to have Polydorus on the left. He would have been newly come to the throne and less experienced than Theopompus. We know that Euryleon, originally from Thebes but "*now a Spartan*" (how he became Spartan, we don't know) commanded the Spartan center. Euphaes and Antander jointly held the Messenian left opposite Theopompus.

Recall that Antander was the commander of either the light infantry or the cavalry (or both) in the Battle of the Ravine. Antander's position with King Euphaes would normally make me think he was the cavalry commander. Owning and breeding horses was the mark of an aristocrat in the ancient world, and light infantry were typically drawn from the poorer segments of society because their equipment was cheaper. This makes me think the Messenian left was some kind of royal cavalry squadron. However, Pausanias points out that there were few cavalry present for the battle and they accomplished little, because back then the people of the Peloponnese were poor horsemen.

Pytharatus commanded the Messenian right opposite Polydorus, and Cleonnis commanded the center opposite Euryleon. If my assumption about the cavalry was correct, that could mean that both Polydorus and Pytharatus commanded light infantry. However, Pausanias also notes that the Spartans used Cretan archers against the Messenian light infantry and specifically points out that neither the Cretans nor the Messenian light troops fought at all, but were held in reserve. The battle was fought entirely by heavy infantry. We are also told that the Spartans had subjugated troops under their command, though whether these were Messenians conquered and forced into servitude, or Laconians from previous Spartan conquests isn't clear. We do know that the Dryopes, driven from their home of Asine by the Argives, had come under Spartan protection and were forced to serve under their command. We hear nothing of the composition of the Messenian army.

Both kings gave their pre-battle speeches (Theopompus gave it for the Spartans, again implying he was the senior king). The Spartan speech was, of course, laconic, consisting mostly of a reminder for the Spartans to fulfill their oath to take Messenia. Euphaes reminded his people of the butchery at Ampheia and that to lose here would mean the same for all of them. It was far better to die a noble death on the battlefield than to suffer the indignity of being butchered and looted by the victorious Spartan army.

Euphaes' words apparently had the desired effect, because the Messenians fought like men possessed, charging for the Spartan lines. The Spartans, Pausanias is careful to point out, also advanced, but did so in disciplined fashion – careful not to break ranks. If Pausanias is describing the actual events accurately, then we are possibly seeing a very early example of the real success of the Lycurgan military system and possible evidence that it was beginning to come into effect even at this very early date. In the archaic period, when individual heroism was predominant and unit discipline not yet the order of the day, the Spartans may have already been ahead of their time, at least as far as heavy infantry went. It is equally possible that Pausanias was misled by his Hellenistic sources who already believed (falsely) that the Spartans were disciplined professionals even at this early date.

But Pausanias describes something else which is also a departure from the hoplite phalanx battles we will see later in this book. After charging into the battle the armies stop and ... yell at each other.

There's a thing I call the "war dance" in modern street brawls. There are some people who are hardened professional fighters, or at least veterans, who can simply go from nonviolence to violence without warning or preamble. But most of us aren't like that. Most of us have to yell and posture and hurl insults to get our blood up to the point where we feel brave enough to throw a punch. We push each other, yell and curse, and most of the time it is directed not at the person we're intending to fight, but at *ourselves* – an effort to overcome fear and force ourselves over the line and into violent action. What Pausanias describes next seems a lot like that to me. The battle lines halted and:

> ... *threatened one another by brandishing their arms and with fierce looks, and fell to recriminations, these calling the Messenians already their slaves, no freer than the helots; the others answering that they were impious in their undertaking, who for the sake of gain attacked their kinsmen and outraged all the ancestral gods of the Dorians, and Heracles above all.*

This war dancing apparently tipped them over into actual fighting and the lines engaged.

Pausanias gives a few details that mark the differences between the Spartans and their opponents. The Spartans were more disciplined and better skilled (Pausanias notes they were "*trained for war from boyhood*," an indication that the Upbringing was in practice at this time). While the Messenians loudly encouraged one another, the Spartans kept silent. The Spartans also were less inclined to individual heroic deeds, preferring to keep formation and work as a unit. More evidence that, even at this early date, they had begun to professionalize their army. They employed a deeper formation (more ranks), and hoped to out-endure the Messenians. I want to remind the reader once again that it's entirely possible that the Spartans *weren't* this disciplined at all, and that Pausanias is either making it up, or being misled by his Hellenistic sources, who believed the laconophilic myths already well established at the time they were writing.

But if this discipline existed, it didn't apply to Sparta's kings, apparently. For in the old heroic style Theopompus broke ranks and rushed out to engage Euphaes in single combat. This single combat caused a surge of fighting throughout the ranks for both armies, but eventually Euphaes and the Messenian left broke Theopompus and the Spartan right, and sent them running. This individual heroic conduct is completely at odds with the idea of an organized, disciplined Spartan army. It may be evidence of the gradual transition (remember, militaries change through a process of gradual reform, not sudden revolution) from the old heroic style of warfare to the new disciplined forms that would be critical for the phalanx to emerge in the classical period. Or, it could be evidence that the Spartans weren't disciplined at all at that time.

Theopompus' rout would surely have resulted in the second Messenian victory of the war, but on the Messenian right Pytharatus had been killed and his leaderless troops were hanging on by a thread. Pausanias notes that neither the Spartans nor the Messenians pursued their routing enemies, but while the Spartans didn't pursue out of discipline and a desire to maintain unit cohesion (as was their "*ancient custom*"), especially in country they didn't know well, Euphaes didn't pursue because he needed to come to the aid of his own routed right wing. In the center, Cleonnis and Euryleon's troops engaged without either side getting the upper hand until nightfall forced an end to the fighting. Keep in mind that night-fighting in the ancient world meant fighting by moon, star and torchlight, and that meant that the ability to see where you were going or tell friend from foe would be extremely difficult.

Pausanias reports that the following morning neither side had the stomach to take up the fight again and instead both sides agreed to a truce to collect and bury their dead. Neither side set up a victory trophy (a field monument made from the captured arms and armor of the enemy dead), which further indicates that they agreed the battle did not have a clear winner. Some scholars believe that Pausanias' mention of a victory trophy is an anachronism, as there are no contemporary mentions of trophies (meaning, the historians discussing them were alive at the time) until after the Greco-Persian War more than two centuries later.

And so, here again we must reckon with the truth of Sparta's military record.

After four years of war, despite superior numbers, training and discipline (if we believe Pausanias), they had lost one battle and ground to a stalemate in a second, having suffered the indignity of seeing their king running from a fight.

Despite this admirable showing by the Messenians, they were unable to sustain the effort. Pausanias points out that they couldn't keep up with the cost of keeping so many towns garrisoned. Their slaves were also deserting to the Spartans. Worse, they were hit with some kind of wide-scale plague (though Pausanias says it "*did not strike everyone*"). These setbacks forced the Messenians to abandon their towns and retreat to an old fortified position on the naturally defensible Mount Ithome, where they extended and upgraded the old circuit walls. Pausanias points out that this position was also at the mountain's most naturally inaccessible point.

And here Pausanias' narrative dips into the incredibly frustrating habit of so many ancient writers – treating myth as if it was reality. Throughout many of the ancient sources, you have to deal with writers talking about the oracles from Delphi as if they were real and as if the outcome of real events hinged on them. I don't doubt that the morale and actions of people were affected by their belief in oracles, but this is a book of history, not mythology and I'm not going to credit oracles and the intervention of gods as even remotely true.

After retreating to their stronghold on Ithome, the Messenians sent a man named Tisis who was "*skilled in divination*" to Delphi to get an oracle that would guide them on how to win the war. Pausanias then says that on his return Tisis was ambushed by the Spartans and fought them off until an unseen presence demanded he be allowed to go free. This is, of course, utter hogwash. The far more likely answer is that Tisis was ambushed by Spartans and simply managed to escape and make it back to Ithome. I won't go into the insane oracle and the wildly misogynistic sequence of events that followed, but suffice to say that the delivery of an oracle at all was demoralizing to the Spartans who according to Pausanias couldn't muster the courage to assault Ithome for another five years.

While it's certainly possible they were demoralized by superstition, it's also possible they were put off by the difficulty of assaulting a fortified position on a high mountain, or even that they attempted yet another unsuccessful siege. Pausanias also implies that the conditions of the oracle weren't properly obeyed, and that this may be why the Messenians ultimately lost the war. Again, that's clearly not true.

There's another possible explanation – the archaeological record indicates that Sparta invaded the Argolid, the region of the northeastern Peloponnese ruled by the city-state of Argos. This could mean that tensions between the Argives and Spartans flared into open warfare during this period, perhaps giving the Messenians a welcome five-year reprieve. This makes sense – remember my earlier mention of the Dryopes assisting the Spartans after being driven from their home of Asine. This town was surely destroyed (archaeologists have found a destroyed layer) by the Argives, possibly in vengeance on the residents for assisting the Spartans, and the date of the destruction is one of the main indicators we have for the end date of the First Messenian War – since the Argives, freed from having to fight the Spartans, could deal with the closer, smaller threat.

Another interesting point here. We know that the Spartans, when they made war during this period, subjugated the population and occupied the territory of the defeated. Keeping this in mind, if we accept that the Spartans did invade the Argolid during this five-year period, then it was either to raid or they were defeated and driven out. However, as we can't be completely certain this invasion occurred, we can't chalk this up as yet another Spartan loss.

The Battle Without Allies

A third battle was fought, and again we don't have an exact location. Pausanias says the Spartans marched against Ithome, but his description makes it sound like a field battle, which is hard to understand since the Messenians occupied a defensible position on good ground.

We have less information than for the prior battle. This battle also isn't named, but I call it "The Battle Without Allies," for Pausanias tells us that the Messenians fought without allies, since the oracle was supposed to guarantee them victory. Far more likely was that the Messenian allies used the oracle as an excuse not to tangle with Sparta. If we believe that the Spartans invaded Argos during the preceding interval, it's possible that the Argives at least were either cowed or licking their wounds following the recent Spartan invasion. We know that the Spartans no longer had the Cretan archers with them and that no sections of either army were broken or routed like last time.

Pausanias notes that champions from both sides met in the middle, another sign that the old heroic style of warfare was still in practice. Pausanias also implies that neither army maintained its formation, which could indicate that the professionalization of the Spartan army was not advanced yet or didn't exist at all.

Euphaes drove hard at Theopompus again, trying to finish the job he started five years ago, but the Spartans got the better of him this time, and he suffered multiple mortal wounds. A huge fight followed as the Spartans tried to drag the dying Messenian king to their side of the battlefield and the Messenians tried to rescue him. Antander was killed trying to save his king. By the time night fell and brought an end to the fighting, the Messenians had recovered their king, but he died of his wounds a few days later. Despite Euphaes' mortal wounding, the battle ended in another stalemate.

Euphaes had no children and was succeeded by Aristodemus as king of the Messenians, even though Aristodemus was ritually polluted by his reaction to the oracle (another implication that the Messenian cause was doomed by the failure to comply with the dictates of the gods).

The war dragged on with both sides maintaining the steady pace of raids into one another's territory. Pausanias notes that Aristodemus maintained a strong alliance with the city-states of Argos and Sicyon, as well as with the city-states of the central Peloponnesian region of Arcadia to the north. The Argives did not publicly declare their opposition to Sparta (perhaps because they were recovering or cowed by the Spartan incursion we discussed earlier), but prepared to take the Messenian side when the time came.

The Battle of Ithome

That time came five years later in a pitched battle apparently prompted by both Spartan and Messenian exhaustion with the length and expense of the war.

Of all the battles of the First Messenian War, we have our most complete information for this fourth battle – which I call "The Battle of Ithome." While the exact location is unknown, the description places it with Mount Ithome to the Messenians' rear, presumably to give them a safe position for retreat in the event the battle went against them.

We know that this time the allies came out in full force. The city-state of Corinth stood with Sparta and the Messenians were joined by troops from Arcadia and "*picked troops*" (elite warriors – though we don't know what made them elite) from Argos and Sicyon. The Spartans put the Corinthian troops in the center, along with their other allied and subjugated peoples, including their helot slaves. The Spartan kings each commanded a wing, in a deeper and tighter formation than in previous battles.

The Messenians created an apparently elite section of their battle line (or possibly the entire battle line) composed of strong and brave Messenians and Arcadians along with the Argives and Sicyonians under the command of Cleonnis. The Messenians were outnumbered and forced to extend their battle line to prevent being outflanked. This would necessarily have thinned their ranks, making a breakthrough more likely.

King Aristodemus himself commanded a reserve force of light infantry. Pausanias gives a fairly detailed description of this force:

> ... *consisting of a few slingers or archers, the bulk of the force being physically suited to rapid assaults and retreats and lightly armed. Not all of them had a breastplate or shield, but those who lacked them were protected with the skins of goats and sheep, some of them, particularly the Arcadian mountaineers, having the hides of wild beasts, wolves and bears.*

Pausanias adds that each of them carried a few javelins, and some of them had thrusting spears. This force was intended to be mobile, possibly to plug a hole in the battle line should the Spartans break through, or to exploit a flanking opportunity. They were kept out of sight of the enemy.

Pausanias reports that the Messenian line held firm as the Spartans attacked, despite being outnumbered. He adds that this was because the Messenians were fielding picked troops against levies, which is confusing if you believe that the Spartans were fielding disciplined, organized soldiers brought up under the Upbringing. It's possible he's referring to the Corinthian troops, to the helots or to other elements of the Spartan army. It's also possible that the Lycurgan military machine was either still gearing up, or not in place at all at this time. At any rate, the Messenians and their allies held firm and the Spartans did not break their line.

And then the Messenians deployed their mobile force, outflanking the Spartans and showering them with missiles.

You can picture the Spartan shock. They were engaged in a tough fight, all their focus directly ahead of them, frustrated that the outnumbered enemy wouldn't give ground and suddenly they began to drop, shot through their sides by sling stones and javelins coming from out of nowhere. If we believe Pausanias' report that the kings commanded the flanks, then it was the elite Peers (if such Peers existed at this time) who took the brunt of this attack. It also illustrates another Spartan failing that we'll see repeated again and again throughout the battles covered in this book – a failure to properly scout, reconnoiter or otherwise get the full measure of the enemy forces and their plans.

Pausanias' description of their reaction confirms that the Spartans being felled by the missiles were members of a social elite, even if they weren't the Peers of later years. Remember that I earlier noted that light infantry were typically of lower social status, unable to afford the more expensive equipment of heavy infantry. He notes here that *"Men are apt to be most annoyed by what they regard as beneath them"* and adds that the Spartans were angered when they charged the light troops, who simply ran away, easily outdistancing their more heavily armored opponents. They then immediately returned to pour the fire back on as soon as the Spartans gave up the chase. The Spartans would see this same tactic repeated against them with equal success roughly 300 years later at the Battle of Sphacteria, and it wouldn't be the last time.

The Spartans were completely unprepared for these hit-and-run tactics. They kept up the fight as long and hard as they could, but clearly the casualties and fatigue of the running combat began to mount and at last Spartan resolve failed. They broke ranks and routed, fleeing the battlefield.

Pausanias specifically points out that they were demoralized by the hit-and-run tactics that ran *"counter to their custom."* Unable to adapt, they were defeated. As I mentioned earlier, routing troops are at their most vulnerable, and while Pausanias does not give a casualty count, he does note that *"it was impossible to count the Spartan losses in the battle, but I am convinced they were heavy."* The Spartans and their allies ran, with the Corinthians having to retreat through enemy territory, likely harassed all the way.

Pausanias is clear that the defeat demoralized the Spartans, and that many of their leaders fell in the battle (though he does not specify who. We can safely assume it was neither of the kings). The Spartans now sent to Delphi for an oracle of their own and received the advice to try trickery instead of open battle. This is an important point when we consider the Spartan reputation for excellence in field battles. The Spartans heeded the oracle, sending 100 spies pretending to be deserters to infiltrate the Messenians. Aristodemus immediately saw through the trick and turned them away, with the magnificent (though probably not real) quote: *"The crimes of the Spartans are new, but their tricks are old."*

The Spartans next tried to fracture the Messenian alliances, but the Arcadians turned their ambassadors back and they did not attempt to reach out to Argos (Pausanias doesn't say why not, but it's further evidence that Sparta pursued a separate war with the Argives in this period, so it may be that relations were too poor to support an embassy).

During this period, the Messenians sent again to Delphi for another oracle (and received an incomprehensible reply), then another as the war dragged into its 20th year. Once again, I am not going to dwell on the specifics of the oracles, because while they may have impacted the morale of the combatants, they certainly didn't directly impact the outcome of the war. What is relevant is that the Spartans used a trick to make it appear as if the oracle had been fulfilled to favor the Spartans and Pausanias implies that Aristodemus was unable to rally the spirits of his superstitious people despite trying to interpret the omens favorably. Pausanias then relates a series of fantastic (and surely false) miracles that foretold victory for the Spartans and defeat for the Messenians. We are also able to guess from Pausanias that while the Spartans were defeated in the pitched battle, they had the Messenians bottled up in their fortress on Mount Ithome, and that food and supply shortages were beginning to tell on the defenders. He makes no mention of it until later in his story, but then notes that the Messenians sought a final battle because of the "*blockade.*"

Despairing of the bad omens and plagued by guilt over past mistakes, Aristodemus committed suicide. This is another indicator that the Messenians were not sitting pretty with the upper hand after their victory in the Battle of Ithome and that they were in fact besieged in their fortress on Mount Ithome. This suicide was the nail in the coffin of Messenian morale. As Aristodemus died without heirs, they had no king to succeed him and so the Messenians raised up Damis, who had commanded the light infantry with him at the last battle, as supreme general. They rejected asking the Spartans for peace terms (again, a thing they wouldn't have even considered despite Aristodemus' death if they had the upper hand, so another point of evidence that they were bottled up in their fortress). Damis took joint command of the army with Cleonnis and a man named Phyleus, and they marched out to face the Spartans for a fifth and final time.

The Last Battle

Pausanias gives almost no information about this final battle, which I call "The Last Battle." All we know of it is that, despite the Messenians' bravery, all their leaders were killed. The implication is that they were defeated and driven back into their fortress where they held out for five more months before melting away – the rich and connected heading to allies in Argos and Sicyon and the priestly class to Eleusis. The commoners, of course, could only return to their towns and villages, there to fall under the Spartan yoke. They were made helots, forming the backbone of the slave class who would support the tiny minority of Peers in their pampered lifestyle for the next three and a half centuries.

Pausanias gives us two quotes from Tyrtaeus to summarize the plight of the conquered Messenians. I've combined them both here: "*Like donkeys worn by their great burdens, bringing of dire necessity to their masters the half of all the fruits the corn-land bears. Wailing for their masters, they and their wives alike, whenever the baneful doom of death came upon any."*

Sparta's record in the First Messenian War

The Last Battle is Sparta's first recorded battlefield victory, and its only recorded battlefield victory in the entire two decades of the First Messenian War. In the end, the Spartans through sheer relentlessness and greater resources held out and wore the Messenians away. But if Pausanias is to be believed, they did this in spite of multiple staggering defeats by an enemy they outmatched and outnumbered. At the end of a 20-year slog, the Spartans were victorious.

And here we should note an incredible irony – the Spartans' legend was formed by their defeat at Thermopylae in 480 BC. Specifically, they are admired because in the mythic mistelling of the story, just 300 of them faced down an army of many tens of thousands of Persians. Their willingness to fight in the face of such a disparity in numbers is a huge part of their claim to fame. Yet, when we reckon the battles I've just recounted, we see the opposite is true – the Spartans fought primarily lopsided battles where they outnumbered their enemies and usually lost anyway.

When we examine their record in the battles we know of, the image of the mighty Spartan warrior starts out on very shaky footing. A single victory, matched against two stalemates and two losses, including one of their kings being defeated, routed and driven from the field. Wherever the roots of Sparta's warrior legend lie, they are surely not to be found in their battlefield record of the First Messenian War.

The Second Messenian War

Sparta's subjugation of Messenia didn't take. Within 40 years, the region was in revolt, an event that widened into another open war that dragged on for almost another 20 years. This war likely happened from roughly 685 to 668 BC (though some scholars say it began at that end date). Again, our main source is the highly dubious Pausanias and his narrative is interwoven with totally unbelievable accounts of gods, oracles and magic animals saving human lives, so we have to treat it very carefully, keeping in mind that we may well be dealing with more myth-making. Some scholars have speculated that Pausanias is telling a history made up by the Messenians in the 4th century BC after they were finally liberated from Spartan domination and set about fabricating their own history. I don't know that that's true, but Pausanias' narrative does form a piece of Sparta's military record and so we have to consider it. Here is the story Pausanias tells, largely a superhero origin story of the Messenian leader Aristomenes.

Pausanias tells us the Messenians burned to be free of the Spartan yoke but made sure of their alliances with Argos and the Arcadians before raising the banner of revolt.

The kings of Sparta at the time were Polydorus' grandson Anaxander for the Agiads, and Theopompus' grandson Zeuxidamus for the Eurypontids.

The Battle of Derae

The war opened with the Battle of Derae (around 684 BC). The word means "hill," but otherwise we have no clue to its location) fought somewhere in Messenia or Laconia about a year after the revolt kicked off. Neither side had its allies and the battle was fought to a stalemate. Pausanias tells us nothing about the battle other than that Aristomenes performed so heroically that the Messenians were for appointing him as their king, and that he declined, accepting the same supreme general position that Damis had held roughly half a century earlier.

This next story is so heroic that my first suspicion is that it can't be true, but it certainly is possible and far too amazing not to include. Aristomenes, eager to do "*deeds worthy of record*," snuck into Sparta under cover of darkness and into the temple of Athena of the Bronze House (the ruins of this building are still visible in Sparta today). There, he dedicated a shield inscribed "*The gift of Aristomenes to the Goddess, taken from the Spartans*." If true, it must have been terrifying, though it stretches belief that even a single man could have snuck over the Taygetus range, into the heart of Sparta, and into one of its most important temples without being detected.

Apparently the episode shook the Spartans so badly that they sent to Delphi for an oracle, which per Pausanias instructed them to seek counsel from Athens. Pausanias relates that Athens, not wanting to help Sparta but also not wanting to defy an oracle, sent the lame, not very smart teacher Tyrtaeus to counsel the Spartans – this is the same famous lyric poet I mentioned before. Again, the story has to be taken with a huge grain of salt, but it is one origin story for Tyrtaeus, where he was from and how he came to Sparta.

The Battle of the Boar's Tomb

A year after the Battle of Derae, the two armies met again at the Battle of the Boar's Tomb in Stenyclerus. Pausanias gives us better order of battle information for this fight. The Messenians were joined by their allies the Eleans, Arcadians, Argives and Sicyonians as well as all those Messenians in exile after their defeat in the First Messenian War. The Spartans had the Corinthians once again, as well as the Lepreans, old enemies of the Eleans.

No other details of troop counts, arms, armor or deployment are given. However, if our dates are correct, this battle was fought right around the time that the warriors on the Chigi vase that I mentioned earlier are depicted. From that correlation, we can guess that the phalanx was coming into existence now, though the transition to the ordered hoplite formation was probably not yet complete. Some scholars have suggested that the Chigi vase might be depicting a battle from the Second Messenian War, perhaps even this very battle.

Pausanias singles out King Anaxander and his guard above all for bravery. Tyrtaeus, Pausanias notes, did not fight, but stood behind the army encouraging the rear ranks to hold firm. Anaxander fought against Aristomenes and his picked guard of 80 men (a huge discrepancy in numbers if Anaxander was fighting with the full complement of 300 *hippeis*, though some scholars argue that the king was protected only by 100 selected from the total corps), and despite their great courage the Spartans were defeated and routed. We saw a Eurypontid king flee from battle in the First Messenian War, and now Pausanias tells us of the Agiad king fleeing in the Second.

Pausanias reports that Aristomenes ordered another Messenian unit to chase the fleeing king and turned his attention to the Spartan line "*where it was strongest.*" The Messenian leader assaulted the line at this point and, perhaps because they were already demoralized seeing their king flee a fight lopsided in his favor, the Spartan line broke and ran with their allies in tow. If we believe that the phalanx was coming into existence at this time, then it's possible that Aristomenes' and Anaxander's units engaged as part of their respective battle lines, possibly on the far right or left, which would allow the victorious Aristomenes to slam into the exposed Spartan flank as Anaxander's unit fled. This would be notably different from the heroic clash between Euphaes and Theopompus out in front of their respective armies in the previous war. This looks a lot more like the clash of phalanxes that would be the hallmark of warfare in the classical era to come.

Pausanias relates that Sparta's nerve was broken by this defeat and that the Spartans would have sued for peace had not the poetry of Tyrtaeus inspired them to continue the fight. He also notes that the Spartans replenished their ranks by drawing on the helots once again.

Aristomenes followed up the victory at Boar's Tomb by raiding the Spartan town of Pharae, a cattle-rustling strike that saw the Messenian hero driving off Spartan herds (which meant he more than likely butchered Spartan helots, who would have been tending to the animals, and not Peers). King Anaxander was alerted to the attack and intercepted Aristomenes, and was defeated and driven off for a second time. Pausanias says that Aristomenes would have chased the fleeing king down had he not been wounded in the buttocks by a javelin. The need to tend to the wound forced Aristomenes to leave off the chase, but he kept the stolen cattle.

He followed this raid with another as soon as he was healed, kidnapping the richest and noblest Spartan women while they were worshiping at the temple of Artemis Caryatis and ransoming them back to the Spartans. Pausanias details a third raid where Spartan women worshipping at a temple of Demeter fought back against the Messenians and even succeeded in capturing Aristomenes, though he later escaped, possibly via a bribe.

The Battle of the Great Trench

The next pitched battle was fought three years into the war at a place called "the Great Trench." Polybius references this battle as well, giving us at least confirmation in another source both for the life of Aristomenes and for this battle.

Pausanias notes that the Messenians were joined by their Arcadian allies (but not the Eleans, Argives or Sicyonians) under the command of Aristocrates, whom Pausanias describes as the Arcadians' "*king and general.*" We are given no troop counts or other order of battle information (save that the Arcadian troops made up the center and left of the Messenian battle line), but we are told that the Spartans won the battle by means of a bribe – the first instance of purchasing victory, according to Pausanias, in the history of Greece.

Pausanias relates that Sparta bribed Aristocrates to betray the Messenian cause. Just as the Spartan and Messenian lines were about to engage, the Arcadian withdrew his contingent, the entire left and center of the Messenian battle line, retreating through the Messenian positions.

We've discussed how tightly ordered and compact the phalanx is, and while we can't be sure how complete the transition to this formation was at the time of the Battle of the Great Trench, we can assume that the withdrawal of troops through a tightly packed line must have forced the Messenians to break ranks to admit their withdrawing allies. Getting those dispersed men back into formation once the Arcadians were through would not have been easy, not counting the incredible blow to Messenian morale from watching their allies abandon them just as the armies closed for action. Unsurprisingly, the remaining Messenian troops were surrounded and crushed, granting the Spartans the first recorded battlefield victory of the Second Messenian War, and that achieved not in a stand-up fight, but through a bribe.

Aristomenes gathered the survivors and fled to a fortress on Mount Eira in northern Messenia. If this seems like a repeat of the retreat to Mount Ithome in the last war, that's because it was (save that the withdrawal to Ithome happened after a good showing in battle, rather than a crushing defeat).

Pausanias reports that the Spartans placed the Messenians under siege, much as they had at Ithome, and just as at Ithome, the Messenians held on – Pausanias tells us they managed to cling to Eira for another 11 years after their loss at the Great Trench, engaging in hit-and-run raids both in their own occupied territory and also over the Taygetus range and into the Spartan home territory of Laconia, stealing corn, cattle, wine, and whatever else wasn't nailed down, and selling captives into slavery.

Pausanias claims that the Spartans, in an effort to make this raiding less profitable, ceased cultivation of any farmland in Messenia, as well as Spartan farmland bordering the region, resulting in political unrest in Sparta *"For those who had property here could not endure its lying idle."* This makes sense if the communal messing system was in place. If a Spartan Peer's land allotment was not producing, he would no longer be able to afford to maintain his mess dues and would be ejected from his mess to descend into the ranks of the Inferiors. Some scholars have also speculated that this description is an indication of the crisis in Spartan land and wealth inequality that spurred the Lycurgan reforms in the first place, though it is impossible to know for sure.

During this period, Aristomenes captured and plundered the Spartan town of Amyclae, one of the original five villages making up the Spartan city-state proper and the site of the second most important of the annual Spartan festivals – the Hyacinthia. He fled before a Spartan relief force could march to rescue the town, but was apparently overtaken by a Spartan army consisting of *"more than half the Spartan infantry"* (it isn't clear if Pausanias is referring to the Peers, or to the Peers plus their subject *perioikoi*) and both kings. According to Pausanias, Aristomenes was now captured but managed to escape due to the aid of both gods and magic animal companions. The story is so outrageous that it's not worth repeating here, but suffice to say that if Aristomenes was actually captured, he made good his escape and found his way back to Mount Eira.

Back at Eira, Aristomenes had more adventures, including a night raid on Sparta's Corinthian allies that saw the Messenians slaughter an entire column in their sleep. He was again purportedly captured, and again escaped (or was released in another very unlikely story).

The Battle of Eira

At last, the fortress on Eira fell due to betrayal when a Spartan deserter noted that the Messenians were shirking guard duty in order to avoid a particularly bad rainstorm. Deserting back to the Spartans, the man led them against the fortress. The Messenians were alerted by their barking dogs, but apparently too late to reestablish the perimeter and the battle quickly descended into a brutal street-to-street and house-to-house fight in the tight urban quarters of the fortress.

Neither side was able to make any headway, the Spartans being unfamiliar with the layout of the town and the Messenians being caught completely unawares. The Messenians realized their desperate situation, and Pausanias describes Messenian women climbing up to the rooftops, ripping up roof tiles to throw down on the Spartans but driven off the roofs by the fierce storm.

The Spartans far outnumbered the Messenians, but their numbers counted for nothing in the tight confines of the streets. The Spartans eventually leveraged this to their advantage, sending idle rear-echelon troops back to camp to rest and eat and then rotating them in to relieve the exhausted troops who had been engaged in the street fighting. The Messenians apparently didn't have the numbers or the organization to match this and after three days, exhaustion and demoralization began to tell. At last, Aristomenes ordered a rearguard to cover the retreat of the women and children (and presumably the most important aristocrats) and led them out of the fort and to safety in Arcadia.

Pausanias says that the Spartans were happy to let them go for fear of *"further inflaming men who had reached the bounds of frenzy and despair,"* but this makes little sense. Either the Messenians fought a successful rearguard action and escaped, or the Spartans were so badly beat up in the running urban fight that they weren't in a position to effectively pursue the escaping Messenians.

In Arcadia, Aristomenes tried to rally a revenge mission, hoping to capture Sparta and trade it back for the conquered territory of Messenia, but was betrayed once again by Aristocrates. This time, however, Aristocrates' treachery was found out, and the Arcadian was stoned to death. This effectively ended any further attempts at liberating Messenia, ending the Second Messenian War with Sparta in firm possession of Messenia. The Messenians were once again reduced to slavery.

Those who had escaped to Arcadia went on to settle even farther afield in southern Italy and Sicily. Aristomenes managed to marry off his daughter to a warlord of Rhodes, and ended his days there, comfortable and at peace. The Spartans, though victorious, were never able to punish the Messenian who had tweaked their nose so badly.

Sparta's record in the Second Messenian War

When we reckon Sparta's battlefield record in the Second Messenian War, we once again get a very different picture from the superwarriors portrayed in popular media. Of the four battles we know of, the Spartans lost one, fought to a stalemate in the other, and won two. Both of those victories were due to treachery (a bribe in one case, and a deserter/spy in the other), rather than simple battlefield brilliance. We again see one of their kings, Anaxander, running from the battlefield not once but twice – the first after his defeat in the Battle of the Boar's Tomb, and again in his unsuccessful attempt to intercept Aristomenes' cattle-drive.

The argument can of course be made that these aren't the *real* Spartans, and that the superwarriors celebrated in popular myth are conclusively *post-* Lycurgan reforms, shaped by the Upbringing and the strict laws introduced by the mythic lawgiver. The argument can also be made that the Lycurgan reforms were initiated as a response to Sparta's abysmally poor performance in the Messenian Wars. Either way, we cannot be sure to what extent these reforms were in place during either of the Messenian Wars, and so we must carefully examine Sparta's performance in later battles in order to truly get their measure.

Fair enough. We will keep going, examining Sparta at war in later years. Fortunately for us (though unfortunately for everyone involved in them), Sparta was constantly at war for its entire history.

Conflict with Argos, Tegea and Samos

The Battle of Hysiae

In the same year as the end of the Second Messenian War (or at least, right around then), the archaeological record shows – backed up by Pausanias – that Sparta once again attempted to punish Argos for its assistance to the Messenians, and possibly to reduce the Argives to the helot status now suffered by the Messenians. The two armies met during the rule of the Argive tyrant Pheidon (probably in 668 BC, just when Eira was finally taken and the Messenians fled into Arcadia) in the Argolid at a place called Hysiae.

That the battle took place in the Argolid shows it was a Spartan invasion (if the Argives were invading, it would have been fought in Laconia). That Argos did not come under the Spartan thumb confirms it was a Spartan defeat. No other information is known about the battle, and some scholars dispute that it was even fought at all. But the archaeology and Pausanias' account make sense, and it's pretty clear that the Battle of Hysiae did indeed take place. The lack of source material means Hysiae must be nothing more than a brief footnote in our examination, but the battle is yet another loss to tally on Sparta's military record, and one much closer to the height of Sparta's glory.

We largely lose sight of Sparta's military campaigns after Hysiae, but the Spartans had to be engaged in the subjugation and consolidation of their hold over what was now the entire southern Peloponnese. There are stories of Sparta's involvement in wars with states to the north, but no major or detailed dissections of battles that we can use here.

It's clear that Sparta's domination over its new helot slave class was shaky and that a lot of attention had to be paid to ensuring that the Spartans weren't overwhelmed by a resentful and recently conquered underclass who vastly outnumbered the beleaguered Peers. Clearly the Spartans found the price to be worth it, or else had a tiger by the tail and feared to let go lest they be devoured. Plutarch sums this up in a quote from the Agiad king Anaxandridas II, when he was asked why the Spartans had the helots work their fields. "How do you think," the king replied, probably looking at the questioner like he was a fool, "we got the fields in the first place?"

Tensions continued between Argos and Sparta, but clearly Sparta was unable to recover from its defeat at Hysiae and lacked the strength to punish their northern neighbor. Yet Sparta clearly still pursued its expansionist policy, and Herodotus tells us that the Spartans still felt confident of their ability to dominate the Arcadians, even though their paid man in the region was dead under a pile of rocks. The Spartans now sent to Delphi for an oracle, which Herodotus tells us predicted that they would capture the Arcadian city-state of Tegea "*to pound with your feet in rhythm, and its beautiful fields for your measuring ropes.*"

The Battle of the Fetters

The Spartans supposedly were encouraged by this oracle and set out for war around 550 BC carrying chains to bind their future helots and measuring ropes to parcel out the Tegean fields as land allotments for future Spartan Peers according to Lycurgan law. As with Hysiae, we have no details whatsoever about the battle that followed, save one – it was a Spartan defeat, and the hopeful warriors who set out to conquer Tegea wound up wearing the chains (fetters) they brought with them to make the Tegeans slaves. Herodotus claims to have seen the very chains in his own time in the temple of Athena Alea. Herodotus also tells us that this was the first of many battles in the Spartan–Tegean war that the Spartans lost, prompting the Spartans to send for yet another oracle, which instructed them to find and repatriate the bones of the mythic hero Orestes.

Herodotus' narrative veers wildly at this point, and we're told a story about the crafty Spartan Lichas finding Orestes' giant bones through a combination of luck and skill. Some modern scholars have suggested that this story is true and that the bones were likely those of a dinosaur or mammoth. I think it far more likely that the story is made up, and that either the Spartans flat-out lied about having the bones or the story was invented as a convenient way of explaining why Tegea wound up in an unequal alliance with Sparta despite having defeated it in so many battles. In the end, the result is the same. Either because the Tegeans believed that Sparta's possession of this holy relic conferred some divine advantage, or because the Spartans finally won the upper hand through military skill or endurance, they defeated Tegea.

But either this defeat was not decisive, or else the Spartans had too much on their hands trying to keep down the helot population of Messenia and Laconia, for they did not subjugate Tegea. Instead they forged a treaty. Tegea became the first member of the military alliance modern scholars would call the Peloponnesian League, which would become a major instrument of Spartan military and foreign policy until its forcible disbandment when Philip II of Macedon (father of Alexander the Great) effectively conquered Greece in 338 BC.

The "League" was a league in name only. It's more accurate to call it a system of bilateral and unequal alliances with Sparta. Each member was allied only with Sparta, not with one another, and while the league had a voting structure (one member, one vote), those votes were not binding on Sparta, and only Sparta could call a meeting of the League. The sole concession League members gained was that Sparta would fight to defend them if attacked, at least theoretically. Further, the League didn't require payment of membership dues or tribute, but League members were required to contribute troops to Spartan military operations, including offensive ones.

While the League absolutely catapulted Sparta into the pole position in the Peloponnese and enabled it to challenge its mortal enemy of Argos, it's important to remember that the League arose from Sparta's failure to subjugate its neighbors. The League was created as an alternative to the relative success that Sparta won in the Messenian Wars against a weaker and decentralized neighbor. Sparta failed to reproduce its conquest of the Messenians even against the relatively small and weak Tegea, and was forced to come up with a political alternative that allowed neighbors to trade some autonomy for relief from Spartan aggression. The League was a smart political move, but it most definitely *wasn't* was a sign of a Sparta that was dominating the ancient battlefield.

The formation of the League, and Sparta's ultimate victory, had clearly begun to tell, however. Yes, it had taken the Spartans a total of 80 years both to subjugate the Messenians in the first place and then to crush their revolt, but they were still, post-Tegea, the undisputed masters of the Peloponnese. Word began to spread that Sparta was a force to be reckoned with, resulting in an embassy from Croesus of Lydia (around 547 BC), a kingdom in what is now western Turkey. Lydia was a powerful kingdom in the 6th century BC, and so rich that the term "as rich as Croesus" is still used today (though probably not by people under the age of 40).

Croesus was worried about the rising power of the Persian Empire to his east, and had received an oracle from Delphi that he believed predicted victory if he went on the offensive. The oracle counseled him to ally with Sparta, and so he reached out to the Spartans, telling them "*the god has declared I should make friends with the Greeks.*" Herodotus tells us that the Spartans had already heard of the oracle, and we've already seen in the Messenian Wars how much stock they put in the Pythia's divine pronouncements, so they were already inclined to accept.

However, it is also very convenient that the Spartans just so happened to be looking for gold to adorn a statue of Apollo, and had sent an embassy to the capital of Lydia at Sardis to buy it. Croesus made a gift of the gold, which went a long way toward inclining the Spartans to agree to be his ally. The deal was sealed, and Sparta sent Croesus a gift of "*a bowl of bronze, engraved around the rim outside with figures, and large enough to hold twenty-seven hundred gallons.*"

But Herodotus notes that the bowl never reached Sardis. There are two competing stories as to why. In the first story, pirates from the isle of Samos off the modern Turkish coast captured the Spartan embassy bearing the gift and stole it (it makes sense that the Spartans would like this story, as it partially justified their later attack on Samos). In the second story, which Herodotus apparently got from the Samians themselves, Sparta was about to set sail for Sardis when news arrived that the capital had already fallen, as

Croesus' ill-advised attack on Persia backfired. First, the Persian king Cyrus the Great forced Croesus back to Sardis and finally captured it in 546 BC, turning Lydia into a satrapy (a province ruled by a governor called a satrap) of Persia. Per this story, the Spartans had no one to give the gift to, so they sold it instead, pocketed the money, and made up the piracy story to explain why they came home without the bowl.

Herodotus gives no opinion on the truth of either tale, but it's yet another hole in the Spartan myth. There are a lot of hints that the supposed wealth-hating superwarriors clearly struggled with the temptations of money. Spartan boys were raised to steal their food, if we believe Plutarch. Is it such a stretch to think they might have applied that skill to other things?

The Battle of the Champions

In 546 BC (or just before), when Croesus was driven into Sardis and put under siege by the Persians, he of course sent to his faithful allies, the Spartans, summoning them to fulfill their oath and come to his aid.

But Sparta had problems of its own. With Tegea wrapped up, it had moved against Argos again, marching to capture Thyraea, a coastal city that formed a vital link to the island of Cythera off the southern coast of the Peloponnese that would make an excellent naval base for coastal raids against Laconia. Sparta likely remembered its inability to effectively respond to the coastal raids of the Messenian Wars and Chilon is reported to have said that he wished the island would sink to the bottom of the sea. To control Thyraea (and the surrounding plain) would provide Sparta with a vital defense against any amphibious assaults from the island.

Argos marched to contest the Spartan attempt on Thyraea, but both city-states were worried about excessive casualties leaving them weak in the face of other possible military commitments. For Sparta, this problem was especially thorny. It had a restive helot population that had previously been in open revolt and a newly subordinate Tegea that had only barely been brought to heel. We can guess that Arcadia, by-and-large, wasn't happy to be cozy with Sparta.

In an effort to limit the damage done by the fighting, the two armies supposedly agreed to a bizarre proposal – instead of a field battle, they would engage in a kind of duel between 300 picked champions from each side.

The full armies of both city-states would deliberately march away, too far to come to the aid of the champions. No prisoners would be taken; the last man (or men) standing from either side would return home to announce the victory. For the losers, presumably, no news would be bad news.

According to Herodotus, this was exactly what happened. The Argives slaughtered the entire Spartan side, with only two of their own, Alcenor and Chromius, left alive. The two victorious Argives then returned home to inform their people they had won the battle, and thus Thyraea.

But Herodotus relates that Alcenor and Chromius had made a fatal mistake. They left the Spartan Othryades still very much alive. Sometime after the victorious Argives left, Othryades somehow had enough strength left to strip the Argive dead of their arms and armor, ritually taking possession of the field and declaring Sparta the victors (since the Argives had left the field, which was the equivalent of a retreat).

If we believe Herodotus, when the Spartans checked the battlefield the next day they found Othryades in possession of the field, and thus claimed the victory. Herodotus tells us that Othryades later killed himself for shame of having survived when his comrades had died.

This story is, of course, obviously false.

Like the popular story of the Battle of Thermopylae, which we will examine in the next chapter, it hinges entirely on the presumption that Sparta's enemies were fools. Alcenor and Chromius knew very well that in order to win the battle, they had to completely kill every member of the opposing force. They also knew that ritual possession of the battlefield was a critical component of victory in late archaic Greece. On top of all this, they knew their city-state was counting on them to get the job done, and that when they did, they would return as heroes.

So, it is totally unbelievable that the two Argives would have left the field without making absolutely sure that every member of the opposing force was dead. They would have taken plenty of time to deliberately slit the throats or stab through the hearts of every corpse, probably several times, to make certain. They would certainly have been reminded to do so multiple times by Argos' leadership before the battle was even fought.

Othryades' incredibly convenient suicide leaves no proof to contest the Spartan claim to victory. It's painfully obvious what actually happened – the

Spartans, faced with yet another defeat, made up a story that one of their own had in fact survived, and when challenged to produce this survivor, claimed he had committed suicide out of shame for being the only survivor.

The Argives' reaction to this proves my point. They were furious, accused the Spartans of dishonesty, and reasserted their claim to Thyraea. This escalated into the field battle they'd hoped to avoid in the first place, and here Sparta won handily. Sadly, we have no details about the fight that followed, only that it was a Spartan victory and apparently one decisive enough to award rulership of Thyraea to the Spartans.

Herodotus claims that it was this battle that resulted in the famous Spartan custom of wearing their hair long. Plutarch claims that Lycurgus said long hair made a good-looking man more handsome and an ugly man more terrifying, which would hint at the custom of wearing long hair beginning much earlier. Herodotus claims that this commitment to long hair was a poke in the eye to the Argives, who made an oath after the loss of Thyraea that their men would cut their hair short and their women would be forbidden to wear gold until the city was recovered.

A final note here – many scholars believe that the Battle of the Champions is a myth and was never fought at all. This is certainly compelling (the story has the tone of a myth), but in the end *all* of Herodotus is problematic and we cannot dismiss his narrative wholesale. We must examine it with skepticism, without throwing it away. Recent scholarship has proven a lot of Herodotus right (such as the excavation of Persian arrowheads from the Colonus hill, which is evidence that at least part of his Thermopylae story is correct). Another possibility is that Herodotus' story of the pre-battle duel is a mythologized description of a pre-battle skirmish between *promachoi* that eventually escalated into a general engagement between two armies. This certainly fits the pattern of how archaic-era armies fought in ancient Greece. It also underscores a pattern that is starting to emerge when we consider how the Spartans fought – that one-on-one, they weren't particularly tough, but that their ability to fight together as a disciplined unit far exceeded that of the other Greeks.

We should remember that Sparta never did honor its alliance with Croesus. For all the gold it received (or took, depending on whose story you believe), Cyrus the Great captured Sardis and captured the king unanswered by even a single Spartan hoplite. Whatever the actual reasons, the Lydian alliance had been a perfect score for Sparta – all of the gold they'd wanted, and not a single Spartan lost.

Assault on Samos

Approximately 26 years after the Battle of the Champions, Sparta found itself embroiled in an effort to unseat a tyrant, something for which it would become famous.

Keep in mind that "tyrant" in the ancient sense doesn't necessarily mean an unjust or corrupt ruler as it does in the modern sense. A tyrant of ancient Greece was simply a leader who came to power outside of the normal channels, usually by seizing it violently. Tyrants could and did rule justly and some were loved by their people. The Greek island of Samos (yes, the same piracy-inclined island involved in the stolen bowl story) was ruled by the tyrant Polycrates, who seized power with his brothers around eight years after the Battle of the Champions, before killing one and exiling the other to consolidate power for himself.

Polycrates created one of the earliest known naval powers, amassing a fleet first of 100 *pentēkonteres*, a kind of early galley roughly 100 feet long and rowed by a single bank of 50 oars, 25 to a side. Later, he amassed 40 of the new style of ship known as the trireme, which I'll describe in detail in the next chapter. Polycrates used this naval might not only for piracy, but also for sea trade and to wage a fairly successful naval campaign of conquest targeting the Greek cities off the Ionian (modern west Turkish) coast.

In 530 BC, the Persian king Cyrus the Great was succeeded by Cambyses II, who continued his predecessor's expansionist policies. At this point, the Persian Empire already controlled Ionia and the Levant (modern-day Syria and Palestine), and Cambyses looked to bring Egypt into the empire. The Egyptian pharaoh Amasis II had been an ally of Polycrates, but the tyrant of Samos went over to the Persians and put his fleet at their service.

This is important to note – Corinth, an ally of Sparta, was a major sea-trading power and any kind of naval power projection, particularly one associated with piracy and trade (as Samos' was) would have made the Corinthians very nervous. Mind you, Corinth certainly wouldn't have objected to piracy in a general sense (indeed, most ancient Greek sea-traders at least moonlit as pirates), but it surely would have objected to *competing* piracy.

Polycrates, being a tyrant, of course had no shortage of political enemies. According to Herodotus, he sent a message to Cambyses asking the Persian king to request that Polycrates send a fleet to aid him in his conquest of Egypt. Cambyses did so, and Polycrates promptly enrolled his political enemies to crew his 40 ships, which were then sent out to Cambyses with *"instructions never to send them back."* It's not clear if Polycrates was expecting the Persians to sink the Samian fleet or send it into dangerous duty against Egypt or something else. Herodotus' narrative gets confused at this point as well, so that it's not clear what precisely became of the fleet.

What we do know is that the fleet of exiles eventually turned back to Samos, possibly defeated Polycrates' loyalists in a naval battle, and drove Polycrates back onto shore. They fared less well in the land battle, and realized that while they could control the waters around Samos, they would never take back their homes without an army. They promptly set off for Sparta to beg the Spartans' aid. Sparta, surprisingly (after so signally failing to help Croesus in his hour of need), agreed. Herodotus is confused as to why (although at least one modern scholar believes that the Spartans were moved by ties of friendship with leading anti-Polycrates Samians). Herodotus says that the Samians claimed the Spartans agreed to help because of aid they had given during the Messenian Wars, but that the Spartans claimed they agreed as vengeance for the stolen bowl I mentioned earlier. The Corinthians *"eagerly joined"* due to some insult, per Herodotus, but I think it's much more likely that the Corinthians saw a chance to neutralize a piratical nuisance and competition for sea trade.

The Samians and Corinthians provided the needed ships for the assault and Sparta acted as the land army. Though we have little more than a paragraph from Herodotus describing the battle, battlefield analysis and archaeology have given us a somewhat detailed picture. We lack troop counts or details on arms and equipment. We know the assault force consisted of Spartans, Corinthians and Samian exiles, but the clear implication is that the land fighting was done either entirely or mostly by the Spartans.

We know almost nothing about Polycrates' force, save that he employed 1,000 mercenary archers (these may have been from Crete, known for its archers, whom we saw in Spartan service in Pausanias' narrative of the Battle of the Kings in the First Messenian War).

We have a good idea of where Samos' circuit wall ran (ancient eastern cities adopted walls before Greece proper. Sparta famously did not build a wall until the Hellenistic age. Plutarch gives us the quote from Agesilaus II that Sparta's young men were its walls, and their spears its boundaries), and from this we can figure out the course of the initial assault fairly well. Greeks under the command of the Spartan king Leotychides also anchored at Samos in 479 BC as part of the maneuvers surrounding the Battle of Mycale, where they defeated the Persians. This gives us a possible landing site for this earlier battle.

This would have Sparta attacking the city at its southwest corner, where the circuit wall runs down to the sea. Herodotus tells us that the Spartans stormed one of the towers there, and succeeded in capturing it. Keep in mind that this kind of tight, urban fighting absolutely neutralizes the phalanx. This would have been an up-close slugfest, possibly relying more on swords than spears for once, in the close confines of wall ramparts and the mount points of scaling ladders. This initial victory was short-lived, however, and Polycrates personally led a countercharge, driving the Spartans out of their bridgehead and forcing them back outside the city wall.

This would have put the Spartans at the base of the sea tower, which was presumably connected by the city wall's rampart to a second tower higher up on a ridge to the north. Polycrates' mercenaries and Samian troops attacked out of a sally port (a door in the wall that would allow defenders to rush out to the attack). This would have given them the high ground advantage, and perhaps Polycrates believed he had an opportunity to defeat the Spartans in a single stroke. It was a bad gamble, for the Spartans immediately rallied and attacked up the slope (it's possible that now, outside the confines of the tower, they could properly form the phalanx and bring their discipline and organization to bear). The sallying force broke almost immediately, which makes sense if you believe that the mercenaries were primarily light-armed archers who wouldn't be able to hold in a stand-up fight with heavily armored Spartan hoplites.

But here the tale takes an interesting turn and gives us an indication that once again Sparta's force wasn't fully professionalized in the modern sense of the word and that the essential humanity of all warriors asserted itself even in the face of legendary Spartan discipline – as the defenders fled back into the city, the Spartans pursued them, killing many. But two of the Spartan Peers, Archias and Lycopas, outpaced their comrades, getting inside the sally port before the defenders could shut it.

We will never know why they did this, but there are only two real possibilities – either the two Peers hoped they could form another bridgehead and keep the sally port open to admit the rest of the army, or they simply lost their heads in the rush of victory, forgot their discipline and gave chase.

I think the second possibility is the correct one, the evidence being that they were the *only* ones caught inside the sally port, implying that the rest of the army kept their heads and their ranks. Herodotus praises the two for bravery and suggests that if the rest of the army had been as brave, Samos would have been taken. He's very likely right, but the reason the army didn't join Archias and Lycopas may have had more to do with discipline than cowardice. The Spartans certainly agreed with Herodotus, naming Archias' son Samios in memorial to his father's glorious death.

At any rate, the effort failed. Once through the sally port, the defenders closed it, trapping the two Peers inside, where they were promptly surrounded and killed.

According to Herodotus, who interviewed Archias' grandson (also named Archias) the Samians so honored the Spartan's bravery that they buried him at public expense.

Polycrates learned his lesson from the defeated sally. He made no further attempts to engage the Spartans in a stand-up fight, but instead stayed bottled up behind his walls. Sparta's reputation for siegecraft remained unimproved. After 40 days camped outside the walls, unable to make any headway, the Spartans finally gave up and left. Polycrates would meet his end later, assassinated by Oroetes, Cyrus' satrap of Lydia.

There is yet another interesting contribution to the Spartan Mirage here – Herodotus tells a second story about the Spartan decision to lift the siege. They were possibly bribed into leaving by Polycrates, who tricked them with electrum-plated lead coins. Herodotus is clear that he doesn't believe this story, but similar coins have been recovered, giving a little more indication that the tale may have been true. Yet another clue that the supposed wealth-hating Spartans, forbidden to use gold and silver coins, were at the very least inconsistent in their adherence to this law.

Another important note – some might argue that siegecraft was generally undeveloped in the ancient world, and that Sparta's inability to effectively take cities was just par for the course. But this isn't true. Sparta's contemporaries the Persians (and their predecessors the Assyrians) had been highly effective at sieges for centuries by the time the Spartans threw up their hands and abandoned their efforts to take Samos. Sparta's poor record at sieges was not necessarily shared by other ancient armies of the period. Indeed, after the Spartan defeat at Thermopylae in 480 BC, the victorious Persian king Xerxes had no problem laying siege to the Athenian Acropolis and dislodging its defenders.

Athenian Entanglement

Sparta's next major military adventure was farther afield to the north, targeting its Attic neighbor and perennial antagonist, the city-state of Athens. The Spartan protagonist was the Agiad king Cleomenes I, the half-brother of the famous Leonidas (the hero of Thermopylae) and the father of Leonidas' wife, Gorgo.

It's important to note two instances of Cleomenes' attitude regarding Persia at this point, because it provides clues to how the Spartans saw their chances fighting the Persians and their reputation as the destroyers of Persian ambitions in Greece. Herodotus gives us the famous story of the Spartan embassy sent to the Persian king Cyrus the Great (probably around 546 BC), warning him to lay off the Greek cities of Ionia. Cyrus' response was magnificent, turning to one of his advisors and asking *"who are the Spartans?"* However, for all their bluster threatening the Persians, the Spartans decidedly failed to honor their alliance with Croesus, as we have seen. Their running fight with Argos (and the Battle of the Champions) is most often blamed, but the hypothesis that isn't usually considered is that the Spartans, having nearly lost wars with tiny city-states such as Tegea, were frightened of taking on the fearsome Persian war machine whose reputation they would surely have known.

You have to remember that in the 6th century BC Persia was the greatest empire in the known (to the Spartans) world, and certainly fielded the largest army. Cleomenes received two more invitations to intervene on behalf of Greek populations suffering under Persian domination – first an appeal from Polycrates' successor Maeandrius, and later from Aristagoras of the Carian city of Miletus, near the modern Turkish village of Balat. Both Greeks appealed to Cleomenes for help and both offered gold to get it. Herodotus credits Cleomenes' "*modesty*" in refusing to help (he even has a great story of Cleomenes' daughter Gorgo warning the king to expel Aristagoras before he is corrupted by him. While Herodotus does a better job than most, this is still one of the few moments a woman takes center stage in the Greek sources' otherwise epic erasure of women), but as we've seen in earlier stories of the Spartan alliance with Croesus and one of the supposed reasons for their abandoning the assault on Samos, they were at least extremely inconsistent about when they were and when they weren't okay with accepting money. In Aristagoras' case, Herodotus tells us that Cleomenes finally refused to assist the Ionian Greeks after hearing that it would take a Spartan army three months' march from the sea to reach the Persian capital at Susa.

I have read scholars theorizing that Cleomenes was cagey, that he was careful, that he was arrogant, but never that he was *afraid*. Keep these incidents in mind – they will be factored in later as we consider Sparta's role in the Greco-Persian War.

But for now, Persia was not high on Sparta's list of worries. Instead, the Spartans were busy unseating tyrants, as we saw in their failed attempt at Samos, and in the reportedly successful attempts at Sicyon and Corinth (both of which wound up as staunch Spartan allies). Sparta began to earn a reputation as a champion of liberty from tyrants, laughable when you consider that it was an apartheid state ruling over a subjugated slave-class. Some scholars have suggested that Sparta's attitude towards tyranny might stem from the stinging defeat it received at the hands of the Argive tyrant Pheidon at the Battle of Hysiae which we examined earlier. Others have noted that Sparta's system of placing extreme checks on the power of the kings, the ephors, and the council of elders indicated a deep-seated fear of one of their own seizing absolute power, fears that would prove well-founded as Sparta moved into the Hellenistic age.

At any rate, Athens came under the rule of the Pisistratid dynasty of tyrants, whose mantle of power eventually settled on the shoulders of one

Hippias. The Athenian aristocratic Alcmaeonid clan bribed the oracle at Delphi to provide omens to Sparta insisting that they intervene and liberate Athens, and Sparta eventually heeded them though Herodotus implies they were reluctant to do so, having been long-standing friends with the Pisistratids (clearly, Spartans could be friends to tyrants when it suited them).

Herodotus gives no details on the composition of the army the Spartans sent, but we do know that it was led by the polemarch (general – literally translates as "war leader") Anchimolius (I am guessing at his title. The first actual mention of a polemarch dates to roughly 31 years after this battle), who was not a member of either the Agiad nor Eurypontid households, but rather a man *"held in the highest regard."* We know that the Spartans attacked by sea, landing at the Athenian "port" (really just a shingle where ships could be beached) of Phalerum (the Athenians would later transfer the bulk of their shipping to Piraeus up the coast) in around 511 BC.

Hippias, meanwhile, hadn't been idle. Forewarned of the attack, he'd sent to the north Greek region of Thessaly and formed an alliance which was immediately honored. The Thessalians sent 1,000 cavalry south under the command of a man named Cineas.

We should pause for a moment here to note that Thessalian cavalry were already famous at this point and would retain their reputation as the finest mounted warriors in Greece for centuries to come. There's a reason that the hoplite infantryman, and not the horseman, became the dominant fighting force in ancient Greece from its earliest days. Greece is mountain-choked, with scarce flat, wide-open spaces suitable for horses to graze and run. Thessaly was an exception and the Thessalians took advantage of it, excelling at riding, horse-breeding and mounted combat. One thousand Thessalian cavalrymen were a serious advantage indeed, especially when you consider that the plain of Phalerum was some of the flattest ground in all of Attica. Further, no source reports the Spartans using cavalry (as opposed to men riding horses and then dismounting to fight) until the following century, which meant that the Spartans almost certainly did not possess troops that could match the Thessalians for mobility and speed.

Herodotus tells us that Hippias prepared the ground around Phalerum to make it more suitable for cavalry maneuvers, clearing it of trees, walls, brush and anything else that might trip up a horse. This would, of course, have been clearly visible to Anchimolius if he'd performed the necessary scouting, and yet Herodotus indicates that the Spartans marched out into the middle of it anyway.

I am normally cautious of any narrative that rests on the notion that one side in a battle were fools (as you saw with my analysis of the Battle of the Champions), but there is a lot of evidence in earlier battles (and in ones yet to come) that the Spartans' inherent conservatism and belief in their own superiority made them quick to reject things they didn't understand and slow to adapt.

We've also seen at the Battle of Ithome that Spartan leadership had a record of failing to adequately scout prior to a battle. When I consider this, Herodotus' description of events makes a bit more sense. Either way, the Thessalians charged and utterly shattered (Herodotus describes the Spartan casualties as "*exceedingly high*") the Spartan position, killing Anchimolius and sending the Spartan army running back to its ships.

The Spartans did not rally or attempt to land elsewhere to try again. Leaderless and broken, they rowed for home, tails between their legs. A note here: Herodotus tells us that Anchimolius was buried in Attica, near where he fell (and indeed that Anchimolius' tomb was still visible at the time Herodotus wrote his famous history) – yet another indicator that "with your shield or on it" is bunk. Nobody carried him home on a shield.

But Sparta was now at the head of the Peloponnesian League and the foremost power in the Peloponnese. It certainly couldn't afford to look weak in front of the Arcadians, Argives and other neighboring states, and it *definitely* couldn't afford to look weak in front of its helot underclass. So, it's not surprising that the Spartans immediately mounted a second expedition, this time marching over land in greater numbers (though again, we don't have a troop count) with Cleomenes at their head.

We have no details of this second assault other than that the Thessalian force confronted the Spartans and was immediately routed and sent running back to Thessaly, with a loss of just 40 Spartans. We do not know why the Spartans were so much more successful this time; it was possibly due to Cleomenes' superior generalship or the larger size of the army. The 2nd century AD Roman engineer Frontinus wrote that Cleomenes reversed the terrain advantage the Thessalians had used against Anchimolius. Where the

Thessalians had prepared the battlefield by clearing it of obstacles, Cleomenes cluttered it with felled trees and made it *"impassable for cavalry."*

If we believe Frontinus here (and we have no reason not to), here is some evidence at least of Spartans both learning from past mistakes and adapting to new battlefield developments. The Spartans clearly had very limited experience of either employing or fighting against mounted men in the 6th century BC. Confronted with crack horsemen for possibly one of the first times in their history, they were caught flat-footed and crushed. In the second battle, with the benefit of experience, they performed much better. We see similar adaptation in other ancient armies, most notably the Romans slowly learning to overcome war elephants in the early 3rd century BC, over the course of two battles in a single year.

With the Thessalians out of the way, Hippias made no further attempt to fight the Spartans in the field and withdrew to Athens' Acropolis. Any modern visitor to the Athenian Acropolis will immediately see that it's an excellent defensible position, on extremely high ground with limited approaches and a complete view of the surrounding area. It is, even today, a fortress in the middle of the city. Even though the Spartans now held the city, they still had their main objective – the tyrant they came to unseat – bottled up in the middle of it.

Now, we well remember Sparta's lousy record on sieges. Herodotus agrees: *"The Spartans would never have taken the stronghold. First of all they had no intention to blockade it, and secondly the Pisistratids [Hippias and his people] were well furnished with food and drink. The Spartans would only have besieged the place for a few days and then returned to Sparta."*

But the Spartans got lucky in that they caught some of the tyrant's family attempting to sneak out of the city. Hippias' love of his family (or at least his inner circle) apparently exceeded his love for power and he agreed to exile in exchange for their return. Hippias fled Greece and traveled to Sardis and the Persian court of Artaphernes, the satrap of Darius I, who had succeeded (after some violence and confusion) Cambyses II as king of Persia. Darius would attempt to restore Hippias to rule over Athens at the Battle of Marathon 20 years later.

It's very likely that Cleomenes and the ephors back at Sparta expected they would be rewarded for this intervention by a new pro-Sparta government at Athens, preferably an oligarchy (rule by a small elite) of the type Sparta preferred. But they didn't get their wish. By removing Hippias, Sparta created a power vacuum that the Alcmaeonid clan rushed to fill. Other aristocratic factions in Athens weren't okay with this and civil strife followed, the end result of which was the Alcmaeonid clan member Cleisthenes extending the vote to every adult male in Athens, making it a democracy.

Don't mistake this arrangement for a modern democracy, however. Athenian citizens, like their Spartan rivals, were a relatively elite bunch. The vote certainly didn't extend to slaves, foreigners living in Athens, women or others denied the franchise of citizenship.

But even so, this development did not make Sparta happy. The issue was exacerbated by one of the figures on the losing side of the Athenian power struggle, a man named Isagoras. Isagoras was a "guest friend" (a kind of formal and ritualized alliance between two individuals in the ancient world that included mutual obligations of hospitality and also material and political support) of Cleomenes. Herodotus strongly implies that Cleomenes had an ongoing affair with Isagoras' wife. Isagoras sent for Cleomenes, asking him to intervene in Athens yet again.

Cleomenes answered his friend's call. Herodotus tells us he returned to Athens probably around 507 BC at the head of "*a small force*" to put his friend in power. Many scholars suggest that this was a private campaign, undertaken by Cleomenes and his supporters without the sanction of the Spartan government. I am skeptical about this. Could a king of Sparta, whose every action might be perceived as representative of the city-state, ever truly act privately? Wasn't a guest-friend of the king effectively a friend to Sparta itself? I find it hard to believe that the ephors could have been ignorant of Cleomenes' actions, and if they knew of it and disapproved of it, why wouldn't they have acted to stop it? They certainly had the power to censure the kings.

It's important to take a moment here to explain Spartan attitudes toward democracy. The Spartans were committed oligarchs. To modern people used to living in democratic republics like the US and the UK, this may seem oppressive, but the Spartans surely did not see it that way. To them, an oligarchy was absolutely free, since the worthy members of society (the wealthy, the aristocrats, the free citizens of the city-state) had a voice in selecting their government. To ancient pro-oligarchs, the idea of letting *everyone* vote was horrifying – tantamount to mob rule. If you gave political power to fools, you were guaranteed to get foolish decisions. Oligarchy (to a Spartan) didn't mean rule by oppressors, it meant rule by the best members of society (always men) – those who were best equipped to make the decisions necessary to ensure the welfare of all, including those who were denied a vote.

At any rate, Cleomenes marched into Athens, banished 700 Alcmaeonid families, and installed Isagoras as tyrant. This, of course, flew in the face of Sparta's reputation for opposing tyranny and badly damaged its reputation across all of Greece.

What happened next couldn't have helped. The Athenians rose up and attacked Cleomenes and his token force, bottling him and Isagoras up on the Acropolis, just as he had done to Hippias three years earlier. Unlike Hippias, Cleomenes hadn't bothered to store enough food and water to withstand a siege. The Agiad king held out for just two days, unable to fight his way through the Athenian mob, before agreeing to a truce that gave him permission to leave. Sparta's king ran home, humiliated. Three hundred of Isagoras' supporters were executed and Cleisthenes returned, becoming *archōn* (chief official).

Whether the debacle at Athens was Cleomenes' private adventure or not, Spartan face was clearly at stake now, and the city-state was faced with a clear threat to its reputation, the kind of thing that could damage its ability to lead the League or even spark a helot revolt. Herodotus tells us that Cleomenes' gathered an army on his own, without informing the Spartan authorities, to avenge this insult, but I find this hard to believe. It seems more likely to me that Sparta could not allow this insult to stand and accordingly authorized a punitive expedition against Athens at the head of a proper army.

Whatever the truth of it, Cleomenes rode out again, this time with his Eurypontid co-king Demaratus. The Athenians, knowing that Sparta would be coming for them, immediately sent an embassy to Sardis asking for an alliance with Persia. Artaphernes knew his master Darius made only one kind of alliance – he accepted subordinates who gave him earth and water as tokens of submission. He demanded this of the Athenians, who promptly gave it, technically making them subjects of the Persian empire. Based on this chain of events, there are some who blame Sparta for the root cause of the later Persian invasion of Greece, and it's hard not to see their point.

Sparta sent to its allies in Thebes and Chalcis (northwest and northeast of Athens, respectively), who joined in the invasion. The Corinthians once again marched beside their Spartan allies. Cleomenes' plan for Athens after the city-state had been crushed pokes another hole in the Bronze Lie, that the Spartans were lovers of freedom, for Cleomenes intended to install Isagoras as tyrant once again. This would be Sparta's *third* invasion of Athens over the course of four years, and its goal was to pretty much put things back to how they were before Sparta had invaded in the first place, only with a different tyrant (one who was personally beholden to Cleomenes) behind the wheel.

It's very likely that Cleomenes justified this state of affairs by telling himself that the combined might of Sparta and Corinth, coupled with the northern offensive from Thebes and Chalcis, would terrify the new Athenian democracy, still recovering from the civil strife that had rocked it since Hippias had been forced out. They would crumple without a fight, and Cleomenes would once again eject Cleisthenes and restore Isagoras, who would rule as Sparta's puppet, extending Spartan influence further in Greece than the Spartans had previously imagined.

But Athens refused to go along with that plan. Rather than divide their forces to face both the northern and southern offensives, the Athenians let Thebes and Chalcis have their gains (they had captured some territories already) and mustered at Eleusis to face the truly responsible party – Sparta. Herodotus reports that the Corinthians suddenly realized that "*they were in the wrong*," turned around and marched home. This is highly unlikely given the fluid morality of Greek military policy. A far more likely reason is that the Corinthians were fine with supporting Sparta when they thought Athens would roll over, but confronted with the possibility of a stand-up fight over nothing more than Spartan pride and ambition, they figured it wasn't worth the risk. It is also a clue that the Corinthians were not sure of victory, which would indicate that they lacked confidence in the Spartan army.

This first crack in Spartan resolve widened into an argument between Demaratus and Cleomenes. Demaratus apparently saw the Corinthians' point and may also have been motivated by a chance to undercut his Agiad rival. At any rate, he began to argue about the wisdom of the whole expedition.

This argument surely leaked to the other League allies in the Spartan army, who now suddenly had an option to avoid a fight and still claim they were complying with their League obligations. "Hey," they could have said, "we were obeying the king. Demaratus said he didn't want to fight." This was the nail in the expedition's coffin. The army melted away almost overnight, leaving a tiny core of Cleomenes and his hardcore supporters – far too few to face the Athenians mustered at Eleusis.

The Athenians, suddenly without a threat on their southern front, executed an about-face, marched north and crushed the Thebans and Chalcidians. Athens' reputation soared. Sparta's sank to an all-time low. Cleomenes headed home in disgrace and a humiliated Sparta passed a law that the two kings would never again be permitted to jointly command an army to prevent such an embarrassment from recurring.

This was a massive reduction in royal military power. Before this new law, either king could muster and lead out an army on his own initiative, either singly or jointly. While one king alone would make the decision to launch a campaign, the other king could join if he wanted. Now, only one king could command an army, which meant the Spartan authorities (the ephors, most likely) got to decide which king would ride out.

This also meant that a king could no longer trade military leadership for political influence, since he couldn't guarantee that he could command the Spartan army in any given campaign. Professor Stephen Hodkinson has argued that this put the military power of the kings firmly under the control of the ephors, and forced the kings to find non-military ways (such as the accumulation and distribution of wealth) to increase their power and influence. If Hodkinson is right (and I believe he is) it's yet another hole in the Bronze Lie. If Spartan society was wealth-hating, totally geared for war, and cared for nothing else, then this seems a very odd way to govern its kings.

There's another point to make here. In pretty much every battle we've examined so far (and pretty much every one we'll see for the rest of the book), Sparta is very careful to march to war only with the help of its allies. This wasn't unusual for any ancient Greek city-state, but it does poke yet another hole in the Bronze Lie. You would think superwarriors wouldn't need help to take on their enemies.

Prelude to the Persian Wars

At this point, we must look to the Ionian coast again, where around nine years after the Spartan failure to conquer Athens (499 BC), the Greek population rose in revolt against Persia. This would have spelled trouble for all Greeks, but was made much worse by Athens and Eretria jumping in and aiding the rebels when they captured and burned Sardis the following year. It made sense for them to do this – the Ionians were fellow Greeks even though they lived on the other side of the Aegean Sea. They shared a language, the same gods and festivals, and many of the guest-friendships I described earlier. But keep in mind that the Athenians had given earth and water to Darius (via his satrap) when they were seeking allies to help defend against Cleomenes' invasion force.

Darius surely saw this as an act of rebellious subjects. Just as the Spartans felt they couldn't afford to lose face when Athens defied them, Darius was not about to let this act go unpunished. Darius supposedly ordered a slave to remind him every day, "Sire, do not forget the Athenians." The Greeks now had Darius' full attention and he sent heralds (as opposed to ambassadors; heralds didn't negotiate) to demand earth and water from them all. In a scene made famous by Miller's *300*, the Spartans threw the Persian heralds into a well, suggesting they would find plenty of both down there.

This is a very important point for us to remember when we consider Sparta's convenient religious excuses for not showing up for the critical Battle of Marathon in 490 BC, and for sending only a tiny token force to Thermopylae ten years later. In both cases, the Spartans pleaded that they were unable to march due to religious concerns (they were celebrating festivals). But heralds were considered sacrosanct in their religion, and their killing certainly incurred ritual pollution. We are certain the Spartans knew this was sacrilege because they even sent two Spartans to Xerxes (who was now king of Persia) to be killed as a way of balancing the divine ledger. Xerxes, far too smart to give up the moral advantage, refused the offer. This is just one example (we'll see many more) of how the Spartans were all too happy to commit sacrilege when it suited them, and then claim religious exemption later when they wanted to avoid a battle.

The Battle of Sepeia

The Argives at the very least gave the Persians a warmer reception. This was unacceptable to a Sparta that had just committed itself to a collision course with the empire. Sparta's relationship with Argos remained tense, and it had been only around 50 years since the two city-states were engaged in open war, so it's no surprise that Sparta decided to preemptively punish Argos for potentially throwing its lot in with Persia (and at the same time satisfy the Spartans' own expansionist policies). Cleomenes marched out again at the head of an army, eager to restore a reputation so badly blackened by his utter failure to bring Athens to heel.

We have no details for the composition of either army, but we know they met at Sepeia in the Argolid. What happened next depends on which source you believe, but all sources are agreed on two points: first, that Sparta won an overwhelming victory, and, secondly, that they did so (once again) by means of a trick.

If you believe Herodotus, then the Argives made the unbelievably stupid decision to mimic every action of the Spartan army – forming up when the Spartans formed up, standing down when the Spartans stood down. This, of course, made it simple for the Spartans to win. They pretended to stand down for a meal, but secretly gave the order to stay in formation. When the Argives mirrored their stand-down, they attacked, took the enemy out of battle order, and won.

I do not believe this at all. Just as with the Battle of the Champions (and with Thermopylae as we'll see in the next chapter), this story rests on the belief that Sparta's enemies were fools. The far more believable story comes from Plutarch, who tells us that Cleomenes agreed to a seven-day truce with the Argives, then promptly violated it and attacked them on the third night, taking them unawares and slaughtering them. When confronted on his deceit, Cleomenes shrugged. "I agreed to a truce of seven *days*. I didn't say anything about the nights."

The Argive survivors of the surprise attack took shelter in a sacred grove nearby. Herodotus tells us that Cleomenes first had his herald call them out one by one by name, saying that their ransoms had been paid and they were free to go (it was customary in ancient warfare to ransom captives back to their families). As each man emerged from the grove, Cleomenes had him murdered.

At last, one of the Argives climbed a tree and spotted the butchered bodies just past the wood's edge. After this, unsurprisingly, the Argives refused to come out. That Cleomenes didn't go in after them is interesting. His army was victorious, the hiding Argives beaten. They would have been wounded, their morale critically low. Why he didn't go in after them will remain an unanswered question, but I wonder if Cleomenes did not have faith in his army's ability to take the Argives on in dense woods where his hoplites would be unable to form an effective phalanx. Could the Argives' reputation as being good one-on-one fighters, possibly seared on the Spartan consciousness after their loss in the Battle of the Champions, have been at work here?

Instead, Cleomenes had his helots set the woods on fire, burning the survivors alive. This was yet another example of the supposedly superstitious and scrupulously religious Spartans' perfect willingness to commit sacrilege whenever it was convenient. Destroying a sacred place was an offense to the gods, but even worse was violating the sacred laws of sanctuary that provided fugitives protection provided they were hidden in a temple (we will see this in play with regard to the famous Spartan Pausanias in the next chapter).

But while Cleomenes defeated the Argives in battle and destroyed their army, he failed to capture the city itself. The reason why is firmly hidden behind the wavering Spartan Mirage. Plutarch tells the story of the Argive poet Telesilla taking command of the Argive women who mounted the ramparts and fighting the Spartans off, sending them packing with heavy casualties. Pausanias expands on this story, making it far more believable – that in addition to the women, Telesilla armed and commanded the slaves and men who hadn't participated in the battle to help garrison the city. Still, this strikes me as unlikely.

What is far more likely is what Cleomenes was accused of upon his return home to Sparta with Argos still untaken – that he had been bribed to leave the city alone. Cleomenes supposedly beat this charge by claiming miraculous omens (including a sign from the goddess Hera when he violated the sanctity of her temple – yet another example of Spartan willingness to commit sacrilege). He was acquitted and continued to rule, but it was clear his star was on the wane. Some scholars have suggested that Cleomenes deliberately didn't subjugate Argos, opting instead to cripple it in a show of force, to avoid upsetting the balance of power in the Peloponnese and frightening Sparta's supposedly subordinate allies in the League. We will likely never know the truth of it.

A final point to note here is that this is one of the earlier battles for which we have a (disputed) casualty count – Herodotus gives us a figure of 6,000 Argive dead in total.

Though it doesn't deal with Sparta's battlefield record, the final chapter in Cleomenes' story is worth telling as it sets the stage for the Greco-Persian Wars we're about to explore.

Sparta, worried about the impending Persian invasion, suddenly found itself thrust into friendship with anti-Persian Athens, despite Cleomenes' horrific record in dealing with that city-state. Athens was at war with the neighboring island city-state of Aegina, which had sent earth and water to Darius and submitted to Persian overlordship.

Cleomenes demanded that Aegina make peace with Athens and give hostages to Athens as surety for its good behavior. For reasons that aren't clear, the Eurypontid king Demaratus opposed this. It's possible that Cleomenes was acting on his own, without the support of the ephors (as was suspected in his assault on Athens in support of Isagoras) and that Demaratus had informed the Aeginetans of this. According to Herodotus, this is exactly what the Aeginetans accused him of.

Cleomenes responded by conspiring with Leotychides, a member of the Eurypontid house who stood to gain by Demaratus' disgrace. The two worked together to cast doubt on Demaratus' legitimate birth and bribed the Delphic oracle to back up their story. It worked. Demaratus was deposed and fled to Persia where he became a trusted advisor to the king, and Leotychides became the Eurypontid king of Sparta. Cleomenes and Leotychides promptly visited Aegina and took ten leading citizens hostage, turning them over to Athens.

That would have been that, but the bribing of the Delphic oracle was found out and Cleomenes fled into exile. Herodotus tells us that he traveled to Arcadia and raised a rebel army there to march on Sparta. Apparently this successfully cowed the government back home, and the Spartans recalled him, restoring him to the Agiad kingship.

Leotychides was handed over to the Aeginetans, but bargained for his life by agreeing to get their hostages back (he failed to deliver on this promise). He remained the Eurypontid king.

Herodotus tells a bizarre story of Cleomenes' recall from exile back to Sparta and how the king, back in power, suddenly went mad, attacking people in the street. One story has it that this madness was brought on by a habit of drinking unwatered wine (the ancient Greeks didn't drink wine straight, but mixed it with water to dilute its potency). In chapter I, I noted that the Spartans supposedly looked down on drunkenness, even forcing helots to get drunk as an object lesson to their youth. So perhaps the story was concocted to show just how far from Spartan virtue Cleomenes had fallen. Or, if it is true, it's an example once again of the glaring contradictions that riddle every aspect of the Spartan legend.

Whatever the reason, Cleomenes was out of control. He was confined in public stocks, and a single helot was set to guard over him. According to Herodotus, Cleomenes convinced the slave to give him his knife and then promptly sliced off bits of himself (what he could reach from being locked in the stocks, which per Herodotus was his lower body) until at last he died.

This is incredibly hard to believe. From his sudden descent into madness, to the decision to confine him in a public stocks, to the decision to guard him with a single helot who, used to being ordered around by any Peer, let alone a king, would surely obey his orders, is too much to swallow.

We know Cleomenes was disgraced. We know forces in Spartan society resented him and wanted him out of the way (his deceitful actions toward Demaratus had to have earned him a lot of enemies, as had his total failure in regard to Athens, and his recent acquittal on bribery charges over his failure to take Argos).

It seems pretty obvious to me that he was assassinated shortly after being "restored" to power in an effort to prevent him from marching on his home city at the head of an army of Arcadian rebels. The story Herodotus was told was concocted to paper over that ugly fact. Who assassinated him will probably never be known, but several scholars have suggested that his half-brother Leonidas did the deed, impatient to take the throne (and probably ready to mount it, if not already acclaimed Agiad king the moment Cleomenes fled into exile). The guilt over this assassination haunted him, and so when a king was called upon to die in the pass at Thermopylae, he took up the post gladly. There isn't a lot of proof to support this story, but it's too good not to tell.

Sparta's Battlefield Performance in the Archaic Period

The archaic period saw Sparta rise from a cluster of villages beside the Eurotas river to the masters of the Peloponnese, but while it had surely advanced in power and prestige, its battlefield performance was decidedly mixed. In the battles we touched on in this chapter, we see that Sparta won just six, while losing *nine* (and in one of those, the Spartan army melted away without a fight), and stalemating three more. On top of this, we saw two Spartan kings fleeing from the battlefield (and one fleeing again during a skirmish over a cattle raid), and one Spartan polemarch killed in battle. We also note that three of the Spartan victories were secured through treachery or trickery, and not through simple warrior dominance.

It's important to note that Sparta's real military advantage may not really have been tied to its military at all. Rather, Sparta appears to have centralized power more rapidly than its enemies, granting it access to more resources and the ability to recover from defeats more quickly than it otherwise would have. This, rather than its vaunted military performance, may have been a greater factor in Sparta's earliest successes.

The height of Sparta's legend was forged in the Greco-Persian War and the battles we will now examine, but would Sparta's reputation match its actual performance on the field?

III

THE GRECO-PERSIAN WAR: THE THERMOPYLAE SPEED BUMP

Xerxes passed over the place where the dead lay and hearing that Leonidas had been king and general of the Spartans, he gave orders to cut off his head and impale it.

Herodotus, *Histories*

It took the Persians from 499 to 493 BC to deal with the Ionian revolt, but deal with it they did. The naval Battle of Lade in 494 BC put paid to the idea of a free and independent Greek community carved out from the Persian Empire's western frontier. Lade was lost when all but 11 of the 60 Samian ships fighting for the Ionian Greeks hoisted sail and fled, the 70 ships of Lesbos panicking and following suit shortly after. This represented a full 34 percent of the Ionian fleet, if Herodotus' ship counts are to be believed, and the vastly shrunken remainder was easily defeated by the Persians.

With this final battle, resistance to Persia effectively collapsed and Darius was finally free to turn his attention to the Athenians, whom his slave had been reminding him not to forget.

You have to remember that Persia in the early 5th century BC was the greatest empire in the world. Darius ruled over lands vast beyond counting, had wealth that even the most powerful Greek city-state could only dream of, and could muster both an army and navy so enormous and well equipped that it would be impossible to stand against it. He could draw on subject peoples from modern India in the east to the coast of modern Turkey in the west and from the southern shore of the Black Sea in the north to Egypt in the south. The title "King of Kings" was certainly justified. The Greeks would have been reasonably terrified at the prospect of a Persian invasion, and resistance truly would have seemed futile to many.

Darius invaded the following year, sending his son-in-law Mardonius to lead a huge army into Greece via a massive amphibious operation. The Persians either lacked reliable local pilots and navigators to advise them, or else took unnecessary risks, because this first transport fleet was caught in a violent storm as it rounded the cape of Mount Athos (one of the three "fingers" of land jutting out from just south of modern-day Thessaloniki in northeastern Greece). Herodotus gives the very likely exaggerated figure of 300 ships lost and 20,000 men killed, but even accounting for exaggeration we can guess that the casualties were extreme. Worse, the disaster emboldened the local Thracian tribes, who attacked the surviving Persians while they made camp, doing even more damage, including wounding Mardonius himself. Mardonius and his army exacted savage retribution against the Thracians, but in the end the expedition had to be aborted. Still, by the end of 492 BC, Persia had pacified Thrace, forced Macedonia to submit to Darius, and captured the island of Thasos off Thrace's southern coast. It was a far cry from Athens, but it was a start.

Darius tried again two years later, making Mardonius stay home (whether to recover from his wound or as punishment for failing in the last expedition, we do not know) and sent another invasion force under Datis, a Persian admiral known for his expertise in all things Greek. With him went the satrap Artaphernes, whom we met earlier. Scholars endlessly dispute the size of the force they commanded (Herodotus gives us a figure of over 600 ships), but most agree it was overwhelming by any measure, certainly enough to challenge all the city-states of Greece even if they united to oppose it. However, other scholars argue (and pretty convincingly) that the Persian army wasn't that much larger than the force the Greeks mustered against it. This belief in a smaller Persian army is definitely the minority view, but we have to note it here and keep it in mind as we describe the events that followed.

Whatever the size of the Persian army, I'm sure you've figured out that the only people the Greek city-states hated more than the Persians were their fellow Greeks. There was no chance that they would unite to oppose anyone. Macedonia and Thrace were already under Persian control and as Datis' fleet island-hopped across the Aegean, the Persians added the isles of Naxos and Delos to their territorial rolls. Finally, they set down on the island of Euboea and took their first real vengeance for the burning of Sardis – sacking the city-state of Eretria, just across the channel from the Attic peninsula and Athens beyond. The Eretrians were enslaved or slaughtered, a grim message of what the Athenians could expect very soon.

The Athenians were joined only by the comparatively tiny city-state of Plataea, contributing just 1,000 hoplites to the Greek cause. These joined the 9,000–10,000 hoplites that scholars believe the Athenians fielded. A drop in the bucket about to be swept away by the Persian tide (again, we're going with the majority estimate of the size of the Persian army here, some disagree!) – some 25,000 infantry and 1,000 cavalry, not counting the 100,000-odd sailors and ships' crew who could also serve as light troops. It was as lopsided a battle as could be imagined and it seemed that nothing would be able to stop the Persians from steamrolling Athens and taking the rest of Greece.

Athens and Sparta were surely not friends and Cleomenes' efforts to subjugate the Athenians' democracy had not been forgotten. But the enemy of an enemy is a friend and Sparta had absolutely buffed its anti-Persian credentials – first by allying with Croesus and warning Cyrus not to bother the Ionian Greeks (so what if they failed to make good on this obligation? they had at least taken some kind of stand), secondly by throwing the Persian envoys into the well, and thirdly by moving against the pro-Persian Argives and Aeginetans. Since the Battle of Sepeia, Sparta was the undisputed master of the Peloponnese and, whether it deserved it or not, its army enjoyed the reputation of the finest heavy infantry in Greece. Its soldiers certainly were inarguably the only *disciplined* and *organized* infantry in Greece, mercenary bands aside.

So, likely holding its nose, Athens sent for Sparta's help. The runner Pheidippides was dispatched, completing the 153-mile, rocky, mountainous route in just a day and a half (this, at least, modern scholars have confirmed is doable by a trained ultramarathoner – which Pheidippides surely was. Since AD 1983 there is an annual Spartathlon run which traces Pheidippides' route. Greek ultramarathoner Yiannis Kouros holds the record of 20:25:00. In 2017, 264 people finished in under 36 hours). Pheidippides found the Spartans in the middle of their most sacred festival, the Carneia, which the Spartans of course claimed they could not possibly violate by sending help before it was complete. Sparta's reputation for strict obedience to religious mandates was well known.

Except when it wasn't. We have already seen multiple examples of Sparta flouting religion when it suited them. In the murder of the Persian envoys, in the bribing of the Delphic oracle (a servant of the god Apollo), in the violation of the Temple of Hera outside Argos, in the burning of the Argive sacred grove. Many scholars argue that these were the personal actions of Cleomenes, and therefore do not reflect on Sparta as a whole. I disagree. Cleomenes was a Spartan king, and despite the limits on Spartan royal power, his person still carried the imprimatur of the state.

The Spartans certainly could have marched to the defense of Greece.

But they didn't.

Scholars have debated the reasons why. It's possible the Spartans were genuinely moved by religious conviction. It's also possible they were concerned about a helot revolt if they sent their army away. But I believe their motives were more cynical.

One of the pillars of the Bronze Lie is the Spartans' reputation as steadfast enemies of Persia. But the truth is that Sparta, like all Greek city-states, acted first and foremost in its own interests – and its own interests were this: Athens was a democracy, which to Sparta meant mob rule. Worse, Athens' success was a stinging slap in the face to Sparta and a reminder to all Greece that Sparta had failed spectacularly to subjugate Athens.

The very best outcome of Datis' invasion force would be for it to bash itself to pieces against the Athenians and their Plataean allies, and then Sparta could either march north and mop up the victorious but weakened Persian army, or better yet stay safely in the Peloponnese – forcing the Persians either to go through an arduous march (with all the dangers of ambush, starvation and desertion that hung over any large ancient army in the field in foreign territory) to reach them, or to chance a sea voyage with the very real risk of destruction by storm. Besides, Sparta's close ally Corinth held the narrow isthmus that any land army trying to reach Sparta would have to cross. Sparta would have a ready buffer and time to plan.

I believe that, hoping for the mutual destruction of the Persian and Athenian armies, Sparta sent Pheidippides north again with the message that its forces would be on their way just as soon as the Carneia was complete.

It's important to note that this is simply my theory – based on what I know of the Spartans and human nature. There are many other plausible reasons (though the sources are *very* spotty on this) why the Spartans may have wanted a delay. Multiple sources, including Plato, Strabo and Pausanias, mention another Messenian revolt, apparently unsuccessful. Scholars have questioned this, since there is so little mention of it, particularly in Herodotus (and you figure he would have alluded to it, since it would be a major factor in Sparta's delayed march). But if we accept these fragmentary accounts, then Sparta was possibly involved in yet another struggle to keep the Messenians under its thumb, and the problem was bad enough that their army couldn't be spared.

The Battle of Marathon

Today, the word "Marathon" means a long-distance race. Some might know that it is named for the Battle of Marathon of 490 BC and that its distance is based on the distance Pheidippides supposedly ran to report the Greek victory to Athens. The word actually comes from the ancient Greek for fennel, which grew abundantly on the plain where the Persians beached their ships and deployed their troops. The plain was flat, broad and perfect for the Persian cavalry who would have plenty of room to maneuver. We should remember the success the Thessalian cavalry had enjoyed against the first Spartan expedition to Athens. Mounted men on good ground could be devastating against a hoplite phalanx – presumably because they could ride around the formation and attack its vulnerable flanks and rear.

And the Persians would have known this, because with them came Hippias, the Athenian tyrant unseated by Cleomenes. Now an old man, Hippias was present to resume his tyranny on behalf of Darius and to rule Athens as a Persian puppet. The only detail yet to be ironed out was the 10,000-odd Athenian and Plataean hoplites occupying a rise at the northwest end of the plain, blocking both of the roads to Athens.

Persian arms, armor and training

We discussed Greek arms and armor in chapter II, and now we have to take a moment to discuss Persian war gear as it's important to the outcome of all battles where Persians fought Greeks. Persia was a vast empire, many times the size of Greece, and composed of subject peoples of varying languages, ethnicities and cultures – all of which were reflected in the army. The "Persians" who disembarked the ships beached at Marathon would have been Iranians, Bactrians, Scythians, Egyptians, Phoenicians, Medes, Hyrcanians and more. There's a tendency to impose uniformity on ancient militaries. It is likely that such a diverse army had diverse equipment (the Scythians, for example, were known to use light hand-axes), but there are some general features worth mentioning.

Most scholars believe that, while there were very likely subject Greeks fighting as hoplites in the Persian army, most Persian troops didn't wear bronze armor. Instead of helmets, most Persian infantry would have worn the *tiara* (yes, the same word as the jeweled headdress in women's fashion), a cloth hood that could be pulled over the face to keep out dust. The few Persians who did wear body armor would have worn linen or leather cuirasses, sometimes covered with bronze scales. They also, by and large, didn't use thick wooden shields in the manner of the Greeks. Instead, they used light wickerwork shields made of cane and rawhide – either small crescent-shaped shields, or huge rectangular ones. Once again, this is just the majority view. There are scholars who believe that at least the elite Persians wore more and better armor than they are usually credited with.

But we will proceed with the majority view, which has the Persians largely unarmored. This near total lack of armor may make it seem like the Persians were defenseless, but it makes more sense when you consider that the Persians didn't expect to close with their enemies. They were, first and foremost, archers – masters of the wood, sinew and horn composite bow, which had much greater power and range than the simple Greek self-bow made of a single flexible piece of wood. The Persians faced their enemies by placing a *sparabara*, "shield bearer," carrying the door-sized rectangular *spara* shield, which they set on the ground and took position behind with a spear. Around nine ranks of archers would line up behind the shield bearer and keep up an absolutely withering rain of arrows until they judged the enemy weakened enough to be charged for close combat. These tactics had worked well enough for the Persians to conquer a vast empire and they advanced to Marathon confident it would work here as well.

Another important note is the nature of Persian arrows. Xenophon tells us of Cretan archers improving their range by shooting Persian-made arrows at a high trajectory. Persian arrow shafts were made of light reeds and their arrowheads were both smaller and lighter than the Cretans'. Such arrows serve very well when you're fighting against other lightly armored opponents (such as the Scythians, Egyptians, Indians and Mesopotamians whom the Persians conquered to build their empire), but they are *much* less effective against an enemy covered nearly head to toe in hard bronze, and carrying a heavy, thick, wooden shield.

There is the famous quote from Herodotus, one of the most repeated Spartan sayings, where the Peer Dieneces is told before Thermopylae that the Persian arrows were so numerous that they would blot out the sun. "Good!" Dieneces supposedly replied, "we'll fight in the shade." Whether or not this exchange ever actually occurred, Dieneces may not have been laughing in the face of death. He may have been informed by the Athenian experience at Marathon that light Persian arrows were largely ineffective against a fully armored Greek hoplite holding his shield high. Seen this way, Dieneces wasn't particularly brave, just confident that he was safe.

One more note on the Persians. Herodotus describes a training regimen, at least among the Persian nobility, that seems every bit as tough as the Spartan Upbringing. Persian aristocrats were trained in riding, handling the spear and the bow, swimming and running, weathering the elements, and standing long watches. Persian nobles were expected to be warriors and clearly trained arduously for that role. We don't have nearly the same detail as we do for the Spartan regimen, but from what we do see, it seems like a Persian noble would be the equal, at least in training, of his Spartan counterpart. Keep in mind that the Spartan Peers were certainly an elite minority. It would be inviting too much of a semantic fight to call them the equivalent of Persian nobles, but it is clear that the elites of both societies were highly trained.

The Greek and Persian armies remained on the field at Marathon for five days, neither army willing to make the first move. The Greeks were probably worried about the vast disparity in numbers, and the Persians were probably nervous to attack a hoplite phalanx dug in on higher ground. We can't be sure why the Greeks finally sounded the advance, and there are multiple hypotheses.

The prevailing theory is that the Greeks' hand was forced when the Persians elected to disembark some ships, loaded with troops, to make an end run around the Athenian position and disembark an army right outside Athens. There was even worry about pro-Persian factions inside the city opening the gates to welcome them. Another theory is that this end-run force was composed of the Persian cavalry (because ancient accounts of the battle don't mention the Persian cavalry at all), taking away one of the Persians' most critical advantages and giving the Greeks the confidence they needed to take the fight to the enemy. I don't like this theory, because it rests on the frankly bigoted theme in so much scholarship on the Greco-Persian War that assumes the Persians were stupid. They were not. In a recent Twitter exchange with Dr Roel Konijnedijk, he noted that it was true that the Persian cavalry aren't mentioned in accounts of Marathon, "but neither were the archers" (who surely must have fought, being the bulk of the Persian infantry). It's a very good point.

Whatever the reason, the Greek force advanced at a run, trusting to their bronze armor and heavy shields to protect them from the light Persian arrows. This proved to be a good bet and the Persians very likely were beginning to feel the sick tinge of panic in their guts when the Greeks smashed into their line like a runaway truck.

In close combat, lack of good armor was only one of several Persian disadvantages. They used shorter, lighter spears with spherical counterbalances as opposed to the Greek butt-spike, which meant that if the spearhead was snapped off, the weapon was useless (again, there is a minority view that the Persians' spears were not shorter, but we're going with the majority view here). Apart from the light hand-axes I mentioned, most Persian infantry would have been armed with the *akinakēs*, a light, straight-bladed long knife. There would have been other weapons as well, but against the hoplite's long, heavy thrusting spear and his either leaf-bladed *xiphos* or cleaver-like *kopis*, they were clearly outmatched.

In order to stretch their line and prevent themselves from being outflanked, the Greeks had thinned their center, which immediately ran into trouble facing the Persians' best troops – Iranians and Scythians who probably had the best equipment out of the army. However the deeper formation of the Greek flanks won out, and then swung inward to envelop the Persians on two sides. The Persians, suddenly finding themselves having to fight in two directions at once, broke and fled, granting the Athenians and Plataeans one of the most legendary upset victories in military history. If you believe Herodotus, over 6,000 Persians were killed at a cost of roughly just 200 Greeks. But that still left over 20,000 Persian troops who had managed to flee the battlefield and disembark on their ships. These set sail for Athens and the Greek troops now raced home, reaching the city just before the soldiers with the Persian fleet, which saw the city well-garrisoned, threw up their hands and left. The Persian invasion of Greece had been defeated.

Once again, I have to at least note the minority view. Some scholars question this story of a race back to Athens because the Persians, per Herodotus, were apparently not in such a hurry to reach Athens that they didn't stop off to pick up prisoners from Eretria.

The Athenians were still binding their wounds and blinking in astonishment at their surprise victory when 2,000 Spartans (if Herodotus is giving us the count of the number of Peers sent, this may be further evidence that the majority had remained behind to deal with the Messenian revolt) finally showed up at Athens' gates, ready to pitch in and do their part in a battle they almost certainly knew had already been fought.

Athens and Plataea had stood up to one of the greatest empires in the ancient world, defeating a threat that would surely have fallen upon all of Greece had the fight gone the other way. The fearless superwarriors of Sparta, famed enemies of foreigners and protectors of Greek liberty, had elected to sit it out.

FOCUS BATTLE: THERMOPYLAE (480 BC) – A SPEED BUMP FOR THE PERSIAN WAR MACHINE

If there is a single event that made Sparta's military legend, a seminal moment when the Bronze Lie was forged, it is the Battle of Thermopylae, fought ten years after Marathon. Nearly everything committed to popular memory about this battle is wrong, including the notion that it was its own battle at all – when in fact it was a holding action meant to delay the Persian army while the far more important naval fight at Artemisium (named for the nearby temple of Artemis), so inextricably linked to Thermopylae that the two actions should be considered a single battle, unfolded.

The Spartan king Leonidas' reply to the Persian king Xerxes' demand that the Spartans lay down their arms (*molōn labe* – "come and take them") has become a rallying cry for the far right around the world, particularly among American "gun rights" advocates such as the National Rifle Association (NRA).

What these right-wing groups always conveniently leave unmentioned is that Xerxes *did* come and take them, and in very short order.

Darius surely smarted from the humiliating and unexpected defeat at Marathon, and began preparing a new expedition to avenge Persian honor and bring the Greeks to heel once and for all. He did not live to see it depart. His death in 486 BC put it to his successor Xerxes I to finish the job, a work further delayed by a revolt by Egypt and possibly Babylon which tied up both the army and the Great King's attention. So, it wasn't until 481 BC that Xerxes finally mustered his army and fleet, wintering them in Lydia (on modern Turkey's west coast) due to storms destroying the bridges he'd constructed across the Hellespont (the Dardanelles – the narrow strait that separates Europe from Turkey). A second bridge was constructed from ships lashed together, and a massive invasion preparation program was undertaken, including the laying in of supply depots along the army's projected path, the construction of roads and the digging of a canal through the Athos peninsula, to allow ships to transit without exposing them to the storms that had scuttled the first invasion attempt in 492 BC.

If these preparations seem extensive, it's because they were. They were also necessary, as Xerxes had assembled what was arguably the largest invasion force in history to that date. As with the army Datis commanded at Marathon, it was drawn from across the massive, polyglot and diverse Persian Empire which stretched from what is now Libya, Turkey and Bulgaria in the west to what is now Pakistan and Turkmenistan in the east. Xerxes had once again sent to the city-states of Greece demanding earth and water (he deliberately omitted Athens and Sparta. There would be no mercy for them), and had once again received it from many of them, and this isn't even counting the already subjugated and loyal territories in Greece's northeast, including Thessaly, Thrace and the kingdom of Macedon. This meant that Xerxes assuredly had Greek troops with him and could count on picking up more along the way.

Herodotus, citing a inscription from the battlefield at Thermopylae, notes one claim that the Persians fielded "three hundred myriads." A myriad is 10,000, which would give Xerxes the outrageous figure of three million troops. This is, quite frankly, impossible. Even if such a massive army could have been mustered, organized and commanded, it surely couldn't have been fed or watered, let alone transported. Herodotus lowers this to a more modest 1,700,000 infantry and 100,000 cavalry, which is also absolutely insane for the same span-of-control and logistical issues I just raised. Modern scholars debate the actual size of this army in circles, with 800,000 combined troops being a number I see repeated. This is still mind-bogglingly large and I am slightly more comfortable with later estimates of a quarter-million combined troops. Even this is, by any standard, ancient or modern, a staggeringly huge army. Herodotus gives the surely false anecdote that Xerxes' host drank whole rivers dry. I align with the minority view that the Persian force was larger than most ancient armies of the period, but probably not a whole lot more than 100,000 troops total. Herodotus and modern scholars both are incentivized to exaggerate the size of the Persian army – the *biggest army ever* makes the story seem more important, and thus more likely to attract a larger and more enthusiastic audience.

We will likely never know the exact size of the army, but the swirling debate makes one thing clear – it was enormous, the biggest army in the known world at that time and easily large enough to roll over any opposition force in Greece. Per Herodotus, the army was so enormous it took seven full days and nights to transit the bobbing, makeshift pontoon bridge across the Hellespont. Xerxes surely advanced into Europe confident that absolutely no one could stop him finally crushing the nettlesome terrorist state to his west. He would put an end to the independence of these backward barbarians who advocated "the lie" in the face of "the truth" of Ahura Mazda, the patron deity of the Persians' Zoroastrian faith.

Whether or not the Persian invasions of Greece constituted a religious war is also hotly debated by scholars. The sources certainly do indicate that both Darius and Xerxes saw the replacement of the lie with Ahura Mazda's truth as a motivating factor. However, how much of a factor isn't clear and is nearly impossible to prove, and unfortunately the argument runs afoul of right-wing agitators who want to conflate the Achaemenid Persian invasions with the inflated bugbear of Islamic Jihad. The two things have absolutely nothing to do with one another and any such comparison is bunk.

We should remember that among the many Greeks accompanying the Persians was the exiled Spartan king Demaratus, chased from his home by the scheming of Cleomenes and Leotychides. He was a critical military and cultural advisor to Xerxes, especially on matters pertaining to Spartans. His role is carefully omitted from *300* (though he does appear in the 1962 film *The 300 Spartans*), which neglects to mention that the Spartans at Thermopylae were facing one of their own greatest luminaries – a former king. Apparently loyalty to Sparta and obedience to its laws evaporated, at least in Demaratus' case, the moment the body politic rejected you.

The army was paralleled by a massive invasion fleet that could provide communications, supply and transport support, 1,327 triremes according to Herodotus, supplied and crewed by Xerxes' seafaring subjects – Egyptians,

Phoenicians, Cypriots, and Ionian and islander Greeks. We actually know a lot about these ships due to the incredible work of Britons John Coates, John Morrison and Charles Willink in the 1980s, who developed largely historically accurate plans for the construction of an Athenian trireme of this period. These plans were used to build the *Olympias*, still in service with today's Greek navy.

Ships such as the *Olympias* were called "triremes" for their three banks of oars, one atop the other (the top bank being a kind of outrigger), manned by some 170 *eretai* (rowers) drawn from *thētes* (the poorest levels of Athenian society), metics (resident aliens) and slaves. Roughly 20 feet wide at the widest point and 130 feet long, these fast, agile ships were equipped with a massive bronze ram. Plutarch tells us that at the Battle of Salamis in 480 BC the triremes carried a fighting complement of 14 hoplites and four archers (Scythian mercenaries, in that case), and the structure of the *Olympias* bears this out, though they certainly could and did carry more or fewer as the operation required. Herodotus mentions fewer, and many scholars give strong arguments for more. A broad deck protected the rowers from the sun and spray and gave the warriors a nice fighting platform to work from in the event of a boarding action (usually accompanied by ramming). Triremes almost always beached stern-first. This is because the added weight of the bronze ram (nearly 500 pounds on the *Olympias*) made the bow ride lower in the water, giving an added boost when launching the ship.

Those Greeks who did not submit to Xerxes' demand for earth and water formed the Hellenic League, a confederation of resisters that included Sparta and Athens (of course, as they had no choice), and also Plataea and Eretria (also of course, given their role in the last Persian invasion), Chalcis, Aegina, Corinth and Ceos. Argos notably did not join, but neither did it actively hinder the Hellenic League, which had sworn to destroy and despoil any pro-Persian city-states, dedicating their wealth to the gods.

Athens' leading politician and general Themistocles had convinced his city-state to use a rich silver strike from Athens' Laurium mines in 483 BC to build a fleet, and Athens had some 200 warships afloat and ready to fight. That said, its crews were nowhere near as experienced as the Persians, who you will recall had already shown their naval skill and strength at Lade 14 years earlier. Despite Athens easily contributing the largest naval force, Sparta wound up with command of the Hellenic League forces on both land and sea, largely due to Peloponnesian allies refusing to serve under Athenian command (hardly surprising given the unequal relationships between Sparta and other members of the Peloponnesian League).

The Hellenic League's strategy was clear – a stand-up fight against such a massive army was insane and there was no sense in looking for a decisive battle. The smart play was to close up the limited land and sea routes into mountain-choked and storm-wracked Greece, and pray that the Persian army's massive size would be its undoing. By delaying the huge host, the Greeks could force the Persians to run out of food and water as they scoured the surrounding countryside for forage and lost ships to the inevitable rough weather off the coastline. It was a risky plan, but it was surely less risky than trying to face the Persians in the field, taking on an army that would outnumber the Greeks by at least ten to one.

The initial choke point was the Vale of Tempe in Thessaly. The Hellenic League sent 10,000 troops under the overall command of the Spartan Euaenetus to hold the pass far enough north to save nearly all of Greece from the ravages of the invading army.

They went at the invitation of the anti-Persian factions of the Thessalians, which wanted to join forces with the Hellenic League to resist the invaders. These factions stood opposed to the Thessalian Aleuad clan, who favored submission to Xerxes.

Here it's worth noting a very interesting word from Thucydides' description of the later Spartan siege of Plataea – *xenagoi*, literally "officers in charge over foreigners." While this word is describing an event more than 50 years after the period we are discussing, it is possible this arrangement existed much earlier. Keep this word in mind. More on it later.

The decision to try to hold the Persians off so far north may have been made not only to bring the Thessalians into the fold, but to try to spare Greece from ravaging. Remember that ancient armies survived mostly on forage, which meant begging, borrowing and requisitioning (stealing) anything that wasn't nailed down in the countryside through which they traveled. There was a reason that ancient armies rarely campaigned in the winter when troops wouldn't be able to harvest neighboring fields, soldiers acting as farmers, butchers and bakers, taking in the crops and livestock of the localities through which they passed.

There are multiple reasons given for why the Greeks didn't make their stand at Tempe. Some say the Greeks were warned off by the pro-Persian king Alexander I of Macedon, who cautioned the Greeks that the Persians simply couldn't be resisted. Others say that a pass by which the Greek position could be outflanked was discovered (this makes the least sense, since it relies on the Greeks not performing basic reconnaissance of the ground before committing troops, an unbelievably stupid thing to do even by ancient military standards. The Greeks, like the Persians, were no fools). The most likely reason was that the Persian army simply moved more slowly than the Greeks guessed (causing supply problems for the Greeks encamped at Tempe and having to forage the surrounding area to keep their troops fed) and then bypassed their position entirely by building another road around the pass and into Thessaly. Of course, technically *any* position can be outflanked (there is literally always a way around a choke point if you're willing to detour far enough), and other scholars have suggested other theories for abandoning Tempe, including suspicion of Thessalian loyalty, and a shortage of supplies for the Greek troops.

Whatever the reason, the Greeks pulled back to the isthmus of Corinth, a natural land-based choke point that would allow the Greeks to hold off an enemy army and keep the Peloponnese safe. This obviously appealed to the Spartans and their Peloponnesian allies. It did not appeal to the rest of the Greeks who lived in Attica and Boeotia north of the isthmus, whose lands would be subjugated and plundered by the Persians. Unfortunately, this left the Thessalians little choice. If the Hellenic League would not protect them, they could do nothing other than submit to Xerxes and adopt a pro-Persian position.

After Tempe, the next logical choke point to stop the Persians was in central Greece at a place called Thermopylae ("Hot Gates"), named for the hot springs that still flow there today. The route was pretty much the only way for a land army to access Greece south of Thessaly (there's another route through the Cephisus valley, but it's mountainous and was probably well guarded by the locals), and narrowed to a tiny corridor sandwiched between the Gulf of Malis to the north, and the over 4,500-foot cliffs of Mount

Callidromus (literally "good running course") to the south. This narrow track ran for roughly four miles east–west between the east and west gates of the pass.

I visited Thermopylae and walked the choke point. It's hard to imagine how narrow it must have been, but in 480 BC the shore of the Gulf was a *lot* closer to the cliffs. So close, in fact, that Herodotus tells us it narrowed to no more than a wagon's width at the east and west gates. It was a space so narrow, that just a few men with good armor and shields, standing shoulder to shoulder, could dig in and hold on against a numerically superior enemy. In such tight quarters, superior numbers would count for nothing.

In other words, it was tailor-made for a hoplite phalanx.

Even better, about halfway between the east and west gates of the pass were the ruins of a wall built by the Phocians to hold off the Thessalians in a past war. The Spartans made sure to rebuild this, which meant they now defended a choke point that was not only tiny, but also fortified.

Here is where the Spartan Mirage asserts itself firmly and we must squint hard to see into it. While academics are more skeptical, nearly every popular account I have read deems the Spartan defense at Thermopylae to be a known suicide mission. These stories credit an oracle from Delphi saying that unless a Spartan king died, Sparta would be destroyed. This oracle is taken seriously by far too many and so it is accepted that Leonidas (not the young and muscular king portrayed by Gerard Butler, but a man over 60, so old in fact he was exempt from military service under Spartan law) marched heroically off to man the pass, with full knowledge that he would not be coming home.

Again, this is a work of history, not mythology, and we have already well established that the Spartans were incredibly cynical when it came to religious observance – pious when it suited them, sacrilegious when it suited them. Some scholars suggest that the oracle was a later story invented to help build the Spartan myth *after* the battle and Leonidas' death, and this makes good sense to me. But the sources are clear – due to the festival of the Carneia once again (as at Marathon) the Spartans suddenly had a very convenient excuse not to send their full army north to hold the pass. Instead, Leonidas chose 300 but only from among men with living sons (again, implying that they knew it was a suicide mission) to carry on the family name.

It's interesting to note that the Carneia had a different prohibition this time. At Marathon, the Carneia meant *no* Spartans could march to battle. At Thermopylae, suddenly the Carneia meant that just one king and 300 Peers could march to battle.

And this number is suspect. The 1st century BC Greek historian Diodorus Siculus writes that Leonidas marched to Thermopylae at the head of 1,000 Lacedaemonians (Spartans – inclusive of Peers, *perioikoi*, Inferiors and helots). Diodorus is clear that only 300 of them were Peers, but he doesn't say who the other 700 were. They were very likely *perioikoi*, and possibly some Inferiors. Each Peer was almost certainly accompanied by at least one helot (Herodotus specifically mentions them as being among the dead) who would have fought alongside their masters. Either way, that's a considerable difference in manpower.

It's also important to note that the other Greek city-states were delayed in contributing troops by the current Olympic festival, which implies that the Spartans would be assured of additional help once it was concluded.

The idea of a suicide mission seems even more laughable when you consider that the brave 300 ... ahem, maybe 1,000 Spartans, were joined by large complements of allied troops. Herodotus tells us of 500 Tegeans, 500 Mantineans, 120 Orchomenians (all three of these city-states were in Arcadia), 1,000 other Arcadians, 400 Corinthians, 200 Phliasians and 80 Mycenaeans. And that's just the allies close to Sparta. Thebes had submitted to Persia, but the anti-Persian faction still managed to send 400 men (probably in the hopes that the Hellenic League would smile on this contribution and not attack Thebes for their pro-Persian stance). Thespiae sent 700, nearly as many as Sparta (if we believe they sent 1,000). The Phocians, who lived just south of the pass, sent 1,000 men, and the Locrians to the east sent 1,000 as well.

We don't know exactly how these troops were armed, but it is safe to assume they were largely equipped as hoplites. The exact numbers are debated, but no matter how you slice it, you no longer have 300 brave men heading off on a suicide mission. You have a tiny contingent of Spartan Peers heading up an army of approximately 7,000 Greeks, nearly as many troops as mustered at Marathon, and on far better ground. Yes, there was still an enormous disparity in numbers, but in the tight confines of the pass, Xerxes' advantage in manpower would be almost entirely neutralized.

Most modern accounts of the Thermopylae story make it seem as if the Spartans alone did the fighting and almost no attention is paid to the thousands of other warriors contributing to the defense. But note the later description of Spartan *xenagoi* commanding units of foreign troops. Remember Sparta's reputation (deserved or not) as the most powerful land army in Greece. Also, remember Sparta's absolutely deserved reputation as the only truly disciplined and organized army in Greece. This raises the possibility of a small Spartan contingent of *officers* and *advisors* leading a much larger allied army in the defense of the pass. In fact, Herodotus even points out that each Greek contingent took its turn defending the pass, presumably giving others a turn to rest, tend to wounds and repair equipment.

However, I must admit that there is no real evidence to support the Spartans acting as *xenagoi* at Thermopylae other than my suspicion based on their numbers. Herodotus' comment that the Greeks took turns in the pass implies that they fought cohesively as units based on their respective city-states. Further, the strength of the Spartans lay in their ability to fight *together*, which would be lost if they were acting as officers. And yet, the use of this term *xenagoi* sticks with me. Modern US Special Forces frequently work as "military advisors" de facto commanding allied troops in running fights around the world. Those relationships are usually based on the disparity in training and professionalism between the American and other militaries. The parallel here between disciplined, organized Spartan troops and other Greek amateurs seems too obvious to completely dismiss.

At any rate, if we believe Herodotus that Sparta could field 8,000 Peers in 480 BC, then Sparta had sent just 4 percent of its available Peers to the most critical action of the Greco-Persian War. We're looking at a well-planned definitively *non*-suicide mission – a well-equipped, sufficiently manned force that had a very real expectation of holding the pass (and more importantly, its neighboring naval choke point at Artemisium) long enough to cause the Persian army to starve and begin to unwind as desertion, failure of discipline, disease and the myriad other problems that would beset any ancient army of that size stuck in one place long enough began to make themselves felt.

That makes a lot more sense than the storybook notion of a fated suicide mission driven by a magic oracle. In fact, Herodotus specifically mentions that more Spartans would be sent as soon as the Carneia was concluded, which meant that Leonidas marched to Thermopylae knowing that help was going to be on the way. Also, recall my previous note on the delay of other Greek forces due to the Olympic festival. All Leonidas had to do was hold on and wait to be reinforced. Hardly the thinking of a man on a suicide mission.

There's another possible reason the Spartans sent so few men. Herodotus tells the story of a council of war called as the Persians appeared and set up camp outside Thermopylae's western gate. Herodotus makes no mention of the Spartans, but the other Peloponnesians argue loudly for abandoning Thermopylae and heading back to the isthmus of Corinth – another choke point that would be just north of the Peloponnesian lands. In other words, the Peloponnesians didn't want to waste their lives protecting territory they didn't live on. Obviously, the Phocians and Locrians who lived right on top of Thermopylae argued against this and in the end Leonidas elected to hold position. Whether or not he did this gladly, we can't know, but it's certainly understandable that the ephors back in Sparta were none too happy about sending any more troops north to defend territory that wasn't theirs than they absolutely had to. Herodotus does add that Leonidas sent for help, though from whom, he doesn't say. Again, not the action of a man on a suicide mission.

There was another factor in the Spartans' thinking. Their old enemy Argos was right on top of them and squarely in the Persian camp. If they marched north with their whole army, what was to stop the Argives from marching on an undefended Sparta? Or from raising the helots in revolt?

At the same time, the Hellenic League sent a naval force of 271 ships (almost 50 percent of them Athenian; the Spartans contributed only ten) to hold the naval choke point at Artemisium roughly 40 miles to the northeast. This choke point was chosen (instead of one much closer to Thermopylae) likely for two reasons. First, the Greeks needed to prevent the Persians from sailing wherever they pleased. In fact, Herodotus tells us that Demaratus even suggested that the Persian fleet raid the Laconian coast in an effort to force the Spartans to return to the Peloponnese and abandon any efforts to fight farther north, but this wise plan was rejected. The other reason was that Artemisium protected the north shore of Euboea, an important island. Without this defense, the Persians could easily have landed on it, sacked Eretria for a second time, and then simply rowed across the channel to march into Attica.

Positioning the fleet at Artemisium was the smart play and the far more critical part of the battle. The Persian land army would be helpless without the logistical support of the nearby fleet and the coastal route theoretically gave large numbers of Persian troops quick access to critical landing points (as the Persian effort to get around the Athenian army at Marathon illustrates). Even the Peloponnesians who preferred fighting at the isthmus of Corinth wouldn't do much good if the Persians could simply bypass it via the gulfs bordering it both north and south. If they were going to stop the Persians, the Hellenic League undoubtedly knew, they had to stop them at sea.

The Persian army arrived at Thermopylae on the same day that the fleet anchored off the coast of Magnesia just north of the Greek island of Euboea, home to the city-state of Eretria that was sacked during the last Persian invasion. Again, we're not sure of the numbers, but no doubt Xerxes was hopeful that the incredible size of the force he'd assembled, speaking a huge array of languages, armed and armored in a wide range of local fashions, would send the Greeks running. The way Herodotus tells it, the Spartans couldn't have cared less. A Persian scout saw them exercising nude out before the Phocian wall, and combing their long hair. This story may or may not be true, but I don't doubt the sentiment. Far from being a suicide mission, Leonidas would probably have been confident that he had a sufficient force to hold the pass indefinitely. That he was outnumbered was mostly irrelevant due to the excellent terrain and the fact that he had enough troops to rotate out the wounded or fatigued with plenty to take their place.

The Anopaia Path – The Law of Competence

The Persians had the option of outflanking the Spartans via the Anopaia Path that went around the steepest parts of Callidromus emptying out behind the Spartan lines. Leonidas would have known that Xerxes was no fool and that the Persians had one of the most sophisticated intelligence networks in the ancient world. Long before the main body of Xerxes' army arrived, he would have sent out scouts to reconnoiter the land and would have had forward observers and intelligence agents interviewing locals and surveying the terrain. The Persians would absolutely have known about the path long before the first of their vanguard even arrived outside the east gate.

It baffles me how many modern scholars just dismiss this. Nearly every book and article on the battle takes Herodotus' story at face value – that Xerxes, master of the greatest and most sophisticated military machine of the classical period, with all of the intelligence apparatus that entails, would simply fail to perform basic reconnaissance. In the end, it is left to the traitor Ephialtes, a local Greek who decided to betray the Spartans and guide the Persians along the path that they otherwise would have missed. In *300*, he is depicted as a physically deformed Spartan, too weak and misshapen to stand in the phalanx, and thus denied his birthright to fight and die with his brethren. It is this rejection by his own countrymen that drives him into Xerxes' tent to betray his people.

At the very least, Ephialtes was not a Spartan. He very likely didn't exist at all and the story of the Persians needing a traitor to guide them is papered over for dramatic effect and as an othering device to paint the Persians as fools. Far more likely is that the Persians recruited *many* local guides in the area long before they arrived at Thermopylae, who provided them with detailed accounts of all the terrain and possible routes through and around the pass, and that this body of local guides became the legendary Ephialtes in Herodotus' narrative.

But let's consider Thermopylae from the revolutionary perspective of "what if we didn't assume the Persians were fools?" It seems like an obvious starting point, but it's one that modern scholars have frankly ignored in nearly all writing about Thermopylae and the result of taking this approach changes everything, as we will see. I have coined what I will refer to henceforward as "The Law of Competence": Never assume ancient commanders were incompetent until ruling out all other possible explanations for their decisions.

I will proceed with my story on this assumption – either there was no Ephialtes, or he was merely one of a huge network of scouts that helped reconnoiter Thermopylae and reported back to the Persian command. Xerxes' local scouts had reported the Anopaia Path to him and he was thinking of how to exploit that as his army filed in. Leonidas, also not stupid, knew that Xerxes would do this, but he wasn't worried. Again, he had ample troops. He deployed the 1,000 Phocians, a sizable force and possibly under the command of a Spartan Peer acting as a *xenagos* officer over the troop. The Phocians were fighting to protect their home territory, they were well commanded and they were more than enough to hold the path long enough to be reinforced if it came down to a tough fight. Leonidas would have been informed by the experience at Marathon and was probably confident that a single Greek hoplite was the match of many Persians.

Leonidas and his Spartans, seeing the Persians arrive, likely weren't naked and hair-combing for long but quickly moved to join the army, armored up, and took up their positions behind the rebuilt Phocian wall. The two armies held position there, Xerxes resting his troops from their long march and probably giving the trailing elements of his enormous army time to catch up, and Leonidas refusing to abandon his perfect defensive position. This wait consumed the first day. On land, the second day mirrored the first. The Persians and the Greeks held position, watching one another.

But at sea, things went sideways for Persia. A horrific storm struck the Persian fleet off Magnesia and the huge armada found inadequate safe harbor to put the ships in. Herodotus describes the seas as boiling and triremes at least (though the Persian fleet would have had many different types of ships, triremes would certainly have figured largely) are notoriously unseaworthy. They are coastal ships, meant to be agile in calm waters for ramming and boarding actions, not to stand off from shore and weather a storm. Long, narrow and with shallow drafts, they roll over easily. A bad storm could make short work of an ancient fleet and that's what happened here.

We don't know the exact number of ships lost, but Herodotus says it was around 400, or a third of the massive flotilla that had mustered to invade. This still outnumbered the Greek holding force roughly 3-to-1, but watching the broken timbers and dead bodies borne on the current had to give the superstitious Greeks (who surely thought the gods were aiding them, as Herodotus confirms) a desperately needed shot in the arm. While Leonidas and his Greeks would not have seen the wreckage, they probably would have noticed the weather and certainly would have heard about the impact. The two positions of Thermopylae and Artemisium were chosen partly because they were easily linked and communications by boat, foot, or horseback, or all three flowed easily between them.

For the third and fourth days, both armies and fleets stayed in place. The Greeks had no reason to move. Their plan was working perfectly; they were forcing the Persians to hold position, letting time and the bellies of hundreds

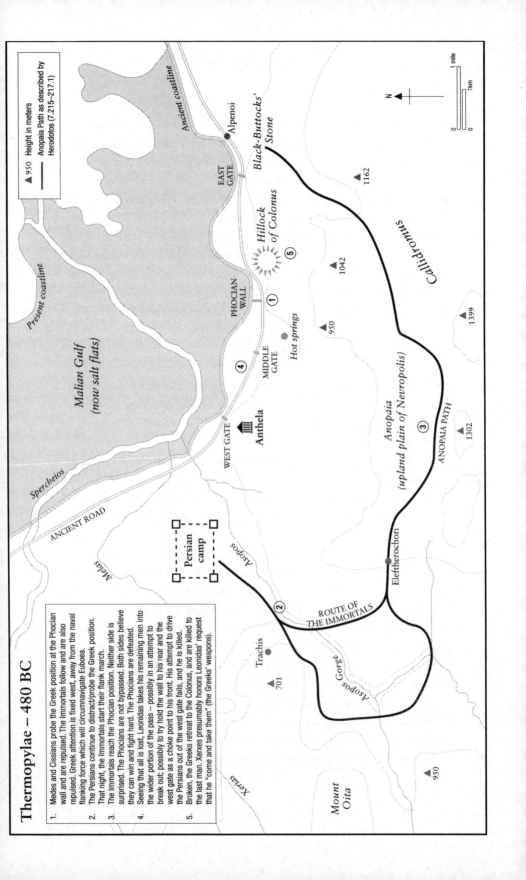

Thermopylae – 480 BC

1. Medes and Cissians probe the Greek position at the Phocian wall and are repulsed. The Immortals follow and are also repulsed. Greek attention is fixed west, away from the naval flanking force which will circumnavigate Euboea.
2. The Persians continue to distract/probe the Greek position. That night, the Immortals start their flank march.
3. The Immortals reach the Phocian position. Neither side is surprised. The Phocians are not bypassed. Both sides believe they can win and fight hard. The Phocians are defeated.
4. Seeing that all is lost, Leonidas takes his remaining men into the wider portion of the pass – possibly in an attempt to break out; possibly to try hold the wall to his rear and the west gate as a choke point to his front. His attempt to drive the Persians out of the west gate fails, and he is killed.
5. Broken, the Greeks retreat to the Colonus, and are killed to the last man. Xerxes presumably honors Leonidas' request that he "come and take them" (the Greeks' weapons).

Height in meters ▲ 950

Anopaia Path as described by Herodotos (7.215-217.1)

N

0   1km
0   1 mile

Present coastline

Ancient coastline

Malian Gulf
(now salt flats)

Spercheios

ANCIENT ROAD

Melas

Xerias

Trachis
▲ 701

Mount Oita

▲ 950

Asopos Gorge

Persian camp

Asopos

Eleftherochori

ROUTE OF THE IMMORTALS

② ③

Anopaia
(upland plain of Nevropolis)

ANOPAIA PATH

Callidromus

▲ 1302

▲ 1399

▲ 950

▲ 1042

▲ 1162

Anthela

WEST GATE

MIDDLE GATE

Hot springs

PHOCIAN WALL ①

④

Hillock of Colonus ⑤

EAST GATE

Black-Buttocks' Stone

Alpenoi

of thousands of men and animals do their slow, insidious work. Herodotus tells us the reason for the Persian delay was the expectation that the Greeks would run. But this flies in the face of the Law of Competence. Xerxes wasn't stupid, nor was his staff. They knew the Greek numbers and supply. They knew they occupied nearly perfect defensive terrain. They would have no doubt that the Greeks weren't going anywhere.

For the Persians, this period was probably a flurry of reconnaissance activity on land, as well as laying in stores and coordinating with the fleet, who were very likely engaged in the arduous and morale-killing task of recovering from the storm – searching frantically for survivors, salvaging wrecks and reckoning the damage and its impact on their plans.

INTO THE PASS

On the fifth day, Xerxes evidently felt his position was sufficiently consolidated and the fleet had sent word that whatever could be done to salvage the disaster of the storm had been done.

It was time.

Xerxes sent Median and Cissian infantry into the pass to assault the Greek position. Both the Medes and Cissians were ancient Iranian peoples. The Medes were the dominant force in the region before the Persians challenged their power and eventually subjugated them. In fact, most Greeks still referred to the Persians as "Medes," though they were a distinct people. These would have been strong troops, representing the trusted core of Xerxes' army.

To hear Herodotus tell it, these men simply launched themselves at the entrenched Greek position and battered themselves against it to no effect, being spitted like pigs at a barbecue, dying in heaps. This again violates the Law of Competence and presumes the Persians were fools. They weren't, and they did no such thing. What is far more likely is that they advanced to bow range, set up behind a wall of *spara*, and then rained arrows on the Greek position. The Greeks, already covered head to toe in bronze and protected to their front by the thick stone of the repaired Phocian wall, raised their shields to form a roof of bronze-faced wood. The Persians had plenty of arrows and they would have kept up the shower for hours, seeking unprotected angles, or waiting for the Greek troops to get tired. But the pass was so narrow that only a few Greeks could stand in the phalanx at a time, and with 6,000 on hand (remember that the 1,000 Phocians had been sent off to hold the Anopaia Path), it was easy to rotate in fresh troops as soon as someone's arm got too tired to keep his shield up.

After a while, the Median and Cissian officers would have realized that the archery wasn't going to work. They also needed to engage the Greek troops proactively to exhaust and wound them, because of a two-pronged plan that Xerxes was even now hatching.

First, the Persians planned to flank the Greek position via the Anopaia Path. Xerxes (or Xerxes' staff) knew that this route was strongly held by 1,000 Phocian troops. His intelligence network would also have informed him that the Phocians were fighting close to home, and would be fierce opponents, but this was no problem. Xerxes detailed his palace troops, "the Immortals," so named because their numbers were never allowed to dip below 10,000. These would have been the ethnic Persians, Medes and Elamites of aristocratic stock, trained to peak performance and superior to the troops of the Persian satraps who served under the King of Kings. They would have been armed with spears and bows, but probably unarmored, their heads covered only by the *tiara*. Some may have had bronze helmets, but these were unlikely to have been as complete as the Corinthian pattern many of the Greeks would have worn. Some may have worn body armor made from leather or linen, possibly with metal scales. Separate from this corps was a hyper-elite unit of 1,000 "Apple Bearers," so named because their spears were counterbalanced with golden apples. Herodotus calls these 1,000 "*the noblest and bravest of the Persians*" and they appear to have served the same role as the Spartan *hippeis*, acting as personal guards to the king. Some scholars lump the Apple Bearers in with the Immortals, and when Herodotus relates that all 10,000 Immortals were to be sent down the path, he makes it sound as though the Apple Bearers were among them. I don't believe that the Apple Bearers would leave their king, and I think it's safer to guess that the Immortals alone were detailed for the march under the command of the Persian nobleman Hydarnes II, whose father and namesake had helped bring Darius I to power.

But this flank march planned for the following day was just half of the Persian plan. The other half came from the sea. The Athenian fleet was stationed at the northeastern tip of the island of Euboea. A fleet circumnavigating Euboea would be completely obscured from the Greeks' view. If they moved quickly and at night, they could sail up the western side of the island and arrive right behind the Greek navy. This, of course, was exactly what the Persians planned to do and every modern account of the battle I have read accepts this.

But there's one thing almost no modern accounts consider – this same route would take the Persian fleet *directly behind* the Greek land position at Thermopylae, where a flanking force could easily be disembarked *behind* the east gate.

This force could then easily link up with the Immortals once they broke through the Phocian defense and trap the Greeks in a pincer. Then, the Persian fleet could sail off and create the same pincer at sea, trapping the Greek fleet at Artemisium. Herodotus says that this fleet's role was simply to prevent the escape of the Greek fleet, but this also doesn't make sense. Having a fleet in their enemy's rear would have presented too good an opportunity to put the Greeks in a pincer to be ignored.

This double-pincer plan was smart, perfectly suited to the terrain, and made the best use of the Persian advantage in numbers and their more lightly armored infantry's greater mobility. In short, it was the smart move, and as we've established, the Persians were very smart. But for this plan to succeed, the Greeks' attention had to be kept facing forward. Leonidas' men at Thermopylae needed to be hyper-focused to the west. He knew the Persians would try the Anopaia Path and was counting on the Phocians to hold them, but he *didn't* know that a naval force would be disembarking marines to his rear, and that had to be kept from him until the time was right. Likewise, the Greek fleet had to be kept at Artemisium looking toward the main body of the Persian fleet and ignorant of the detachment of 200 Persian ships, moving around the east side of first Sciathos, and then Euboea, rounding the island to head up the Euripus Channel, bottling the Greek ships inside.

This view much better explains what happened next than the traditional story – that the Medes and Cissians threw themselves recklessly against the Greek phalanx, dying in huge numbers for no good reason. Again, this makes sense only if we view the Persians as a wild, untrained rabble, rather than the army of one of the most advanced civilizations of its time. But I do not doubt that, with their inferior weapons and armor, the Persians got the worst of the close combat once they gave up the archery and charged.

Though this is disputed, I believe the Persians' spears were shorter than the Greeks' and they lacked butt-spikes, which meant they would have been rendered useless if they broke. Their light axes would have had some impact, but they would have to get close enough to use them and the Greeks were sure not to cooperate. Their cane and rawhide shields were sturdy enough to fend off arrows like their own, but they would be easily punched through by a hoplite spear or split by a chop from a heavy Greek cleaver-sword.

We must also give credit to the Spartans here. These were not the same men who had formed the warband in Messenia, cheering while their king broke ranks to engage in heroic combat in front of the line. The 300 Spartans at Thermopylae knew that their position would stand or fall based on the cohesion of their phalanx. There could be no gaps in the line the Persians could widen to create a fatal breach. Their Boeotian, Locrian and Arcadian comrades might be only part-time warriors, but they were clearly at the top of their game. They would have been kicking legs, shoving shoulders, bellowing at the men around them to hold the line. These Spartans would have keenly felt the pressure of their reputation. They knew the other Greeks were looking at them to lead, that if their will faltered, the battle would be lost.

Still, the Persians they faced were no rabble. They were highly trained, brave men, and they would have made the best of a bad situation, seizing Greek spears and trying to rip them from their wielder's grasp; one man hooking the top of a Greek shield with his axe spike, yanking it down to expose the holder to a thrust from his comrade's spear. They fought in earnest, likely unaware of the larger plan, believing that it was their job to break the Greek line and clear the pass.

But their commanders, and certainly Xerxes, knew better. This was a probe, an attack intended to take their measure and sound out their weaknesses, to weaken the enemy with wounds and fatigue. But above all this, it was an attack planned to grab the Greeks' attention and focus it firmly to the west, away from the Anopaia Path and the naval flanking force that would soon be sailing around Euboea to attack them from behind.

However, the Greeks could not have known this. As far as Leonidas was concerned, he had no word from the Phocian position that the Anopaia Path had been taken by the enemy. The Medes and Cissians were trying to break through here and now, and he and his men fought ferociously to make sure they failed. When, at long last, the horns sounded the recall and the Medes and Cissians withdrew, the hoplites would have thrust their spears into the earth to stand upright on their butt-spikes and leaned on them, panting, helmets propped up on the backs of their heads, shields grounded, resting against their legs. In this posture, they could ease their tired muscles, but still be ready to snatch their arms back up in an instant.

They didn't have long. Even now, the Persian commanders were mustering the Immortals – the same men who were assigned to march the Anopaia Path were turning out into ranks to make a second attack on the Greek position. Leonidas and his men would well know the reputation of this corps, and would have been able to identify them by their dress. The committing of the Immortals surely signaled that Xerxes intended to break through from the west. Leonidas' eyes were fixed firmly on his enemy, and away from the unprotected shore of the Malian Gulf to his rear.

And he might have remained ignorant if not for a deserter from the Persian fleet, a salvage diver named Scyllias. Herodotus identifies him as a Thessalian, so he was likely one of the Greeks who submitted to the Persians either during the early campaigns around Marathon, or in the rush to seek Persian favor once the Hellenic League abandoned Tempe. As a diver, he could presumably swim hidden under the water for long periods and used this to make good his escape. Herodotus turns to the reader and admits that he doubts Scyllias could have swum that far and that he came by boat. However he arrived, Scyllias surfaced among the Greek ships, got himself hauled aboard a trireme, and promptly gave his report that the Persians were sending a fleet around Euboea to attack the Greeks from behind.

The Greek fleet took counsel from this decision and determined it would launch after dark and head back down the channel, intercepting the flanking fleet and catching it by surprise. In the meantime, however, the Greeks decided to try themselves against the main Persian fleet before them. Herodotus tells us this was motivated by a desire to see how the Persians fought at sea, but that makes little sense and again violates the Law of

Competence, which holds just as true for Greeks as it does for Persians. Far more realistic is that the Greeks, like the Persians, were seeking to misdirect and make sure that the Persians didn't suspect they were aware of the flanking force by instigating a battle.

Herodotus tells us the Persians were taken completely by surprise seeing the heavily outnumbered Greeks rowing to the *attack*. They scrambled to launch from the beach at Aphetae, just opposite the Greek position off Artemisium.

Here we have to pause to describe an ancient naval maneuver known as the *diekplous*. Literally meaning "rowing through and past," it's a fancy word to describe a simple tactic. When presented with enough space between two enemy triremes (and keep in mind you'd need space not only for your hull, but also for your oars) or if your line of ships was longer than the enemy's, you simply rowed your ship past the enemy, keeping as close as possible. Scholars debate whether part of this maneuver involved shipping your oars at the last possible minute so that your hull sheared off the enemy's oars, sparing your own. At any rate, as soon as your bow passed the enemy's stern, you cut hard to port or starboard (depending on which side you passed) and then rammed the enemy in the quarter or stern. The Greeks were horrifically outnumbered in this engagement, which meant they would be intensely vulnerable to this tactic.

Themistocles, the Athenian commander responsible for the existence of Athens' navy and certainly for its naval strategy despite Sparta's overall command, ordered the ships to form into a circle sterns in, rams pointing out. Some scholars dispute that this would be possible with 271 ships and I agree with them. It is far more likely that they formed a half-moon line, bowing out toward the enemy. This would still make the *diekplous* impossible and accommodate that many ships.

Herodotus doesn't give many details about the battle that followed, but the Greeks clearly got the better of it, capturing 30 enemy ships. Ramming prow to prow was a risky proposition for both ships, which meant that if the Persians wanted to come to grips with the Greeks, they would have to board, and then all of the close-combat advantages of the hoplite marines (better armor and weapons) would come into play. Some scholars dispute this, saying that Greek marines would have been armed more lightly than their land-based colleagues. However, Greek ships were slower and bulkier than their Persian counterparts, and also likely carried greater numbers of marines, even if they weren't armed and armored as heavily as hoplites.

Meanwhile, back on land, the Immortals were essentially repeating the Medes' and Cissians' performance from earlier in the day. Here, if we believe Herodotus, the Spartans executed a brilliant maneuver that punished the elite unit severely. The Immortals, likely having learned from the poor close-combat performance of the Medes and Cissians, stood off and tried their luck with arrows. Either impatient, or worried that some of the shots were beginning to tell, Leonidas ordered his troops to make a feigned retreat.

Remember that, whatever the commanders knew of the Persian flanking strategy, the rank and file, even of a palace unit, did not. As far as they were concerned, the Greeks were finished. They returned their bows to their cases, hefted their spears and charged. Herodotus implies that this charge was mad and disorganized, but this violates the Law of Competence and flies in the face of what we know of the Immortals – that they were highly trained troops. If the feigned retreat story is true, then I would suspect the Immortals did indeed pursue, but did so in ordered fashion.

The result was the same: when they reached the Greek position, the Greeks turned, re-formed and engaged. Too close to use their bows, the Persians were forced to fight in the Greeks' preferred style of close-combat. Whatever their elite status, the Immortals' equipment was still not a match for that of the Greeks, who made short work of them. Some scholars argue that only a disciplined force such as the Spartans could pull off such a complex maneuver, but I disagree. I have participated in enough reenactments to know what this entails – an about-face, a quick march to the rear, and then, on the order, another about-face and dressing the line. This is more tricky than, say, marching in a straight line, but it was hardly beyond the ability of Greek hoplites.

Nightfall signaled the end of the fighting on both land and sea, but there were still Persian losses to come. Once again, a terrific storm blew up, catching the Persian flanking fleet off Euboea's unprotected eastern shore, utterly wiping them out. The coastline there is rocky and inhospitable, offering no sandy shoreline to beach ships. The Persians had no choice but to try to ride out the weather, or make their way through it. Not a single ship survived.

The Greek fleet would have sent word to Leonidas as soon as Scyllias spilled the beans about the Persian plan, but we don't know if that runner would have arrived yet. As lookouts stationed on Euboea reported the wreckage of the Persian flanking fleet, another one would have been sent with a follow-up message to the tune of, "Hey, remember that fleet we were warning you about? No sweat. The gods took care of it."

As the sun rose on the sixth day of the twin battles, things were looking good for the Greeks. They'd held position on both land and sea, and Xerxes' first major maneuver had failed utterly. The sixth day proceeded exactly as the fifth – Xerxes funneled infantry into the pass to probe the Greek front and they were repulsed with reportedly heavy losses. Herodotus is short on details for this day's land fighting, save pointing out the rotation and resting of the Greek troops and noting that all the contingents (not just the Spartans) got a turn standing and fighting. As I mentioned earlier, while Herodotus describes this only on the second day, I believe this was the plan of action throughout all of the fighting.

At sea, things went even better for the Greeks. Reinforcements arrived from Athens in the shape of 53 ships presumably with stores and full crews. With the Persian fleet already down by hundreds of ships, this modest boost to the Greek naval ranks went a long way toward evening the odds. More important was the boost to morale provided by this development coupled with the sight of the wreckage and drowned corpses of the Persian flanking fleet. Herodotus confirms that the Greeks saw the gods favoring them and mustered the courage to try another attack. It was again successful, though we have no details other than that it was carried out at the same time of day and that they attacked the "Cilician squadron" (Cilicia was a coastal region of the Persian Empire in what is southeast Turkey today) of the Persian fleet, sinking it and returning to their position at Artemisium before nightfall.

THE BATTLE TURNS – THE IMMORTALS SET OUT

But darkness brought the execution of the second prong of Xerxes' flanking maneuver. Presumably the damaged Immortals replenished their ranks, the most promising Persian warriors being promoted to take up new positions so that the fixed number never fell below 10,000. Otherwise, it was a reduced force that set out on the Anopaia Path, navigating by moonlight. If we assume horrific casualties from the previous day's fighting, say 20 percent, then you would still have more than 7,000 Persians on the march to confront 1,000 Phocians.

Here, Herodotus' story becomes impossible to accept. According to him, the Immortals caught the Phocians essentially napping (he describes them scrambling for their weapons and armor) despite the huge number of Persian troops broadcasting their approach via the dead leaves crunching under 7,000 pairs of feet. The Phocians had deployed no scouts, set up no watches, deployed no pickets – a massive violation of the Law of Competence that I just can't believe.

What Herodotus describes next is even more unbelievable. Hydarnes was caught just as unawares as the Phocians were. Expecting the pass to be unguarded and terrified that he might be facing more Spartans, he reportedly asked his guide (Ephialtes) to identify the enemy. Ephialtes replied that they were Phocians, which calmed Hydarnes enough to sound the attack.

This is obviously untrue. First, it utterly violates the Law of Competence by leaning entirely on the premise that Hydarnes and indeed the entire Persian high command were fools. The far more likely scenario is that Hydarnes knew full well the path was guarded, by whom, and how many they were. As mentioned above, his troops were likely guided along the Anopaia Path by several locals hired for the purpose (whom Herodotus mashes together into the character of Ephialtes). But even if Hydarnes had found himself facing 1,000 Spartans, he would have done so at the head of seven times their number (at least) of his own troops and this time not at a choke point just a wagon's breadth wide at its narrowest point and protected by a stone wall. He would have been confident in his advantage and pressed the attack, and he would have been right to do so.

I've hiked one theoretical route for the Anopaia Path, beginning at the tiny Greek village of Vardates and heading east around Callidromus. It isn't known exactly where the Phocians held their position blocking the path, but it was almost certainly east of the modern mountain village of Eleftherochori – where the ground widens into a broad and relatively flat mountain plain. When I hiked it, the ground was broad and flat enough to soak up the rain that had been falling steadily for several days, turning it into a treacherous, muddy bog.

One thing Herodotus does get right is that Hydarnes ordered his troops to stand off and rain arrows on the enemy. But the rest makes no sense at all. Herodotus tells us that the Phocians, feeling that all was lost, withdrew to the highest point on the battlefield, abandoning their blocking position on the path, and prepared to hold out to the last man. The Immortals, under orders to flank the Greek position in the pass below, simply shrugged and bypassed the Phocians, marching on to take up position behind Leonidas' troops.

This again violates the Law of Competence, because it is spectacularly stupid. If what Herodotus says is true, then the Persian palace troops simply marched along, leaving 1,000 enemy troops *in their rear*. Even more unbelievable, the Phocians were on their home turf and knew the ground intimately. The Persians knew they would be *descending* toward Leonidas' position, which meant that not only would they be leaving the Phocians behind them, they would be ceding them the high ground, an unforgivable tactical error. Herodotus' story makes sense only if the Persians were complete fools. And, as we've already established, they weren't.

Here's what I think actually happened (and to be fair, I cannot prove this, I am speculating). The Phocians, deployed to hold the path and fighting on their home territory, put their shields up and weathered the storm of arrows as their comrades had in the pass. The Immortals, under pressure to clear the path and move into position behind Leonidas, gave up on archery and closed for "shock" hand-to-hand combat. As we've already seen, their inferior weapons and armor put them at an extreme disadvantage, but on the comparatively open terrain of the Anopaia Path (when we consider the extreme narrowness of the Thermopylae pass), they were able to spread out and use their greater numbers to their advantage. The Phocian hoplites were occupied fighting two or three Persians in front of them, defenseless against the Immortals who attacked them from behind, thrusting their daggers into the gaps between corselet and helmet, severing spines, or hamstringing the Greeks with sharp blows from their light axes.

The Phocians would have known that losing here meant their farms and homes would be looted and burned, their treasure taken for prizes, their wives and children slaughtered or sold into slavery. They would have fought like men possessed, making the Immortals pay dearly for every inch of ground. But in the end, the Persian numbers overwhelmed them. Perhaps they were wiped out to the last man. Perhaps Hydarnes paused for a moment, panting, surveying the heap of corpses before him, his own mingled with the Greeks, and admired the bravery of the Phocians and (maybe) the Spartans who led them. We know the Persians honored the brave among their enemies from previous encounters described by Herodotus, even sparing the lives of captives who had fought well against them.

But however bravely the Phocians had fought, in the end they had lost, and Hydarnes led his Immortals down from the heights and into the Greek backfield. Persian deserters had already brought word to Leonidas of the night march, and the Phocian scouts had been streaming in with the dawn to give him the news of the fight on the path and its outcome. As the sun rose, Leonidas' scouts would have confirmed the reports, seeing the 7,000 or so Immortals (minus the casualties they took in the fight on the path, which I assume were light) making their way down.

Many scholars ask why, if Leonidas knew he would be flanked by the Anopaia Path, he sent only 1,000 Phocians to guard it. I would argue that the Spartans had the example of Marathon, where Greek hoplites had won out against a vastly larger number of Persians, as an object lesson that 1,000 hoplites would be more than enough to hold the position, even against a numerically superior foe.

DIVISION IN THE RANKS

At this point the story again takes yet another unbelievable turn. If we accept Herodotus' narrative, then Leonidas held a council of war and concluded that they were about to be overrun. According to Herodotus, opinions were sharply divided, with many of the Greeks being in favor of abandoning the position before they were cut off by the Immortals descending from the heights.

This makes good sense. The Peloponnesian allies were already on record as wanting to defend from the isthmus of Corinth. Why should they die so far north? The Locrians, hearing of the Phocian annihilation, may well have been desperate to get back to their own families to evacuate them, or to mount a defense closer to home. Herodotus then has Leonidas *dismiss* the majority of the army, sending the men home because he was not confident they were committed to the fight. This doesn't make sense to me. The Greek goal was to delay the Persians as long as possible and with 6,000 Greeks (minus the Phocians and whatever other casualties they had taken so far, which I believe were light), they could still defend the ground in two directions, especially when you consider that the force outflanking them was comparatively small. I believe Leonidas argued to hold position and faced mutiny in his forces, as Cleomenes did outside Athens in 506 BC.

The Peloponnesian allies defied Leonidas' orders to hold position, shouldered their arms, and marched home, leaving the remaining Spartans, 700 Thespians and 400 Thebans to finish the fight. It isn't clear how much time passed between their departure and the Immortals' arrival cutting off the road home, but perhaps the dust kicked up by their exit mingled with that swirling from the Immortals' approach as they deployed in ranks to block the remaining Greeks' retreat.

Some scholars argue that Leonidas' decision to remain (along with the Thespians and Thebans) was a selfless sacrifice – a move to delay the Persian cavalry, who would surely have ridden down the rest of the retreating Greeks if they did not have something to occupy them for the time being, but I doubt this is true. Leonidas most likely cursed the departing Greeks for cowards and would have been more than happy to see them run down by Persian horsemen if his duty wasn't to prevent any Persians from passing his position.

And so the seventh day dawned with the Greeks on land reduced to a tiny fraction of their already small force. Remember that the Spartans were *not* just 300. They were 1,000, and that's not counting that each of the Peers would have had at least one helot attendant who very likely was fighting alongside them (as we saw from the battles from the archaic period). This would put the Spartan numbers at at least roughly 1,300 (minus some casualties). Adding in the Thespians and Thebans, we still have a force of 2,000 or so (again, accounting for casualties). Still more than enough to hold the pass.

However, Leonidas made a surprising decision, if Herodotus is to be believed – he marched the full force into the wider portion of the pass, abandoning the Phocian wall, and took the fight to the Persians.

AN ATTEMPT TO BREAK OUT? LEONIDAS FALLS

Herodotus seems to be implying that Leonidas was guided by the oracle and fulfilling the terms of his suicide mission, seeking to do as much damage to the Persians as he could and selling his life dearly. I do not believe this is true. So what really happened? With his force greatly reduced, multiple explanations are possible – firstly, that Herodotus' story is false and Leonidas did not advance, but rather withdrew to the location of his last stand, the small hill of Colonus.

We have some evidence that this is the location of the final Spartan defeat. Many Persian arrowheads currently on display at the Archaeological Museum at Athens were supposedly excavated from that exact site (though some archaeologists dispute this). Another possibility is that Leonidas was seeking to recreate the conditions of Marathon, looking either to break through the Persian army or else to rout it with a charge. This theory makes more sense if we believe the Persian force was smaller than is commonly believed.

There's an interesting version of this story told by Diodorus Siculus – a night attack where Leonidas led the remaining Greeks in an effort to storm Xerxes' camp and kill the Great King himself. This is completely at odds with Herodotus' narrative, and so most modern historians dismiss it. But I wonder if Diodorus is misinterpreting or is at least influenced by an earlier lost source that indicated that Leonidas' decision to move out from the Phocian wall was motivated by a last-ditch attempt to break out and perhaps even reach Xerxes' camp in the hopes that by cutting off the snake's head, the body would slither away.

Another possibility is that Leonidas was attempting to consolidate his position – trying to drive the Persians back so he could hold the narrower west gate, and then defend the Phocian wall in the other direction against the Immortals now attacking him from the east.

Here's my best guess (and no historian can make more than a guess based on the sources available to us now) – Leonidas did not have a good count on the number of troops massing to his rear beyond the east gate. No doubt the panicked Phocian runners who brought the news of the defeat on the Anopaia Path inflated them in the telling. Leonidas would have known only that a great number of Xerxes' very best troops had cut off the passage behind him. With most of his army melted away, he knew that his ability to hold the pass was fatally compromised. He had enough men to man the gaps both east and west, but exhaustion and wounds would soon take their toll and he no longer had the reserves to keep rotating fresh troops in. It is also possible that the Immortals descended from the heights *inside* the east gate, which meant Leonidas' ability to close off that choke point was lost.

Because this was most decidedly *not* a suicide mission, Leonidas then had to figure out what to do next – a plan that would damage the enemy and keep his own people alive. Faced with the devil he knew (the Persian army in front of him beyond the west gate) or the devil he didn't (the Immortals behind him), he chose the one he knew, and the *salpinges* (long, straight trumpets used by the ancient Greeks) sounded the advance into the teeth of the enemy. His ultimate motive (whether to drive the Persians back and secure the west gate, to break out, or to kill Xerxes) will remain a mystery.

I imagine the Persians would have had much of the same reaction as they witnessed the Greek charge at Marathon – jaw-dropping disbelief that anyone would be so mad. Even with casualties and the detachment of the Immortals, the Persians outnumbered the Greek force somewhere in the neighborhood of 10-to-1. The Greeks had been fighting nearly nonstop for three days, their armor would have been dented and cracked, ragged rents visible in the linen and leather of their cuirasses, strips of bronze peeling back from the notches in their heavy shields. Some of them may even have been wielding their spears with the butt-spikes facing out, the heads having snapped off long ago. Others may have abandoned broken spears altogether and advanced with their swords drawn.

The Persians would have heard the Spartan shouts echoing across the distance, calling on the hoplites to dress the line, to make sure the shields remained locked, leaving no gaps for Persian arrows to exploit. The Spartan helots would have jogged along the flanks, animal skins or linen wrapped around their left arms. One or two may have scavenged a Persian wicker shield. In their right hands they would have carried javelins or slings, or even heavy rocks.

The Persians would have answered as at Marathon, ordering the *sparabara* to plant their shields, the archers aiming high and letting their light arrows arc down to shower the advancing Greeks. If we believe that the Spartans were acting as *xenagoi*, they might have bellowed to their charges "'ware arrows! Shields up! At the run now, lads!" The heavy, round shields would have come up, the arrows pattering off them harmlessly, here and there the small three-edged heads finding purchase to quiver in the thin covering of bronze. Here and there a hoplite would hiss as a lucky shot grazed his bare thigh or arm. The helots would not have been so lucky. They would have dashed into the phalanx, seeking cover behind their better-armored masters (as Tyrtaeus' poems tell us they did), but more than a few of them would have died screaming, the arrows easily penetrating their thin clothing.

And as at Marathon, the Greek line would have raised the paean and charged. The Persians might have gotten another volley or two off before the Greeks reached the massive *spara* and either ripped them aside or blew straight through them. Once again, the Persian inferiority of equipment would tell and many of them would have died, spitted through by the heavy Greek spears, limbs ripped off by the powerful strokes of *kopides* cleaver-swords. Where they fell, the Greeks would have trampled them, eyes front, but bronze lizard-killers stabbing down to make sure the wounded did not rise to trouble them again. The Persian line would have recoiled. It may even have bowed. Some of the levy infantry might have dropped their weapons, terrified by the relentlessness of the Greek assault, trying to claw their way back through their own troops to reach safety. Leonidas may have even dared to hope that his plan would work, looking up at Xerxes' palatial command tent, or the throne from which the Great King watched the battle unfold.

He may have believed they could make it.

But 2,000 men were not 7,000, and in the wider expanse of the pass, the Persians could bring their numerical superiority to bear. The phalanx was highly effective when its flanks were secure, but that was impossible now, and the hoplites on the left and right of the line would have found themselves having to fight in two directions at once. Distracted by the enemy to their front, the enemy to their side would be able to slip behind their guard, burying a spearpoint or an *akinakēs* in an exposed armpit or neck. Worse, the exertion of the contest would be telling, the few lucky arrows piercing feet or arms making movement slow and painful. The archers brave enough not to flee would be shooting point blank into the

Greeks' faces, not bothering to arc their missiles now. Some of these might find the small holes in the Corinthian helmets, the soft eyes open wide behind them. A shudder might have run through the phalanx as the Greek charge slowed.

The Persians would have seen this, taken heart, surged forward.

And then Leonidas fell.

Herodotus gives no details surrounding the king's death, only that he *"proved himself extremely valiant."* The fact that the Persians were even able to reach Leonidas shows how badly mauled the phalanx was at this point. As the king, he would have been surrounded by *hippeis*, the youngest and best of the Spartans sent out on the expedition. Further, the other Greeks would have known how important the king's life was to the morale of the remaining force, and would have fought like lions to defend him. Perhaps Leonidas channeled Theopompus for a moment, driving forward to take the fight to the enemy. Perhaps Xerxes' troops punched through his bodyguard and took the fight to the king themselves. The enormous respect the king commanded is shown by the terrific effort the Greeks made to recover his body (we would expect this from the Spartans, but not the Thespians and Thebans). Four times they threw the enemy back in their desperate attempt to drag Leonidas' bloody corpse into their own phalanx. Herodotus tells us the Persians lost their own notables in this meat-grinder, including at least two brothers of Xerxes.

At last the rearguard or helot lookouts would have raised the call. The Immortals were streaming in through the east gate. If the Greeks remained where they were, they would be crushed in open ground from both before and behind. They retreated, fighting the whole way, weapons breaking, pieces of armor stripped away as straps snapped, or cast off as ragged rips in the bronze turned a helmet into a blade cutting its wearer.

They wouldn't have bothered with the Phocian wall now. It would do them no good against the Immortals racing toward them from behind it. Instead, they withdrew over it and up to a small hill (the Colonus) where they rested the king's body in the center and formed a circle around him – splintered shields overlapping as best they could, many armed with little more than the broken nub of a sword blade held by its hilt in the hope the jagged edges could still do some good. They would have watched in grim defiance as the Persians swirled, completely surrounding them, a tiny island of Greeks in a sea of enemies.

It was at this point that the surviving Thebans threw down their arms and surrendered. Their home city-state had already submitted to Persia. Perhaps the enemy would view them kindly for that? They bet wrong. Many of them were shot dead by Persian arrows even as they advanced with their weapon hands open and empty to show they meant no harm. The rest were taken behind the lines and branded with Xerxes' mark to herald their future as Persian slaves.

Herodotus' account of the final moments of the remaining Greeks is graphic. They fought with the stubs of their spears and the jagged hilts of their snapped swords, and when these failed, they fought with their fists and teeth. At long last, the Persians judged them so exhausted that they were no longer worth the effort of a close assault. The officers ordered their troops to stand off and shower the Greeks with missiles. With their armor battered and stripped, their heavy shields shattered, the Greeks could do nothing more than throw up their hands against the storm of arrows, javelins and thrown rocks, all falling like some hideous metal storm, burying them utterly.

The final casualty count is not known. Certainly hundreds of the allied Greeks whom Herodotus does not bother to count by their *poleis*. He does tell us that 4,000 Greeks in total died and he reckons the helots separately, so we can guess that he is referring only to hoplites here. The 298 Spartans (two were sent away – one as a messenger, and one with an eye affliction so severe that he could not fight; both survivors would later commit suicide after being shunned by their community for having the temerity to live when their countrymen had died) amounted to just 7 percent of the total Greek dead and their loss was just a fraction of Sparta's total muster. Thespiae, meanwhile, had contributed 18 percent of the total casualties. Their contribution went nearly completely unnoticed until they finally received a monument on the battlefield at the shockingly late date of 1997. We have the name of their *stratēgos* (general) Demophilus, but nothing more. Both *The 300 Spartans* and *300* give him a cameo.

This still leaves some 3,000 other allied Greek dead, whose contribution was boiled down in Miller's *300* to the throwaway dismissal of "Brave amateurs. They do their part." And of course the helots who would have done their masters' cooking and cleaning, who would have bound their wounds, repaired their armor and passed up spare spears to replace the ones that broke, all before joining the Peers to fight in the pass, are completely ignored. We can't say with certainty how many were there. There may have been as few as 300 (one for each Peer), or as many as 2,100 (seven for each Peer, the number given for the Battle of Plataea the following year). It's possible that some escaped the battle and their flight, as with their contributions, wasn't reported, but it's far more likely that they stood and fought alongside their oppressors, doggedly holding the pass and the tiny hill to their last breath.

The Greek defense at Thermopylae had been wiped out to the last man. The fleet at Artemisium no longer had a reason to hold its position now that the Persian land army could simply march past it unmolested. It quit the cape and withdrew south to Salamis.

Xerxes' losses had been higher than he would have liked, but the truth was that the Great King could easily absorb the casualties and each mouth permanently closed by a Greek spear thrust was one less that would need water and food. Herodotus reports Xerxes as flying into a rage at Leonidas' defiance, ordering his body desecrated, the head severed and fixed to a stake for the benefit of his passing army. He gives the Persian losses at the absolutely insanely inflated figure of 20,000, but accuses Xerxes of burying all but 1,000 immediately to hide the extent of the damage. I am more inclined to believe that 1,000 was closer to the actual extent of the Persian loss, with Herodotus doing what he could to rehabilitate the Greek reputation following what could be reckoned only as a devastating defeat.

Even with the losses to the Persian army, the Greek strategic objective – to delay the Persians long enough to starve their army out – had utterly failed. The Achaemenid land army had been delayed for a grand total of three days and could now march unopposed into Greece, straight for the prize that had eluded it ten years before – the towering Acropolis of Athens, just 130-odd miles to the southeast. That the delay had been so paltry was reinforced by Xerxes' decision to remain in the pass for the following two days, opting to take time to rest and regroup after the taxing fight rather than race on toward his objective.

The Hellenic League must have been horrified. In just three days, their strategy of delay and starvation had completely unraveled. Not only had they lost critical ships and men in the sea fight at Artemisium, but some 4,000 hoplites lay dead in the pass, and the head of a Spartan king was fixed to a pole. In a brilliant and critical review of *300*, historian Tom Holland theorized that Themistocles, known to be a master spin-doctor, immediately set about disseminating the story of a heroic last stand in a desperate effort to shore up Greek morale, which must have been teetering on the brink of collapse. What was a slaughter must somehow be repackaged and sold as a glorious last stand if the Greeks were to have any hope of staying in the fight. The legendary Spartans hadn't been little more than a speed-bump under the wheels of the Persian war machine. No! They had obediently stood their post as surely all Spartans must (never mind that we have seen Spartans, and even Spartan kings, fleeing previous battles), commanded by their laws to conquer or die!

This foundational myth is made most famous by the poem composed by the turn of the 5th century BC poet Simonides of Ceos, which has been translated time and again, but whose most famous rendering is still engraved on a memorial placed at the site: "*Go tell the Spartans, thou who passest by, That here, obedient to their laws, we lie.*" Surely someone was dispatched to tell the Spartans, but that was of little concern to Xerxes who no doubt had his troops strip the enemy dead of their weapons and armor for the king's treasury, for reuse among his own troops, or possibly to build a trophy for the benefit of his Greek troops.

"Come and take them," Leonidas had said of his arms.

And in the end, Xerxes had done precisely that.

In the wake of the battle the cities of central Greece submitted to Xerxes wholesale with the exception of wounded Thespiae, Phocis and Athens' ally Plataea (whose citizens, having fought at Marathon, probably thought they could expect little mercy). These citizens sheltered in the Peloponnese and the Persians put their empty cities to the torch. Athens, completely defenseless, was evacuated. The identity of a Greek *polis* was in its citizens, not its city. If the people could be saved, then the city could be repopulated when the Persians had moved on. Leonidas' brother Cleombrotus oversaw the fortification of the isthmus of Corinth, no doubt with some degree of relief that if there was another land battle with the Persians, it would be fought where it should have been in the first place as far as the Peloponnesians were concerned.

A few diehards held out on the Athenian acropolis, older volunteers who trusted to an oracle which told them to put faith in Athens' "wooden wall." Most Athenians read this to mean the wooden hulls of the fleet and evacuated to Salamis and the navy's protection, but these hardliners thought they meant the wooden defenses built around the Acropolis. These few volunteers on the Acropolis were wiped out in short order and Xerxes' army put Athens' most sacred places to the torch. Salamis' shore is some 20 miles away from the city, and the Acropolis is Athens' highest point. The refugees must have watched in horror as the blaze rose into the night sky.

Xerxes' fleet pursued the Greeks to Salamis and engaged them there. The Spartans had little role in the battle (they contributed just 16 ships to the fleet, which was under the command of a Spartan admiral), but brilliant admiralship by Themistocles and the Athenian contingent managed to secure a crushing victory.

In fact, the real Spartan contribution was almost to lose the battle before it started. A panicked counsel of war was held as the Greek fleet saw the fires of the Athenian Acropolis and received word that the Persians had taken the city. The Peloponnesians, led by the Corinthians, were of course for withdrawing the fleet to the isthmus, probably to make their stand in the open waters of the Saronic Gulf. This was a disastrous strategy – since it would again allow the Persians the advantage of deploying their superior numbers (still much greater than the Greek fleet despite the mauling they'd taken both on the way to and at Artemisium). The Spartan admiral Eurybiades – nominally the commander of the Greek fleet – agreed with this plan and approved it.

Themistocles rightly realized that if the fleet withdrew, it would never reach the isthmus intact. Rather, each contingent would sail away to protect its home waters and all chance of mustering a fleet big enough to take on Xerxes would evaporate. And even if the fleet somehow managed to hang together, it would be enveloped and annihilated in the open waters off Corinth. Their one chance to win was to fight where they were, in constrained straits like those at Artemisium, which alone could give the heavier Greek triremes the advantage. The Corinthian contingent tried to shout Themistocles down, but the Athenian reminded them (and all the assembled commanders) that Athens had the strongest navy, and should they decide to turn that strength against another Greek city-state, they would be powerless to stop them. The message foreshadowed Athenian naval bully diplomacy in the years to come, but it also worked for now and allowed Themistocles to continue his appeal unopposed. As a final gut punch, he threatened Eurybiades that if he did not use his power as admiral to order the entire fleet to stand and fight, then the Athenians would evacuate their entire fleet to southern Italy and start a new colony there, leaving the Greek navy so short-handed that they wouldn't have a hope of defeating Xerxes.

The argument worked. The Spartans agreed to hold the line, but *only* under Themistocles' threat and with the greatest reluctance. This argument would flare up again, and to be fair to Eurybiades and the other Peloponnesians, they were terrified for their families and homes, which were still vulnerable to Xerxes' land army, even now ravaging Attica. If the Greek fleet were defeated at Salamis, they would be unable to assist with the defense against the land army as it marched farther south.

Themistocles then sent word to Xerxes in either a betrayal, if you believe some scholars, or a brilliant act of deception, if you believe others. I think he was hedging his bets, trying to make sure that whoever won, he would be in the winner's circle. At any rate, the plan worked exceedingly well and the Persian fleet, already badly scarred by the successive storms off Magnesia and Euboea, and then the naval combat at Artemisium, fought at Salamis and was defeated with the loss of an additional 200–300 ships and the subsequent shattering of its morale. It may still have outnumbered the Hellenic League fleet, but it was clearly not in a position to conduct effective operations in a foreign theater and withdrew across the sea and back to what is now the modern Turkish coast.

I want to note here that I am following Herodotus closely in my understanding of how Salamis played out. Some scholars believe this to be pro-Themistocles propaganda (I have already mentioned that Themistocles was a master spin-doctor) and that more credit should be given to Eurybiades, the Spartan in command of the Greek fleet. I personally do not align with this, but it's important that it be pointed out. Like so many things in ancient Greek history, there is always a plausible opposing view.

Xerxes, too, had been in the field far too long. His empire was vast and sprawling, and ancient kings ruled largely through the force of their personality. Without his physical presence, eventually his various satraps would decide that they were doing just fine without him and rebellion would begin to bloom. He could surely claim that he'd done what he set out to do. The third Persian expedition had been an unmitigated success. A Spartan king was dead. Fully half of Greece had submitted to Persian authority. Athens was a smoking ruin.

Xerxes made his way back to his winter palace at Susa, leaving Mardonius behind to complete the subjugation of Greece with the bulk of the land army, now swollen with Thessalian and Boeotian Greeks who had submitted to Achaemenid rule. The biggest challenge, how to supply the Persian army through the winter, was now solved with the fall of Boeotia – the Persian troops now had ample lands to feed both men and animals, and with Thebes having submitted, they wouldn't have to worry about a hostile population poisoning food and water supplies or attacking foraging parties. Mardonius could take the winter to bide his time, and then move south to finish the job.

Mardonius sent King Alexander of Macedon once again to negotiate with Athens, clearly with an eye toward taking possession of the victorious Athenian fleet. Why fight any longer? Life could go on as it had before. The Persians were gentle masters, as Alexander could personally attest. The Athenians rejected the embassy and called on the Spartans to march north from the isthmus to assist them once again, to stop Mardonius' army *before* it could ravage Attica a second time.

As before with Marathon *and* Thermopylae, the Spartans *again* tried to use a religious festival as an excuse to advance their own goal – a fight at the isthmus that would protect the Peloponnese and the rest of Greece be damned. This time it was the Hyacinthia rather than the Carneia that provided the convenient excuse and it took the Athenian threat of going over to the Persians and willingly surrendering their fleet to Mardonius (who could use it to land troops anywhere on the Peloponnesian coast at will, or to otherwise terrorize Laconia from the sea, completely bypassing the fortifications at the isthmus that the Spartans had made the cornerstone of their defense) to force the Spartans to march north.

The Battle of Plataea

But march north they did in 479 BC, under the command of Leonidas' nephew Pausanias, serving as regent for Leonidas' son Pleistarchus, who was too young to assume the Agiad Spartan throne. He was joined in command by his Agiad cousin Euryanax.

The panic the Spartans felt over the possibility of an Athenian defection was displayed by the size of the Spartan mobilization – a full 5,000 of the vaunted Peers (roughly 63 percent of the total muster) along with seven helots for each Peer, for a total of 35,000 light infantry, causing some scholars to speculate that the Spartans wanted to bring along the majority of the fighting helot population for fear they would revolt with so many Peers away from home. There is merit to this argument, but I think they simply wanted the light infantry force, as the helots could be relied on (due to Stockholm syndrome, most likely) to fight loyally beside their masters, as we saw in the Messenian Wars and at Thermopylae. They were followed shortly after by another 5,000 hoplites from among the *perioikoi*.

Mardonius, realizing his terms were rejected and possibly alerted to the Spartan march by pro-Persian Argos (which was clearly too weak to stop the Spartans or their Peloponnesian allies from marching north) sacked and burned Athens a second time. He then marched back north, seeking to do battle in open country where he could bring his superior cavalry to bear and draw on support from friendly Thebes. He built his fortified camp on the Asopus river just before Thebes and made ready to greet the Greeks. The 10,000-odd Lacedaemonian hoplites linked up with a huge complement of allied troops, totaling roughly 40,000 heavy infantry per Herodotus. For once, the Spartans supplied the largest contingent by far, with substantial contributions from Tegea (1,500), Corinth (5,000), Sicyon (3,000), Troezen

(1,000), Phlius (1,000), Megara (3,000) and, of course, Athens (8,000). None of this counts Sparta's 35,000 helots or any of the allied light infantry, which brought the number of Greek troops to a staggering 80,000 by modern scholarly assessments. This enormous force took up position in the foothills of the Cithaeron range that separates Attica from Boeotia. Facing them across the river was Mardonius' force, likely the same size or slightly larger, but with a marked superiority in both missile capability and cavalry. Further, the Persians now had a stronger hoplite close-combat capability due to their Theban and Thessalian subjects.

The battle strategies were clear – the Greek forces needed to convince Mardonius to attack them on the hilly ground where their cavalry would not have the advantage, and Mardonius needed to draw the Greeks onto the plain where his horsemen could shoot or ride them down at their leisure. An initial effort to harass the Megarian contingent with cavalry started out effective, but was neutralized when the Athenians sent out a highly mobile and adaptive archer-hoplite team (the heavy infantry sheltering the archers), which stopped the attack and killed Masistius, its commander. He was well loved by the Persians, and the Greeks played on this, parading his body in a cart before the Greek troops (an action that mirrored Xerxes' abuse of Leonidas' body after Thermopylae). The Greeks shifted position to take advantage of the sole water supply, with the Spartan contingent in the honored place on the right hand of the line.

The two armies stared one another down for the next eight days, the Greeks refusing to come out onto the plain where Mardonius could employ his cavalry, and Mardonius, chastened by Masistius' death and failure, refusing to bring the fight to them. He continued harassing cavalry attacks, but was unable to provoke the Greeks into abandoning their position. He settled instead for attacking their supply lines, and successfully ambushed and captured a wagon train of provisions bound for the Greeks.

Here the Spartans engaged in some interesting behavior that flies in the face of their legend. Herodotus tells us that Mardonius finally lost patience, or was goaded by his own supply problems, and prepared to force a battle even if it meant attacking the Greek position. Alexander of Macedon warned the Greeks of this, and Pausanias gave the order that the Athenian contingent, which was positioned facing the Persian infantry, should switch positions with the Spartan contingent, which was facing the Persians' Greek allies.

Pausanias' supposed reason for this switch was that the Athenians had more experience fighting Persians, having faced them at Marathon, whereas the only Spartans who had ever fought a Persian were rotting in a heap at Thermopylae. Herodotus is clear that he believed Pausanias was providing a flimsy excuse as cover for the fact that he was genuinely afraid to face Persians in the field. Scholars dismiss this, but they do so *very* quickly and with arguments that seem laconophilic.

The fact is that no Spartan had yet fought a Persian and lived. Certainly Themistocles' propaganda about the glorious Spartan defeat at Thermopylae was probably already making the rounds, but since none of the defenders at Thermopylae had survived to relate the tale to Pausanias, both he and Euryanax may well have seen the Persians as daunting opponents. Certainly the Athenians had bested them before, but maybe that put Pausanias in the mind that *only* Athenians could best them, and it was better to be safe than sorry. Even if we don't accept that Pausanias, Euryanax or any other Spartan polemarch present at Plataea was afraid, they may have, driven by Spartan conservatism, preferred the fight they knew (*ōthismos* against other hoplites like the Thebans) to the strange and foreign battle of the barbarians.

It cannot be proven either way, but it must be accepted as a possibility that this move was driven by the mighty Spartan superwarriors being frightened of an opponent. We have already seen that the Spartans used excuses to cover far more likely reasons for refusing to engage an enemy – most notably religious festivals, their reasoning for missing Marathon, sending a token force to Thermopylae, and almost failing to report for Plataea. This switching places between Athenians and Spartans happened twice; when Mardonius noticed the exchange and mirrored it so that Spartans faced the Persians again, Pausanias switched the contingents back, only to have Mardonius mirror the move a second time.

At this point, Mardonius realized the Spartans were trying to avoid fighting his Persian troops and sent a herald to accuse them of cowardice and challenge them to a mass duel. The Spartans again, very possibly out of fear, did not answer.

The next Spartan failure came in their inability to secure the one water source for the Greeks, allowing Mardonius' troops to poison it. With their supply caravan intercepted and their only water source destroyed, the Greeks couldn't stay put. August in Boeotia is brutally hot, and men under all that armor need a great deal of water frequently. The Greek line would have to move somewhere where it could be supplied. Such a move would make the men intensely vulnerable to being attacked piecemeal as their formation broke up for the march, outflanked or taken in the rear, individual units being crushed by the lighter and more mobile Persians.

Worse, the plan was to move the army under cover of darkness to hopefully keep from alerting the Persians, or at least to delay pursuit. Moving an ancient army of this size would be incredibly difficult in broad daylight, and nearly impossible in pitch darkness with troops not using artificial light for fear of alerting their enemies.

And here, another remarkable Spartan failure occurred. In the face of a need to retreat, the vaunted Spartan discipline completely broke down. In the council of war where the retreat had been agreed, the Athenians and Spartans were designated to guard an "island" of land formed by the splitting of a nearby stream. Overnight, the Greek center withdrew to this island. But when the designated time of departure arrived, the Spartans on the right didn't move. The Athenians on the Greek left waited, probably with well-founded suspicion based on previous Spartan failures to launch (Marathon, Thermopylae and even this very battle), and finally sent a herald to find out what was going on.

The herald was shocked to discover Pausanias and Euryanax arguing with one of their subordinate *lochagoi* who straight up refused to obey orders. Amompharetus, the commander of the one of the Spartan *lochoi*, felt that retreating would shame Sparta and simply wouldn't do it. Never mind the fact that remaining in place surely meant that the troops would weaken from thirst and eventually be overrun. Herodotus reports that Amompharetus was furious he hadn't been consulted in the original council of war, and that he threw a heavy rock threateningly close to the feet of his commanders, claiming it was his "voting pebble" (in ancient Greece, pebbles were sometimes used to cast a vote) and that he wasn't going anywhere.

Pausanias' response was essentially, "You're insane. Fine. Stay here and die." He then asked the herald to let the Athenians know they were moving out *without* Amompharetus and his *lochos*. Recall Thucydides and

Xenophon's descriptions of the *lochoi* in chapter II. We do not know if the numbers were the same at the time of Herodotus' narrative, but if we accept that they were in the same ballpark, we are talking about the Spartan commander *abandoning* a senior officer and roughly 500 hoplites who simply refused to obey orders for reasons of pride. The number may well have been double that. If we accept that this was the obal army, with each *lochos* representing one of the Spartan five core villages, then Amompharetus likely commanded 1,000 men and this doesn't even count the helots and other light infantry attached to his unit. This is a critical point that modern scholars praising the vaunted Spartan organization and discipline don't adequately address.

Ancient armies functioned by consensus to a much greater extent than modern ones, and neither Pausanias nor Euryanax was a king, but this was still an appalling breakdown in the chain of command. It is possible that Pausanias had lost Amompharetus' respect when he switched the Spartan position to avoid fighting the Persians and then when he refused the challenge to the mass duel.

Worse, Pausanias' argument with Amompharetus took the entire night, and dawn found the Spartans pulling back in complete and plain view of the enemy. Still worse, they were out on their own, unsupported by the Greek center which had already withdrawn. Amompharetus, realizing that he had been left alone, finally admitted that he was going to be cut off and wiped out, sucked up his pride, and followed Pausanias who was moving south through the foothills of the Cithaeron range in the hopes that the broken ground would protect the troops from cavalry. The Athenians also got underway, but crossed open plains where they were exposed.

Amompharetus caught up with Pausanias outside a temple of Demeter just as the Persian cavalry caught up to them. Mardonius, thinking he'd caught the Spartans out alone, sent his infantry to join them. The Athenians marched to their aid, but were intercepted by Mardonius' Greek subjects who pinned them in place. The Greek allies of the center (per Herodotus) did not move to help until after the fighting was done, but this doesn't make sense. For one thing, Herodotus discusses the Tegeans and, for another, he discusses Theban cavalry catching and slaughtering other allied Greeks, which wouldn't have been possible if they weren't closer to the action.

What happened next is tough for a modern person to accept. While the Persian *sparabara* set their shields and ranks of archers behind them showered the Spartans with arrows, Pausanias refused to allow his troops to move, seeking favorable omens from the gods before advancing into battle. This sort of thing was typical for ancient Greek armies of the period, but of course can be interpreted by a modern and far less superstitious person as Pausanias being paralyzed by terror or hoping to hold position until rescued by the Athenians or other allied Greeks.

We have already seen on several occasions that at least the Spartan king Cleomenes was more than willing to commit sacrilege when it suited him, but Herodotus is willing to give the Spartans the benefit of the doubt here, describing Pausanias' decision in neutral terms. Herodotus indicates that the Spartans were sitting or crouched, sheltering behind their large, heavy shields from the storm of Persian arrows that were still thick enough to cause some casualties.

At last the same Tegeans who had defeated the Spartans and forced them to wear their own chains just over 70 years earlier had had enough. They weren't going to sit there until enough Persian arrows got lucky and their numbers were reduced to uselessness. They rose and charged the enemy.

Herodotus tells us that at the same time the omens became conveniently favorable for Pausanias and he was permitted by the gods to attack.

The conclusion a modern reader draws seems pretty obvious – shamed by a much smaller allied city-state taking the lead and likely still stung by the damage to his reputation from switching positions with the Athenians and declining the mass-duel, Pausanias took the Spartans into the fight. This is certainly what I thought when I first read Herodotus' account; however it's important to note that ancient Greek armies really were governed by their superstitions, and that Herodotus' account is usually pretty quick to call the Spartans out, which he doesn't do here.

Whatever the truth of Pausanias' motivations, he did finally lead his troops into the teeth of the enemy.

Here, after a litany of indecision, fear and failure, the Spartans finally had their moment.

The goal of this book is to demythologize the Spartans and an important means of doing this is highlighting the conflict between their known actions and their legend as superwarriors. However, this focus can detract from the fact that the Spartans were indeed excellent heavy infantry, quite possibly some of the finest in Greece. When they at last overcame their terror at facing the same barbarians who had slaughtered their king and comrades at Thermopylae and advanced to close combat, they were in their element.

We have seen that Sparta was a conservative society, jittery and unsure when confronted with the new and the strange. Phalanx-based close combat with a known enemy to their front was something the Spartans knew well, and their comfort with the medium showed.

Herodotus is clear that the Persians sold their lives dearly, but the Spartans were clearly buying, and their greatest purchase was Mardonius. The Persian commander, possibly attempting to rally his flagging troops, was taken down along with his "*best thousand*" (possibly the Apple Bearers). With their commander killed in plain sight, Persian morale evaporated and the line broke.

The Spartans pursued them back to their fortified encampment where once again their inability to conduct siege warfare, apparently unimproved since the Messenian Wars, asserted itself. Herodotus tells us they "*lacked experience in assaulting walls.*" We can imagine their only missile troops, unarmored helots armed mostly with rocks, taking on Persian expert archers securely positioned behind their ramparts.

That might have been the end of the Spartan role then and there, but fortunately the Athenians defeated the Theban phalanx and joined the Spartans. The Athenians apparently had greater siege expertise (or else the numbers necessary to overwhelm the defenses), as they successfully breached the walls and permitted the combined Greek forces to storm the Persian camp.

Once again, it was tiny Tegea and not mighty Sparta, whose forces were the first through the breach. Herodotus notes that they plundered Mardonius' personal tent, though he doesn't mean this as a compliment to Tegean bravery, but more likely as a criticism of their lack of discipline.

The resulting slaughter of the remaining Persians, both during the rout and pursuit to the camp, and after the breach, was horrific. Modern historians disagree about the exact number, but some figures are as high as 90,000.

The relative losses on the Greek side were a tiny fraction of this (Herodotus says fewer than 200 and Plutarch fewer than 2,000), making it a victory every bit as triumphant and lopsided as Marathon.

The destruction of Mardonius' army effectively ended Persian territorial ambitions in Greece. The Persian Empire was far from being knocked down and would still play a major role in Greek politics and particularly in Spartan military adventures, but the Persians would never again seek to directly conquer the Greek people beyond the Ionian coast.

Pausanias, who in my opinion was at best incompetent and at worst a vacillating coward, was the hero of the hour. The accolade would absolutely go to his head, with disastrous consequences (and providing another shining example of the Bronze Lie) in the near future.

Mycale

But there was still one more battle to be fought to bring the Greco-Persian War to a close. Following Salamis, the victorious Hellenic League fleet sailed to Samos in pursuit of the fleeing Persian navy. It was led by the Spartan king Leotychides, the same man who'd partnered with Cleomenes to bribe the oracle at Delphi.

The Persian fleet, broken down and demoralized, refused to risk a sea battle and instead beached its ships on the Ionian coast, then drew up and fortified its position at the base of Mount Mycale. There, it linked up with a Persian land force stationed to guard Ionia under the command of the Persian nobleman Tigranes. The Persians doubted the loyalty of the Ionian Greeks in their army, in particular the Samians (whom they disarmed) and the Milesians (whom they sent away). Herodotus claims that word of the victory at Plataea reached the Greeks as they prepared to do battle (though this is disputed) with an unsurprising boost to Greek morale. The sizes of the relative armies are again disputed, but modern scholars seem to be comfortable with around 40,000 Greek troops facing 60,000 Persians.

The Spartans were *once again* slow to attack. The Athenians on the left of the Greek line advanced and engaged the Persians immediately. Herodotus excuses the Spartan slowness by reporting that they had to traverse "*a ravine and high ground"* to reach the enemy. But this makes me cock an eyebrow when I consider Spartan reluctance to fight at all in every single one of the battles of the Greco-Persian War. Looking at Sparta's record in the last two fights, I can surely be forgiven for suspecting that *not* fighting may have been something of an established Spartan military policy.

At any rate, the other Greeks had no need of Spartan help to defeat the Persians. Herodotus tells us the Athenians, Corinthians, Sicyonians and Troezenians broke the Persian line themselves, sending the Persians running for their camp (Herodotus says they pushed extra hard in their eagerness not to share the glory with Sparta, but I believe it's equally possible the Spartans deliberately hung back to give their allies time to soften the enemy up).

I freely admit I don't have additional evidence other than Sparta's past record of avoiding fights, but whatever the reason for the delay, the Spartans at last arrived and *"assisted with finishing off the remaining men."* In other words, the Spartans turned their legendary might loose on a demoralized and already broken enemy. The victorious Greeks burned all of the remaining Persian ships, effectively destroying the Persian navy (minus the Phoenicians, who had been sent away before the battle) and eliminating any threat of a Persian return to Greek shores. With this final battle, a mop-up operation really, the Greco-Persian War ended in a resounding Greek victory.

Sparta's Record in the Greco-Persian War

The decisive victory of the Greeks over the Persians was not due to Spartan might. The entire war was marked by Spartan hesitancy, reluctance to fight, bad generalship, and a demonstrated desire to make its allies do the heavy lifting.

Sparta sent a token force to Thermopylae, where Leonidas failed to properly secure the Anopaia Path, resulting in his force being outflanked and annihilated. Its warriors marched to Plataea only when the threat of Athenian defection forced them to. Plataea was absolutely won by Spartan strength of arms, the slaying of Mardonius being the key point in the battle. But otherwise, the fight was marked by Pausanias' cowardice and indecision, and Amompharetus' disobedience to orders.

Plataea was won *in spite* of Spartan unprofessionalism and lack of discipline and courage, *not* because of the Spartans' status as history's greatest warriors. At Mycale, the Spartans may have hung back to let their allies do the hard work, before stepping in to mop up an already defeated enemy. Even if they truly were delayed by bad terrain, the delay proved only that the other Greeks had no need of Spartan help and were perfectly able to crush the Persians on their own. On the naval front, the Spartans contributed insignificant token forces at both Artemisium and Salamis (though the fleet was under the command of a Spartan admiral).

But we cannot deny Sparta its victories, whatever caveats we must put in place when considering them. In the four major actions of the Greco-Persian War (Thermopylae/Artemisium, Salamis, Plataea and Mycale) the Spartans had suffered defeat at just one – the one that was most responsible for founding their legend as the greatest warriors the world has ever known – the blood-soaked pass of Thermopylae.

But this can also be viewed from the opposite angle – that of the four major actions of the Greco-Persian War, Sparta made a substantial contribution to just one victory (Plataea), and was primarily responsible for the greatest defeat (Thermopylae) which ironically launched the legend we still wrestle with today.

Pausanias and Leotychides

Before we move on to Sparta's next great era of military conflict in the Peloponnesian Wars, we should take a moment to consider the careers of both Pausanias and Leotychides.

While in hindsight we can see that the defeats inflicted on Persia at Salamis, Plataea and Mycale had ended any threat it might pose to Greece, that wasn't at all clear to either the Greeks or the Persians at the time. The war was still very much ongoing as far as the Hellenic League was concerned and operations would need to be continued. The first matter to be settled was how to handle the pro-Persian city-states of Greece – most notably among these Thebes and the region of Thessaly.

Pausanias was still the nominal overall military commander for the League and the hero of Plataea (however undeserved), and so it fell to him to handle Thebes. He laid siege to the city for 20 days until the Thebans agreed to hand over their pro-Persian leadership, whom Pausanias promptly executed without trial and without consulting any other members of the League, supposedly as a reaction to Theban plans to bribe the judges assigned to try them. Herodotus also mentions that Pausanias spared the children of one Theban leader who fled, an unusually humane act by the standards of the day.

But Pausanias then slipped into egomania. He had spoils from the victory over the Persians dedicated to Apollo with an inscription specifically naming himself as the man who had defeated the Persians. This was simply too much, not just for the other members of the League, but for the Spartans, who had the inscription altered, scratching off Pausanias' name and replacing it with a list of the Greek city-states who had contributed to the victory.

Not only were Pausanias' actions troubling, they were yet another glaring contradiction to the myth of Spartan selflessness and the Lycurgan ideal of the erasure of the individual and the total subservience to the collective good of the state. Pausanias clearly viewed himself as a great individual and was working hard to build a cult of personality to celebrate and perpetuate that idea.

Another foundation stone of the Bronze Lie – that Spartans despised money and had enough only for their basic needs – is knocked loose when we consider the actions of the Eurypontid king Leotychides.

As Pausanias marched to punish Thebes, Leotychides did the same for Thessaly, moving against the Aleuad clan of Thessalian nobles who were the most diehard pro-Persians in the region. In order to do this, Leotychides had to draw off Spartan troops from the Hellenic League forces currently at Byzantium (modern-day Istanbul), where they were stationed to keep an eye on possible Persian counterstrikes into Europe. The League's commanders were not happy with the prospect of losing the best heavy infantry of their army to deal with a people who, while certainly not friends, were not an active threat to remotely the same degree as even a defeated Persia. They probably suspected the real motivation behind this punitive expedition – Sparta attempting to spread its influence across the rest of Greece and to force unequal alliances on other city-states as it had done in the Peloponnesian League.

Leotychides' expedition failed horrendously. The Thessalian superiority in cavalry and Sparta's inability to adapt to the demands of siege warfare meant that the expedition made little progress. When at last the Aleuads bribed the Eurypontid king to wave off the expedition, he accepted the money gladly, probably having realized that since he was going to be forced out of the north anyway, he might as well head home with his pockets full. Both Herodotus and Pausanias report that the bribe was discovered (a glove full of silver in his tent). The ephors recalled Leotychides to Sparta to face trial for bribery. Leotychides fled to Tegea and was deposed *in absentia* and succeeded by his grandson, Archidamus II. He never returned to Sparta and died a decade later. The story of his love of money would surely have raised eyebrows at the time as much as it does now – directly clashing with the legend of Sparta's hatred for wealth.

Meanwhile, Pausanias was hardly covering himself in glory. The high-handed, egotistical behavior evidenced by the inscription continued, making enemies of the League, until the ephors finally recalled him. It's not clear why they sent him back to resume command of the League, though some scholars have said the move was to prevent the Athenians from doing so. Pausanias' command gave him jurisdiction over high-ranking Persian prisoners at Byzantium, whom he was subsequently accused of having freed deliberately in an effort to court Xerxes' favor.

We have to pause in the story here to note our source – Thucydides. Before he was a historian, Thucydides was an Athenian general fighting against Sparta in the Peloponnesian Wars, a series of events that impacted him dramatically. He appears to be making an effort at being impartial, but we have to take his opinions on Sparta with a grain of salt. He certainly wasn't positively inclined toward it. Also, in writing about Pausanias, he was covering events that occurred before he was born.

Thucydides relates that Pausanias received a letter from Xerxes thanking him for returning the prisoners and responding to Pausanias' proposal that he would aid Xerxes in return for being made satrap of Greece. While possible, this is tough for me to believe.

Even if Xerxes agreed to this, he had just lost both his expeditionary land army and navy and Pausanias certainly didn't have the native support to conquer Greece on Persia's behalf. For once, I side with a Spartan, and believe this was a story told to discredit Pausanias and Sparta in general, possibly as a reaction to Pausanias' high-handed and arrogant behavior after arriving at Byzantium.

Thucydides accuses Pausanias of even taking on Persian style – dressing as a Persian and surrounding himself with Median and Egyptian bodyguards. While I certainly believe that Pausanias was an egomaniac and was absolutely attempting to build a cult of personality for himself, I don't know that he would have physically imitated the customs of a people whom he would have regarded as barbaric (this is an unpopular opinion. Many scholars believe this is exactly what a conqueror of a foreign people would do – as a way to show off the spoils he had won – and there are numerous examples of this among the Greeks, including Alexander the Great). But my position is bolstered by a story from Herodotus, telling us of Pausanias' reaction after having captured Xerxes' personal tent, which had been left with Mardonius at Plataea:

> *Pausanias summoned Mardonius' bakers and cooks and told them to prepare a meal of the sort they made for their former master. The order was obeyed; and when Pausanias saw ... everything prepared for the feast with great magnificence, he ... ordered his own servants to get ready an ordinary Spartan dinner. The difference between the two meals was indeed remarkable ... Pausanias laughed ... saying "look at the folly of the Persians who, living in this style, came to Greece to rob us of our poverty."*

Whatever Pausanias' behavior may actually have been, it was bad enough that the Athenians forcibly expelled him from Byzantium. He fled to Colonae and continued corresponding with the Persians (per Thucydides) until the Spartans finally brought him back to Sparta once more. Suspicion against Pausanias continued to grow, and Thucydides notes that he may have conspired not only with Persia, but also with the helots with the aim of leading a coup and seizing control of the Spartan government.

This strikes me as even less likely than Pausanias' seeking to betray Greece to a Persia he himself had only just been so instrumental in defeating. In the end, Thucydides reports that Pausanias was betrayed by one of his couriers, bearing a treasonous letter to Persia. The suspicious courier, having opened and read the letter, discovered that Pausanias instructed the recipient to murder the man who brought it (presumably to ensure there would be no proof it had been sent), and promptly betrayed him to the ephors who finally had the proof they needed to put him to death.

Pausanias fled for sanctuary to the temple of Athena, where he could not be killed without incurring ritual pollution (though we have seen that the Spartans were happy to violate this when it was convenient). According to Diodorus, Pausanias' own mother set the first brick to wall him into the sanctuary and the ephors followed suit. They waited until he was on the brink of starvation before dragging him out to die in the street where his corpse would not foul the sacred space.

How much, if any, of this wild story is true is impossible to know, but the general tone is clear – Pausanias was hungry for both power and fame in direct contradiction to the Spartan myth of selflessness and prioritization of community over individual glory. This was allowed to grow for far too long, eventually resulting in an implosion that must have been humiliating for Sparta and personally ruinous for the man himself.

Sadly, more ruin was yet to come, not just to Sparta, but to all of Greece at Spartan hands.

IV

THE PELOPONNESIAN WARS: FLOUNDERING AT SEA, SURRENDERING ON LAND

Nothing that happened in the war surprised the Greeks so much as this. It was the opinion that no force or famine could make the Spartans give up their arms, but that they would fight on as they could, and die with weapons in their hands: indeed, people could scarcely believe that those who had surrendered were of the same stuff as the fallen.

Thucydides, *History of the Peloponnesian War*

Greek politics following the Greco-Persian War are a tangle of alliances, double-crosses, military feints and dramatic speeches that is challenging to follow for even dedicated historians of the period. Fortunately for the purposes of this book, we're interested only insofar as they shed light on the Bronze Lie and give us an opportunity to compare Sparta's battlefield record to the legend of its military greatness.

If the period of the Peloponnesian Wars could be summed up in a single sentence, it would be this – with Persia removed as an immediate threat, the Greeks turned on each other.

I will add that the Peloponnesian Wars were fought in three phases. Sparta did not win a single one of these. Rather, Athens lost each one, almost as if the Athenians were deliberately trying. You can judge for yourself in the description that follows.

Sparta saw the purpose of the Greco-Persian War as having been achieved. Persia was pushed out of Greece and badly mauled enough that it wouldn't be coming back anytime soon. Sparta's focus was where it always was out of necessity – on keeping the army at home to prevent a helot revolt and to ensure its unequal "allies" in the Peloponnesian League didn't get any funny ideas about collaborating with them. Athens didn't accept this position. The entire Ionian coast was populated by Greeks and some of those cities had been colonies of Athens. The Athenians at least *claimed* to be concerned with protecting the Ionian Greeks and punishing the Persians (as well as preventing any future invasion), but later events would prove that these were thin veneers covering expansionist and imperial ambitions. Athens formed a league of its own, the treasury and meeting place of which was on the island of Delos, sacred to Apollo. This lent its name to the Delian League, which rapidly became a tribute-taking, brutal-handed imperial master of much of Greece, with Athens firmly at its helm.

The damage to Sparta's reputation from Leotychides' misadventure and Pausanias' disastrous end was severe. The Spartans' abdication of responsibility for pursuing the war against Persia couldn't have helped. But Herodotus' cohesive narrative ends with the close of the Greco-Persian War (save for a few brief comments on later events in book IX of his history). Thucydides takes up the tale, but his focus is entirely on Athens and we're left trying to piece together fragments of evidence in order to understand what became of Sparta prior to the outbreak of hostilities.

Two Battles with Arcadia

We know that the Arcadian city-states, previously reliable allies of Sparta, threw off their obligations and that two battles were fought to bring them to heel. We know next to nothing about either one – we have only offhand comments by Herodotus and the turn of the 4th century BC Greek orator Isocrates, but the fact they were fought at all so soon after Plataea and Mycale is an indicator of how rapidly Sparta's star had fallen. We know one of these two battles was fought between Sparta and an Argive–Tegean alliance and that Sparta won. We don't know when the battle was fought, presumably between 478 and 470 BC. The second battle was fought at a place called Dipaea probably in 470 BC and was between Sparta and "*all the Arcadians, save the Mantineans.*" Both battles were Spartan victories, though the first could hardly have been decisive, otherwise the second wouldn't have been necessary.

Spartan–Athenian relations, tense at the best of times, continued to sour. First, the Athenians used a trick to rebuild their city walls (demolished by the Persians) against Spartan objections. Sparta leaned on the incredibly disingenuous argument that if the Persians came back, they would be able to make use of a captured Athens' walls. Sparta had no walls of its own, anyway. Of course, this is a very easy argument for a city-state like Sparta to make, being situated in one of the most naturally defensible locations in all Greece – protected from sea approaches by an intensely hostile shore and otherwise surrounded by inaccessible mountains navigated only via easily guarded passes. Athens enjoyed no such natural protections and Themistocles, who appears to have well earned his reputation as one of the great cunning minds of his age, enacted a skillful delaying maneuver, stalling the Spartans with promises of an embassy to discuss the matter while every able-bodied Athenian scrambled to rebuild the city's walls. By the time the Spartans realized what was going on, the walls were already standing and Athens was able to look to its own defenses.

Sparta's attempt to convince the Athenians not to refortify their cities included an offer to use Sparta's army to protect them. Apart from being insultingly arrogant (Athens had its own army that had proved abundantly capable of protecting the city at Marathon), it's pretty clear that this was a double-edged offer. On the one hand it sent the message "If you don't rebuild your walls, we have an army that will protect you." On the other hand it also sent the message "If you attempt to rebuild your walls, we have an army that will destroy you."

The Spartans took the news that the walls had been rebuilt without much upset. The sources seem to imply that they had simply been trying to do what was best for all of Greece and were now at least relieved of any obligation to protect Athens, but I don't think this was the case at all. We have seen Sparta's horrendous record of assaulting fortified positions dating all the way back to the Messenian Wars. I think that once the Spartans were confronted with walls already in place, they realized there was nothing they could do about it.

The burgeoning Athenian Empire had continued to attack Persian possessions since Mycale and in 469 BC its famous general Cimon led the Athenians to a decisive naval and land victory at Eurymedon on Turkey's coast. Continued Athenian heavy-handed imperial expansion, helped by their powerful navy and the tribute they took in from the members of the Delian League, raised tensions, as did fighting between Athens and Sparta's allies including Corinth and Aegina. Sentiment grew among the Peloponnesians that Athenian power had to be checked and that Sparta was the city-state in position to pump the brakes. This would very likely have been sparked by an appeal in 465 BC from the Greek island of Thasos, off the coast of that strip of modern-day northern Greece that runs south along the Bulgarian border. The Athenians were in the process of laying siege to the island, very probably to get hold of a lucrative gold mine and trading ports.

The Athenian victory at Eurymedon had once again smashed the Persian army and navy and rendered them unable to respond to any request by Thasos for help (there is a minority view that Eurymedon was only a minor engagement with little impact on Persian power). The only other power able to oppose Athens was Sparta, and it was to Sparta that Thasos sent for assistance. An invasion of Attica would force the Athenians to bring their army and navy back to face a threat much closer to home. According to Thucydides, Sparta agreed. This might have sparked the Peloponnesian Wars as early as 464 BC, but nature (or if you're thinking like an ancient Greek, the gods) had other plans.

Poseidon earthshaker intervenes

Before they could respond to the Thasian appeal, Sparta was racked by a powerful earthquake, arguably one of the worst in its history.

The sources give a mythological explanation for this and I'll examine it only because it again illustrates the supposedly hyper-religious Spartans' willingness to commit sacrilege whenever it was convenient. Thucydides tells us the earthquake was caused by angering Poseidon (in addition to being god of the sea, Poseidon was known as "earthshaker" and deemed responsible for earthquakes) when the Spartans dragged fleeing helots from his temple where they were seeking sanctuary. Of course it is not true that Poseidon caused the earthquake, but I don't doubt that the Spartans gladly violated their own laws of sanctuary in pursuit of fleeing helots.

The earthquake all but flattened Sparta. The sources give unbelievable figures – that only five buildings in all of Sparta remained standing, that 20,000 were killed. I can't help but roll my eyes at these exaggerations, but one thing is clear – this earthquake was powerful and it had a terrible impact on Sparta. It also underscored how tense and fragile matters were between Sparta and its subject population, for the very first action of Archidamus was to turn out the Spartan army in anticipation of the helot uprising that would surely follow.

The Third Messenian War – The Battle of Stenyclerus and the Second Battle of Ithome

And follow it did. Sparta now (464 BC) faced perhaps the worst helot revolt to date (its third, if you believe that a helot revolt delayed the Spartan response to the Athenian appeal at Marathon). The uprising was so bad that it even sucked in two of the *perioikoi* towns and it got off to a good start for the rebels.

The Spartan Peer Aeimnestus, who according to Herodotus had killed Mardonius with his own hands, either took on the Messenian army with just 300 of his own troops, or else was caught out while campaigning in Messenia. At Stenyclerus, the same place where the Spartans had been defeated at the Battle of the Boar's Tomb and had to watch in humiliation as their king Anaxander fled the field, Aeimnestus and all his 300 were annihilated.

The rebels apparently made their base on the same Mount Ithome that had been the Messenian base of operations under first Euphaes and later Aristodemus more than 250 years earlier. It's hard to tell from Herodotus' offhand comment, but he implies that a field battle was fought between the Messenian army at Ithome and the Spartans and that the Spartans won.

Afterward, it seems the Messenians were bottled up in the mountain fortress and that the Spartans, as ever completely unable to assault a fortified position, had to appeal to allies to help them breach the Messenian walls. Thucydides tells us that the siege of Ithome dragged on for a *"great length"* and that the Spartans specifically asked for Athenian help due to their skill at sieges.

The Athenians, surprisingly, responded. Scholars dispute why they did this, but it's important to remember that Sparta was hardly unique in its appetite for slave labor. While the Athenians didn't have a slave social caste as the Spartans did, they were slavers on an epic scale themselves. The silver mines which had provided the fleet that had previously beaten Persia and now advanced Athens' ever-growing empire were worked by thousands of slaves in absolutely horrible conditions. The Athenians, however they may have felt about Sparta, would not have liked the idea of a successful slave revolt anywhere in Greece, nor would they have been happy about the balance of power being so radically upset on their southern border, very likely to the advantage of a previously pro-Persian Argos and competing sea power Corinth. Some may argue that the Athenians did liberate helots, but the counterargument may be made that this was done more out of a desire to harm Sparta and advance Athens' politico-military objectives than out of any opposition to slavery, even the caste-based slavery the Spartans practiced. In addition to all of this, Cimon (the victor of Eurymedon) was pro-Spartan and strongly argued that it was in Athens' best interest to keep Sparta stable and strong, likely because he saw a strong Sparta as the key to a stable Greece able to resist any further Persian attempts to invade. Not only was Cimon a leading Athenian, he was a guest-friend of leading Spartans and had even named one of his sons Lacedaemonos (Spartan). So, perhaps it's not all that surprising that Cimon marched south at the head of 4,000 Athenian hoplites to help Sparta out.

Shortly after they arrived, the Spartans dismissed them. Why they did so isn't clear. Some have theorized that the Spartans were concerned the Athenians would be sympathetic to the helots (though the Athenians were slavers, their slaves were mostly non-Greek and they would have likely been troubled by the fact that the helots were all Greeks). Others have speculated that the Spartans worried that the Athenians were engaging in ground reconnaissance with an eye toward a future invasion of Sparta, mapping and surveying, sounding out the local populations, noting routes and terrain.

This doesn't make sense to me. The Spartans were not stupid. They would certainly have known the Athenians would gather this intelligence once they were in country before they even invited them. I believe there is another answer, one that is not captured in the ancient sources, some deal or slight or political machination that is lost to us. But regardless, no sooner had Cimon and his 4,000 arrived than they were ordered to depart, and they marched back to Athens rightly furious, to tell the tale of a serious diplomatic slight that wounded Athenian pride. The Athenians were enraged. Cimon was cashiered and Athenian policy toward Sparta took a decidedly hostile turn.

In the end, the Spartans were unable to storm Ithome and eject the rebels. The Third Messenian War was ended by negotiation, a deal that allowed the Messenian rebels to leave, on the condition that if they ever returned, they would immediately be reduced back into helotage. The Athenians settled them in the city of Naupactus on the Corinthian Gulf, a move that simultaneously removed a thorn in Sparta's side, but also gave aid and comfort to Sparta's enemies.

I can't imagine the Spartans were grateful. Athens further inflamed tensions by allying itself with Megara in that city-state's war against Spartan-allied Corinth. Tensions between the two great powers spiraled toward open war.

The Peloponnesian Wars Begin

However things still didn't come to blows until 460 BC, when Sparta was defeated by an Athenian–Argive alliance outside Oenoe. We know of the battle from Pausanias' description of a painted portico but have no other details of the order of battle, troop counts or why it was fought.

Herodotus gives us one throwaway line that the Spartans captured the city of Halieis in the Argolid, but again provides no further details.

Tanagra

The Battle of Tanagra is the first battle in what most scholars call the First Peloponnesian War for which we have any surrounding information. It was fought in 457 BC when Sparta intervened in a dispute between the Dorians and Phocians in central Greece. Keep in mind that the Spartans were descendants of the Dorians, so marching to support Doris was at least ostensibly a kinship matter.

However, some scholars suggest there are two other reasons the Spartans marched at the head of a very large army to deal with such small city-states (according to Thucydides it comprised 1,500 Peers and 10,000 allied troops under the command of Nicomedes, regent for Pausanias' son Pleistoanax, the Agiad king still too young to take the field).

First, Athens had begun construction of its famous long walls that linked the city to its sea ports at Piraeus and Phalerum. Once complete, these walls would provide Athens with a fully protected connection to the sea, one which Sparta could not answer given its long history of inability to take fortified positions. Secondly, Thucydides also mentions that there was some hope in Sparta that a pro-Spartan faction in Athens might overthrow the current government. Having a strong army in central Greece positioned Sparta to take advantage of this coup, if it should come to pass.

The Phocians (who you'll recall fought alongside the Spartans at Thermopylae) were certainly no match for such a massive army and Sparta quickly settled the contest in favor of Doris. However, the Athenians reacted strongly to the nearby Spartan presence (a good indicator that there was more to the Spartan decision to march than just a squabble between Phocis and Doris), blocked both the sea and land routes back to Sparta, and then mustered out 14,000 hoplites, including their entire citizen-phalanx and other allied troops (Thucydides mentions 1,000 Argive troops and an unspecified number of Thessalian cavalry). Athens then marched its army out of Attica and into Boeotia to confront the Spartan force.

The two armies met at Tanagra and again we have almost no details on the actual conduct of the battle save two facts – the Spartans won and there were serious casualties on both sides (although we have no exact numbers other than that 400 Argives fell). The Spartan victory at Tanagra didn't stick, however. Two months after the battle, the defeated Athenians returned and asserted control over central Greece. Even after victory in battle, Sparta proved unable to truly project power outside the Peloponnese.

Numerous sources discuss aggressive Athenian coastal operations against members of the Peloponnesian League. Sparta didn't care to, or was unable to, respond. Later, the Athenians assisted the Egyptians in revolting against their Persian masters, which prompted the first in what would become a trend of political moves by Persia toward Sparta – the giving of money. Both Thucydides and Diodorus Siculus tell us that the Persians sent their envoy Megabazus to bribe the Spartans to invade. The money was accepted, but the Spartans didn't act on it as Thucydides describes it as being *"spent in vain."* But here again is another glaring contradiction we must mark, another pillar of the Bronze Lie. The Spartans, famous wealth-hating xenophobes and enemies of Persia, who had forced the Persians out of Greece in 480–479 BC, were happily taking their gold around 25 years later.

Sparta and Athens entered into a five-year peace in 451 BC, likely due to pressures on both sides – Athens had just suffered a costly failure of an expedition in Egypt, and Sparta was concerned with Athenian expansion and Athens' alliance with Argos. Sparta also made a "generational" peace (the time of a single generation, or 30 years) with Argos, another indication that Sparta either felt weak or was worried about an increasingly aggressive Athens.

Athens had moved the Delian League treasury to Athens to keep it safe from Persia in 454 BC, but the move was a sign of Athens' real goal, which was imperial domination of Greece and expansion beyond. League dues were mandatory and attempts to withdraw were seen as a rebellion against Athens to be crushed by military force.

Athens supposedly concluded the Peace of Callias with Persia in 449 BC, but this is disputed, with good arguments on both sides. However, I tend to align with those who agree that the peace was real, as evidenced by the inarguable ending of hostilities on both sides at the time of the peace.

Sparta intervened against the Phocians once again during the five-year truce, kicking them out of Delphi, only to have control of Delphi returned to them by Athens as soon as the Spartans left.

Athens suffered a defeat at the hands of Boeotian troops in 447 BC, news of which may have contributed to the subsequent revolt of the island of Euboea and the city-state of Megara the following year. Sparta finally saw its chance and sent an expeditionary force under the command of the Agiad king Pleistoanax to invade Attica.

The army *"ravaged the land"* according to Thucydides, which probably means it burnt crops, robbed homes, killed locals and generally caused mayhem. What it didn't do was capture any significant human settlements (or at least, if it did, our sources don't mention it), or fight any pitched battles against the Athenians or their allies. This is very likely due to Sparta's continued inability to assault a fortified position, and we're left with the image of the Spartan army acting like a pack of bandits, while the Athenians and their subjects and allies watched carefully (but not too worried) from their walled towns.

However, we also have to remember that Sparta hadn't achieved "field superiority" (having completely destroyed its enemy's army), without which, no siege can be successfully conducted. Athens may have been bottled up behind its walls, but its fleet could still deliver marines and supplies, and its army could theoretically march out to threaten any besiegers or at least harass them. So, in this case it may not be Sparta's deficiency in siegecraft, but more its failure to achieve the basic requirements of a successful siege that prevented it from making a better showing of its invasion.

Whatever the cause, Athens itself was never under any serious threat. After determining that the Spartans weren't going to be able to do anything more than fruitlessly raid, Pleistoanax apparently gave up and went home. Once back in Sparta he was accused of accepting an Athenian bribe to leave Attica. This may have been political scheming, but we've seen enough reporting of Spartan tendencies to both take and give bribes (a glaring contradiction to the Lycurgan wealth-hating ideal. What use does a people who only use heavy iron money have for gold?) to consider the possibility that it might have been true.

Regardless of the truth of the charges, both Pleistoanax and his advisor Cleandridas fled into exile, making Pleistoanax the fourth Spartan king (after Cleomenes, Demaratus and Leotychides) to be driven out of the Spartan government due to charges of corruption or illegitimacy. Pausanias was not a king, but he was a member of a Spartan royal house and a powerful figure in Spartan society.

With Pleistoanax out of the way, the Eurypontid king Archidamus was able to secure peace with Athens in 445 BC (Archidamus was a guest friend of the Athenian leading statesman Pericles). Archidamus is probably my favorite of all Spartan kings, practical and peace-loving, repeatedly displaying an attribute so badly lacking in all leaders, but in Spartans in particular – the ability to take the long view. Again and again, Archidamus was sober and coolheaded, advocating always for peace, and if peace could not be had, then for a slow and cautious approach to war, not taking on fights that Sparta couldn't win. Unfortunately for Archidamus, Spartan kings were not particularly powerful and the rest of the government did not share his cautious and measured approach to foreign policy.

But for now, Sparta negotiated another generational (30 years) peace. It lasted less than half that time.

The Archidamian Phase of the Peloponnesian Wars

Perhaps the greatest irony is that the second outbreak of fighting in the Peloponnesian Wars is named for the man who argued most strongly against it and who took up command of the Spartan war effort only with the greatest reluctance. The "Archidamian War," as it is popularly known (more correctly, we should call it the Archidamian phase of the Peloponnesian Wars), broke out in 431 BC and Thucydides is pretty clear in placing the blame squarely on Athens. I'm inclined to believe him, considering that he was an Athenian general whose loyalties lay firmly with that city-state. He tells us that *"the growing power of Athens was obvious. The Athenians began to interfere with Sparta's allies to a level that Sparta could no longer tolerate."*

The war almost broke out as early as 440 BC, when Samos revolted against Athens and begged for Spartan aid. Sparta brought the question up for a vote of the Peloponnesian League, but the proposal was opposed by Corinth and the plan scrapped.

In Sparta's reliance on Corinthian approval to go to war, we see another glaring hole in the Bronze Lie. It's certainly a compliment to Sparta that it relied on its allies and was careful to ensure that they were fully on board with any proposed military expedition before risking another humiliating disintegration of its army as Cleomenes had done in 506 BC. But it also shows that Sparta was just as reliant on diplomacy and coalition-building as it was on brute strength or warfighting skill. The suicidally brave mythical Spartans in *300* wouldn't have cared that the Corinthians didn't want to fight. The real Spartans cared very much indeed.

Athens proceeded to conquer Samos. Seven years later, Athens then went on to make a treaty with the island of Corcyra (modern-day Corfu – just off the coast of northwestern Greece and southwestern Albania), which it defended against Corinth (Corcyra was originally a Corinthian colony). Athens responded to Corinth's attack on Corcyra by mounting its own aggression against the Corinthian colony of Potidaea on the opposite side of Greece (on the left-most of the "three fingers" descending from below modern-day Thessaloniki in northeastern Greece), ripping down one of its walls.

This clinched it for Corinth. It wasn't about to approve Sparta going to war against Athens for Samos, but it was furious about the defense of Corcyra and now the Athenians were messing with one of its other colonies on the other side of Greece. Both Potidaea and Corinth asked for Spartan aid, and this time Sparta agreed. Emboldened by the promise of Spartan assistance, Potidaea rebelled against Athens and the Athenians put the city under siege.

A delegation of Greek city-states (including Megara, Aegina and Corinth) with grievances against Athens arrived demanding that the Spartans put up or shut up. After hearing the arguments, Sparta agreed to their allies' request. It would declare war on Athens. But first, it had to send to Delphi for an oracle to be sure that Apollo approved of their decision.

The oracle's response was so unusually clear that I suspect that the Pythia had once again been bribed – Sparta should immediately invade Attica, confident that Apollo would be on its side. Even with this unambiguous answer from the god, Sparta *still* called another meeting of its allies, including those who hadn't attended the previous meeting, and put the matter to a vote.

Here again we see a bald-faced example of the Bronze Lie. The superwarriors of Sparta did not advance confidently to battle, assured they could defeat any army thrown against them. Even with divine approval, they still refused to make a move without being totally sure they had allied support. This is sensible and reflects well on the Spartans, but it does *not* hold up the popular image of superwarriors who are brave unto death. Sparta clearly relied as much on diplomacy and consensus building as it did on its spears.

Thucydides narrates the Corinthians stumping in support of the Spartan position, and even the Boeotians under Thebes chimed in, angry with Athens over past defeats after Tanagra. In the end, the majority voted for war.

The Spartans now sent multiple embassies to Athens to demand that the Delian League come to terms. These embassies were rejected (after a stirring oration by Pericles, which Thucydides relates) as I'm sure the Spartans expected. Athens did appear to negotiate and even agreed to submit the disputes to arbitration, but the undercurrent was always clear – Athens could never meet Sparta's demands. There was no official declaration of war, but both sides knew it was coming, and soon.

Sparta mustered out the full roll of its allies. Thucydides notes the massive mobilization that responded to the call (a damning indictment of how badly Athens had upset the Greeks with its high-handed imperialism):

> *The Spartans had the whole Peloponnese south of the isthmus of Corinth except the Argives and Achaeans (for these were friendly with both Athens and Sparta); of all Achaea, only the Pellenians answered the call; but later all the rest did the same; and outside the Peloponnese, the Megarians, Locrians, Boeotians, Phocians, Ambraciots, Leucadians and Anactorians. Of these the Corinthians, Megareans, Sicyonians, Pellenians, Eleans, Ambraciots, and Leucadians provided ships; the Boeotians, Phocians and Locrians, cavalry; and the rest of the cities, infantry.*

This massive army easily rivaled the joint muster for Plataea and must have been a truly daunting force. But the Athenians could draw on a huge network of allies (and subjects) of their own.

However, the Athenians' real advantage was the absolutely insane Spartan battle plan of repeating Pleistoanax's failed effort to ravage the Attic countryside. The Athenians very likely knew that no matter how large their army was, the Spartans were just awful at sieges and wouldn't do well trying to take Athenian fortified positions.

Archidamus very clearly saw that this was a terrible idea. Thucydides gives him an impassioned speech where he essentially says:

> This is insane. The Athenians have a massive naval empire. Even if we utterly destroy the crops on the Attic plain, they can harvest crops elsewhere in their domain and import whatever they need by sea, which we'd be powerless to prevent since we can't stop their navy.

If we're going to beat Athens, we have to stir up revolt across their empire and we don't have the money, the ships or the crews to do that. We need to build our war chest, and we also need to build alliances with those who can fund the effort and provide a navy – this includes Persia.

But being right isn't the same as being convincing. His influence may have been partly eroded by the many public humiliations of Sparta's kings and royal regents over the past three quarters of a century. He also faced the same problem all political moderates face, even today – war and conflict are more exciting and garner more popular support than complex and moderate diplomacy. It's far easier to bang on a podium and call for an invasion than it is to call for sober and careful consideration of how to untangle a political knot.

Archidamus also faced a demographic problem – his arguments appealed to the minority of older Spartans who had experienced war and knew its horror first hand. These sympathetic voices were drowned out by a clamor of younger men who were impatient to be tested in battle.

Given all of this, Archidamus was overruled and took up his command of the giant Peloponnesian League army with what I can only imagine was the greatest reluctance.

He started things off in truly Archidamian fashion – sending yet *another* embassy to inform the Athenians they were about to be invaded. This ambassador was unsurprisingly sent away by a people busily preparing for the invasion he'd come to announce. It was likely a formality, but from what I know of Archidamus' character, I don't doubt that even now he hoped that sanity could prevail and both sides be pulled back from the brink of what he knew would be a horrifically costly and fruitless war. Here again we see the glaring contradiction to the Bronze Lie of Spartan warrior supremacy – the brave Spartans, masters of war, first into a fight and last off the field, always willing to conquer or die, being led by a peace-loving, rational, deeply conscientious king, looking for off-ramps to conflict at every opportunity.

But there's a more cynical spin to be taken on Archidamus – that he wasn't peace-loving or conscientious at all, but simply thought Sparta was getting into a fight it couldn't win.

The siege of Oenoe

Pericles, no fool, immediately made his holdings around Athens public land to prevent any blackening of his reputation when Archidamus spared them from ravaging due to their guest-friendship, and thus put the thought into Athenian minds that Pericles might sympathize with the Spartan cause.

Archidamus was still bent on peace and thus opened the war in spectacularly embarrassing fashion with a siege of the Attic fortress at Oenoe in the hopes that the action would force the Athenians to come to terms. Once again, the preconditions of a successful siege – the defeat of Athens' army and navy – were not met, and so the outcome was a forgone conclusion. Athens didn't come to terms, and Sparta's playing to its weakness in siege warfare resulted in an embarrassing defeat when it was forced to abandon the attempt.

His hopes for a negotiated settlement abandoned, Archidamus now sought to convince the Athenians to come out from behind their walls by ravaging the plains all around Athens – Eleusis, Thria and finally Acharnae to the north of the city. Things shook out exactly as Archidamus had predicted. The Athenians stayed safe behind their walls, sending cavalry out to try to harass the Spartan army (which was protected not by its own cavalry – the Spartans were much too rigid and unadaptive to really invest in this critical military role – but by the horsemen sent from their Boeotian allies) and were otherwise just fine. Archidamus finished out the campaigning season and marched back home having accomplished absolutely nothing, precisely as Pleistoanax had done before him. At least he avoided charges of bribery on his return.

Archidamus invaded a second time in 430 BC and this time campaigned for well over a month, laying waste to the plain all around Athens. This time Athens did sue for peace, but it had nothing to do with Archidamus' futile second ravaging. Rather, Athens was a victim of a horrific plague that killed a huge portion of its population, who were crowded together behind walls trying to wait out the Spartan campaign. The Spartans had inadvertently found a way to use the Athenians' defensive posture against them. Of course, the Spartans had no reason to accept the peace terms and so rejected them.

Pericles died from the plague in 429 BC, the same year that Archidamus invaded again.

The relief of Methone – Brasidas emerges

Through it all, the Athenians scoured the Peloponnesian coast, again exactly as Archidamus had predicted. Thucydides tells us that they sent a fleet of 100 ships, plus another 50 from Corcyra, which would have enabled them to put a substantial force of marines on shore, not to mention rowers fighting as light troops. Thucydides gives a figure of 4,000 infantry and 300 cavalry.

We hear our first tale of Spartan heroics in this portion of the war, when the Athenians assaulted the town of Methone on the southwestern coast of Messenia in 430 BC. The Spartan hero Brasidas, who would go on to cover himself in glory, launched his celebrated career by driving through the Athenian army with just 100 men, according to Thucydides. This tiny band (minus a few casualties) managed to reach the town and garrison it, forcing the Athenians to move on (presumably because they didn't have the time to sit down for a siege. They were probably also worried about remaining too long so deep in enemy territory). For this brave action, Brasidas became *"the first celebrated at Sparta in this war."* What this means is debated, but I assume it indicates he was decorated or awarded some honor.

The Spartan town of Prasiae on the Laconian coast fared less well, sacked and burned by the Athenians the following year. These maritime raids proved to be as ineffective as Archidamus' land campaigns. Sure, the Athenians could cause trouble on the coastline, but they couldn't march far inland, nor could they take and hold territory (as Brasidas' rescue of Methone proved) for fear of being cut off and stranded behind enemy lines.

That same year, a Spartan fleet of 100 ships bearing 1,000 hoplites under the admiral Cnemus attacked the Athenian-aligned island of Zacynthus off the northwest coast of the Peloponnese. It can't really be counted as a battle, since all the force did was ravage the island before determining that the inhabitants wouldn't submit, at which point the Spartans gave up and sailed off. Thucydides does not confirm this, but I again suspect there was a fortified town in play that Cnemus realized he wouldn't be able to effectively storm. This would certainly fit with Sparta's battlefield record thus far. There's also the possibility that the Spartan fleet was concerned about being caught out at sea, an indication that even at this early date they weren't confident of their ability to take on the Athenian navy.

Assault on Stratus

The following year (429 BC), Cnemus continued his poor battlefield record with an abortive invasion of the western Greek territory of Acarnania at the behest of the Spartan allies the Ambraciots and Chaonians. Control of Acarnania would hopefully force Zacynthus to surrender, as well as threaten Naupactus, where Athens had settled the rebellious helots at the end of the Third Messenian War.

Cnemus sailed to the coast, evading 20 Athenian ships keeping watch off Naupactus under the command of Phormio. He then disembarked his 1,000 Spartan hoplites, quite possibly the same ones who had just previously ravaged Zacynthus to no avail. Here he was joined by a substantial allied force. Thucydides tells us the Chaonians sent 1,000 infantry, and notes unspecified numbers of Ambraciots, Leucadians and Anactorians, as well as "*barbarians*" (non-Greek Balkan peoples), the Thesprotians and Molossians. Meanwhile, a large allied fleet would protect the Spartans from any sea-borne Athenian or Athenian-allied attacks.

But Cnemus didn't wait for the arrival of his fleet and instead advanced immediately on the Acarnanian capital of Stratus, thinking to quickly take it and win the campaign. He divided his army into three divisions, himself in command of the Spartans on the left. The plan was to camp in sight of the Stratian walls and see if the enemy would submit without a fight (a plan that clearly showed Archidamus' influence and also that Cnemus had not learned how ineffective this had proved at Oenoe). There was now either a signal or communications failure, or else the Chaonians (and the barbarian units) who made up the center of the battle line simply weren't in the mood to be so cautious.

While the right and left wings made camp, the center advanced on their own. The Stratians, no fools, realized they had a golden opportunity and ambushed the advancing allied center, slaughtering the Chaonians. The barbarian troops, seeing all was lost, ran for their lives. The Acarnanians played this win smartly – they didn't pursue the fleeing troops, but instead sent slingers (Thucydides tells us the Acarnanians were known for their skill with this weapon) to harass the camps. At nightfall, Cnemus withdrew under cover of darkness, then made a brief truce to recover the dead before sounding a final retreat. The army disbanded afterward.

Rhium and Naupactus

Meanwhile, the allied fleet arrived to assist, 47 ships in all, not dreaming that Phormio would attack them with just 20 ships of his own. But the allied fleet was composed of heavily laden transports and they also underestimated the absolute dominance of Athenian naval skill at this point in the war. The initial fleet Themistocles had convinced Athens to fund with its silver strike half a century ago was now crewed by seasoned and veteran sailors, and they made short work of the Peloponnesian fleet (the Spartans contributed very few ships themselves) just off Rhium, capturing 12 ships and their crews.

The survivors joined a new Spartan fleet at the shipyard of Cyllene and were once again placed under Cnemus' command. Apparently, one military failure followed by a genuine disaster was not enough to erode Spartan confidence in the man, yet another example of the Bronze Lie. Spartan military "professionalism" (really discipline and organization, as the Spartans were not true full-time professional soldiers in the modern sense of the word) would mean that men would be promoted or fall from grace based on their performance in combat. But in reality, Spartan military leaders rose or fell based on all the typical factors in the ancient world – networking, patronage, wealth or connections to leading families.

This new Spartan fleet of 77 ships threatened Naupactus, forcing Phormio to sail to meet them, still with just 20 ships of his own. Phormio, to his credit, sent for reinforcements, but the additional ships were diverted to Crete and didn't arrive in time to help.

The Spartans succeeded in forcing nine of Phormio's 20 ships to beach themselves, and chased the rest into the harbor. It looked as if that was the end of it, but the last ship in Phormio's fleet looped around an anchored merchantman and rammed one of the Spartans' Leucadian allied triremes, sinking it (Thucydides reports the Spartan Peer Timocrates, who was on board, committed suicide out of shame).

The sudden and unexpected assault apparently completely threw the Spartan fleet into confusion and Phormio, probably unable to believe his luck, immediately took advantage of the opportunity, moved to the attack and routed the much larger force, capturing six more ships before the Spartans could flee.

The battle effectively ended any Spartan naval operations on the west coast of central Greece and firmly established Athens' reputation as the strongest navy in the region. Sparta was justifiably terrified of Athens on the water, so much so that the following year it sent no aid when the Ionian island of Mytilene rebelled against Athens. The Spartans did send a fleet of 40 ships to Mytilene in 427 BC under the admiral Alcidas, as conveniently late as the Spartan march on Marathon. Mytilene had of course already fallen by the time the fleet arrived and Alcidas declined to use his ships to retake the city, or to raid or stir up further revolt among Athens' Ionian subjects. Thucydides is clear that Alcidas fled, and his narrative makes it plain that the Spartan admiral was terrified of Athenian naval dominance.

Corcyra

Fleeing back to the Peloponnese with his 40 ships, Alcidas was reinforced by another 13 from the Leucadians and Ambraciots. He took his enlarged fleet on to Corcyra, which was locked in its own internal struggle between pro-Spartan oligarchic and pro-Athenian democratic factions. This struggle crippled their naval defense – 12 Athenian ships and another 60 Corcyrean – because the Corcyrean crews turned on one another in the latest phase of their own civil war. Alcidas was able to divide his fleet – 20 ships to take on the disordered Corcyreans, and another 20 for the Athenians. The Spartans won, captured 13 Corcyrean ships, and ravaged the coastline.

It was Sparta's first recorded naval victory against Athens, but its luster was tarnished by the decision to flee at the sight of another 60 Athenian ships inbound to even the odds.

Cnemus had one small redemption at the end of his previous disastrous performance, though he had to share it with the hero Brasidas. The Megarians convinced the two to stage a surprise attack on the Athenian port of Piraeus, but this plan was aborted when fear of failure and possibly contrary winds forced them to turn aside and attack Salamis instead. Thucydides is clear that he believed that if they'd been able to overcome their fear, they would have successfully taken Piraeus.

The attack on Salamis took the Athenians completely by surprise. The Spartans were able to tow away three warships and lay waste to much of the island before the Athenians sent both their fleet and a ground force to respond. By then, the Spartans had withdrawn. It was a small, raiding victory, and it increased Athenian vigilance and defensive measures over their most critical port, but it was very likely the shot in the arm the Spartans needed after their defeats outside Stratus and at Rhium and Naupactus.

The siege of Plataea

Back on land, Archidamus had marched again as early as 429 BC against the Athenian allied city of Plataea, inhabited by the same brave men who had stood with Athens against the Persians at Marathon while the Spartans made their excuses. Here, Thucydides narrates a fascinating episode in the history of Spartan warfare.

We see, in pretty good detail, Archidamus' efforts to improve the Spartan record on siege warfare. It's a rare glimpse of the Spartans adapting and improving, a sliver of the humanity beneath the Bronze Lie.

The Plataeans naturally invoked the promise Pausanias had made to them following the defeat of the Persians in 479 BC, that the Spartans would always protect Plataea. Archidamus was, quite clearly, violating this oath (with all the religious pollution that entailed. More proof that the Spartans threw religion in the trash whenever it suited them). Archidamus replied that he was happy to honor the oath if the Plataeans would return to neutrality, which of course they couldn't do as the Athenians had previously taken members of the Plataean leading families hostage as a hedge against this very thing. Archidamus finally offered to *rent* their city and surrounding lands, giving the Plataeans leave to depart. He had to know the Athenians would never allow this, and he was right. In the end, the Plataeans made ready to defend their city with a tiny garrison of 400 Plataeans and 80 Athenians. We don't know the size of Archidamus' army, but it clearly overwhelmingly outnumbered the defenders. Here we see the first use of the Greek word *xenagoi*, which I mentioned earlier, indicating that Spartan officers commanded other Greek troops in the siege operations.

Thucydides describes the leapfrogging of attack and defense in great detail. The Spartans first raised a siege mound – a ramp of earth building up to overtop the city wall.

The defenders countered by building their own inner wall that continually grew higher than the siege mound. They then dug through the base of their own wall and began removing dirt from the Spartan siege mound. The Spartans then used reed mats and clay to wall off the base of their own mound, forcing the defenders to both tunnel around that and raise yet another inner wall. The Spartans responded by employing rams, and the defenders used ropes both to yank the rams up and topple them over and to swing heavy wooden beams down in front of the walls to ... well ... ram the rams. The Spartans responded by starting a massive fire which burned too hot for the defenders to put out ... until the weather did it for them.

At long last, the Spartans had to settle down to a long siege, making sure they had walled the city off from either escape or help. This wall was manned in shifts all the way through 427 BC, when Plataea was finally stormed and taken. However, one of the reasons the city fell was that fully half the defenders had successfully broken out and escaped in a daring nighttime operation. The remainder were executed in a show trial.

Olpae

The next major land engagement came the following year when the Spartan Eurylochus led 3,000 allied hoplites against Naupactus in a joint operation with the Aetolians (Aetolia is a region in central Greece). They were opposed by the Athenian general Demosthenes, who would win fame for his performance at the joint Battle of Pylos and Sphacteria the following year. Delay and indecision on Eurylochus' part allowed Naupactus to be reinforced, and the Spartan-led allied troops wound up engaging the Athenians and their allies under Demosthenes outside Olpae. Among the troops that Demosthenes led were Messenians, no doubt eager to settle their generations-old score with the Spartans.

The battle began well for the Spartans and their allies, with Demosthenes in real danger of being outflanked, but a force of Athenian-allied Acarnanians ambushed the Spartan-allied force, killing Eurylochus and sending the remaining troops into a panic.

Demosthenes' forces won after suffering around 300 casualties, compared to 1,000 on the Spartan-allied side.

Demosthenes allowed the Spartan second in command Menedaeus to escape along with the Peloponnesian allies, leaving the other allies in the lurch. Thucydides was clear that this was a secret arrangement between

Demosthenes and Menedaeus and done deliberately to show that the Spartans were "*men that treacherously advanced their own interest.*" But the fact remains that Menedaeus *accepted* Demosthenes' offer, thus proving the Athenian right. In Menedaeus' acceptance of the chance to save his own skin, we see another example of the Bronze Lie. One of the most famous quotes from Herodotus is the Spartan king Demaratus' surely apocryphal words, warning Xerxes that by Spartan law, Spartans "*must abide at their post and there conquer or die.*" Menedaeus, Spartan that he was, clearly did not get that particular memo.

The sad punchline to all this futile fighting on sea and land, neither of which accomplished much of anything in terms of the relative power between Sparta and Athens or the leagues they both commanded, was Archidamus' death probably around 427–426 BC. He had done everything he could to prevent the outbreak of war, and worked hard to curtail it even as it wound its way along. It would continue, still bearing his name, for another four years.

FOCUS BATTLE: PYLOS AND SPHACTERIA (425 BC) – CONQUER OR DIE?

It's worth taking some time to dive deep on the Battle of Pylos in 425 BC, which includes the fight for the island of Sphacteria, barely more than 300 feet from the mainland at its closest point. This fight was a veritable catalog of Spartan errors, foolhardy tactical decisions and failures of vigilance that resulted in disaster as whole armies were literally caught napping. Most importantly, the battle gave us the event that shocked the Greek world – the surrender of 120 elite Peers, rather than their dying with their weapons in their hands as Leonidas and his 300 (or 298) had so famously done 55 years earlier.

Pylos was Sparta's lowest point during the Archidamian phase of the Peloponnesian Wars. To be fair to the Spartans, the battle is also full of acts of incredible heroism, tenacity and devotion to duty, but it is in the *balance* of Spartan actions that we see the truth. At Pylos and Sphacteria we see *human beings*, full of all the glorious valor and wretched cowardice we expect of *all* people. There is absolutely no evidence, literary or material, that in the 55 years since Thermopylae Spartan martial values had been significantly degraded. These were the same supposedly great warriors that held (actually, as we have seen, failed to hold) Thermopylae against Xerxes. The outcomes of the battles at Pylos and Sphacteria were utterly different, under surprisingly similar conditions, as we will see.

THE ARCHIDAMIAN WAR: SPARTAN RIGIDITY AND ATHENIAN MOBILITY

The Archidamian phase of the Peloponnesian Wars had been raging for six years by the time of the Battle of Pylos, with the established rhythm of thrust and counterthrust – the Spartans, superior on land, invaded Attica, ineffectually laying waste to Athenian crops, and the navally superior Athenians raided the coast of the Peloponnese.

We have already discussed the Spartans' rigid conservatism and how it impeded them from adapting to developments in military tactics and technology. It was one of their greatest cultural failings and it hit them particularly hard in this instance. Athens, safely protected behind its long walls, expertly employed cavalry sorties to harass and contain Spartan invasions into Attica. Sparta, on the other hand, never invested heavily in cavalry and relied mostly on its Boeotian allies to keep its columns safe. But the Boeotians were operating to the north and Sparta lacked a mobile force to deal with Athenian raiding parties which would appear out of the mists at will anywhere they liked on the Peloponnesian coast.

Even worse, as we'll see in the description of the battle, the Spartans didn't invest heavily in light troops. These fell into two major categories: *psiloi* (literally, "the naked people") and specialist light infantry with real expertise, such as *peltastai* (anglicized as "peltasts" – named for their mostly wicker or hide *peltē* crescent-shaped small shields), usually armed with javelins, or archers. *Psiloi* were usually too poor to afford any significant weaponry and certainly not the incredibly expensive *hopla* and usually had to content themselves with a strip of hide or cloth as an improvised shield. Like a medieval peasant levy, *psiloi* used whatever weapons were to hand – farming implements, scavenged blades, improvised spears and, more often than not, whatever rocks they could find on the battlefield. Rowers from the Athenian fleet would often double as *psiloi* in land battles, as was certainly the case on Sphacteria.

Sparta, as we'll see, viewed missile combat as "*effeminate*" (Thucydides puts this description in one Spartan's mouth). This attitude does not seem to have changed much over the years. Plutarch quotes the Spartan king Archidamus III nearly a century later saying "*Men's valor is no more,*" upon seeing a catapult in action for the first time. Each Peer went into battle with at least one helot attendant who would continue the custom of ensuring that his noble master would never have to do any actual work – cooking meals, dressing wounds, pitching tents, carrying and repairing weapons and armor and generally attending to any and all tasks other than the actual fighting. But, as we saw at Thermopylae and Plataea, the helots did fight, loyally and bravely, for their Spartan oppressors. This corps of slaves gave the Spartans much of their light infantry and missile capability at Pylos and Sphacteria.

One note before I go on here – as we've already seen, the Peloponnesian Wars were not a struggle strictly between Athens and Sparta, but a conflict between the Delian League and the Peloponnesian League with their respective *poleis* at the center of operations. That said, for ease of understanding and flow, in the story that follows I will always refer to the Delian forces as "the Athenians" and the Peloponnesian forces as "the Spartans." I of course mean the various nationalities involved on both sides.

TAKING PYLOS: BAD WEATHER SETS THE STAGE

In 425 BC, the Spartans sent a fleet of 60 ships against Corcyra under the *navarchos* (admiral) Thrasymelidas. The Athenians in turn sent a fleet of 40 triremes sailing south along the west coast of the Peloponnese to assist. The fact that they were able to sail such a large fleet at will along the very heart of Sparta's sphere of influence is a strong indicator of Athens' almost complete naval supremacy.

The Athenian fleet had three senior officers – the legendary Demosthenes, whom we saw victorious outside Olpae and whose tactical genius would be proven at Pylos, and his much less famous colleagues Sophocles and

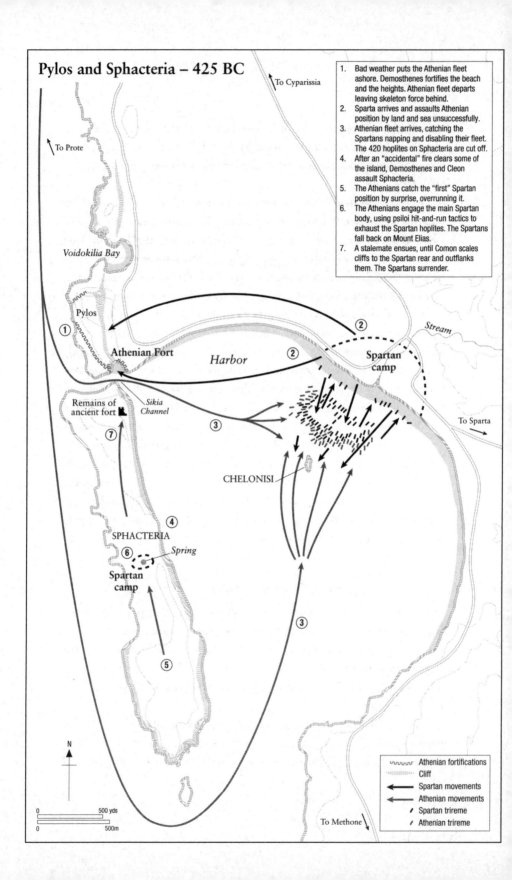

Pylos and Sphacteria – 425 BC

To Cyparissia

To Prote

Voidokilia Bay

Pylos

① Athenian Fort

Harbor

② ②

Spartan camp

Stream

To Sparta

Remains of ancient fort

Sikia Channel

③

⑦

CHELONISI

③

SPHACTERIA

⑥ *Spring*

④

Spartan camp

⑤

N

1. Bad weather puts the Athenian fleet ashore. Demosthenes fortifies the beach and the heights. Athenian fleet departs leaving skeleton force behind.
2. Sparta arrives and assaults Athenian position by land and sea unsuccessfully.
3. Athenian fleet arrives, catching the Spartans napping and disabling their fleet. The 420 hoplites on Sphacteria are cut off.
4. After an "accidental" fire clears some of the island, Demosthenes and Cleon assault Sphacteria.
5. The Athenians catch the "first" Spartan position by surprise, overrunning it.
6. The Athenians engage the main Spartan body, using psiloi hit-and-run tactics to exhaust the Spartan hoplites. The Spartans fall back on Mount Elias.
7. A stalemate ensues, until Comon scales cliffs to the Spartan rear and outflanks them. The Spartans surrender.

ᔕᔕᔕᔕ	Athenian fortifications
⠿⠿⠿	Cliff
←	Spartan movements
←	Athenian movements
✓	Spartan trireme
✓	Athenian trireme

0   500 yds

0   500m

To Methone

Eurymedon. The three argued as they approached the island of Sphacteria, with Demosthenes wanting to put in on the inviting sandy beach of Pylos' natural harbor to "*do what was wanted there*" as Thucydides puts it, presumably to raid or build an outpost in Sparta's backyard. Sophocles and Eurymedon disagreed, having heard that the Spartan fleet was behind them at Corcyra, and confident (with good reason after Phormio's victories) that even though the Spartans outnumbered them, the Athenians could easily beat them at sea. The three leaders argued until, if you want to think like an ancient Greek, the gods intervened, and a storm blew in that forced the fleet to beach in Pylos harbor.

The fight at Pylos and Sphacteria hinged on the ancient Greek trireme of the 5th century BC, which we examined in chapter III. The seas were rough until the Athenian fleet was safely east of Sphacteria, which provided a natural breakwater for the interior bay (modern-day Navarino Bay). Demosthenes took advantage of this turn of events and tried again unsuccessfully to convince his colleagues to fortify their position. Again, the gods intervened and the bad weather kept the fleet on shore (triremes were notoriously unsafe in rough water and could only hug the coast safely). Eurymedon and Sophocles may have not been fans of Demosthenes' goals, but that didn't make them fools. They had landed right in the middle of Sparta's backyard and they knew it wouldn't be long before the Spartans arrived in force to destroy them. At last, they consented to fortify their position, which they did, enclosing the headland at the north of the bay surrounded by rocky shore and massive cliffs, which they also walled off.

Thucydides points out that the Athenians had no building tools or equipment and did all this work with their bare hands – another indicator that they were deeply concerned about an impending Spartan attack. This task seems less daunting when you estimate that the Athenians had somewhere in the neighborhood of 8,000 men at Pylos. That many hands can do a lot of work quickly.

The weather had cleared by the time this work was finished and Eurymedon and Sophocles would delay no longer. They set off for Corcyra in the hopes of catching the Spartan fleet. They left Demosthenes with just five triremes and their crews – about 75 hoplites and 20 archers. This may not seem like much even to hold a fortified cliff, but keep in mind that the nearly 1,000 rowers would also have doubled as *psiloi,* and in some cases specialty light troops if they could afford the gear and had the training.

ASSAULT BY LAND AND SEA: SPARTA REACTS

It was impossible to keep such a massive deployment on Sparta's home turf secret, but remember that this was long before radio communications and the chain of oral messages that brought the Spartans news was probably confused and panicked. One thing they were certain of – a large Athenian force had landed unexpectedly on the southwest coast and was digging in.

Sparta's response was massive. Just 15 days into his invasion of Attica, the Eurypontid king Agis II turned his army back around and marched for Pylos. Word was immediately sent to Spartan allies to muster troops to throw the Athenians out. Messages also recalled the Spartan fleet of 60 triremes from Corcyra. Either Thrasymelidas was aware that Eurymedon and Sophocles were sailing to intercept them (a fight the Spartans would surely have lost against the navally dominant Athenians in open water), or he got incredibly lucky, dragging his ships across the isthmus of Leucas and totally evading the Athenians. It's worth noting yet another major departure from the Spartan legend here – the great warriors *avoiding* a fight, even one where they were as surely outmatched as they were at Thermopylae. The Spartan fleet sailed into the harbor and beached their ships on the sandy shore just southeast of Demosthenes' fortified position, disembarked their troops and set up camp.

Meanwhile, Demosthenes had sent two of his five precious ships under skeleton crews (to preserve his limited manpower) to locate Eurymedon and Sophocles and warn them that the Spartan fleet they were looking for was not at Corcyra, but at Pylos, and they needed to return as quickly as possible.

Demosthenes also had help from Messenians most likely out of Naupactus, who still burned with hatred toward the Spartans for their earlier conquest and reduction to helotage in the Messenian Wars. These provided precious shields, some manpower and vital intelligence on Spartan movements. They arrived in a kind of mini-trireme of just 30 oars called a *triakontēr,* manned by pirates who were only too happy to risk their lives to bloody the nose of the Spartan oppressor.

Sparta planned a simultaneous land and amphibious assault. We don't know the exact numbers, but we can be certain they outnumbered the Athenians by a staggering amount. The Athenians digging into their fortified positions must have watched the scores of triremes unloading on the beach and seen the dust kicked up by the enormous land army marching toward them. With just three ships now trapped on their tiny fortified stretch of sand and their backs to the sea, I can only imagine the terror they must have felt as they readied for the Spartan attack. Their one hope lay in the arrival of the Athenian fleet. It's unlikely with the Spartan encirclement of their position that they had word that Demosthenes' messengers had gotten through, and the fleet was even now rowing hard to rescue them.

The Spartans were worried about Sphacteria, the island just off Pylos. Thucydides tells us that *"fearing that the enemy might make use of the island to operate against them,* [the Spartans] *carried over some heavy infantry there, stationing others along the coast."* This force rotated in and out, but the unit that wound up occupying the central part of this story was under the command of the Peer Epitadas and consisted of 420 hoplites. Some of these would have been *perioikoi*, but we know at least 120 of them were the elite Peers, Sparta's most precious resource.

Keep in mind that the *oliganthrōpia*, Sparta's acute manpower crisis driven by wealth inequality, bad inheritance laws, cultural rigidity and the casualties of constant warfare, was already well underway. Herodotus tells us that 8,000 Peers were available at Thermopylae (of which only 300 were sent). Per Thucydides, these had dwindled to 2,500 in just 62 years. This means that the Peers stationed on Sphacteria may have represented over 4 percent of the total population. Losing them would be a blow Sparta could not easily sustain. In addition to the hoplites, there were probably another 500 or so helots on the island, but ancient historians almost never speak of the poor and enslaved, and we are left largely guessing at their numbers, equipment and role. Odds are that most if not all of these helots would have fought as *psiloi*.

As Sparta closed the land and sea arms of the pincer, Demosthenes rallied his troops and reminded them that, outnumbered as they were, they could still hold the Spartans off. "Their numbers won't help them in this small space! You Athenians know what it's like to assault a beach! You know that if we don't run in terror from the splashing of the oars and the looming hulls we can beat them! Dig in and hold on! We stop them *here* at the water's edge!"

It was more than just a nice speech. The beach was held on the landward side by towering fortified cliffs that the Spartans had no real way to scale (they hadn't had time to build real siege equipment, to include scaling ladders, in their rush to reach Pylos). The seaward side was tiny. The beach itself was minuscule, the sandy portion suitable for beaching a trireme already occupied by the Athenians. This forced the Spartans either to stand off, deploying troops into shallow water, or to try to beach on the rocks, with the consequent risk of damage to the ships.

Thucydides tells us that this is exactly what happened. It's important to note that while a trireme could be as much as 20 feet wide, the constantly moving oars extended much farther. A ship isn't like a car. You can't apply brakes and just stop it. It is constantly moving, drifting. To avoid tangling your oars with the ship next to you, much greater distance has to be maintained. The bay must have been crowded with triremes desperately backing oars as they tried to hold position, avoid fouling the oars of their neighbors, and find water shallow enough to drop off their assaulting troops.

At last Brasidas, the hero of Methone we met earlier, had had enough. Thucydides quotes him in a speech nearly as dramatic as Demosthenes': "You protect your ships while we lose the land! Run them aground! Get on that shore any way you can! Drive these men from their position!" His helmsman complied, deliberately wrecking his trireme on the rocks. Brasidas ordered the gangplanks dropped, each only wide enough to admit one Spartan marine at a time. Brasidas, in true Spartan fashion, made sure he was the first to set foot on the gangplank, leading by example.

It was brave, noble, dramatic, the stuff of Hollywood action flicks.

It was also unforgivably stupid.

Keep in mind that each gangplank could accommodate a single warrior. While the beach was small, it was certainly large enough for the Athenians to spread out. This means that Brasidas faced the far end of the gangplank surrounded by anywhere from three to five Athenian opponents.

But, if we interpret Thucydides correctly, he didn't even make it that far. Thucydides tell us that "*he was cut down by the Athenians, and after receiving many wounds fainted away.*" But even more significant is that Thucydides tells us he fell back into the ship's bow. This tells us two things: first, that Brasidas' trireme had beached bow first, and secondly, that he was taken out by missiles, because if he had gone any distance down the gangplank, he would have fallen onto the beach or into the water. I'm reminded of the harrowing opening scene to the 1998 hit World War II film *Saving Private Ryan* which depicts a Higgins boat dropping its gangplank, only to have the entire crew massacred by machine gun fire before they can disembark.

The results were less dramatic in the 5th century BC, but we can guess from Thucydides' use of "*many wounds*" that Brasidas was peppered with sling stones, javelins and arrows. I picture him falling backward into his ship. There's a punchline to the foolhardy exercise – Thucydides tells us that Brasidas' shield slipped off his arm and fell into the sea.

Most people know the quote from Plutarch, "come back with your shield or on it," the Spartan admonition that it was better to die in battle than cast the shield aside and flee. As discussed above, this quote is likely apocryphal and highly debated (the Spartans buried the dead where they fell or in the nearest friendly territory), but the scholarly consensus is that losing one's shield was highly shameful. The Agora Museum in Athens currently displays a shield believed to be taken from the Spartans at battle and dedicated by the Athenians based on the inscription:

"ΑΘΗΝΑΙΟΙ ΑΠΟ ΛΑΚΕΔΑΙΜΟΝΙΩΝ ΣΚΠΥΛΟ" ("the Athenians from the Spartans at Pylos"). We have no indication that this is Brasidas' lost shield.

Amazingly, Brasidas survived his foolhardy display, but you can imagine how the sight of one of their great heroes felled before he could even come to grips with the enemy must have impacted Spartan morale. Remember how superstitious ancient warriors were and the Spartans most of all. Perhaps this was interpreted as a sign of the gods' disfavor. And it was only the first of multiple Spartan mistakes, as we'll see.

This scene was repeated across the narrow stretch of Athenian-held beach. The Spartan triremes did their best to discharge troops to take it by storm and they were met by committed Athenian resistance at every point. The overwhelming numbers of the Spartans counted for nothing charging down narrow gangplanks or trying to scale sheer cliffs topped with the hastily built Athenian fortifications.

The fighting went on for the rest of that and the following day, but the Spartans could make no headway. A ragged cheer must have risen from the exhausted Athenian ranks as the Spartans withdrew simultaneously from both the land and sea attacks.

But the Athenians were hardly out of the woods. They clung to a tiny patch of ground, walled in atop their cliffs, hemmed in on their scrap of beach. The Spartans completely surrounded them on both land and sea and Demosthenes had to know that his little band of hold-outs wouldn't last long without some way to get supplies.

For now, though, it was enough to strip off their armor and collapse exhausted on the sand, leaving the few unlucky souls stuck with lookout duty to sound the alarm when the Spartans inevitably came on again. They'd made a good accounting of themselves. History would not record them as cowards. But they were hopelessly outnumbered and cut off from support. When the Spartans renewed their assault, Demosthenes must have known they were done for.

And then, from the peak of the northwest cliff, the lookout would have raised the cry that would have set every Athenian heart blazing.

Ships had been spotted rowing south. Their masts and rigging had been stripped off and left on shore; they were moving under oars ready for battle.

The Athenian fleet had returned.

And even better, it was *bigger* than it had been when it left, an additional ten triremes of reinforcements having padded out its ranks. Fifty ships bore down on Sphacteria, ready to meet the Spartans in open water.

CAUGHT NAPPING: THE SPARTANS LOSE THEIR FLEET

The natural harbor at Pylos is entered by two channels, one big one south of Sphacteria and one tiny one north of it. The northern channel, known as the Sikia, can easily be blocked by two triremes. Keeping in mind that there were 420 hoplites and their helot attendants on the island, that meant the Spartans could harass any Athenian ships bottled up in the Sikia with missile fire if they got close enough and could dispatch anyone unlucky enough to go into the water and swim for the southern shore.

Eurymedon and Sophocles must have drummed out all their crews, readying their archers and hoplite marines to meet the Spartans to the west of the island, or readying themselves for a bloody fight in the close confines of the channel.

Miraculously, neither happened.

The Athenian fleet divided and sailed through both the northern and southern channels completely unopposed. Beyond Sphacteria, the smooth waters of the bay welcomed them. The Spartan fleet was visible on the beach, its crew in a panic at the approach of the Athenians, scrambling to shove the triremes out to sea. Incredibly, the Spartans had been caught napping.

No literary source confirms this, but Demosthenes' troops had to be cheering themselves hoarse on shore. The Athenians were absolute masters on the water and the still surface of the bay allowed their gifted helmsmen and skilled rowers to show off their talents to the utmost. The Spartans had barely managed to launch most of their ships before the Athenians slammed into them, bronze rams staving in their hulls, archers raking their decks with arrows. Thucydides tells us that within moments many Spartan ships were sunk or sinking and the rest were backing oars, desperately trying to get away from the unstoppable Athenian tide. The Athenians captured five of the Spartan triremes right off the bat, one with its crew still on board (and presumably taken prisoner). The rest were dragged frantically up onto the beach in the hopes that the Spartans would be better able to defend them from the shore than on the water.

But the Athenians weren't fools. They played to their strength, continuing to ram and disable the Spartan ships in the shallow water. Here and there, they directed their crews to throw lines around the enemy triremes, towing them out into the water where they could be captured.

Almost immediately, it became apparent that the landlubbing Spartans had all but lost their fleet, leaving the Athenians the undisputed masters of the harbor, the bay and the water all around the island of Sphacteria – where 420 Spartan hoplites watched in horror, realizing that they were about to be cut off.

The Spartans on shore realized this too and rushed madly into the ocean to try to drag their captured triremes back. Thucydides describes the scene as the Spartans engaging in a *"sea battle on land"* in reference to the Athenians smashing and capturing their ships even while they were drawn up on the shore, and the Athenians engaging in a *"land battle on the sea"* in reference to the fierce hand-to-hand fighting in the water as the Spartans desperately sought to win back their captured ships.

When the fighting was finally done, the Spartans had managed to get their ships back (except the first five that had been captured), but their fleet was hopelessly disabled, and they were confined to the shore. The battle was clearly over, and the usual post-battle rituals ensued. The victorious Athenians set up a trophy of captured arms and armor (and possibly a ship's ram or two), likely on the tiny island of Chelonisi in the center of the bay, returned the Spartan dead, and secured the captured ships. They then immediately began patrolling the shores off Sphacteria, making certain the Spartans there could neither escape nor receive aid.

The defeated Spartans, lacking any chance of getting back out onto the water without being immediately crushed by the Athenian fleet, could only watch helplessly from shore.

The news of the stranded Spartans on Sphacteria sent shock waves through the city. Thucydides says *"the authorities,"* by which he likely means at least one of the kings, the ephors and members of the *gerousia*, immediately went out to Pylos and an armistice was declared.

The terms of the armistice were humiliating for the Spartans. They were ordered to turn over the entire fleet – *all* 60 ships they had just fought so hard to keep. If they did this, the Athenians would permit them to send a small amount of food and supplies to the stranded Spartans (under watchful Athenian eyes, of course) and both sides would refrain from fighting while Sparta sent envoys to Athens to negotiate a larger deal to secure the release of what now could only be termed the Spartan captives. The 420 hoplites and their attendants were still armed, armored and capable of fighting, but Sphacteria was a prison nonetheless.

That the Spartans agreed to these terms shows how desperate they were to retrieve their captured countrymen. It's also a stunning refutation of the Spartan myth of selfless sacrifice. In the Thermopylae myth, the Spartans had gladly thrown away 300 Spartan lives to preserve Sparta's sacred honor. We have heard time and again about Spartans who committed suicide rather than live with shame. The number on Sphacteria was not that much greater than at Thermopylae and the price the Athenians demanded, 60 triremes, would certainly set back the Spartan war effort significantly, particularly in a domain where Athens was already dominant. Judging from the Thermopylae story, we'd reasonably expect the Spartans to shrug and say, "Those are Spartans, they will find a way back to us or die trying."

But of course, the 420 men on that island were fathers and sons, brothers and cousins. They were loved and needed and their return was hotly desired by a society that, like *all* human societies, cared for its members.

Thucydides' quoting of the Spartan delegation's speech at Athens underscores this. These are not the words of haughty strongmen. The Spartans do everything but beg for their people back. "*We beg you to take our words, not in a hostile tone, nor as if we were lecturing the ignorant, but rather as a suggestion to intelligent judges.*" A far cry from the laconic, warlike quips put in the mouths of Leonidas and Dieneces at Thermopylae. The stark difference between the mythic Spartans at Thermopylae and the all too real ones at Pylos is abundantly clear.

The only vaguely warlike portion of the speech was the Spartan warning that amounted to "the wheel turns," noting that the Spartans might be in a bad position now, but the Athenians' turn would eventually come. But this warning is clearly contextualized by the rest of the speech as a desperate attempt to convince the Athenians to make peace, which Sparta offered on absolutely intimate and unconditional terms.

I have said before that Sparta did not win any phase of the Peloponnesian Wars. Rather, Athens lost each one. The Spartan overture was an incredible opportunity tossed in the trash by Athens. Thucydides tells us the general consensus was to grasp for concessions (including the return of critical *poleis* that they knew Sparta would never relinquish), but special consideration has to be reserved for Cleon, an Athenian populist who rose to power in the wake of Pericles' demise.

We have to take what we know of Cleon with a grain of salt, as it's clear that Thucydides hated the man and did his best to present him in the worst possible light. But, if we believe Thucydides, Cleon blasted the Spartan delegation, accusing them of deceit and double dealing. The Spartans endured this with something approaching dignity and returned to Pylos with nothing accomplished. The armistice was canceled and Sparta resumed its land-based assaults on the fortified position on the cliffs and beach. Meanwhile, Athens reinforced its fleet up to 70 triremes and continued to patrol around the island, day and night.

The travel to and from Athens, inclusive of the negotiations, took 20 days, during which the scorching Greek summer meandered from boiling July into blistering August. The Spartans on the island began to starve.

Sphacteria has just one spring in the center of the island, brackish and weak. The Spartans called for volunteers to run the Athenian blockade, promising pay to any freeman, or freedom to any helot who would risk his life swimming or boating to the island under cover of darkness to deliver critical supplies. You might be surprised to think that any of these got through with 70 Athenian triremes around the island, but keep in mind that Sphacteria is roughly 1.2 square miles and that the western shore gets some pretty rough seas depending on the weather, tough going for a patrolling trireme. Also keep in mind that the 5th century BC was a world lit only by fire, without spotlights, flares or any other means to pick out a single swimmer or small fishing boat with a floating net full of supplies in tow.

The Athenians had supply problems of their own, with Spartan troops likely making it impossible to forage on the land. All the needed food and fresh water had to be brought in by sea, where fortunately the Athenians were in complete command. A stalemate ensued, with the Spartans on Sphacteria holding doggedly on and the Spartans on the shore unable to dislodge the Athenians from their holdout on Pylos. Meanwhile, supplies dwindled and the Athenians began to struggle to keep themselves fed and watered as well.

As we've already seen, the Athenians were incredibly fickle when it came to military policy and as soon as the thrill of the engagement dwindled into the slog of a siege, they regretted refusing the Spartan peace overture. They blamed Cleon (rightly, in my opinion). Cleon lied about the situation at Pylos and then tried to pin the responsibility on someone else, saying that the Athenian Nicias, his main political rival and one of the *stratēgoi* (generals) for the year, should lead a force to Sphacteria to capture and kill the hold-outs there. "If I were general, that's what I'd do!"

The plan backfired. Nicias and the other *stratēgoi* replied that if Cleon wanted to do this, he was welcome to try. Cleon, no warrior, immediately tried to backpedal, but the damage was done. Thucydides sets the scene clearly:

> *Nicias repeated his offer, resigned the command against Pylos and called the Athenians to witness that he did so. And as the crowd does, the more Cleon shrank from the expedition and tried to back out of what he had said, the more they encouraged Nicias to hand over his command, and shouted for Cleon to go.*

At last, terrified but unable to back out, Cleon was forced to agree to lead an army to Sphacteria to face the Spartans.

Cleon was nothing if not a masterful politician. As soon as he realized he couldn't get out of it, he immediately stated that he wasn't afraid of the Spartans and that he would accomplish the mission without bothering a single Athenian citizen (to be fair to Cleon, nearly all male Athenian citizens of his rank would have had some experience training as hoplites). Instead, he would take only allied troops currently in Athens, men from Lemnos and Imbros, as well as some Thracian peltasts – probably expert light infantry and crack javelineers. He also took 400 archers, likely Scythian and Cretan mercenaries. With this force, Cleon swore he would end the stalemate on Sphacteria in 20 days. He departed in the midst of heckling and laughter.

While Cleon was making his way to Sphacteria, the Athenian cause had an unexpected stroke of luck (or a deliberate smart move, depending on whether or not you believe Thucydides). The Athenian patrols were putting in on the shore of Sphacteria to take meals and get off the trireme for a while, probably keeping close to the ship, ready to launch if the Spartans sought to engage them. One of these sailors, making a cooking fire for his lunch, started a forest fire (it's also possible the fire was deliberately set). The fire spread across the island and by the time the smoke cleared, a large part of the ground cover was burned away.

Thucydides doesn't report any reaction on the part of the Spartans on the island, but you can imagine them fleeing the smoke and fire, racing to those patches somehow spared by the flames, coughing and choking. If any died in the blaze, Thucydides doesn't tell us.

This was a huge boon to the Athenians. It made the Spartans on the island more vulnerable to missiles from Athenian archers, *psiloi* and peltasts. More importantly, it eliminated the Spartans' ability to hide and strike from ambush. Sphacteria had been reduced to a blackened, clear (though not level) field. Any fight now would be a field battle – and one that would not favor the hopelessly outnumbered, starving and smoke-addled Spartans.

With the island clear, Demosthenes was now able to see the exact number of the Spartans and where they were located. He immediately began to put a plan into motion to storm the place. Just as this was getting moving, Cleon arrived and the two forces linked up. They immediately sent a message to the main Spartan camp on the shore at Pylos, demanding the surrender of the men on Sphacteria. This move surely announced their intention to the Spartans both on the island and on shore, but it was clear there was nothing they could do to stop it regardless. The Spartans, perhaps stung by their reception at Athens, refused terms. Cleon and Demosthenes waited another day and then launched their assault.

ASSAULT ON SPHACTERIA

They landed their assault force on both sides of the island, some 800 hoplites and around ten times as many light troops – *psiloi*, archers and peltasts. We don't know the exact extent of the fire. It would take a pretty epic blaze to completely deforest 1.2 square miles and we can infer from the lack of reported Spartan casualties that the fire didn't completely consume the island. But we also know from Thucydides' descriptions of Demosthenes being able to see Spartan numbers and positions from the shore of Pylos that the land had to be relatively clear.

Which makes the Spartans' next mistake hard to believe.

First – you need to understand the island. Sphacteria is narrow and cigar-shaped, running pretty much north–south. Its northern end, which forms the southern boundary of the Sikia channel, is its highest point, forming a cliff-peak that is called Mount Elias in the present day. From the heights of Mount Elias, the island runs pretty much gradually downhill until it flattens out at the one spring I mentioned earlier, about halfway along the island's length.

Thucydides tells us that the Spartans had set up a *"first"* outpost on the southern end of the island consisting of 30 hoplites (he gives no indication of how many of these were Peers, but we should assume as least one to act as an officer). The *"main"* portion of the Spartans held the island's center, sticking close to their one water source. Another small force held the heights at Mount Elias on the island's north end.

We don't know exactly where the Athenians put ashore, but Thucydides does tell us they began their assault before dawn with the 800 hoplites, while it was likely still dark, and *"moved at a run"* toward the Spartans' southern outpost.

Now, I get that it was dark, but what happened next is mystifying. Keep in mind that the island had been largely cleared of cover by the fire, granting a clear view of the assault force. Also remember that Demosthenes and Cleon had just demanded the stranded Spartans' surrender the day before, clearly signaling their intent to assault the island. This information was surely conveyed to the Spartans on the island by signals or blockade runners. Heck, Sphacteria was close enough to the Pylos shore in places that they could probably just yell it across to them.

You'd think the Spartans would have set watches, that it would have been impossible to take them by surprise.

And yet they were taken by surprise, totally and completely.

Thucydides reports that, as with the fleet's initial arrival in the harbor, the Athenians came upon the southern outpost completely unawares, *"the men being scarcely out of bed and still arming."* Thucydides gives the excuse that the Spartans thought *"the ships were only sailing as usual to their positions for the night,"* but this makes absolutely no sense to me. Either way, you can picture the Spartans hearing the crunching of Athenian feet on the ash carpet the fire had left on the island, scrambling up and racing to their weapons, only to be cut down before they could even grab their spears.

It was an unforgivable lack of vigilance and may be an indication of how starved and exhausted the Spartans were after more than two months of being stranded on Sphacteria in the grueling summer heat. They'd have picked the place clean within days, and relied entirely on the short rations the blockade runners had been able to sneak to them.

It is also another deflation of the Spartan myth of warrior supremacy. The placement and keeping of watches is the most basic and fundamental aspect of any military operation. This was the *second* utter failure to observe even this basic principle of warfare (the first being allowing the Athenian fleet to catch them unawares), with the same disastrous consequences. If we assume an equal number of helots were killed at the southern outpost, then the Spartans had already lost 7 percent of their force on Sphacteria without a single Athenian casualty.

Day broke as this bloody act was completed and now Demosthenes put his *psiloi* ashore:

> ... *all the crews of over seventy ships, except the lowest rank of oars, with the weapons they carried, eight hundred archers, and as many peltasts, the Messenian reinforcements, and all the other troops on duty around Pylos, except the garrison of the fort.*

This was a staggering force to take on just 390 Spartan hoplites and their helot attendants and is a tremendous compliment to the Spartans, clear evidence of their reputation as masters of infantry battle.

Demosthenes split his overwhelming force into companies of 200, ordering them to seize every rise on the island. The huge force completely surrounded the Spartans, pelting them with missiles from all sides.

The Athenian hoplites, meanwhile, stood off and grounded their spears, watching from a distance. The Spartans behaved exactly as expected, marching to fight the kind of battle they preferred – hoplite to hoplite – shield against shield.

The Athenian *psiloi* made this impossible. With every step, the Spartans were peppered with javelins, rocks, sling stones and arrows, denting bronze, piercing cloth and flesh, shattering bone. The helots would have done their level best to return fire, but keep in mind that the Spartans a.) didn't prioritize missile combat, thinking of it as an effeminate way to fight, and b.) were very careful not to provide military training to helots for fear it would be used against them when those helots inevitably revolted. So, we can imagine the helots were no match for the better trained, better fed and better rested Athenian missile troops. Eventually casualties would have begun to mount and at last the Spartan heavy infantry tried to deal with the *psiloi* themselves.

Certain members of a hoplite phalanx were sometimes designated *ekdromoi* (runners-out). These would have been younger, fitter men, judged able to exit the phalanx to fight in skirmish order against lighter troops (this tactic was likely tied to the trend of jettisoning heavy armor that we discussed in chapter I). There's some evidence that *ekdromoi* were more lightly equipped than other hoplites in earlier times, but by 425 BC, nearly all hoplites had given up body armor, the closed-face Corinthian helmet, and in some cases even the bronze greaves. It's likely that most of the Spartans would have been equipped only with the *aspis* shield, their spear and the open *pilos* helmet, a conical affair that protected only the top and back of the head, leaving the face, ears and neck entirely open.

This choice reflects the Spartan disdain for missile weapons. In a stand-up fight with other heavy infantry, this helmet makes a lot more sense and is a worthwhile risk for the improved visibility, hearing and heat dispersal. But against a shower of missiles, the Spartans must have quickly regretted the choice. Thucydides hints at this, saying "*their caps would not keep out the arrows,*" which I believe is a reference to the *pilos'* open face.

The *ekdromoi* dashed out from the Spartan phalanx, killing a *psilos* here and there, but even lightly armed as they were, they couldn't match the speed of the *psiloi*, many of whom wore no armor at all and carried no shields. Some may have even fought nude. While this made them more vulnerable to wounds, it made them *much* faster than even the fastest Spartan hoplite. Thucydides describes the Athenian *psiloi* fleeing from the Spartan attempts to close with them, then dashing back to start peppering them with missiles the instant the Spartans gave up the chase.

He's also careful to describe the dust and the noise made by such a huge number of combatants, pointing out that within moments, the Spartans could neither see nor hear the commands of their officers. And as the August dawn came on in earnest, it would only have gotten hotter and hotter, until even the simple *pilos* bronze cap must have begun to feel like an oven, the *aspis* shields as heavy as anvils. At last the Spartans had had enough. They retreated in good order to the north, harassed all the way, to the occupied heights of Mount Elias.

The main body was wounded and exhausted, but at least they could be relieved by the fresh troops holding the high ground and I can imagine them collapsing as their comrades surged forward, locking shields against the storm of missiles, anchoring their flanks on the homemade walls the Spartans had thrown up during their long occupation. The troops of the main body would have been desperate for water, but there was none to be had unless it had been stockpiled on the heights (unlikely, given the short supply), as they were so far from the island's single spring. The break from the fighting would have been something, but it is likely that the majority of the Spartan troops were wounded and exhausted and unable to do more than rest while their fresh comrades held the line.

And hold it they did. The Athenians may have been running low on missiles at this point (having to be resupplied by sea) other than the rocks that were plentiful enough. They were also attacking uphill and likely exhausted themselves from the running battle they had just fought on the center of the island.

A stalemate ensued, with the Spartans able to keep the Athenians from surrounding them again, but with nowhere else to go, the sheer cliffs of Mount Elias at their backs. Here the two forces settled in, the Spartans appearing intent on holding the high ground to the last man. The Athenians no doubt were thinking of Thermopylae and the heroic struggle of the 300.

Or perhaps not.

Thucydides makes a critical point regarding the running fight with the *psiloi*, one that speaks most importantly to the clash between the legend of the Spartans and the reality of fighting them. The Athenians:

> *... were now more familiar with his* [the Spartan Peer's] *aspect and found him less terrible, the result not having justified the fears which they had suffered, when they first landed in slavish worry at the idea of attacking Spartans; and accordingly their fear changing to disdain, they now rushed all together with loud shouts upon them, and pelted them with stones, javelins and arrows, whichever came first to hand.*

In other words, the Athenians had been terrified because of the *legend* of Spartan prowess, but when they actually faced them in battle, they quickly realized that they were just men, like any other. With that realization, they had pressed their attack home. Even before the final stalemate, Sphacteria had fatally punctured the myth of Spartan supremacy for thousands of Athenians.

But there was a final Spartan lapse yet to come. The remaining Spartans focused all their attention to the front and downhill, relying on the sheer cliffs of Mount Elias to protect their backs.

This would have been a sound strategy if the cliffs had been truly too steep to scale.

But they weren't.

Comon (we have his name from Pausanias, not Thucydides), the commander of the Messenian allies, noticed this immediately and asked Cleon for a detachment of troops to find a way around into the Spartan rear.

Thucydides spells out beautifully what happened next:

> *Upon receiving what he asked for, he* [Comon] *started from a point out of sight in order not to be seen by the enemy, and creeping on wherever the cliffs of the island permitted, and where the Spartans, trusting to the strength of the ground, kept no guard, succeeded after the greatest difficulty in getting round without their seeing him, and suddenly appeared on the high ground in their rear, to the dismay of the surprised enemy and the still greater joy of his expectant friends. The Spartans thus were between two fires, and in the same dilemma, to compare small things with great, as at Thermopylae, where the defenders were cut off through the Persians getting around by the path, being now attacked in front and behind ...*

He was absolutely right. This was *precisely* the same scenario as Thermopylae, with the exhausted Spartans spun up and ready to repeat the same performance, selling their lives dearly. Holding their post until death.

But there was one key difference. At Sphacteria, the Spartans surrendered.

Their capitulation had to be as shocking to the Athenians as it would later be to the entire Greek world. Thucydides tells us the negotiations were held with Styphon, son of Pharax, the Spartans' third in command. Their commander, Epitadas, had been killed in the fighting. Their second in command, Hippagretas, was thought dead, though Thucydides notes he was still alive but left for dead among the corpses. Thucydides also tells us that most of the Spartans immediately surrendered the instant the Athenian herald made the offer, underscoring that this was *not* an unpopular decision by a weak junior commander. This was the overwhelming desire of *most* of the Spartan troops.

We must give the Spartans on Sphacteria credit. They held out under brutal conditions – they endured searing heat, lack of supplies and one of the most lopsided running fights in ancient history. Thucydides tells us they endured on Sphacteria for an incredible 72 days, surviving solely on what blockade runners could ferry across. By any measure, they performed extraordinarily well.

But they also put the final nail in the coffin of the Spartan warrior myth. These men, not even two generations after Thermopylae, wanted to *live*. Their desire to return home to their families, to continue breathing the sweet air, was more important to them than Demaratus' quote from Herodotus that I gave earlier – that Spartans *"must abide at their post and there conquer or die."*

Spartans were humans. And, as with all humans, the desire to keep on breathing is more powerful than any law or ideal in the world.

Thucydides conveys the utter shock at this unexpected turn:

> *Nothing that happened in the war surprised the Greeks* [note that Thucydides says this surrender shocked all of Greece, not just the Athenians] *so much as this. It was the opinion that no force or famine could make the Spartans give up their weapons, but that they would fight on as they could, and die with them in their hands: indeed people could scarcely believe that those who had surrendered were of the same stuff as the fallen ...*

Cleon, amazingly, was as good as his word. A total of 292 Spartans were taken alive. Of these, 120 were the elite Peers. The rest, we can assume, were *perioikoi*, as helots would not have been mentioned. The Spartans had suffered a horrific 30 percent casualty rate in the assault.

Thucydides closes the story of the battle with an indicator that the shock at the surrender rattled the Spartans as much as it did the rest of the Greeks, but not so much that they abandoned their own legend. Faced with direct and concrete proof of their own humanity, the Spartan prisoners rejected it, scrambling for an excuse, a reason to justify their failure.

The answer they settled on was the "effeminate" choice of missile weapons to lay them low. Thucydides has one of the Spartan prisoners referring to the Athenian arrows as "spindles," comparing them to the main tool used for the weaving of cloth. In other words, women's work. In response to a barb from an Athenian ally, this Spartan complained that an arrow couldn't tell a coward from a brave man. The implication was that missile weapons made combat random and somehow unfair. In matched combat, hoplite to hoplite, the Spartans would have won. This is probably true, but warfare is a constantly shifting, adaptive field, as the Athenians clearly understood. Here, as we have already seen and will see in later chapters, Spartan conservatism was ultimately a disabling casualty.

The defeat at Sphacteria shifted the momentum of the Archidamian phase of the Peloponnesian Wars. Where before it was a grinding stalemate, Athens now suddenly seemed ascendant. Helots deserted to the free Messenians now garrisoning Pylos. The Spartans continued to plead both for peace and for the return of their captured Peers, demands that Athens, thinking it had the definite upper hand, denied. But what Thucydides leaves unmentioned is the shift in the reputation of the Spartan hoplite. Thousands of light-armed troops would have returned from the fight at Sphacteria to spread the story of their experience there – the tale that, when you went toe to toe with a Spartan, even a vaunted Peer trained under the brutal Upbringing, he bled and died like other men, fled like other men, and surrendered like other men.

The Spartans were, of course, terrified by the presence of a Messenian-garrisoned Pylos. They had fought three long and bitter wars against their helot population and they rightly understood that the temptation to desert would be too high for many helots to resist. Thucydides tells us that they dealt with this using treachery that's pretty unsurprising from the society that invented the crypteia. The Spartans announced they would free those helots who had given the "*best service in war*" (another indication that helots did indeed fight). When 2,000 of these helots had been put forward, the Spartans put "*crowns on their heads and went in procession about the temples*" before spiriting them away and slaughtering them all. The goal, of course, had not been to reward the best helot warriors, but to identify the ones who were most likely to threaten the Spartans should they join their Messenian comrades garrisoning Pylos. Scholars dispute whether or not this story is true, but it certainly fits with what else we know of Spartan treatment of helots.

The summer after Sphacteria, Nicias took advantage of Sparta being knocked back and led the Athenian fleet to ravage the Laconian coast. He first captured the island of Cythera, precisely what the Spartans had feared for centuries. It became the perfect base for Athenian coastal raiding with fast triremes and light-armed troops. This move forced the Spartans to finally get the message on their need for a mobile, light-armed force (exactly what they had lacked on Sphacteria). Thucydides tells us the Spartans raised a troop of cavalry and archers *"against their custom."* It's an important note in Sparta's military history, like Archidamus' adaptation during the siege of Plataea. The Spartans were slow to adapt, but that doesn't mean they didn't do it at all.

Perhaps as a reaction to slaughter of the 2,000 helots, or if you believe the story is false, as an alternative to it, 700 helots were equipped as hoplites, assigned to Brasidas' command and sent north. The reward for these *brasideioi* (Brasidas' men) was the promise of freedom once they had proved their loyalty by serving in battle.

The Athenians made clear that another invasion of Attica would result in the execution of the Spartan Peers captured at Sphacteria. This was a loss that the Spartans, deep in the grip of their Peer manpower shortage, were simply unwilling to accept. However, that threat did not apply to northern Greece, where the Macedonian king Perdiccas II agreed to support Spartan operations against Athenian interests in Thrace.

That Brasidas undertook this mission commanding a helot force probably means that with Pylos garrisoned and Nicias raiding the Laconian coast, the Spartans absolutely couldn't send an army of Peers abroad. It's also a possible sign that the helot massacre didn't work and that the helot population remained as restive and dangerous as before, possibly even more so if word of the murder spread and inflamed anger among the families of the slain 2,000. Brasidas also hired an additional 1,000 Peloponnesian mercenaries, no doubt doing double duty as both troops and minders for their *brasideioi* colleagues in case they got the idea that maybe avenging their people on Brasidas seemed like a sweeter prize than freedom.

No doubt as Brasidas mustered at the isthmus of Corinth, the generation-long peace with Argos was on his mind. In just three years, it would expire, potentially bringing a powerful enemy into the war on Athens' side. But he didn't have time to worry. Athens aided a pro-democracy faction at Megara, taking the city's port of Nisea. Megara wasn't in Attica, so Brasidas was free to intervene without risking the lives of the captured Peers. He took his 1,700 to Megara, and was joined by a substantial force of Corinthian, Sicyonian and Phliasian allies. This already sizable force was joined by an equally impressive muster of Boeotians – their cavalry did the only fighting of the event, skirmishing with Athenian horsemen before breaking off. Brasidas' army and the Athenians engaged in a standoff, until the Megarians, seeing the Athenians refused to attack a superior force, admitted Brasidas into the city. This can't be reckoned as a battle, but it was surely a Spartan victory (Athens kept the port of Nisea).

The encounter surely boosted Brasidas' morale as he turned back to his initial mission, moving his men to Thrace to join Perdiccas. Thucydides relates a fairly impressive story of Brasidas cleverly outmaneuvering the Athenian-allied Thessalians to cross their territory without a fight, reaching Perdiccas in short order. But this was just the first example of Brasidas' skill as a commander. Whatever stupidity he displayed in his suicidally brave charge down the gangplank at Pylos was made up for by the cunning he showed in Thrace. Through a combination of flat-out lies, intimidation and artful diplomacy he convinced the cities of Acanthus and Stagirus to revolt against the Delian League.

But the real prize in the north was the Athenian-allied city of Amphipolis, which in addition to providing critical resources to Athens also controlled the crossing of the Strymon river. In a daring surprise attack, he placed the city under siege and offered safe passage to anyone who wished to leave, as well as promising not to pillage the goods of those who remained. Eucles, the Athenian general stationed inside the city, sent a desperate plea for help to the nearest Athenian force – seven ships stationed at nearby Thasos under the command of none other than Thucydides, the very writer whose account forms pretty much our sole narrative for most of the Peloponnesian Wars.

Brasidas' offer was too good to pass up and the city surrendered without a fight before Thucydides could arrive – he wound up picking up the refugees who fled under the terms of Brasidas' offer, including Eucles.

Assault on Eion

Thucydides put in at the nearby city of Eion, garrisoning it with his own troops and the refugees. Here, there was a fight, and one that went badly for Brasidas. Thucydides references himself in the third person, describing how he defeated Brasidas' attempts to take Eion by both land and water. Thucydides doesn't lavish himself with praise for this successful defense and Athens surely didn't either. Thucydides' home city blamed him for the loss of Amphipolis and sent him into exile for the next 20 years.

Meanwhile, Brasidas' taking of Amphipolis certainly sent the message that the Peloponnesian League was the winning horse to be backed in the north. Three more cities revolted from the Delian League in rapid succession. He then took the city of Torone (on the middle of the three "fingers" of land extending south from modern-day Thessaloniki) with the help of some pro-Spartan traitors who opened the gates for him. Again, while this is a Spartan victory, it can't be reckoned a battle. Thucydides notes that the only potential resistance was a garrison of 50 Athenian warriors asleep in the marketplace who all fled the moment Brasidas' army came howling through the open gate.

While this doesn't speak positively of Sparta's battlefield record, it most certainly *does* speak positively of Brasidas' cunning. He was proving incredibly successful at taking cities *without* a fight. Thucydides describes his brilliance in a great passage:

> For Brasidas both showed himself otherwise very moderate, and also gave out in speech that he was sent forth to recover the liberty of Greece. And the cities which were subject to the Athenians, hearing of the taking of Amphipolis, and what assurance he brought with him, and of his gentleness besides, were extremely desirous of innovation, and sent messengers privily to bid him draw near, every one striving who should first revolt.

The point is abundantly clear – Brasidas is counted one of Sparta's greatest war leaders *not* for his performance on the battlefield, but because of his ability to avoid battles altogether. Is it possible that the wounds he took at Pylos taught him a valuable lesson? That he maybe rethought the wisdom of charging in headlong? We can never know, but one thing is certain – the

Brasidas who marched north into Thrace was surely a different man than the one who lost his shield at Pylos.

Brasidas might have liberated all of Thrace from the Delian League, but his own government cut him off at the knees. Desperate to get the captured Peers back, they negotiated a one-year peace with Athens. This may also have been partially driven by a desire to undercut Brasidas, whose success and fame had to be bothering the Spartan leadership who had already repeatedly demonstrated a cultural tendency to knife their own. Despite the peace, two more cities rebelled from the Delian League and went over to Sparta. Brasidas garrisoned them against future attack.

Lyncestis

Brasidas then joined Perdiccas in the Macedonian king's campaign to conquer the Macedonian "Lynx's Land" of Lyncestis. A battle was fought against a combined Illyrian and Lyncestian army in 423 BC, which initially went well for Perdiccas and Brasidas, but when a force of Illyrian mercenaries whom Perdiccas had hired went over to the enemy, the king lost his nerve. He withdrew his Macedonian troops and their allies during the night, leaving Brasidas and his force cut off and heavily outnumbered.

But Brasidas' cunning covered him in glory once again. He formed his heavy infantry into a square with his light troops in the center. He also made good use of the *ekdromoi* – the same runners-out that the Spartans had used less successfully at Sphacteria. After a rousing speech, he began to have this box-formation crab-step its way to the rear, fighting off the enemy the entire way. The formation moved painfully slowly, allowing the more lightly armed and quicker Illyrian troops to encircle it. Brasidas quickly realized this would surely mean the end if he didn't act. He gave the order for 300 picked troops to break through the encirclement and take a nearby hill which his army could use as a rallying point. These 300 carved a bloody and victorious path to the objective and secured it. The rest of the army followed and was able to move from there to safety. It was a Spartan defeat, to be sure, but one so brilliantly and courageously managed that it prevented what could have been a catastrophe.

The whole event had a punchline – the Spartans, furious at being abandoned by their Macedonian allies, pillaged Perdiccas' territory in response. The Macedonian king, enraged at having his lands despoiled, went over to Athens. After all of Brasidas' success gaining allies without fighting, he finished by losing his most important ally when he actually did fight. Perdiccas proved himself a very powerful ally to Athens, effectively preventing any meaningful Spartan reinforcements from reaching the north.

With Perdiccas' defection, it seemed that Brasidas' luck had finally turned. In his next attempt to take a city (Potidaea) by surprise, his scaling ladder was discovered by a sentry, forcing him to wave off.

Amphipolis

Brasidas' luck finally ran out completely in 422 BC, when the one-year truce ended and Athens sent Cleon north at the head of a sizable army. He retook Torone, then linked up with Perdiccas and together they prepared to retake Amphipolis. Brasidas marshaled an army to defend the city and conceived another daring tactical plan to punch a hole in Cleon's center with a picked band of 150 warriors. Cleon lost his nerve as the Spartan army mustered, but bungled his own withdrawal, leaving his army open for attack. Brasidas took advantage of the confusion and mounted a devastating strike that killed Cleon and 600 Athenians and allies. Amphipolis remained secure at the cost of just seven Spartan lives.

Sadly, one of them was Brasidas, expiring just after he learned he had won. He was named a hero and interred in Amphipolis. A silver urn mounted on four lion's feet and crowned with a golden wreath of oak leaves is still displayed at the Amphipolis Archaeological Museum. Scholars dispute whether or not it contains his remains, but I believe that it does.

The Peace of Nicias

Cleon and Brasidas had been major voices for the continuation of the war, and with both of them dead, Athens and Sparta had had enough (Thucydides is clear that Cleon was a major obstacle to peace on the Athenian side). In 421 BC Pleistoanax (recalled from exile likely with some help from a bribed Delphic oracle) and Nicias agreed to the Peace of Nicias.

The Peers captured at Sphacteria were finally returned and Athens agreed to aid Sparta in the event of an attack or a helot revolt. The Archidamian phase of the Peloponnesian Wars was over six years after the death of the man it was named for, and after a decade of futile battling back and forth that accomplished nothing at the cost of countless lives. Both Athens and Sparta remained much as they had been when Archidamus argued against starting hostilities in the first place.

Sparta's record in the Archidamian phase of the Peloponnesian Wars

Sparta's battlefield performance during the Archidamian phase was lackluster at best. Of the 12 battles we've discussed, they won just three, losing the other nine. Most critically, the surrender of the Peers at Sphacteria had severely damaged Sparta's reputation in ways that would surely embolden its enemies in the coming years. It also saw the killing of Eurylochus and Menedaeus' willingness to sell out his allies to save his own skin. Even Sparta's victories were tarnished – Archidamus' taking of Plataea *after* allowing half the defenders to escape, the victory at Corcyra followed by fleeing in the face of Athenian naval reinforcements.

A Stillborn Peace

The Peace of Nicias was arranged for 50 years, long enough to let memories of the atrocities fade and for a new generation of politicians to come to the fore, hopefully people who would be less warlike than their fathers.

It was a fool's hope. The promised 50 years of peace lasted only eight before Athens and Sparta were once again in open war.

The peace was fraying even as it was made. One of the conditions was the return of Amphipolis to Athens, a concession the Spartans were unable to make in the face of overwhelming Amphipolitan resistance. The Athenians answered this by refusing to return Pylos.

However, neither side could have prepared for the emergence of the Athenian statesman and general Alcibiades, whose good looks and personal magnetism were matched only by his utter ruthlessness and desire for personal gain. He was ardently opposed to peace with Sparta and worked tirelessly to unwind the fragile truce from the moment it was agreed.

Considering the return of the 120 Peers captured at Sphacteria to Sparta, we must think back to the two Spartan survivors of Thermopylae in 480 BC. Both were ordered away from the battle – one of them (Aristodemus) due to an eye infection, and the other (Pantites) sent on a diplomatic mission to Thessaly. Both men were ostracized and publicly humiliated for having the temerity to live, and both committed suicide (Aristodemus by charging out of the line at Plataea, and Pantites by hanging himself).

But that was two men at a time when the body of Peers was much larger. Now, Sparta was confronted by having to deal with 120 of the highest-ranked members of their society. By Spartan law, they should have been punished as "tremblers" and denied the ability to serve in government or buy and sell, but these were men from rich families, highly connected and influential. So, it is not surprising that at first they weren't punished at all. Punishment came later and only when the Spartan authorities feared that failing to do so might start a revolution. What punishments were administrated were later rescinded (though we're not sure exactly when), possibly as the rich families of the former captives spread around money and influence to undo the sentence.

In the end, the Peers were reintegrated into Spartan society. It seemed that surrendering had become socially tolerable in Sparta after all, provided that enough Peers did it at once and that their families were connected enough and had deep enough pockets to stand up for their relatives.

The 700 hundred *brasideioi* were another problem. They were free now, but still had the memory of the oppression they'd suffered as helots, albeit now coupled with military training honed by campaigning at Megara and in the north under Brasidas. Sparta settled them mostly around Lepreum on the border with Elis, which couldn't have helped the already high tensions with that city-state.

Sparta also allied with Thebes which technically violated the Peace of Nicias (the Thebans hadn't signed on to the treaty, and so were ineligible to be allies). Alcibiades seized on this to goad Athens into making an anti-Spartan alliance with already aggravated Elis and also Mantinea and Argos, with whom Sparta's 30-year peace had finally expired. The proverbial ink on the Peace of Nicias wasn't even dry before new battle lines were being drawn.

Thucydides reports that in the summer of 421 BC Pleistoanax led a Spartan army to liberate the Parhassians from Mantinean control and to demolish a Mantinean fort. Thucydides notes that the Mantineans marshaled to fight but apparently thought better of it and retreated without engaging the Spartan army. No battle appears to have been fought, but Pleistoanax ravaged the region and likely deepened the animosity between Sparta and the new Argos–Elis–Mantinea axis, and no doubt their Athenian backers.

This may seem like an act of Spartan aggression, but it was at least partly justified as Mantinea had been aggressively expanding its own power while Sparta was occupied with Athens. This ambition was beginning to seriously threaten Spartan security and prompted Pleistoanax to act.

Argos, feeling emboldened by its new alliance and still burning from its historical enmity with Sparta (I doubt the Argives would ever forget what Cleomenes had done to them), marched on Sparta's ally of Epidaurus. King Agis II mustered the army to respond ... and promptly came up with a wealth of religious excuses (unfavorable omens when the pre-border-crossing sacrifices were made and also the festival of the Carneia) as to why they couldn't go to war. Both Thucydides and Diodorus seem convinced that the religious objections were genuine, and Thucydides is hardly a pro-Spartan partisan. This is hard for me to accept based on previous religious excuses for Sparta delaying or avoiding a fight, but I must admit at least the possibility that Agis believed he was limited by religious restrictions.

And also this – Agis II was the son of Archidamus II, the same king who had struggled in vain to end the phase of the Peloponnesian Wars that bear his name. It's possible that his son was impressed by his father's efforts and tried to imitate them, seeking off-ramps to conflict. If this is true, it is commendable, but also another hole poked in the Bronze Lie of supremely brave Spartans spoiling for a fight whenever possible.

Epidaurus

In 419 BC, Sparta garrisoned Epidaurus against the Argives, giving Alcibiades the justification he needed to accuse Sparta of violating the Peace of Nicias. This tiny garrison (just 300 Spartans – we don't know if they were Peers or not – under the command of one Agesippidas) managed to repel an Argive attempt to take the city by storm in the winter.

By the following summer Agis finally sprang into action. He marched on Argos with a full muster, including all of the allies. The Argives matched him with an army nearly as large and both forces maneuvered in what looked like to be an intensely bloody battle. At the last minute, however, the Argive general Thrasyllus brokered a deal with Agis and got the Spartan king to agree to a four-month truce. The negotiations appear to have been largely secret and impromptu, and Agis did not inform his commanders or allies of what was happening. As far as they knew, the two armies had drawn up for battle, maneuvered, and at the moment of ignition, everything was called off and both sides were suddenly at peace.

Agis marched home to a furious Spartan government and public disgrace that would dog him for the rest of his career. Thrasyllus was stoned by his people and barely escaped with his life. Alcibiades then arrived with Athenian troops to aid in the now cancelled battle. His presence convinced the Argives, Eleans and Mantineans to violate the newly agreed truce and occupy the city of Orchomenus in northeastern Arcadia.

With this news, Spartan rage at Agis erupted. The government decided to destroy his home and to fine him 100,000 drachmas for his unauthorized truce which had now resulted in the capitulation of Orchomenus. Agis pleaded for a second chance to lead the army to victory. This reprieve was granted, but only under strict supervision. Ten Peers were assigned to him to oversee his decisions on his next campaign.

It was a humiliating and unprecedented measure and lends credence to the suspicion that Agis acted out of fear, both in his previous refusals to march and in his making the truce when he had the opportunity to give battle. We also have to consider the possibility that Agis was acting not out of fear, but out of a genuine desire to bring about peace, contrary to more aggressive interests in the Spartan government who assigned the ten supervisors to ensure that Agis did as they wished.

First Mantinea

But the assignment of the supervisors also likely motivated him to heroic levels of bravery in his next stand-up fight. The opportunity came almost immediately when the Argive alliance marched against Tegea minus the Eleans, who left in a huff after their proposal to march against the settled helots at Lepreum was rejected. Agis clearly had something to prove and in this he was aligned with a humiliated Sparta – smarting from its failed efforts to check Athens in the Archidamian War, followed by its failure to check Argos and its allies (which now included Athens). Thucydides tells us that it was the largest muster of Spartans yet, though they wound up sending the oldest and youngest hoplites back, possibly to guard against a helot revolt at home. The Spartans entered the territory around Mantinea and laid waste to it, also sending for their northern allies, who were unable to arrive in time due to having to travel through enemy territory to reach Mantinea.

Modern scholars estimate that the Spartans still had a slightly larger army. This was due partly to the presence of Arcadian allies, and partly to a sizable contingent of *neodamōdeis* (around 2,000). The *neodamōdeis* or "New People" were freed helots along the same lines as the *brasideioi*. These freed slaves were likely created after the *brasideioi* marched north in 424 BC, but before they returned. Unlike the *brasideioi* for whom freedom was a reward for loyal service, the *neodamōdeis* were freed immediately upon signing up to serve.

Many of these *neodamōdeis* joined the *brasideioi* in garrisoning Lepreum, helping to provide an effective buffer for Sparta against its enemies (evidenced by the Eleans withdrawing their contingent when Argos' other allies marched on Tegea). This model of freeing slaves who agreed to serve was now used again to provide the Spartans with a quick and easy muster of new hoplites, though they were likely of far lower quality (and far worse equipped) than the Peers. That Sparta would even consider this as an option is an excellent example of the strain of the *oliganthrōpia*, as the declining number of Peers strained Sparta's ability to field an effective army.

It turned out to be a very good thing Sparta had assigned Agis supervision. The Argive alliance force took up a position on high ground that would have given it a distinct advantage in an assault. Agis prepared to charge it anyway, desperate to redeem himself after his humiliation. Thucydides tells us that he would have committed the Spartan army to a likely disastrous position if one of the ten supervisors (Diodorus gives his name as Pharax) hadn't warned him not to "*cure evil with evil*" and convinced him to withdraw after the two armies were just a stone's throw away from each other.

I doubt this distance. It is extremely risky to try to maneuver, and especially to retreat, when you are that close to an enemy. A withdrawing army is *always* less cohesive than an advancing one. The act of walking backwards is more challenging than that of moving ahead, especially when you're dealing with thousands of men (modern scholars estimate that Agis' army was around 9,000, not counting the still-enslaved helots). A competent commander could easily have taken advantage of this withdrawal, executing a charge that could throw the withdrawing army into confusion and turning retreat into rout. It's likely that Thucydides exaggerates and the decision to withdraw came before the two armies were anywhere near one another. Diodorus gives a slightly different narrative, but I prefer Thucydides.

However, Agis listened to his advisor (or more likely obeyed his orders), and withdrew to Tegea where he diverted a stream to try to flood Mantinean fields in the hopes of provoking the Argive allies to quit their position and come out to fight. I cannot believe this plan worked (the harvest had already been taken in anyway), but you have to remember that the Argive general Thrasyllus had been just as vilified for cowardice as Agis had. The current Argive commanders no doubt were under similar pressure to have a battle and prove they weren't cowards, and so they did quit their position and turned out to fight the following morning. Meanwhile Agis, finished with his flooding operation, marched back to Mantinea. In a move now familiar to us when we consider Spartan commanders, he utterly failed to deploy scouts or reconnoiter the ground and as a result blundered smack into the enemy.

Thucydides' description of the Spartan order of battle for this fight is one of our best glimpses of the organization of the Spartan army and forms the basis for much of the description provided in chapter I. He also provides excellent and important details in describing the phalanxes advancing on each other – noting how the Spartans kept their ranks dressed and moved in a slow and disciplined manner, careful not to create gaps in the line. He describes the use of pipers (*aulos* players) to keep the troops in step. He also describes the inevitable drift to the right as each hoplite sought to take shelter behind the shield of the man beside him.

But despite their disciplined advance, the Spartans' celebrated discipline failed just as critically as it had at Plataea 61 years earlier. Owing to the rightward drift I just described, Agis realized that the left of his battle line was in danger of being outflanked and enveloped (if you're not familiar with these terms, please jump to the appendix on the fundamentals of ancient battle; I lay out everything out there) and he gave the order for the *neodamōdeis* and Sciritae (the special troops I described in chapter I) to shift left, creating a gap in his line. He then gave a second set of orders to the Spartan polemarchs Aristocles and Hipponoidas to lead their troops to plug the gap.

They refused.

Just as Amompharetus refused to comply with Pausanias' orders at Plataea, the two Spartans refused to obey their king. This hole in the Bronze Lie is big enough to drive a truck through. Sparta's legendary discipline completely collapsed in the face of commanders who believed their individual initiative trumped the strategic aims of their king.

The fatal gap remained open.

Agis, seeing the destruction of his army unfolding before his eyes, issued desperate orders to the *neodamōdeis* and Sciritae to slide right again, as being outflanked would be a lesser evil than a giant breach in his line, but he was already too late. The allied right, held by Mantinean troops, saw their moment and took it. Shouting their war cry, they charged toward the gap in the Spartan line.

The results were entirely predictable. A phalanx could only fight straight ahead. It was intensely vulnerable on its flanks, and the gap provided the Mantineans with the opportunity to roll up the exposed flanks not only of the *neodamōdeis* and Sciritae, but also the leftmost of the Spartan Peers. They were joined by 1,000 "chosen warriors," Argive hoplites specially selected as the most elite of their army. They rolled over the Spartan left like a rogue wave, utterly shattering it.

That should have been the end of the battle. However, the Mantineans and Argives displayed the same lack of discipline showed by Aristocles and Hipponoidas. Instead of swinging left to roll up the entire Spartan line, they pressed on to the Spartan baggage train in the hopes of looting it. This was a common problem with ancient armies and turned the fortunes of more than one ancient battle.

This failure of the allies' discipline gave Agis the chance he needed to turn things around. The stand-up fight in the center was a traditional *ōthismos* push of hoplite against hoplite and here the Spartans absolutely excelled. They broke and routed the Argives and isolated the Athenians who held the allied left. They would easily have enveloped and routed these as well, but Agis was now forced to send his whole army to rescue the Spartan left, giving the Athenians a chance to retreat covered by their cavalry.

It's important to point out what an unprecedented maneuver this was, truly beyond the capability of other armies of the period. Agis managed to maneuver not just a a small unit, but his entire army – the Peers, the *perioikoi* and the allied troops – while maintaining the critical cohesion necessary to permit a phalanx to be victorious.

The Mantineans and elite Argives also fled in the face of the entire Spartan army bearing down on them. Agis did not pursue, because of Spartan discipline (if you believe Thucydides) or because Pharax forbade it (if you believe Diodorus).

It was, by any measure, a stunning and decisive Spartan victory. Agis had achieved his much-sought-after redemption. Most importantly, it had been a set-piece battle on mostly level ground – phalanx against phalanx between relatively equally matched armies. It was the win Sparta so desperately needed to restore the reputation of its hoplites after their humiliation at Sphacteria. They had proven, undeniably, that it was a mistake to count them out.

Agis must have wept with relief. His compatriots had surely lost all confidence in him, to the point where the Agiad king Pleistoanax marched out with the old and young hoplites who had been sent back, to aid his co-king whom everyone surely expected to lose. The allies also finally arrived. Both armies, receiving news of the victory, had no recourse but to march home, reconsidering Agis' reputation on the way.

Thucydides confirms how much this victory did to restore the reputation of Spartan arms:

> … *in one battle they wiped away their disgrace with the Greeks; for they had been thought cowards for the blow they received on the island* [Sphacteria] *and with imprudence and slowness to act on other occasions. But after this, their failures were considered to be bad luck, and they were thought to be the same as they had been.*

Sparta used the victory effectively, extending an olive branch to the Argives, who took one look at their broken army and eagerly accepted it. They ignored

Alcibiades' pleading and switched sides, allying with Sparta. Sparta also concluded a 30-year peace with Mantinea and returned Lepreum to Elis.

In this new period of seeming Spartan momentum, Argos' democracy was overthrown and replaced with a pro-Spartan oligarchy (in 417 BC). But the transition was short-lived. Argive democrats rose against the oligarchs while Sparta was celebrating yet another religious festival, and this time the Spartans (after some dithering) ignored the religious restriction and marched on Argos in yet another example of Sparta's absolute willingness to commit sacrilege when it suited them. Unfortunately, they arrived too late and headed home once they realized it, leaving their oligarch allies to their fate. It wasn't until the winter of 416 BC that Sparta finally sent Agis against Argos in force, but he failed to take the city and had to content himself by capturing nearby Hysiae and carrying out a horrific massacre of prisoners.

Alcibiades, opportunistic as ever, sent aid to the Argive democratic faction and conducted his own purge of those Argives suspected of being pro-Spartan. Despite the open warfare of Mantinea and the bald-faced Athenian aid to Sparta's enemies, neither side renounced the Peace of Nicias. The treaty was less than a joke, but it remained technically in force.

Another expedition against Argos was called off due to religious excuses, and an Athenian-supported Argos continued to thrust and counterthrust with Sparta for the rest of that year. Sparta appeared cautious, and a kind of stalemate had ensued with neither side showing real advantage.

And then Athens threw everything away.

The Sicilian disaster

Alcibiades, charismatic, opportunistic, and as it turned out, completely wrongheaded, won his argument for an invasion of Sicily. It is certainly a testament to Alcibiades' charm and influence that he was able to convince Athens to engage in this intensely foolish and aggressive adventure so soon after the defeat at Mantinea (which he'd also strongly pushed for). A massive fleet was funded and equipped (barely. Money was a major problem and delayed the expedition's departure) and by 414 BC it was attacking Syracuse, the main city-state of Sicily. Athens made a good initial showing, but the Athenian lack of cavalry limited its success, as Syracuse was known for its horsemen. However, Syracuse's levy hoplites were undisciplined and lacked strong leadership. Athens could claim a technical victory in its initial contact, but Syracuse still remained stubbornly in enemy hands. Syracuse sent to Sparta for aid and, as it was originally a colony of Corinth, Sparta came under pressure from that city-state as well.

Athens' invasion (under the partial command of Nicias) was ostensibly to defend Athens' allies, but everyone knew Athens' real motive was high-handed imperialism, a fact that Alcibiades would later confirm.

This is because the Athenian switched sides.

Athenian politics gave a new definition to the term "eating their own" and when Alcibiades was accused of sacrilege and sentenced to death *in absentia*, the Athenian wisely made a break for it and went over to Sparta. The sacrilege he was accused of is too interesting not to mention. The *hermai* of Athens were essentially pillars with the head of a god (usually Hermes) at the top and a stone penis and testicles at the anatomically appropriate height. To a modern viewer they look ludicrous, but they were revered by the ancient Greeks, and just before the Athenian fleet someone went through Athens marring all the stone faces. This may seem ridiculous to a modern reader, but to an ancient it was a serious act of sacrilege. We will never know who really committed the vandalism, but the blame was laid squarely at Alcibiades' feet.

The Spartans were only too happy to talk to Alcibiades, whose loyalty to Athens extended only as far as the Athenians' to him. The Athenians wanted to execute him? Not if he executed them first. He revealed the purpose of the Athenians' mission to Syracuse (which was hardly a revelation to the Spartans) and also gave them some critical and extremely sound advice (it seemed Alcibiades reserved his good counsel for the enemies of his home city). First, he told the Spartans that what the Syracusans lacked was discipline and leadership. While the Spartans should certainly send troops, what the Syracusans really needed was an *officer* who could train them, organize them and lead them to victory. Secondly, he advised the Spartans to capture and fortify the Attic village of Decelea, to the north of Athens. A Spartan military force there would be in a position to intercept food imports from the sea, could ravage the Attic countryside, and could also complicate access to Athens' silver mines.

Sparta was convinced to send an expedition to Syracuse, but was reluctant to invade Attica to distract the Athenians, ostensibly on account of not wanting to invoke divine wrath due to violating the peace. Indeed, the Syracusan plea had requested this very thing.

Instead, Sparta elected to invade Argos, and did some likely ineffectual ravaging before an earthquake halted its operations. This was possibly an effort to goad the Athenians into breaking the peace (and incurring any subsequent divine wrath). Unfortunately for Sparta, Argive retaliation was much more successful, as they carried off "*a great booty*" according to Thucydides.

Sparta followed with another major invasion that summer, which brought 30 Athenian ships raiding the Laconian coast in response. This was the excuse Sparta needed to formally end the Peace of Nicias and act on Alcibiades' advice. An expedition was sent to Syracuse and the Spartans prepared to take and fortify Decelea.

Yet as with Thermopylae, Sparta's commitment to the contest was half-hearted. Whether this was due to Sparta's manpower shortage, political maneuvering, or doubt over Alcibiades' story, we can't be sure.

The Spartans did at least send a capable commander. Gylippus had originally been a *mothax*, a kind of social inferior who was still free, but of lesser status. A *mothax* was usually sponsored by a rich family of a Peer, and clearly enjoyed some prestige. The position was a path back to the status of full Peer for the children of Peers who had lost that status, possibly due to inability to pay their mess dues.

Not only was Gylippus now a full Peer, but he was the son of Cleandridas who had been an advisor to Pleistoanax. This likely meant that Gylippus' family was close to the king now that he was back in power. Further, Cleandridas had been exiled in southern Italy and had obtained citizenship in a city-state there. This meant his son likely had connections in the western Mediterranean, which would absolutely come in handy on an expedition to Sicily.

This decision to appoint a commander with political connections in the region is an indicator of wise and careful thinking, but it is *also* another glaring hole in the Bronze Lie. Far from relying on brute strength, Sparta leaned hard on the "soft" power of diplomacy, and leveraged family relationships, guest friendships and other non-violent means of providing military advantage.

Sparta's trust in Gylippus proved well placed. Sparta still hadn't rebuilt the fleet it had lost at Pylos over a decade earlier, and so Gylippus set out on four

Corinthian ships. Two of them had Corinthian crews, the other Spartan – but the Spartan crews were helots and recently freed *neodamōdeis*. This almost certainly was a result of Sparta's manpower shortage, and very likely reflected a cautious desire to retain the Peers at home not only to keep an eye on the remaining helots, but also as a hedge against Argos or further Athenian coastal raids.

The small number of ships wound up saving Gylippus, for the Athenian fleet at Sicily thought the tiny Spartan fleet simply a pack of pirates and made no serious move to intercept it. Gylippus landed at Himera on Sicily's north shore. The city came over to the Spartan cause, provided badly needed arms and armor, and sent other Sicilian Greeks who came to Gylippus' banner. By the time the dust had cleared, Gylippus stood at the head of some 3,000 well-equipped infantry and 200 cavalry and he promptly set off east to Syracuse.

Meanwhile, the Athenians had taken the heights of Epipolae just to the north of Syracuse and built two forts commanding it. The northern one was at Labdalum on the northern edge of the heights. From the more southerly of the two (a round fort) they began building walls south to Syracuse's harbor to cut the city off from the interior of Sicily. The Syracusans had tried building counterwalls to cut off the path of the Athenian walls, but the Athenians had easily stormed these and captured them. They'd also put their fleet into Syracuse's harbor and taken it.

This, coupled with the initial defeat of the Syracusan forces when the Athenians landed, had crushed morale. The Syracusans were on the verge of surrender when Gylippus showed up with badly needed troops and much more badly needed confidence. Gylippus may have been a *mothax*, but he still would have gone through the brutal Spartan Upbringing and was clearly possessed of the discipline for which the Spartans were (somewhat unjustifiably) famous. He took command of the Syracusan troops (they were in such poor shape that Thucydides tells us they couldn't even form a line) and clearly instilled some kind of order and discipline in them. He also engaged in some showmanship intended to boost critically low Syracusan morale – sending a herald to the Athenians granting them a truce of five days to pack up and leave. He had to know this offer would be refused, and it was, but it must have done much to stiffen the Syracusans' spines.

Assault on the Labdalum fort, assault on the Athenian wall, the battle between the walls and the battle beside the walls

The next day, Gylippus began the slow work of reversing Athens' gains. He used his army to distract the Athenians while he sent another force to successfully surprise and capture the northern of the two Athenian forts (the Labdalum fort) on the Epipolae heights. This gave the Syracusans yet another morale boost, and also a point from which to build a third cross wall to prevent the Athenians from further walling off Syracuse.

Gylippus tried an assault on the Athenian siege wall itself, but was driven off. He suffered another defeat when he foolishly took on the Athenians in between the two armies' respective walls where the space was too tight for the Syracusan cavalry to deploy effectively. The Athenians beat Gylippus' troops in a stand-up infantry battle, and in a move utterly uncharacteristic for any ancient general, let alone a Spartan, Gylippus took personal responsibility for the loss, saying it was his fault for choosing ground where the Syracusans' advantage in cavalry and light infantry couldn't be employed.

His honesty clearly worked to shore up his troops' morale, and when he faced the Athenians again shortly after, he was careful to pick ground where the Syracusan cavalry and light infantry had room to maneuver. The advantage told and the Athenians were driven back with their left flank utterly routed. Even better, the defeat allowed Gylippus' troops to finish their counterwall and effectively put an end to Athenian efforts to cut Syracuse off.

Storming of the harbor forts, the attempt on the round fort, and the night defense of Epipolae

Gylippus had his next success in 413 BC, when he stormed and captured Athenian forts controlling Syracuse's harbor while the Athenians were busy defeating the Syracusan navy. It was a near repeat of the distraction-surprise attack tactic he'd used to take the Labdalum fort the previous year, and it worked brilliantly.

He was less successful in his efforts to storm the Athenian circle fort, but his overall success brought more and more Sicilian Greeks to the Syracusan cause. With Spartan help the Syracusans were holding and maybe even gaining momentum, but they were a long way from ejecting the Athenians and winning outright. If Athens had withdrawn, it might have been able to regain some of its footing and at least have been able to declare a stalemate.

Instead, in perhaps the greatest blunder of all the Peloponnesian Wars, it doubled down.

Athens sent Demosthenes, the hero of Pylos, in command of another massive fleet only slightly smaller than the first one – some 73 ships with nearly 5,000 hoplites and even more light-armed troops. This fleet was still underway when the Syracusan navy finally defeated the navy of the original Athenian invasion in Syracuse's harbor. Arriving, Demosthenes displayed all of the bravery and determination he had shown at Pylos and immediately set out first to ravage the land outside Syracuse, and then to storm the heights of Epipolae in a night attack, with the goal of taking the Syracusan crosswall.

Night attacks were incredibly risky propositions in the ancient world. Even a bright moon and abundant torch light made for murky and confused fighting, with difficulty distinguishing friend from foe. Already superstitious ancient warriors were much more easily frightened in the dark, and critical unit cohesion and morale became a touch-and-go thing. The Athenians were initially successful, but seem to have become strung out pursuing their defeated enemy, and at last the enemy rallied and utterly crushed them. Thucydides is clear that the confusion of the night operation was a major part of the Athenian loss: "*Wherefore at the last, falling one upon another in different parts of the army, friends against friends, and countrymen against countrymen, they not only terrified each other, but came to blows and could hardly again be parted.*"

With this defeat, Athenian morale was finished. Nicias, ill and terrified of the vengeance Athens would take on him when he returned (he had surely learned the lesson of their treatment of Alcibiades), refused Demosthenes' insistence that they give up the fight and retreat. The Syracusans built a chain of boats across the harbor, trapping the Athenian fleet inside and then crushing their attempt to break out. Utterly broken, the Athenian army of some 40,000 tried to retreat overland, only to be stalked and annihilated by the Syracusans and their Spartan allies. Demosthenes and Nicias' columns were separated, with 14,000 of Demosthenes' troops killed and 6,000 taken prisoner. Nicias' entire column surrendered, with the deathly ill general personally giving himself up to Gylippus.

The two-year expedition had ended in complete and utter disaster for Athens, costing it two fleets, two land armies and two of its best commanders for absolutely no gain at all. Thucydides' summary makes plain the magnitude of the catastrophe:

> *For being wholly overcome in every kind and receiving small loss in nothing, their army and fleet and all that ever they had perished (as they used to say) with a universal destruction. Few of many returned home. And thus passed the business concerning Sicily.*

Gylippus argued for keeping both Demosthenes and Nicias as prisoners. Taking Demosthenes back to Sparta would have been a real coup for the Spartans, who were still eager to avenge Demosthenes' actions at Pylos. But the Syracusans had suffered terribly over the last two years and were in no mood for that. Both generals were executed without trial, and the prisoners were worked to death in Syracuse's stone quarries. The disaster had crushed Athenian morale, shattered its reputation and respect abroad, and significantly set back its military capability. It was an inflection point in the long slog of the Peloponnesian Wars, one from which Athens would never recover.

A final note on Gylippus. Like so many other Spartan luminaries, his heroism was later drowned in charges of financial malfeasance as he was accused of embezzling part of a shipment of silver (booty taken from Athens) bound for Sparta in 405 BC. Like so many other great Spartans, he likely fled abroad, never returning to Sparta to face charges of stealing public funds. In love of money, it seems, the former *mothax* was every bit equal to a lifelong Peer.

The Decelean Phase of the Peloponnesian Wars

In 413 BC Sparta heeded Alcibiades' advice and built the fort at Decelea, visible from Athens. King Agis himself commanded the force stationed there, in a nod to the importance of the position. The troops were able to supply themselves by raiding the countryside and could easily be reinforced overland from Sparta and other allies. Exactly as advertised, the position proved perfect to intercept shipments of imported food, and also traffic from the silver mines, and to serve as a constant threat to the Athenian countryside. It also served as the ideal rallying point for escaped Athenian slaves. The position was so critical that it lent its name to the final phase of the Peloponnesian Wars – the Decelean War.

The shock to Greece from the Syracusan disaster was every bit as great as after Pylos. Athens' star was clearly on the wane, and opportunists surged forward to take advantage. The island of Chios reached out to Sparta seeking to revolt, as did other anti-Athenian factions across Greece and Ionia. More importantly, Darius II, the illegitimate grandson of the same Xerxes who'd faced Leonidas at Thermopylae, ruling the still vast and powerful Persian Empire, ordered his satraps Tissaphernes and Pharnabazus to reach out to the Spartans with offers of financial aid. The Spartans, great enemies of Persia, so famous for boldly standing against Darius II's grandfather, eagerly accepted. They also accepted assistance from the Syracusan navy, which now had direct and immediate experience fighting against the Athenians on the water.

Effort to detach the Chian navy

An effort to secretly detach the Chian navy from Athens was horribly bungled, and the Athenians caught the fleet and killed its Spartan commander, Alcamenes. Frightened, Sparta almost lost the nerve to send a fleet to help with the Chian rebellion, but Alcibiades once again employed his opportunist's charm to convince the Spartans to go through with the operation. The Spartans sent him along as an advisor to the expedition's captain, the Spartan Chalcideus.

Another possible reason for sending Alcibiades was that he had allegedly cuckolded Agis and impregnated his wife, Timaea. Spartan culture allowed a great deal of sexual freedom to women (compared to the rest of Greece at the time. Certainly not by modern standards). Spartan society did approve of polygamy, but only for women. A woman could be legally married to a second man and was permitted to have sex with him, with the agreement of her husband. But this arrangement occurred only out in the open, and didn't cover adultery or secret trysts. Even more importantly, it didn't extend to the wives of kings, since any child born of that union wouldn't have a royal father.

Spartan troops deploy from column-of-march into the phalanx. While certainly not "professionals" in the modern sense of the word, their discipline and organization outstripped the amateur standard of Greek warfare. (Artwork by Adam Hook, © Osprey Publishing)

Reconstruction of the *aspis* shield showing the "Argive grip" and heavy wooden construction. This proved to be a critical advantage against Persian arrows in the Greco-Persian War. (Artwork by Steve Noon, © Osprey Publishing)

Thucydides describes the Spartan "sworn bands" as "generally" eight ranks deep. These ones are six deep, with the *enōmotarchoi* (officers) positions circled. Far right is possibly the *lochagos* (overall leader). (Artwork by Steve Noon, © Osprey Publishing)

Pre-hoplite Spartans. Note the "dipylon" figure-8-shaped shields and multiple spears without butt-spikes. Early Spartan *aristoi* war bands might have featured warriors like these. (Artwork by Richard Hook, © Osprey Publishing)

A Spartan proto-hoplite battles an Argive warrior. While much of his panoply looks hoplite-esque, he carries two spears suitable for throwing as well as thrusting.

(Artwork by Giuseppe Rava, © Osprey Publishing)

An archaic period Spartan warrior, showing the bell cuirass, greaves, spear, shield, Illyrian and Corinthian pattern helmets, and crests. The lambda wasn't painted on Spartan shields until much later.
(Artwork by Steve Noon, © Osprey Publishing)

Spartan warriors at the end of the archaic period, as hoplite warfare began to take hold. We can still see more complete armor (thigh and forearm protection), later jettisoned.
(Artwork by Richard Hook, © Osprey Publishing)

Reconstruction of the battle depicted on the Chigi vase. It is possibly the Battle of the Boar's Tomb in 683 BC, or another from the Second Messenian War.
(Artwork by Richard Hook, © Osprey Publishing)

Spartan kings as they may have appeared *circa* early 6th century BC. The shield patterns are based on votive lead offerings dedicated at the temple of Artemis Orthia in Sparta. (Artwork by Richard Hook, © Osprey Publishing)

A *circa* early 5th century BC Spartan officer addresses allied hoplites. Thucydides speaks of *xenagoi* – Spartan officers in command of allied troops. (Artwork by Angus McBride, © Osprey Publishing)

A Persian scout spies Spartan troops ball-playing at Thermopylae in 480 BC. This carelessness may have been due to confidence in their superior position and equipment, rather than suicidal bravery. (Artwork by Steve Noon, © Osprey Publishing)

Author's photo of Mount Callidromus (modern Kallidromo) from inside the Thermopylae pass. This guarded the Spartans' southern flank in 480 BC. (Myke Cole)

The legendary Spartan last stand on the Colonus in 480 BC. Herodotus tells us their weapons, armor, and shields were in much worse condition than is shown here.
(Artwork by Richard Hook, © Osprey Publishing)

The Spartans, outflanked and realizing their position is hopeless, make a mad drive to the west at Thermopylae in 480 BC. It fails, and King Leonidas is killed.
(Artwork by Steve Noon, © Osprey Publishing)

The Battle of Thermopylae in 480 BC is often touted as having somehow stopped the Persians. It did nothing of the sort. Here, Achaemenid troops capture the Athenian Acropolis. (Artwork by Peter Dennis, © Osprey Publishing)

The Battle of Salamis in 480 BC did far more to thwart Persian ambitions than Thermopylae. However, the Spartan role in this battle appears to have been minimal. (Artwork by Peter Dennis, © Osprey Publishing)

A rower's-eye-view of conditions on an early 5th century BC trireme like those employed at the Battle of Salamis.
(Artwork by Peter Dennis, © Osprey Publishing)

The Spartans take omens again and again at Plataea in 479 BC, refusing to charge the Persians despite a storm of arrows. Some interpret this as an indication of fear.
(Artwork by Steve Noon, © Osprey Publishing)

The supposedly iron Spartan discipline breaks down completely at Plataea in 479 BC, when Amompharetus refuses orders to move from a bad position, compromising the entire army. (Artwork by Richard Hook, © Osprey Publishing)

Possibly shamed into action by the Tegeans, the Spartans finally charge the Persians at Plataea in 479 BC. Note the unarmored helots armed with rocks, or carrying spare spears. (Artwork by Peter Dennis, © Osprey Publishing)

A 5th century BC Spartan *aulos* player and trumpeter can be seen here. Thucydides tells us the Spartans used music to keep their troops in step when advancing into battle.
(Artwork by Richard Hook, © Osprey Publishing)

Helots chase down and kill an Athenian hoplite. This slave caste, unarmored and often armed with nothing more than rocks, provided critical light infantry support to their Spartan oppressors.
(Artwork by Angus McBride, © Osprey Publishing)

Author's photo of the island of Sphacteria, seen from the Pylos shore in 425 BC, where the Spartan ships were likely beached. In modern times, Pylos is further south. (Myke Cole)

In a tactically foolish move, Brasidas rushes down the gangplank at Pylos in 425 BC. His grievous wounding may have sandbagged Spartan morale. (Artwork by Peter Dennis, © Osprey Publishing)

Catching the Spartans completely off guard in the bay off Pylos in 425 BC, the Athenians either capture or disable the Spartan fleet and maroon their troops on Sphacteria.
(Artwork by Peter Dennis, © Osprey Publishing)

The Spartan Peers are unable to come to grips with Athenian light troops on Sphacteria in 425 BC. Defeated by hit-and-run tactics, the Spartans retreat to high ground.
(Artwork by Peter Dennis, © Osprey Publishing)

Retreating to Mount Elias on Sphacteria in 425 BC, the Spartans are outflanked. Realizing their position is hopeless, they surrender. The move shocks Greece and defangs their legend. (Artwork by Peter Dennis, © Osprey Publishing)

Spartans build a *tropaion* after their victory in the First Battle of Mantinea in 418 BC. Such trophies were constructed largely of arms and armor stripped from the defeated dead. (Artwork by Steve Noon, © Osprey Publishing)

Spartan officers (denoted by helmet crests) and a warrior, resting after the First Battle of Mantinea. Note the artist's depiction of the mustacheless beards, per the supposed custom.
(Artwork by Richard Hook, © Osprey Publishing)

Gylippus arrives in Syracuse at the end of the 5th century BC. He marches at the head of freed helots – *neodamōdeis*, one of Sparta's critical answers to its manpower shortage. (Artwork by Peter Dennis, © Osprey Publishing)

Spartan-supported forces successfully defend Epipolae in 414 BC. Night operations were incredibly risky in the ancient world, where the lack of artificial light and communications made disastrous confusion almost certain. (Artwork by Peter Dennis, © Osprey Publishing)

Circa late 5th century BC Spartan and allied hoplites are surprised by cavalry on a road. Spartan failure to adequately scout or invest in intelligence operations was a factor in much of their military record. (Artwork by Angus McBride, © Osprey Publishing)

"Spartan" naval troops, all of whom are allies or mercenaries. Sparta never truly invested in developing a native naval capability, and was heavily reliant on external sources.
(Artwork by Richard Hook, © Osprey Publishing)

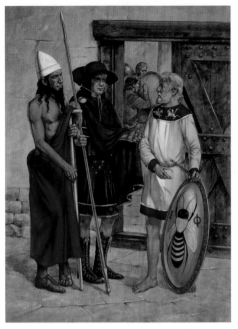

An early 4th century BC Spartan officer inspecting military wares. Note his *pilos* cap. Some scholars believe that these were worn instead of bronze *pilos* helmets in battle. (Artwork by Richard Hook, © Osprey Publishing)

Mercenaries in Spartan service, *circa* early 4th century BC. Facing an increasing manpower shortage, Sparta made increasing use of mercenaries throughout its military history. (Artwork by Richard Hook, © Osprey Publishing)

Defeated at Coronea in 394 BC, the Thebans still manage to break through the Spartan line, badly wounding the Spartan king in the process. (Artwork by Adam Hook, © Osprey Publishing)

Spartan troops wheel to face the enemy at Coronea. Thucydides describes Spartan maneuvers as simple and easy to understand, but they were at a high level compared to their almost entirely amateur opponents. (Artwork by Steve Noon, © Osprey Publishing)

Author's photo of the battlefield of Leuctra, where Sparta's power was finally broken in 371 BC. The photo is taken from the likely location of the Spartan camp, looking north. (Myke Cole)

A Spartan cavalryman rides down a fleeing Theban, *circa* early 4th century BC.
Sparta was never known for its cavalry, frequently relying on allied support to fill the role.
(Artwork by Richard Hook, © Osprey Publishing)

The legendary Theban Epaminondas is killed at the Second Battle of Mantinea in 362 BC. Despite the battle being a Theban victory, Epaminondas' death spared the Spartans. (Artwork by Angus McBride, © Osprey Publishing)

A Spartan hoplite and armored *perioikoi*. Note that by the middle of the Peloponnesian Wars, most of the heavy armor had been jettisoned leaving just the helmet and shield. (Artwork by Steve Noon, © Osprey Publishing)

Author's photo of Mount Evas (sometimes spelled "Euas," modern Tourles), where the Spartan left was positioned during the Second Battle of Sellasia in 222 BC. (Myke Cole)

THE SPARTAN RECORD

Battle	Date (approx.)	War (if applicable)		Outcome
The Ravine	739 BC	First Messenian	⊗	Defeat
The Kings	738 BC	First Messenian	⊕	Stalemate
Without Allies	733 BC	First Messenian	⊕	Stalemate
Ithome	728 BC	First Messenian	⊗	Defeat
Last	724 BC	First Messenian	✕	Victory
Derae	684 BC	Second Messenian	⊕	Stalemate
Boar's Tomb	683 BC	Second Messenian	⊗	Defeat
Great Trench	682 BC	Second Messenian	✕	Victory
Eira	669 BC	Second Messenian	✕	Victory
Hysiae	669 BC		⊗	Defeat
Fetters	550 BC		⊗	Defeat
Champions – Duel of 300	546 BC		⊗	Defeat
Champions – Battle	546 BC		✕	Victory
Assault on Samos	520 BC		⊗	Defeat
First Assault on Athens	511 BC		⊗	Defeat
Second Assault on Athens	510 BC		✕	Victory
Punitive Expedition against Athens	507 BC		⊗	Defeat
Sepeia	494 BC		✕	Victory
Thermopylae/Artemisium	480 BC	Greco-Persian	⊗	Defeat
Salamis	480 BC	Greco-Persian	≈✕	Victory
Plataea	479 BC	Greco-Persian	✕	Victory
Mycale	479 BC	Greco-Persian	✕	Victory
Campaign against the Aleudae	c. 478 BC		⊗	Defeat
Tegea	c. 474 BC		✕	Victory
Dipaea	470 BC		✕	Victory
Stenyclerus	464 BC	Third Messenian (post earthquake revolt)	⊗	Defeat
Second Battle of Ithome	464 BC	Third Messenian (post earthquake revolt)	✕	Victory
Oenoe	c. 460 BC	First Peloponnesian	⊗	Defeat
Halieis	c. 460 BC		✕	Victory
Tanagra	457 BC	First Peloponnesian	✕	Victory
Siege of Oenoe	431 BC	Archidamean	⊗	Defeat
Relief of Methone	431 BC	Archidamean	✕	Victory
Assault on Stratus	429 BC	Archidamean	⊗	Defeat
Rhium	429 BC	Archidamean	≈⊗	Defeat
Naupactus	429 BC	Archidamean	≈⊗	Defeat
Siege of Plataea	430–427 BC	Archidamean	✕	Victory
Corcyra	c. 427 BC	Archidamean	≈✕	Victory
Olpae	426 BC	Archidamean	⊗	Defeat
Pylos/Sphacteria	425 BC	Archidamean	⊗	Defeat
Assault on Eion	424 BC	Archidamean	⊗	Defeat
Lyncestis	423 BC	Archidamean	⊗	Defeat
Amphipolis	422 BC	Archidamean	⊗	Defeat
Defense of Epidaurus	421 BC	Peace of Nicias	✕	Victory
First Mantinea	418 BC	Peace of Nicias	✕	Victory
Assault on Labdalum fort	414 BC	(Syracusan Relief)	✕	Victory
Attack on Athenian wall	414 BC	(Syracusan Relief)	⊗	Defeat
Battle Between the Walls	414 BC	(Syracusan Relief)	⊗	Defeat
Battle Beside the Walls	414 BC	(Syracusan Relief)	✕	Victory
Storming of harbor forts	413 BC	(Syracusan Relief)	✕	Victory
Failed attempt to take circle fort	413 BC	(Syracusan Relief)	⊗	Defeat
Night defense of Epipolae	413 BC	(Syracusan Relief)	✕	Victory
Attack on Chian navy	412 BC	Decelean	≈⊗	Defeat
Assault on Athenian fort on Chios	411 BC	Decelean	⊗	Defeat
Naval battle off Chios	411 BC	Decelean	≈⊕	Stalemate
Eretria	411 BC	Decelean	≈✕	Victory
Cynosemma	411 BC	Decelean	≈⊗	Defeat
Abydus	411 BC	Decelean	≈⊗	Defeat
Taking of Cyzicus	410 BC	Decelean	✕	Victory
Cyzicus	410 BC	Decelean	≈⊗	Defeat
Cerata	409 BC	Decelean	⊗	Defeat
Chalcedon	408 BC	Decelean	⊗	Defeat
Defense of Byzantium	408 BC	Decelean	⊗	Defeat
Assault on Athens	407 BC	Decelean	⊗	Defeat
Notium	406 BC	Decelean	≈✕	Victory
Mytilene	406 BC	Decelean	≈✕	Victory

Battle	Date	Campaign		Result
Arginusae	406 BC	Decelean	≈⊗	Defeat
Aegospotami	405 BC	Decelean	≈✕	Victory
Selymbria	403 BC		✕	Victory
Assault on Phyle	403 BC	Athenian Insurgency	⊗	Defeat
Dawn raid on pro-Spartan camp	403 BC	Athenian Insurgency	⊗	Defeat
Munichia	403 BC	Athenian Insurgency	⊗	Defeat
Piraeus	403 BC	Athenian Insurgency	✕	Victory
Siege of the Elean gymnasium	401 BC	Elean	⊗	Defeat
Cunaxa	401 BC		⊗	Defeat
Siege of Larisa	399 BC		⊗	Defeat
Assault on the Bithynian camp	399 BC		⊗	Defeat
Cavalry duel near Dascyleium	395 BC		⊗	Defeat
Sardis	395 BC		✕	Victory
Pharnabazus' attack on foragers	395 BC		⊗	Defeat
Herippidas' raid on Pharnabazus' camp	395 BC		✕	Victory
Haliartus	395 BC	Corinthian	⊗	Defeat
The Nemea	394 BC	Corinthian	✕	Victory
Cnidus	394 BC	Corinthian	≈⊗	Defeat
Coronea	394 BC	Corinthian	✕	Victory
Rearguard action against skirmishers in Locris	394 BC	Corinthian	✕	Victory
Battle in the gulf around Achea and Lecheum	393 BC	Corinthian	≈⊗	Defeat
Battle of Corinth's long walls	392 BC	Corinthian	✕	Victory
Lecheum	391 BC	Corinthian	⊗	Defeat
Methymna	390 BC	Corinthian	⊗	Defeat
Ambush outside Abydus	390 BC	Corinthian	⊗	Defeat
Agesilaus' engagement with the Acarnanians	389 BC	Corinthian	✕	Victory
Chambrias' ambush of Gorgopas	387 BC	Corinthian	⊗	Defeat
First Olynthus	382 BC		✕	Victory
Second Olynthus	381 BC		⊗	Defeat
Cleombrotus' march to Plataea	379 BC	Boeotian	✕	Victory
Theban cavalry raid	378 BC	Boeotian	✕	Victory
Thespiae	378 BC	Boeotian	⊗	Defeat
Alcetas' capture of the Theban fleet	377 BC	Boeotian	✕	Victory
Cleombrotus' 2nd attempt to enter Theban territory	376 BC	Boeotian	⊗	Defeat
Naxos	376 BC	Boeotian	≈⊗	Defeat
Alyzeia	375 BC	Boeotian	≈⊗	Defeat
Tegyra	375 BC	Boeotian	⊗	Defeat
Second Corcyra	373 BC	Boeotian	⊗	Defeat
Leuctra	371 BC	Boeotian	⊗	Defeat
Orchomenus	370 BC	Boeotian	✕	Victory
Defense of the pass against the Arcadians	370 BC	Boeotian	⊗	Defeat
Argive entry at Tegeatis	370 BC	Boeotian	⊗	Defeat
Pallene	369 BC	Boeotian	⊗	Defeat
Asine	369 BC	Boeotian	⊗	Defeat
Caryae	369 BC	Boeotian	✕	Victory
Tearless Battle	368 BC	Boeotian	✕	Victory
First Sellasia	365 BC	Boeotian	✕	Victory
Initial intervention in the Elean-Arcadian	365 BC	Boeotian	⊗	Defeat
Cromnus	365 BC	Boeotian	⊗	Defeat
Defense of Sparta	362 BC	Boeotian	✕	Victory
Second Mantinea	362 BC	Boeotian	⚖	Stalemate
Defeat of Tachos	c. 361 BC		✕	Victory
Megalopolis	331 BC		⊗	Defeat
Third Mantinea	294 BC		⊗	Defeat
Defense of Sparta against Pyrrhus	272 BC		✕	Victory
Corinth	265 BC		⊗	Defeat
Second Megalopolis	262 BC		⊗	Defeat
Mount Lycaeum	227 BC	Cleomenean	✕	Victory
Leuctra	227 BC	Cleomenean	✕	Victory
Dyme	226 BC	Cleomenean	✕	Victory
Second Sellasia	222 BC	Cleomenean	⊗	Defeat
Third Mantinea	207 BC		⊗	Defeat

Key

Victory: ✕ Stalemate: ⚖ Defeat: ⊗
Naval battle: ≈

This meant that, even if the accusation against Alcibiades were untrue, just the insinuation would likely have enraged Agis. It was an interesting episode in Sparta's history, given the foundation myth of Menelaus and Helen.

The expedition was an initial success. Chios did rebel, and Alcibiades worked with Tissaphernes to repeat Brasidas' strategy in the north of Greece – attempting to whip up anti-Athenian revolts along the Ionian coast and meeting with reasonable success. The Athenians responded, tapping 1,000 talents (a talent was about 73 pounds) of, probably, silver to fund a counterstrike. What followed was a whirlwind of naval thrusts and counterthrusts during which Chalcideus was killed. Spartan naval efforts were put under the command of their admiral Astyochus in 411 BC who avoided battle, likely because he was justifiably cautious of engaging the still superior skill of the Athenian navy unless he had an overwhelming advantage.

Assault on the Athenian fort on Chios

Astyochus did move swiftly to ensure that the Chians remained pro-Spartan, working with the Spartan harmost (*harmostēs*, a kind of governor) Pedaritus at Chios to crush those who wanted to switch sides after the Chians suffered numerous defeats fighting the Athenians. This didn't stop Pedaritus sending word to Sparta complaining that Astyochus wasn't providing enough needed help when Athens built a fort on Chios' northern coast.

Sparta responded similarly to the way it had done to Agis after his shameful truce, sending a board of advisors to supervise Astyochus. These advisors managed to anger Tissaphernes by opposing the terms of the treaty he'd negotiated with Sparta.

Plutarch suggests that Alcibiades, realizing that Agis' hatred of him would eventually make him an enemy of Sparta, was advising the satrap to aid neither Sparta nor Athens too much, but to play one against the other. Plutarch makes it clear that Tissaphernes "... *completely surrendered to the flatteries of Alcibiades* ..." but Thucydides points out that Tissaphernes was already planning to move ahead with his own plans, and simply used Alcibiades as his patsy.

Tissaphernes withheld payment for Astyochus' fleet, possibly at Alcibiades' instigation. However, recent scholarship has strongly refuted this idea of

Persia playing Athens and Sparta against one another at Alcibiades' direction, once again reminding us that Plutarch is at best an unreliable source, needing to be taken with a healthy grain of salt.

Astyochus convinced Rhodes to revolt from the Delian League and grant him a place to spend the winter, while Pedaritus unsuccessfully led the Chians against the Athenian fort on the coast of Chios. The attack failed, killing Pedaritus.

If we believe Thucydides and Plutarch, then Alcibiades was truly the most gifted influencer in human history. After dragging both Athens and Sparta into expedition after expedition, and then winning over Tissaphernes, he now switched sides *again*, promising Athens' noble families that he could convince Tissaphernes to help the Athenian cause if they would just give up democracy and institute oligarchic rule. The leading Athenians actually accepted this plan, igniting fury among many Athenians who still blamed Alcibiades for the disaster at Syracuse.

One of these, Phrynichus, even went so far as to offer to betray the Athenian fleet to Astyochus if it would stop Alcibiades from being accepted back into Athens' good graces. Astyochus, in what was perhaps the worst strategic blunder in Spartan history, *declined* the opportunity and instead reported to Tissaphernes. While he had squandered Sparta's chance to destroy the Athenian fleet in a single blow, he did manage to secure a new formal treaty with Darius II, which was worse for the Greeks, as it acknowledged the right of the Persians to rule all the Greeks in Asia Minor (modern Turkey's west coast) just to secure the money needed to pay the fleet. The agreement showed the Spartans were feeling the pinch, and were probably terrified of their unpaid sailors deserting to the Athenians and the defeats at sea that would surely follow.

Naval battle off Chios and Eretria

The Spartans now sent the Peer Dercylidas to incite revolt in two important cities on the Hellespont. This was critical, because it put Sparta in position to intercept shipments of grain from the Black Sea bound for Athens. At the same time, Pedaritus' successor Leon led a naval squadron against the Athenian navy off Chios. The battle was a stalemate, but the Athenians did win back one of the rebellious Hellespontine cities and checked Dercylidas.

Alcibiades' gambit in Athens paid off, and an oligarchy of 400 took over, eventually expanding to a rule by the 5,000 leading citizens of Athens. It's true that Sparta preferred oligarchy to democracy, but not if that meant accepting Athens' position as an empire. King Agis tried to take advantage of the unrest by marching on Athens (hoping that the city would simply go over to him, as a fellow oligarch) but there was still too much bad blood, and once he saw that Athens was manning the walls to fight him, he wisely retreated.

The Spartans took advantage of the chaos to send a fleet under Agesandridas to try to raise the island of Euboea in revolt against the Delian League. The Athenians responded with their own fleet, which they sent to their old ally Eretria, which had marched alongside them in the attack on Sardis (in 498 BC) and suffered the Persian response. But this was not the same Eretria they had once known. Pro-Spartan elements in the city signaled Agesandridas the opportune moment to attack, and the Eretrians slaughtered those Athenian sailors who washed ashore in the crushing naval defeat that followed. Euboea rose in revolt, cutting off yet another critical source of supply to Athens.

Cynossema

Agesandridas failed to follow up the victory with an attack on Athens or its ports. Thucydides is clear that if Agesandridas had taken Athens' port of Piraeus, it would have brought the entire Athenian empire crashing down:

> But here, as on so many other occasions, the Spartans proved the most convenient people in the world for the Athenians to be at war with. The wide difference between the two characters, the slowness and want of energy of the Spartans as contrasted with the dash and enterprise of their opponents, proved a great advantage, especially to a naval empire like Athens.

Superwarriors, indeed.

Meanwhile Mindarus, the Spartan admiral replacing Astyochus, managed to slip his fleet past the Athenians and sail to the Hellespont in support of the anti-Delian revolts there. With Euboea already cut off, the Athenians couldn't afford to let the Spartans interdict critical grain shipments. Athens sent a fleet under Thrasybulus to intercept. Outnumbered, Thrasybulus refused to engage for five days and was nearly crushed when the fleet finally sailed out to fight off Cynossema.

Mindarus drove the center of the Athenian fleet aground and forced the right and left apart. Victory seemed assured, but the vaunted Spartan discipline clearly didn't extend to the navy (which was largely composed of Syracusan allies; the only Peers would have been a few officers), which lost order and cohesion in pursuit of fleeing Athenian ships. Thrasybulus rallied and attacked, breaking Mindarus' squadron and sending panic through the rest of the Spartan ships.

The Syracusan contingent of the Spartan fleet fled, and the battle was a narrowly won Athenian victory that proved that, even outnumbered and practically beaten, the Athenians were still more than a match for the Spartans on the water.

Abydus

With this victory, the Athenians held position on the Hellespont, ready to respond to the Spartans and keep the shipping lanes open for grain coming from the Black Sea. Mindarus sent to the Rhodian commander Doreius to sail north from Rhodes with reinforcements. Doreius did as he was bid, but was driven ashore by bad weather. Pharnabazus sent an army to support him from the land, and Mindarus launched his fleet from Abydus to rescue him from the sea. Thrasybulus had been watching for this moment, and launched to intercept the Spartan fleet. Once again, the Athenians were outnumbered, but advanced confident in their superior seafaring skill. The ensuing battle was a stalemate, with neither side being able to gain the upper hand.

It might have gone on like this until nightfall forced both sides to withdraw, but 18 more ships appeared on the horizon. Both fleets held their breath to see whom they served, and cheers burst from the Athenians as the newcomers ran up the red flag that indicated it was Alcibiades leading Athenian ships from Samos. The Spartans' nerve failed, and they ran, rowing hard for Abydus. Their formation broke apart in their rush for safety, allowing the Athenians and their allies to pick them off in detail. By the time the Spartans reached Abydus, they had lost 30 ships.

Athens might have finished the Spartans once and for all if the revolt of Euboea hadn't required them to detach a substantial portion of their fleet to deal with matters there. Alcibiades' double dealing finally caught up with him as well; when he met with Tissaphernes, the satrap had him arrested and thrown in prison (probably to show the Spartans whose side he was really on). Alcibiades escaped after only a month, an indicator that Tissaphernes' action may have been just for show.

Taking Cyzicus

After two defeats, it was a minor miracle that Mindarus was left in command of Spartan naval efforts, but the third time is a charm, as they say. This third time came the following year when Mindarus partnered with Pharnabazus to take the Anatolian city of Cyzicus. This land operation should be noted. The composition of the army isn't exactly clear (it's possible the Persian contribution was siege engines), but clearly Spartan (mostly *perioikoi* under the command of Peers. It's important to note that no Peers fought as rank and file during Sparta's overseas campaigns between 413 and 386 BC) and allied troops cooperated in a land operation with the same Persians they had fought at Thermopylae, Plataea and Mycale to reduce and capture a fellow Greek city – another gaping hole in the Bronze Lie. In the captured city, Mindarus mustered his new fleet (funded with Persian gold) of some 80 ships.

Alcibiades, having escaped Tissaphernes, was back in command of the Athenian fleet alongside Thrasybulus, the veteran of Cynossema and Abydus. The Athenian fleet sailed past the Spartan base of Abydus at night to conceal its size. It then settled on the modern-day island of Marmara, just off the coast of Cyzicus. Here, Alcibiades broke off a detachment of just 20 ships, and made for Cyzicus while the rest of the fleet stayed tucked away out of sight.

Mindarus bought the trick like it was on sale. He launched from Cyzicus with his entire fleet, chasing the fleeing Alcibiades until he was out in open water. At this point Thrasybulus appeared with the rest of the Athenian fleet and cut off Mindarus' retreat.

Outnumbered, outmaneuvered and attacked from front and rear, Mindarus fled for the beach where Pharnabazus' troops could help him. As at Abydus, the Spartan formation became strung out, and the Athenians picked off the fleeing Spartans one by one. Diodorus describes the chase: "*Alcibiades, pursuing him vigorously, sank some ships, damaged and captured others, and the largest number, which were moored on the land itself, he seized and threw*

grappling-irons on, trying by this means to drag them from the land." Pharnabazus'
Persians now came to the rescue and began driving the Athenians back. The
remaining Athenian admirals landed their troops and joined in the land
battle, which turned ugly for the combined Spartan–Persian army. After hard
fighting, the Athenians held the field. Mindarus lay dead and the entire
Spartan fleet (which would have consisted of very few actual Spartan ships)
had been captured, except for the Syracusan ships, which had been burned
before their sailors fled the field.

It was a devastating loss. In a single blow, Sparta had lost its entire fleet
despite substantial Persian assistance. Mindarus had been decisively
outmaneuvered, humiliated and crushed. The state of Spartan morale is best
summed up in a famous note from Hippocrates, Mindarus' second in
command, sent back to Sparta. "Fleet destroyed. Mindarus dead. The men
starve. We don't know what to do." Sparta, whipped, frightened, having
suffered three major naval defeats in the span of a single year, finally got the
message – Athens simply couldn't be beaten on the water. Even the disaster at
Syracuse couldn't make a dent in its naval supremacy. An embassy was sent to
Athens in humiliation to beg for peace.

In a development that should surprise absolutely no one, Athens refused.
Mantinea had chastened it on land, and now Athens had more than made up
for it on the sea. Why should Athens agree to peace? Sparta had no fleet.
Persia's gold and its army hadn't helped. Surely, the Spartans were finished.

As with Syracuse, it was a proud and foolish decision.

Pharnabazus' commitment to Sparta's success ran deeper than Athens
guessed, and Persia's riches were endless. The Spartan survivors had hardly
begun to regroup before the satrap was clothing and rearming them, providing
them with ample timber to start cutting beams to build new ships. Agis sallied
forth from Decelea, most likely in an effort to distract the Athenians in the
wake of their victory (and to boost Spartan morale), but the Athenians called
his bluff and he fled, losing some of his rearguard to Athenian skirmishers.
Meanwhile, the grain shipments the Spartans had fought so hard to stop came
sailing through under the protection of the Athenian fleet. The Spartans sent
Clearchus in command of an allied fleet of 15 ships to reinforce Spartan-held
Byzantium, losing three to Athenian raiders en route. The Athenians,
meanwhile, concentrated on expanding their hold over the Ionian coast at the

expense of Persia. In 410 BC, Sparta finally dealt with Pylos, blockading the Messenian and rebel helot garrison by sea and assaulting the walls. Athens sent aid by sea, justifiably confident in its ability to defeat the Spartan blockade, but fell victim to a storm. (Diodorus tells us the Athenians were so furious with the admiral that they put him on trial for treason. He bribed his way out.) In the end, the Spartans did not capture the city, but instead received its surrender on the condition the garrison was allowed to depart under a truce. It was some consolation after the triple naval disasters to have finally plucked the thorn out of their paw that had festered there for the past 15 years.

Cerata and Chalcedon

Sparta wasn't the only city-state to regain territory lost for over a decade. The following year, Megara finally recaptured its port of Nisea after nearly as long, only to have Athens dispatch an army to take it back. An allied army of Spartans, Megarians and Syracusans marched out to meet them. The two armies clashed at Mount Cerata, and the Athenians soundly thrashed the Spartan-led force, forcing them to withdraw. (Diodorus doesn't say the force was led by Spartans, but it is unlikely they would have ceded leadership to any of their subordinate allies. Only 20 Spartans were killed, the majority of the casualties being absorbed by the Megarians.)

That same year, Alcibiades laid siege to Spartan-controlled Chalcedon by the Hellespont. Hippocrates, the Spartan governor, led his own troops and the Chalcedonians out to fight the Athenians while Pharnabazus' men were kept back by the Athenians garrisoning their siege wall. The hoplite battle was evenly matched until Alcibiades' cavalry superiority shifted the scales. The Spartan failure to adequately invest in cavalry, with their insistence in leaning on their own inflated reputation as the masters of hoplite warfare, stung them yet again. Hippocrates was killed and the Spartan-led army routed. Pharnabazus was forced to agree to take Athenian envoys to Darius II in order to save his own skin.

Defense of Byzantium

Alcibiades laid siege to Byzantium next, the Spartan-held city presenting the greatest obstacle to the safe shipment of grain to Athens. Clearchus held the city against assault and worked tirelessly to keep his starving troops fed as the city was blockaded and cut off. Unfortunately, Byzantium's defenders needed Clearchus' personal leadership to stiffen their spines, and they betrayed the city to the Athenians while their commander was meeting with Pharnabazus to gather badly needed money. Clearchus' garrison fought like lions in the city's market, but once the Athenians promised that no harm would come to the Byzantines, they switched sides, and the Spartans' (and other foreign troops') fate was sealed.

Alcibiades was triumphant. His star crested as he took back every Spartan-controlled city in the region except the naval base at Abydus. The way to the Black Sea was secured and it seemed that Athens was on the verge of ending this war in its favor once and for all.

No one could have believed that in less than five years, all would be lost and it would have Sparta's boot on its throat.

One of the main reasons for this reversal of fortune sailed to take command of the fleet that same year. His name was Lysander. He had been a *mothax* like Gylippus owing to his family's poverty, but he claimed descent from the line of the demigod Heracles himself. He was the lover of the later Spartan Eurypontid king Agesilaus II, a position that aided both men enormously. Very little is known of his early life, but it's likely he rose from poverty due to the strength of his personality and his ambition. Some scholars cast him as Sparta's Alcibiades – cunning, brilliant, ruthless and intensely competent. He certainly proved those attributes in the years that followed.

Perhaps only slightly less important to the ultimate Spartan victory in the Peloponnesian Wars than Lysander was the Persian prince Cyrus the Younger, Darius II's teenaged son, sent out as the satrap of Lydia and Phrygia and commander of the army stationed in Asia Minor. Lysander charmed him as much as Alcibiades had Tissaphernes, convincing the young prince to open his coffers to the point where sailors in the Spartan fleet were paid more than their Athenian counterparts. Lysander's thinking was that the higher pay would encourage skilled rowers to desert the Athenian cause and come over to the Spartan fleet. This strategy would turn out to be devastatingly effective.

Assault on Athens

Meanwhile, Agis assembled a truly massive army and marched on Athens in 407 BC, hoping to take advantage of the fact that most of the city's manpower was abroad dealing with the Ionian coast and the Hellespont. Athens garrisoned the walls with boys and old men, and once Agis' Boeotian allied cavalry were defeated by Athens' horsemen, he retreated. Humiliated, he challenged them to battle the following day, and Athens' badly outnumbered and extremely inexpert force marshaled outside the city walls to face him. Agis, likely easily goaded into mistakes by the shame he'd earned before the Battle of Mantinea, rashly attacked, bringing his troops into missile range of the walls. His army was shot through with arrows and he was forced to retreat yet again. He tried to make up for this double humiliation by ravaging the Attic countryside, but his reputation was surely further stained.

With this latest humiliation, things were still looking very good for Athens. Despite their control of Decelea, Sparta had signally failed to close the sea route to the Black Sea, to make real inroads in Ionia, or to significantly threaten Athens itself. All they had was Persian support.

It would prove to be enough.

Notium

The tide turned the following year when Alcibiades left command of the Athenian fleet at Notium to his steersman Antiochus with strict instructions not to attack the Spartan fleet, which was stationed across the water at Ephesus about midway down modern Turkey's west coast.

Antiochus disobeyed his commander, sending out a token force of ten ships to try to lure the Spartans into battle as Alcibiades had done at Cyzicus to such great effect. Lysander took the bait, but the results were the exact opposite. He sank Antiochus' own ship and then turned out his entire fleet of 90 ships, chasing the bait force back to its harbor where the Athenians were completely unprepared to face the entire might of the Spartan fleet. They deployed in desperation to try to save their beleaguered bait force, but the rapid launch put them into the water out of all order and Lysander was able to thrash them soundly, capturing or sinking 22 Athenian ships before the rest of the fleet could retreat inside the harbor. Antiochus at least would not have to answer for his rash action. He'd lost his life, likely when his flagship went down in the initial attack.

In retrospect, the victory was not that great. Twenty-two ships out of a fleet of some 80 was a significant loss, but not so great that the Athenians couldn't recover. But the writing was on the wall: after years of being on the naval back foot, Lysander and Cyrus had finally figured out how to beat Athens at sea – the higher pay offered by the Spartan fleet was starting to tell as experienced rowers deserted the Athenian fleet to work for higher wages serving Sparta. Most importantly, the message had been sent to both sides – Sparta had engaged Athens in a stand-up naval battle and won. Athens' fleet was no longer unbeatable. In Lysander, Sparta finally had an admiral who could go toe-to-toe with the mightiest navy in the world. In Cyrus, Sparta finally had a source of money that could give him the navy to do it.

The source of so much of the Athenian navy's success, Alcibiades, was roundly blamed for the defeat. He had sailed off and left the fleet under the command of a friend, rather than a seasoned board of admirals who would have known better than to tempt Lysander. He was drummed out of Athens and fled to Thrace. The other Athenian commanders, including Thrasybulus, were deposed with him, depriving Athens of badly needed effective naval leadership. As it had in the Syracusan expedition, Athens displayed relentless commitment to losing the war to Sparta.

Lysander meanwhile was replaced by the new admiral for the year (admirals were allowed to serve for only a single year), Callicratidas. By all accounts, Lysander didn't want to give up power, and he worked to build alliances with leadership in all the cities allied to Sparta. These alliances were with Lysander personally, and not with Sparta, a departure that would be shocking if the Spartan ideal of selfless sacrifice for the state were always true.

But Lysander's interest in his own personal ambition is another glaring contradiction to the Lycurgan ideal of selflessness and prioritization of the Spartan state over personal glory. As with Pausanias, Lysander certainly had no problem promoting his own cult of personality.

Callicratidas arrived with his own substantial reinforcements, and now commanded a truly enormous fleet of some 140 ships. Paying that many rowers was a challenge. Callicratidas refused to take Cyrus as a patron, and so Cyrus' purse mostly closed with the departure of Lysander, evidence that their personal relationship was the driving factor in Cyrus' support (Lysander's personal magnetism matched Alcibiades'). This forced Callicratidas to be aggressive in search of plunder. He assaulted the Athenian position on Chios, taking it, then plundered another Chian city, selling the Athenians into slavery to pay his fleet.

Mytilene

Conon, the Athenian admiral in command after Alcibiades was cashiered, sailed the Athenian fleet to the region off modern Turkey's west coast, hoping to catch the superior Spartan-led fleet unawares. Instead, the two fleets sighted each other off Mytilene and Callicratidas gave chase. Conon stopped fleeing when the front Spartan-led ships outdistanced the rest of their fleet, and turned his own ships to fight, no doubt hoping to pick them off. But this was not the same Spartan navy that had been defeated under Mindarus. The skilled rowers held position and their marines kept the ships from being boarded long enough for the rest of the fleet to catch up. It was Conon's fleet that wound up divided, and the Athenians lost 30 ships before securing the remaining 40 in the harbor covered by Mytilene's fortifications and fleeing overland to the city. The city and its harbor were blockaded and placed under siege. Conon ran the blockade with two ships, one of which got through to beg the Athenians to send help.

Arginusae

Athens' response was massive and immediate. Golden statues of Nike (the goddess of victory) were melted down to provide critical gold. Citizens, metics and slaves alike were turned out to man a massive Athenian and allied fleet of some 150 ships which sailed to the Arginusae islands near Mytilene. Callicratidas' success at Mytilene had loosened Cyrus' purse strings, and he used the money to reinforce his own fleet to 170. He took 120 of them to meet the Athenian fleet, leaving 50 to maintain the blockade of Mytilene. That he was willing to take on the Athenians despite being outnumbered was a testament to Spartan naval confidence and an indicator of how many skilled rowers the higher Spartan wages had been able to attract.

As I have done so often in this book, I have to point out that relatively recent scholarship attacks our main source on Callicratidas and his decision-making (Xenophon's *Hellenica*) and advances different views, but I'm going with the majority view here.

The two fleets formed lines of battle, the Athenian ships crewed by less-experienced and worse-trained rowers than the higher-paid Spartan fleet (Xenophon specifically points out that the *"Athenians were inferior in seamanship"*), their decks likewise crammed with amateur marines drawn from the widest recruitment pool possible. The Spartan fleet was better equipped, better trained, and most importantly, had the critical morale advantage. By all accounts it should have won.

But weather prevented the night engagement that Callicratidas desired, and then the admiral made an error similar to Brasidas' foolhardy rush down the gangplank at Pylos. Xenophon has Callicratidas' Megarian pilot warn him against rushing to engage the enemy. The Spartan admiral's response is dramatic, brave and incredibly stupid: *"Callicratidas, however, said that Sparta would fare none the worse if he were killed, but flight, he said, would be a disgrace."*

This was, of course, exactly what happened.

Callicratidas' ship rammed an enemy vessel with the admiral up on deck, and the resulting shock to the Spartan ship threw him overboard where he either drowned or was crushed between the colliding hulls. The sudden death of their admiral had to have been a shock to Spartan morale, and the Spartan right, where he had commanded, quickly disintegrated. The Spartan left held on a bit longer, before turning and fleeing for their lives. All told, 77 Spartan and allied ships were sunk, to a cost of just 25 on the Athenian side.

The problem for the Athenians was that the crews of those 25 ships were still in the water around Arginusae and desperately in need of rescue. Athens divided its command, sending its senior admirals against Mytilene where Conon was still blockaded, and leaving two junior admirals to carry out the rescue of the shipwrecked Athenian crews. A storm arose that prevented them from completing either operation.

The Spartan Eteonicus, hearing of the defeat, elected to lie about it. Xenophon tells us he directed a messenger *"to sail out of the harbor in silence and not talk with anyone, and then to sail back immediately to his fleet, wearing garlands and shouting that Callicratidas had been victorious in battle and that all the ships of the Athenians had been destroyed."* He then withdrew his blockading force to Chios where he was joined by the remnants of the defeated Spartan fleet.

The popular narrative is that Athens once again proved that no good deed went unpunished. The admirals, despite having won a great victory and then being prevented from following up on it by a force of nature, were put on trial for failing to rescue the sailors from the sunken ships, convicted and executed. The move, in a single stroke, deprived Athens of its greatest admirals and provided a powerful disincentive for talented naval officers to agree to serve.

However, more recent scholarship (in the last 20 years) makes the argument that the trials and executions were actually driven by charges of financial crimes against these admirals, and that these admirals made false accusations against their rivals in order to save their own skins. This more recent view paints a much kinder picture of Athenian justice.

But even if we accept that Athens didn't bungle the handling of the admirals post-Arginusae, it certainly wasn't done with its efforts to assure its own destruction. Sparta *again* sued for peace in the wake of this major defeat, and Athens once again refused. This marked the third time in the long stretch of these wars that Sparta, and not Athens, had tried to negotiate an end to hostilities after a major defeat (the other two being after Pylos/Sphacteria and Cyzicus). Athens wouldn't get the chance to refuse again.

Sparta had learned its lesson: every admiral it had put in charge of its fleet – Astyochus, Mindarus and Callicratidas – had been a spectacular failure. Only one had brought the Spartans anything like reliable success – Lysander, and he had served his term limit. However, he'd also worked tirelessly to build a cult of personality that served his ambitions, not only among Sparta's elite and its allies, but also with Prince Cyrus. The members of that cult now joined a chorus asking for him to be restored to command of the fleet. Sparta complied the only way it could. Since the law was clear that a man couldn't serve as fleet admiral twice, Lysander was sent as a "secretary" (*epistoleus*) to the Spartan admiral Aracus. Aracus was surely made aware that his title was merely a formality. Lysander was in charge.

With Lysander back at the helm, Cyrus was quick to funnel money to the Spartan fleet, bringing it rapidly back to full strength. He immediately put the fleet into action restoring oligarchies in cities that had gone back to Athenian-style democracy, including in Miletus even though it was a Spartan ally. Cyrus' affection for Lysander was so great that he turned the income of his province over to the man.

Cyrus was later arrested by his brother Artaxerxes on the death of their father, Darius II, but pardoned after the intercession of his mother. This gave a hint of future conflict to come, one in which Sparta would have a role.

Aegospotami

With this extra money from Cyrus' province, Lysander fully reconstituted the Spartan fleet up to 170 ships, and set off on a series of campaigns against Athenian-held cities in the region. At last Lysander seized Lampascus, which provided him with the perfect striking base from which to cut off Athens' Black Sea grain shipments once again.

Athens of course had no choice but to try to bring him to battle with its own fleet of 180 ships, once again much more poorly crewed and equipped. It had gotten lucky with Callicratidas' headstrong foolishness at Arginusae (if we believe Xenophon, whose account of Callicratidas at Arginusae is disputed). It would not be so lucky again against Lysander.

The Athenian fleet beached near Lampascus where it could keep an eye on Lysander. Alcibiades himself came down to the beach to advise the Athenian admirals that their position was poorly chosen. It would be difficult to supply their troops, and the position lacked a decent harbor to refit their ships. Alcibiades also offered the services of an army of Thracian troops that he had charmed into being willing to support the Athenian cause. The disgraced general was ignored and sent packing.

He was to be proven exactly right.

We have conflicting accounts from Xenophon and Diodorus on how the Battle of Aegospotami unfolded. Diodorus tells us the Athenians attempted another luring maneuver with a small decoy fleet as Antiochus had done at Notium, and that it failed just as spectacularly. I find this hard to believe. However inexperienced the new Athenian admirals may have been, they surely would have heard of what happened at Notium and been determined not to repeat the same mistake. Xenophon's account is much more believable – that the bad position of the Athenian fleet forced its crews to range too far from the beach in an effort to find food. Lysander launched from Abydus while they were still out foraging, and captured the vast majority of their ships while they were still on the beach with no naval fighting at all. Considering the poor Athenian morale and the fact that their fleet couldn't afford to compete with Spartan high pay for veteran rowers, the Athenian crews would have been undisciplined and amateur. This is exactly the kind of breakdown in discipline we can expect in such a force. Lysander's fleet, on the other hand, was hardened, professional and motivated. In short, the Spartans were ready to take full advantage of Athens' lapse.

Sparta's victory was total. Athens' fleet was utterly annihilated. Only nine ships escaped (Conon was on one of them). Sparta took the rest of the fleet, including 3,000 Athenian crew made prisoner. Exhausted and enraged by decades of atrocities on both sides of the war, Lysander butchered all of them. Athens, with no fleet to oppose him, could do nothing but watch in horror.

With this master stroke, the Peloponnesian Wars were effectively over. Lysander took a victory lap, bringing city after city over to the Spartan cause. Only Samos and Athens held out. Both were placed under siege. Lysander sailed to Attica where a Spartan army was already ravaging the countryside, but no serious effort was made to take Athens by storm.

There was no need. With no Athenian fleet to keep the sea lanes open, and the Decelean fort dominating the Attic routes, Athens was at long last completely deprived of food. The citizens of both Athens and Samos bravely starved until 404 BC, then at last threw open their gates. Sparta marched onto the Acropolis and set its terms – Athens would demolish its long walls, take back its pro-oligarchy exiles, keep no more than 12 ships in its navy, and above all hold the same friends and enemies as Sparta.

After nearly 30 years of devastating war that had convulsed Greece in misery at the cost of tens of thousands of lives, and that had seen Persia's power rise, Sparta had finally won. It was, at long last, the undisputed master of Greece.

It would hold its mastery for less than a year.

Sparta's record during the Peace of Nicias, in Sicily, and in the Decelean phase of the Peloponnesian Wars

While it's a stretch to call the Peace of Nicias an actual peace, and while the fighting in Sicily technically doesn't fall into either the Archidamian or Decelean phases of the Peloponnesian Wars, Sparta remained locked in combat with Athens throughout these intervening years. In the nine battles of this interim period between the two phases, Sparta's record is excellent, winning six and losing just three, and those three minor defeats that underpinned the ultimate victory in Sicily. Much of this good record can be credited to the dedication and endurance of Gylippus, and also to the discipline and organization of the Spartan army yielding major dividends at the First Battle of Mantinea. However, even that great victory was marred by an appalling breakdown in discipline as Agis' subordinate commanders refused to close a fatal gap in the line, almost costing Sparta the battle. Indeed, that near-catastrophe almost never got the chance to come to pass, as Agis' hot-headed desire for redemption almost spurred him to throw away the battle at the outset by attacking from a disadvantageous position. Assigning him supervisors to oversee him turned out to be prescient indeed.

The Decelean phase of the Peloponnesian Wars can be truly said to have been won on the sea. Sparta's performance certainly improved, including the overall victory and the end of the decades-long series of conflicts that had rocked an entire generation. Yet when we look at the 16 fights we examined in this phase, we find Sparta losing ten, and grinding to a stalemate in one more, leaving just five outright victories – all but one of these won at sea.

All of these sea victories resulted inarguably from one critical resource – Persian gold necessary to build and outfit the Spartan fleet and eventually to attract the most skilled crews. It can certainly be argued that Sparta didn't battle its way to victory in the Decelean phase of the Peloponnesian Wars. Rather, it purchased it with someone else's money.

The one land victory (the taking of Cyzicus) was a joint operation with the purportedly hated Persian enemy, suddenly Sparta's erstwhile friend and ally and likely providing the critical siege skill that Sparta lacked and had still failed to develop.

Additionally, the victory at Eretria was accomplished via a betrayal inside that city. Sparta's attempts on open land, where its hoplites were reputed to dominate, were a litany of embarrassing failures as Agis II struggled to redeem himself. Lastly, we must acknowledge that one of the key strategies that arguably won the Decelean phase was suggested not by any Spartan genius, but by the Athenian Alcibiades, who clued Sparta into the opportunity presented by fortifying Decelea.

Archidamus' argument before the Archidamian phase of the war kicked off – that Sparta needed to ally with Persia to obtain the gold it would need to face Athens at sea – proved out to be prescient and correct. That said, we have to consider the very real possibility that the ancient source for giving credit to Alcibiades for Sparta's winning strategy was Alcibiades himself, which of course makes it much more doubtful. That said, we cannot prove the sources wrong in this regard, and so I lean toward taking them at face value, though in the end we cannot be sure.

V

MASTERS OF GREECE?
SPARTA SQUANDERS ITS
HEGEMONY

*For victory, if the gods are kind, will return to us our country and
homes, freedom and honors, children, to those who have them,
and wives. Happy, indeed, are those of us who shall win the victory
and live to behold the gladdest day of all! And happy also he who is slain;
for no one, however rich he may be, will gain a monument so glorious.
Now, when the right moment comes, I will sound the battle cry . . .
then let us all, with one spirit, take vengeance upon these men
for the outrages we have suffered.*

Thrasybulus to the Athenian exiles before the Battle
of Munichia, Xenophon, *Hellenica*

404 BC saw Sparta at the head of a massive naval empire that spanned all
of Greece and well into the Balkans. It might have spanned the west coast

of modern Turkey as well as the islands there, but Sparta's debt to Persia was too great to ignore. Every Spartan of note knew that Persian money had made this victory possible, and Persia's price was clear and simple – domination of the Greeks of Asia, without interference from the Greeks of Greece. Sparta now willingly tugged its collective forelock and let Persia proceed. A central pillar of the Bronze Lie, that the Spartans were enemies of the Persians, xenophobes who kept a European Greece free of oriental influence, was proven laughably false. Gone were the days when Sparta would send a delegation to Cyrus the Great, warning him to keep his hands off Greek people wherever they might find themselves. This new Sparta had bigger concerns.

The first of these was to consolidate Spartan power by cracking down on the democratic factions in the city-states across Greece. Pro-democracy leaders were massacred and Spartan garrisons, led by military governors, installed. In their place, Lysander set up decarchies – ruling councils of ten men, all loyal to him. Sparta now had the Athenian treasury and more importantly the tributary city-states which were still required to pay into it. Sparta's reputation, already suffering from 30 years of protracted war, defeat after defeat, rejected attempts to make peace, the debacle at Sphacteria, and the final reliance on Persian gold, now plummeted as Lysander's heavy hand squeezed Greece entirely – butchering political opponents, replacing them with his personal friends. But the worst blow to Spartan prestige was the city turning its back on the Greeks abroad, leaving them to suffer under the Persian yoke.

Other Spartans didn't help matters. The egomania of men like Pausanias and Lysander was not an isolated thing. In 403 BC, Clearchus was sent to Byzantium to aid the government there in a war against Thracian tribesmen. No sooner did he arrive and recruit an army of mercenaries than he took control of the government. Diodorus tells us that he used a festival as an excuse to gather the leading Byzantine men together and massacre them, slaughtering the city's chief magistrates and strangling 30 leading citizens. He then levied false charges against the wealthy of the city (presumably as an excuse to appropriate said wealth) and then had them either executed or exiled.

Tarnished Victory – The Athenian Insurgency, The Elean War, and Spartan Actions in Asia Minor

Selymbria

At last, Sparta sent an army against Clearchus under the command of Panthoedas. Clearchus fled to Selymbria where he could be more assured of the population's loyalty. There, he fought a field battle against Panthoedas. He was defeated and shut up in Selymbria, which was placed under siege. Clearchus escaped the siege in the night and fled to Persia.

In Persia, he managed to secure a leading role in Prince Cyrus' army during Cyrus' rebellion against his brother Artaxerxes. He would be with that army during its defeat at Cunaxa two years later. Xenophon, a major source for much of this book, would campaign alongside him. The epic journey of the defeated Greek mercenary army, the famous "March of the 10,000" from deep in hostile Persia back to Greece, is the subject of Xenophon's most famous work, the *Anabasis*.

Sparta also threw its weight behind the vicious Syracusan tyrant Dionysius. Diodorus tells of the Spartan emissary Aristus who was sent ostensibly to overthrow the tyranny, but in the end betrayed the Syracusan dissidents and executed them in the hope of ingratiating Dionysius to the Spartan cause so they could call upon his services later.

Diodorus is abundantly clear about how this impacted Sparta's reputation, for Aristus had "*made strong the tyrant by betraying those who put their faith in him, and by such conduct brought disgrace both upon himself and upon his native land.*" Sparta's reputation had been made on the overthrow of tyrants (when it suited them). The story of Polycrates of Samos was probably well known. This glaring contradiction was not lost on Greece, and served only to reinforce the impression left by the depredations of Lysander and Clearchus.

Sparta also immediately added two powerful new enemies – Corinth and Thebes, who both insisted that Athens be made to pay for its role in the war. The city should have been razed, they argued, its inhabitants all sold into slavery. But far more concerning to Corinth and Therese was the money taken from the remains of the Athenian treasury, the gold and silver statues adorning the city, the riches plundered from its leading citizens. All of it had gone to Sparta. Corinth and Thebes felt robbed of their share of the loot. The result was a simmering anti-Spartan axis, a coalition including the traditional enemies of Argos and Athens, only now with the much larger, richer and more powerful Corinth and Thebes added as well.

Diodorus, Xenophon and Plutarch all argue that the influx of money into Sparta turned society on its head. I do not believe this at all. We have already seen throughout Sparta's history that the iron money myth of the old Lycurgan model was most likely not true, and that gold and silver coinage had been a fact of life in Sparta for a long time. There is clear evidence of the taking and giving of bribes, the seeking of riches, and all of the normal human tendencies of greed and wealth building. It's possible that Sparta's sudden enrichment may have proved difficult for the city-state to get to grips with, but it is not as if the state was previously without wealth and suddenly came into it.

But there's even more proof that Sparta's refusal to use gold and silver money is just another part of the Bronze Lie. Between 448 and 420 BC, leading Spartans competed and won the four-horse chariot race at the Olympic Games eight out of nine times. In 396 and 392 BC, Cynisca, the sister of the Spartan king Agesilaus, had winning teams (though she didn't drive the chariots herself, this did technically make her the first woman to win an Olympic event).

The cost of competing in the four-horse chariot race was enormous. You had to breed and raise champion horses. You had to hire a crew and support staff and construct or buy a state-of-the-art chariot.

And not only did these Spartans win the events, they even commissioned bronze statues to commemorate their victories. Cynisca appeared to be aware of how significant her win was, for she commissioned *seven* statues, one for her, one for her charioteer, one for the chariot, and another four for each of the horses. The statues came with an inscription (Xenophon claims the inscription was Agesilaus' and not Cynisca's idea) reading "*Kings of Sparta are my father and brothers, [I] Cynisca, victorious with a chariot of swift-footed horses, have erected this statue. I declare myself the only woman in all Greece to have won this crown.*"

These statues were very likely made by foreign sculptors, and even if they were made by Greeks, those sculptors would have been paid enormous sums, almost certainly in silver and gold.

Lysander certainly made the most of his wealth. Plutarch tells us that he ordered a bronze statue of himself put up at Delphi. He also notes that Lysander *"was at this time more powerful than any Greek before him had been, and was thought to cherish a pretentious pride that was greater even than his power"* and made no protest when the people of Samos voted to rename their festival of Hera to a festival of Lysander. Furthermore, Plutarch tells us that Lysander kept poets in his retinue who were clearly there to write songs of praise about him (he gave the poet Antilochus a cap full of silver as a reward for a particularly fawning poem). The displays of wealth and the deliberate cultivation of fame and personal glory are, yet again, contradictions to the legend of wealth-hating Spartan selflessness. The sources are in universal agreement that Lysander was a brilliant commander and a skilled diplomat, and that he *knew* he was these things and clearly felt that his qualities should elevate him above other men. He took to the life of a celebrity.

But Lysander's glory complicated Sparta's leadership situation. There was the usual rivalry and tension between the Agiad king (now Pausanias, the son of Pleistoanax, who had died in 409 BC) and the Eurypontid king (still Agis II, who had repeatedly marched on Athens to such little effect until Lysander's naval victory made Athens' defeat inevitable). But now there was a third player – Lysander, enormously popular and with many powerful men in many cities across Greece that were personally loyal to him.

This constant scheming and jockeying for position cannot have helped to improve Sparta's reputation among its now subject peoples.

In 403 BC, just a year after Athens' surrender, matters finally came to a head and Greece erupted into violence. Lysander had established the "Thirty Tyrants," an oligarchic ruling council in Athens made up of men personally loyal to him. This Thirty was led by Critias, the famous student of Socrates. Lysander garrisoned the city with 700 hoplites to enforce the council's will. With this small force, the council initiated a corrupt reign of terror that was marked by its excesses – accusing and executing political rivals or those whose property they wanted to confiscate.

Phyle

Thrasybulus, the respected Athenian admiral whose command we just examined, was exiled to Thebes when the Thirty took control. In 403 BC, driven by the excesses of the Spartan puppet government, he returned with just 70 other exiles. They seized the fortress of Phyle on Mount Parnes, on the border of Attica and Boeotia. The Thirty turned out an overwhelming force of 3,000 infantry and an unspecified number of cavalry. They laid siege to Phyle, but were unable to take it. Xenophon describes Thrasybulus' force resisting the initial Spartan-allied Athenian assault (while Xenophon doesn't specify this, it's very likely that Thrasybulus' force had already grown well past 70 men, as other exiles and disaffected Athenians came over to his army).

Still, however determined Thrasybulus may have been, he would surely have eventually been starved out by the overwhelming enemy force. But a snow storm blew in, so severe that the Spartan army was forced to break the siege and march back to Athens *"after losing a goodly number of their camp followers by the attacks of the men in Phyle."*

Back in Athens, the Thirty worried that Thrasybulus might plunder the surrounding countryside, and sent the army back out to keep watch on his force, which had now grown to 700 men.

Rather than risk being shut up in the fortress, Thrasybulus marched his force out by night and hid them *"three or four stadia"* away (according to Xenophon. A *stadion* was approximately 600 feet, for a total of 1,800–2,400 feet, or a little less than half a mile) from the Spartan force. Why the Spartans did not deploy scouts or send out patrols to detect an ambushing force, Xenophon doesn't say, but it certainly matches previous Spartan failures to adequately scout an area or set watches when battle might be imminent (Sphacteria being the most glaring example). If they did post scouts, they failed to detect Thrasybulus' force, and the exiles mounted a dawn raid on the Spartan camp.

The surprise was total, with Xenophon telling us that the Athenian exiles caught two of the enemy *"still in their beds"* and completely routed both the Spartan and pro-Spartan Athenian infantry and cavalry, killing 120 hoplites.

They pursued the fleeing enemy for a little less than a mile, then returned to the site of the attack and set up a trophy before looting the camp and taking the captured arms and equipment back to Phyle. Pro-Spartan Athenian cavalry rode out to the site to see if they could rescue anyone, but all of the Spartan and pro-Spartan Athenian force was dead or fled, so they returned empty handed.

Terrified, Critias and the Thirty engineered the arrest of leading figures in the Attic town of Eleusis, in order to create a fallback position should it become necessary to abandon Athens. It was a smart move. The victory before Phyle eroded faith in Athens' pro-Spartan government and trumpeted Thrasybulus' fame across the region. His ranks continued to swell with other exiles and anti-Spartan Athenians who fled the oppressive regime for a chance to strike back.

Just five days after the dawn raid, Thrasybulus had enough troops to leave 200 men to garrison Phyle and march another 1,000 to the Athenian port of Piraeus. Here, he took the hill of Munichia that overlooked the port.

Munichia

It was a deliberate provocation, a clear display that the pro-Spartan government of Athens was too weak to keep an enemy army from showing up on its very doorstep. It couldn't allow this to stand; it had no choice but to come out and fight.

Xenophon doesn't give us exact numbers on the pro-Spartan side, but we know they grossly outnumbered Thrasybulus and his 1,000 men, forming a phalanx on the Munichia hill ten ranks deep with the light infantry stationed behind it. Meanwhile, the pro-Spartan forces formed up in a phalanx 50 ranks deep. While we would need to know the exact frontage of the formation to properly understand the disparity in numbers, we can guess that it was vast, probably at least 3-to-1. The "*Laconian hoplites*" (likely the actual Spartans who made up the garrison of Athens) were on the right, and the pro-Spartan oligarchs (including Critias) made up the left. The entire pro-Spartan force advanced on the hill.

Thrasybulus' pre-battle speech is a good object lesson of how much the Spartan hoplite's reputation had suffered in the last nearly 30 years of war. There is no indication that the Athenian exiles regarded them as particularly frightening opponents. Thrasybulus simply reminded his men that they had just defeated this same enemy a few days ago and sent them running. It would be easy enough to do it again. Xenophon also has Thrasybulus noting the advantage of his position "*because they are marching up hill, they cannot throw either spears or javelins over the heads of those in front of them, while we, throwing both spears and javelins and stones down hill, shall reach them and strike down many.*"

This proved true. The Athenian exiles were able to soften the much larger pro-Spartan force with missile fire while their enemy was still attempting to advance into range. At this point, Thrasybulus ordered the charge and the full mass of his hoplite phalanx launched itself down the hill, letting the weight of its weapons and armor add to the crunching impact that would begin the *ōthismos*.

The pro-Spartan phalanx, already bloodied and slowed by Thrasybulus' missiles, broke apart. *Ōthismos* became rout. The relatively light casualties on the pro-Spartan side (some 70 dead) may indicate that the pro-Spartan force broke instantly, or possibly began running before Thrasybulus' force even made contact. Among those 70 dead was Critias himself, but the most critical casualty was any prestige the Thirty had remaining. Their reputation was utterly broken. After two battlefield defeats by inferior forces, they could not hope to rule by fear any longer.

Piraeus

The following day, the Thirty were deposed and fled to Eleusis. A council of ten was set up in their place. But if Thrasybulus had hoped this new government would be willing to make concessions, he was sadly mistaken. The new government in Athens immediately sent word to Sparta begging for help.

Sparta, surely humiliated by its inability to keep Athens under control so soon after it had surrendered, appointed Lysander to deal with the matter. The Thirty were Lysander's personal men, and he favored a policy of violent reprisal. He rode out for Eleusis to raise an army to end Thrasybulus' ambitions brutally and completely. His brother Libys commanded the Spartan fleet to blockade Piraeus and prevent Thrasybulus' men from being supplied by sea.

Xenophon tells us that after Lysander left for Eleusis, Pausanias persuaded the ephors to let him lead out the full army of the Peloponnesian League against Thrasybulus. Xenophon has Pausanias moved by envy and a desire for glory to take up the mission to deal with Thrasybulus while Lysander was still busy raising troops. But when I consider Pausanias' actions in the days that followed, I believe he understood that Thrasybulus' success was due to the Thirty's high-handed and corrupt government, and saw a critical lesson in the swelling of Thrasybulus' army from 70 men to over 1,000 in just a few days.

Athens would be pacified only through clemency, not massacre. Thrasybulus' men must be beaten, but then concessions would have to be made.

Notably, Sparta's Boeotian and Corinthian allies refused to accompany the Spartan expedition to Athens. This refusal can't have endeared them to Sparta, and is a sign that not even a single year after the defeat of Athens, Sparta's hegemony over Greece was not remotely a settled thing.

Arriving at Piraeus, Pausanias ordered Thrasybulus' exiles to disperse and go home. Not surprisingly, they refused. Xenophon doesn't tell us the exact size of Pausanias' army, but he tells us Pausanias sent up two *morai* (divisions) of Spartan troops (around 1,150 men) and three squadrons of pro-Spartan Athenian cavalry to engage the exiles.

Once again, Thrasybulus was likely badly outnumbered but still managed to beat back the attack. As Pausanias withdrew, Thrasybulus sent out light troops to harass his retreat, which enraged Pausanias.

The king responded by committing the cavalry and younger, faster infantry to pursuing Thrasybulus' light infantry. They killed 30, chasing the survivors back into Piraeus. They apparently blundered into the rest of Thrasybulus' army here, who peppered them with missile fire, killing two Spartan polemarchs and an Olympic victor who was one of Pausanias' bodyguards. Thrasybulus then engaged with his hoplites and the Spartans were driven back once more.

Pausanias, hard pressed, rallied his troops on a hill where he "*formed an extremely deep phalanx and led the charge against the Athenians.*" Thrasybulus foolishly "*did indeed accept battle at close quarters*" despite the Spartans holding high ground and Thrasybulus having a marsh at his back. The overwhelming impetus of the deeper Spartan phalanx shoved the Athenian exiles back into the marsh where their footing must have been treacherous. In the end, they broke and ran, with another 150 killed. The Spartan force lost only 13 dead, all buried outside the Cerameicus gate of Athens. This tomb was found and excavated in 1930 – four intact skeletons showing war wounds were found.

Xenophon tells us Pausanias set up a trophy to celebrate his victory, but is also careful to note that the king felt kindly toward the defeated and immediately set to work reconciling the exiles with the oligarchic faction in Athens. Both Thrasybulus and the pro-Spartan oligarchs sent emissaries to

Sparta, who in turn sent 15 officials to work with Pausanias to negotiate a settlement. In the end, Athens' democracy was restored, almost all of the exiles were pardoned, and the insurgency was quelled.

This speaks highly of Pausanias, who showed not only military skill and valor, but a keen politician's and intelligence officer's grasp of the situation on the ground and the maturity and foresight to make the moves that were in Sparta's best interests – as Corinth and Boeotia's refusal to march with Pausanias showed, Sparta clearly wasn't in Greece's good graces, and an insurgency in Athens would very likely have sucked in Argos, Elis, Mantinea and likely Corinth and Thebes too. It is very possible that Pausanias did what he did because he knew it was Sparta's only hope to avoid another flare-up of the civil wars that had dominated Greece for a generation.

He surely avoided this, but he also clearly illustrated that, just a single year after Athens' surrender, Sparta was master of nothing. The city-state was not in a position to dictate policy to anyone, not even its recently crushed rival, which, though forced into alliance with Sparta, still had its democracy back, with many of its heroes, including those like Thrasybulus who had taken up arms against Sparta, alive and unharmed. This was very likely a *better* outcome for not just Sparta but all of Greece, but it certainly wasn't an indicator of strength.

Indeed, Pausanias' actions so enraged some leading Spartans that he was put on trial immediately after, but was acquitted when all five ephors voted in his favor. Voting to condemn him was his rival co-king, Agis.

The Elean War

The following year, Agis was back in the field, leading the Spartan army against Elis for its refusal to liberate its subject towns (the Eleans, quite rightly, told the Spartans they'd be happy to do so just as soon as the Spartans liberated their *perioikoi*), and also to pay Elis back for barring Sparta from the Olympic Games. Pausanias (the geographer, not the king) tells us that Agis interpreted an earthquake as a sign from the gods to disband his army and call off the campaign. This is possible, but with so many other examples of Spartans using religious reasons to avoid fighting, it's equally possible Agis didn't feel confident in his forces, or was worried about the enemy, and used it as an excuse.

The following year, Sparta mustered to invade Elis again and this time Athens sent troops in support – the wise clemency of Pausanias (the king, not the geographer) was paying off. Athens may have once again been democratic, but it was firmly in the Spartan camp now. Thebes and Corinth once again refused to send troops, a harbinger of things to come.

We get our story of the Elean War from two sources, Xenophon and Diodorus, and each tells it from the point of view of a different king. Xenophon tells us that Agis ravaged the Elean countryside and advanced on the city where he'd likely pre-arranged for a pro-Spartan revolt to occur. It did, but failed, and Agis withdrew without attacking the city proper, establishing a fort similar to the one that had been so successful for the Spartans at Decelea (the Greeks used the word *epiteichisma* to describe this kind of fort. The word literally means "a stronghold in enemy territory" and it is roughly the equivalent of the modern Forward Operating Base – FOB). According to Xenophon, Lysippus, the Spartan commander of this fort, raided the countryside until the Eleans could take it no more and surrendered. Diodorus tells a very different story from Pausanias' point of view. He has the king march out at the head of 4,000 Spartans and even more allies (but not the Thebans or the Corinthians) and, after the customary ravaging, lay siege to a gymnasium *"in a careless manner"* thinking his army was too powerful to be opposed. One thousand elite Aetolians, allies of the Eleans, made a surprise attack against his force and routed it, killing 30. Diodorus shows how the defeat shook Pausanias and changed his invasion strategy. When the king:

> ... *saw that the city would be hard to take, he traversed its territory, laying it waste and plundering it, even though it was sacred soil, and gathered great stores of booty. Since the winter was already at hand, he built walled outposts in Elis and left adequate forces in them, and himself passed the winter with the rest of the army in Dyme.*

Note, once again, the Spartan king's willingness to plunder *"sacred soil."*

The following year, Agis died on his way home from Delphi after tithing some of the treasure taken from Elis. The throne should naturally have passed to his son Leotychides, but of course Leotychides was (possibly correctly) thought to be the illegitimate son of Alcibiades, who had allegedly seduced

Agis' wife Timaea and cuckolded the Spartan king. The only other candidate was the same Agesilaus we discussed earlier when we called into question the Spartan practice of infanticide – the man born with a club foot, and who had somehow still managed to graduate the Upbringing (which kings were never supposed to go through) with flying colors.

Xenophon tells us now of an oracle from Delphi warning the Spartans to beware a "lame king." The oracle is so convenient that we have to consider the possibility that the Pythia was again bribed to invent it in an effort to sway the choice in favor of Leotychides, since it's pretty clear that a lame king would surely mean the guy with the club foot. But Lysander, Agesilaus' lover, intervened, weighing in with his considerable influence on behalf of his man. He interpreted the oracle to mean that "lame king" referred to the lameness of Leotychides' parentage and not Agesilaus' foot. Lysander was incredibly powerful and influential, and in the end his argument won.

Agesilaus would prove to be one of Sparta's most famous and controversial kings. While scholars debate whether or not he was personally at fault, he undeniably presided over Sparta's most drastic and sustained period of decline.

Cunaxa

I mentioned the Battle of Cunaxa, when the Persian prince Cyrus sought to overthrow his brother Artaxerxes and take the Persian throne. His mercenary army was commanded in part by the Spartan Clearchus, fled from his ouster by his own people after he turned tyrant. As Cyrus assembled his army, he called in his debt with the Spartans, who had won the Peloponnesian Wars largely thanks to his gold. Their response was lackluster – they sent the Peer Cheirosophos with 700 hoplites as well as naval support. The popular view is that the Spartans, along with some 10,000 (13,000, if you count the light troops) other Greek mercenaries fought exceedingly well in the battle that followed, routing the Persian troops of Artaxerxes, who were still, nearly 90 years after Marathon, unable to face Greek hoplites in a stand-up fight and ran as soon as the Greeks charged. The battle would very likely have been a victory if Cyrus hadn't attempted to rush his brother and got himself killed by a javelin. Cunaxa was a fight to put Cyrus on the throne, and with the death of Cyrus, the reason for the battle evaporated, and with it Cyrus' army.

However, a minority view advances the very convincing opinion (because it complies with the Law of Competence) that Artaxerxes deliberately had his troops retreat in an effort to draw the slow hoplite heavy infantry away from the rest of Cyrus' line. It was only Cyrus' charge (the one that got him killed) that saved the Greeks from being cut off, outflanked and destroyed.

Clearchus would later be assassinated during a parley, but the majority of the "10,000" who marched back to Greece after the battle reached it safely (largely, we should point out, because the light troops protected the slow, plodding hoplites from Persian missile troops that harassed them the whole way). Cunaxa may not have been a victory for the Spartan state, but a significant Spartan force participated, under Spartan leadership (Clearchus), and so it must be counted when we consider Sparta's combat performance.

With Cyrus' death, Sparta's main ally in Persia was gone. As far as Artaxerxes was concerned, Sparta was a Persian client who had allied with Cyrus, and was therefore still in open rebellion against Persia. Tissaphernes received most of Cyrus' provinces and immediately attempted to extend his rule over the Ionian Greeks, who sent to Sparta for help. While Sparta was all too happy to abandon the Greeks in Asia to their fate in exchange for Persian money, it seemed that deal died with the man who had given them most of it – Cyrus. In an echo of the warning Sparta had sent to Cyrus the Great so many years ago, it promptly sent a warning to Tissaphernes to leave the Ionian Greeks alone. Just as with Cyrus the Great, Tissaphernes ignored it and laid siege to the Ionian city of Cyme.

Sparta responded with an army, but a typically weak one for its overseas expeditions during this period. It was commanded by the Peer Thibron, and consisted only of 1,000 *neodamōdeis*. The rest of the troops were Peloponnesian allies (4,000) and 300 Athenian cavalry (Xenophon mentions that Athens' restored democracy used this as an opportunity to take out their garbage, sending horsemen who were "*some of those who had served as cavalrymen in the time of the Thirty, thinking it would be a gain to the democracy if they should live in foreign lands and perish there*"). It's possible Sparta was hoping to campaign on the cheap in the hopes that the Ionians would contribute their own forces. If so, this assumption proved correct, as Thibron added another 2,000 Ionian Greeks to his troops.

Thibron was forced to keep out of the plains by Persian cavalry who would have ridden rings around his almost entirely heavy infantry force, but Xenophon notes that his army was finally joined by the remains of the "10,000" who had made the trek back to Greece from Cunaxa, and these reinforcements finally emboldened him to take the offensive. Xenophon tells us that Thibron took seven cities by "*voluntary surrender*" possibly due to friendly relationships (two of the cities were held by descendants of the Spartan king Demaratus). Xenophon does mention that Thibron took some "*weak*" cities by storm, but describes only an unsuccessful siege of Larissa, where Thibron's effort to cut off the water supply was confounded by constant raids by the defenders, until at last the ephors sent word for him to lift the siege and invade Caria.

Here we have to pause to note that Xenophon believed that Thibron had tried to kill him when the two had served together, and certainly had a bone to pick with the Spartan. This definitely raises the concern that Xenophon paints an excessively negative picture of Thibron's campaigns.

On the way to Caria, Thibron passed through Ephesus, where Dercylidas was waiting to replace him in command. Thibron, like so many Spartan commanders, was put on trial when he got home, "*for the allies accused him of allowing his soldiers to plunder their friends* [the Greeks of Asia]." Unlike Pausanias after Piraeus, he was convicted and exiled.

According to Xenophon, Dercylidas had a score to settle with the Persian satrap Pharnabazus who had somehow slandered Dercylidas to the point where the Spartan was punished, being forced to stand guard duty. Dercylidas never forgot the insult, and immediately worked out a truce with Tissaphernes, turning his attention to Pharnabazus' holdings to the north. Xenophon points out that Dercylidas was every bit the commander that Thibron was not, and that he managed to control his troops and keep them from harming the goods or territory of their Ionian allies. In a single day, three more cities voluntarily came over to the Spartan cause, and another three followed later after some coaxing.

A seventh city, Cebren, well-fortified and garrisoned, held out for five days (while unfavorable sacrifices supposedly kept Dercylidas from attacking) before finally throwing open its gates on the fifth day (more likely, Dercylidas was working on betraying the city from the inside and so used the religious excuse for the delay while his operatives went to work). Another two cities admitted him after a careful combination of diplomacy and threats. In his string of successes, Dercylidas reminds me a lot of Brasidas and his campaigns in northeastern Greece – that he made great gains by *not* fighting, rather than risking a battlefield decision. But it's worth pointing out that neither Dercylidas nor Thibron was successful in besieging any strongly held city. Poor siegecraft, it seems, remained a Spartan trait.

Assault on the Bithynian camp

Dercylidas followed this success by wintering his troops in Bithynia on the north Turkish coast. There, he made an alliance with the Odryssian Thracian king Seuthes, detaching 200 hoplites to serve as a guard for the Odryssian camp. These 200 were attacked by Bithynian Thracians after Seuthes' loot.

Xenophon describes how in a mirror of Ithome and Sphacteria, the Greek troops were unable to come to grips with the enemy:

> ... the Bithynians, while they gave way at whatever point the Greeks rushed forth, and easily made their escape, since they were peltasts fleeing from hoplites, kept throwing javelins upon them from the one side and the other and struck down many of them at every sally; and in the end the Greeks were shot down like cattle shut up in a pen.

These were likely not Spartan hoplites, but they were almost certainly Spartan-led, and Sparta's inability to deal effectively with the harassing tactics of light troops had clearly not improved much over time. Of the 200 detached, only 15 made it back to the main Spartan camp.

While Dercylidas did win additional cities in subsequent years, he didn't fight any battles that shed light on Sparta's military record. The balance of power for the Asian Greeks didn't substantively change, save that the Persians recruited Conon, who rather tragically commanded for Athens during the Peloponnesian Wars, into their navy. We can't be certain that Conon's entry into the war made the Spartans fearful, but I can't imagine they were thrilled. Conon had been badly mauled fighting the Spartans, yes, but he was also a veteran of fighting them, and the recent flare-up at Athens (and the concessions it forced) surely didn't incline them positively toward taking on Athenians on land or at sea. This may have played into the decision to send Agesilaus personally to the coast of Asia Minor.

Another possible factor was a conspiracy that very nearly touched off Sparta's fourth serious helot revolt. One of the Inferiors, by all accounts a talented and smart man named Cinadon, chafed at the status differential between himself and the Peers and plotted a conspiracy to grant equal rights to Inferiors and helots alike. This plot was eventually betrayed, and scholars are divided on how close it came to fruition. Cinadon was sent on a secret mission with the *hippeis*, who promptly arrested and interrogated him, dragging out the names of his co-conspirators. All were tortured and executed.

It was under the shadow of this conspiracy that Agesilaus raised his troops in 397 BC. Thirty Peers accompanied their king, a rather generous number for Spartan overseas expeditions in this period. Agesilaus' forces were more typical for this era – 2,000 *neodamōdeis* and 6,000 allied troops. It is possible that this deployment of *neodamōdeis*, as we've seen before, was an effort to get restive helots fighting in the field instead of plotting at home, driven by terror over the near miss with Cinadon's conspiracy.

Lysander, Agesilaus' lover and quite arguably responsible for his kingship, accompanied him (Xenophon has Lysander convincing Agesilaus to take on the expedition). Xenophon notes that Lysander was hoping to reestablish the ruling-councils of ten, who had been personally loyal to him, and disbanded by order of the ephors. It also seems that Lysander was hopeful his relationship with Agesilaus would restore him to the former power he'd enjoyed when the Peloponnesian Wars were in full swing, but he was to be disappointed, and quickly.

In a foreshadowing of things to come, we saw the Corinthians and Thebans repeatedly refuse to contribute troops to Sparta's recent expeditions. Now, they went a step further. Not only did they refuse to contribute troops (and this time Athens joined them in the refusal), but two boeotarchs (senior military officials from the Boeotian League, of which Thebes was the principal member in a slightly similar manner to Sparta's position in the Peloponnesian League and Athens' in the Delian League) intervened and forbade Agesilaus from sacrificing at the Boeotian sanctuary at Aulis before departing for the Ionian coast (Agesilaus was trying to imitate the likely mythic sacrifice of Agamemnon before departing for Troy). Xenophon even has them throwing the sacrificial offerings off the altar. Agesilaus was furious. He never forgot the insult, and Thebes and Sparta were never reconciled. Both Plutarch and Xenophon agree that this fury at Thebes was responsible for Sparta's eventual downfall at Theban hands.

For his first year in Asia Minor, Agesilaus' operations were mostly confined to ravaging and diplomacy. Xenophon relates that Tissaphernes delayed Agesilaus with promises of peace while he secretly reinforced himself with an army sent by Artaxerxes. Xenophon does note that Lysander upstaged his king:

> ... since the people all knew Lysander, they beset him with requests that he should obtain from Agesilaus the granting of their petitions; and for this reason a very great crowd was continually courting and following him, so that Agesilaus appeared to be a man in private station and Lysander king.

The two quarreled, with Agesilaus reversing Lysander's dictates, and Xenophon tells us that at last Lysander asked the king to send him north to the Hellespont where he proved successful in inducing additional revolt to Sparta's cause. But the story shows a rift developing between the two leaders, and one that would never fully heal.

Cavalry duel near Dascylium

There is only one battle of note during this long general stalemate between Agesilaus' expeditionary force and the Persians, a cavalry scrap around 395 BC near Dascylium in Anatolia (where the Persian satrap Pharnabazus had his headquarters – modern Ergili, Turkey). It was a skirmish, really, but it reinforced a critical lesson to Agesilaus and, unlike other Spartan commanders who almost famously failed to adapt, Agesilaus took the lesson – Sparta was weak in cavalry, and it couldn't hope to fight the incredibly skilled horsemen of Persia unless this was remedied.

The battle itself was an accident – the Greek and Persian cavalry squadrons both climbing the same hill in order to scout the surrounding area, and then blundering into each other at a distance of four plethra (about 400 feet), much too close to disengage. We can infer from Xenophon's description of the "phalanxes" of cavalry that Pharnabazus' Persians outnumbered Agesilaus' Greeks (normally, I would expect these to have been pro-Spartan Athenians and Boeotians, but we have seen that both refused to contribute allies to this expedition) – for the Greeks were drawn up four deep, while the Persians were "*many men*" deep with a frontage of 12. The Greeks clearly hesitated (possibly an indication of lack of experience or skill among Spartan or Peloponnesian allied horsemen), but the Persians were master cavalrymen. They quickly sensed their advantage and charged. Not only were they better horsemen, but they had better equipment. Xenophon specifically notes the cornel-wood shafts of their spears holding up in the combat, while the (presumably ash) shafts of the Greek cavalry snapped under strain. In the end, the Greeks lost 12 men and the Persians just one.

It was hardly a major fight, but it was certainly an instructive one. Indeed, Xenophon indicates the lesson was hammered home: "*And perceiving that, unless he obtained an adequate cavalry force, he would not be able to campaign in the plains, he resolved that this must be provided, so that he might not have to carry on a skulking warfare.*"

Agesilaus then engaged in a remarkable display of Spartan adaptivity that echoed Archidamus' efforts during the siege of Plataea – he assigned the richest men in the region (raising horses and equipping horsemen was wildly expensive) the duty of providing cavalry to his army. In a particularly brilliant stroke he allowed these rich men to provide *any* horseman, not necessarily the rich man himself. This allowed the rich to buy off military service, and ensured that Agesilaus would still receive a properly equipped cavalry. He followed this with putting his entire army into competitive training, setting up games with prizes for physical condition among his heavy infantry, horsemanship among his cavalry and shooting accuracy among his missile-armed troops. Xenophon also reports multiple times that Agesilaus paid attention to preparing markets in the towns where he stationed his armies, ensuring his troops had ready access to fresh equipment and the means to make repairs. It also surely drove commerce to the cities he used, which endeared the populations to him – the very opposite of the plundering that Thibron was accused of.

Sardis

In the spring, Agesilaus judged his forces to be ready and marched on the same Sardis the burning of which had arguably touched off the entire conflict between Persia and Greece over a century earlier, and where the Persian satrap Tissaphernes made his headquarters. Tissaphernes, caught off guard, raced north to intercept him.

Here again we have two diverging accounts – one from Xenophon and the other from the unknown author of the Oxyrhynchus papyrus, one of a huge collection of documents mostly dating from Ptolemaic and Roman Egypt discovered at the turn of the 20th century AD. Xenophon has Agesilaus' advance on Sardis completely unopposed (indeed, he was able to ravage the countryside for three days until Tissaphernes caught up with him), while the papyrus tells us that the Spartan army was harassed by Persian missile fire and cavalry the entire way, forcing Agesilaus to march his hoplites in a hollow square with the baggage in the center. Unable to engage the more mobile Persian force, Agesilaus was finally forced to stage an ambush which forced the Persians to flee, and then unleashed his recently acquired and trained cavalry and light troops in pursuit, killing 600.

Xenophon tells us that after three days unopposed, Tissaphernes sent his cavalry to massacre Agesilaus' camp followers (likely in the hopes not only of plunder, but of drawing Agesilaus' own cavalry into a fight the Persians were confident they could win). Tissaphernes made a critical mistake, however, letting his cavalry extend out too far from the army; meanwhile, Agesilaus was able to send both his light infantry and his fastest heavy infantry (the youngest and most athletic of them) in support of his own horsemen. The Persian cavalry, overwhelmed by Agesilaus' combined-arms force, broke and fled. The Greeks pursued and sacked their camp. Xenophon specifically notes that Agesilaus captured the Persians' baggage camels and then took them back to Greece.

I personally favor the Oxyrhynchus narrative. In observance of the Law of Competence (which says the Persians were not stupid), I find it impossible to believe that a highly mobile Persian force, fighting on its home territory, with extensive knowledge of the countryside could a.) fail to locate Agesilaus' army and b.) fail to catch up with it once it was located. I also think that both Xenophon and the Oxyrhynchus historian are describing the same battle at the end of both narratives. In addition, modern scholarship points out that Xenophon's personal hatred of Tissaphernes may have colored his story.

The victory spelled Tissaphernes' doom. Artaxerxes lost confidence in his satrap and sent as a replacement Tithraustes, who was also charged with collecting Tissaphernes' head (scholars argue that Tissaphernes was in fact assassinated by political rivals, and not on the king's orders). Tithraustes had barely washed the blood off his hands before he offered Agesilaus very favorable peace terms – If the Spartan king would leave Persia, the Asian Greeks could govern themselves free from Persian control. Agesilaus agreed to a six-month truce during which he would direct his efforts against the territory of Pharnabazus, but Xenophon makes it clear that he was high on his success and had no intention of abandoning a war that was showering him in both wealth and glory. In fact, Agesilaus' success inspired the Spartan government to take the unprecedented move of placing him in combined command of both the Spartan land army *and* fleet. It is possible that this was a move intended to sideline Lysander (Sparta's most successful admiral and the obvious candidate) by his political enemies, who had likely gotten wind of the falling out between the two former lovers. Agesilaus delegated the naval command to his brother-in-law Peisander.

Xenophon has Agesilaus marching against Pharnabazus' territory in Phrygia and winning some cities by force, but we don't have enough details to see how they impacted Sparta's combat record. He proceeded into Paphlagonia (on the northern coast of modern Turkey where it borders the Black Sea) and won the alliance of its king, who was brought over by the rebel Persian satrap Spithridates, who'd been convinced to rebel by Lysander. Thus reinforced, Agesilaus plundered the area around Pharnabazus' palace in Dascylium until the satrap caught him flat-footed.

Pharnabazus attacks Spartan foragers

This is another small engagement that can barely be termed a battle, but it's interesting to examine because it is practically unique – Agesilaus' troops, high on their success and not thinking they were in danger, were out foraging without posting scouts or performing sufficient reconnaissance of the area. Pharnabazus seized the chance to deploy 400 cavalry and two scythed-chariots – modified war chariots with horizontal cutting blades projecting from the wheels, carriage or horse's yoke. These failed spectacularly in later battles, but were incredibly effective here.

Keep in mind that foraging in ancient armies was usually accomplished by light-armed troops, and that the strength of these troops was their missile capability and mobility. Fighting in dispersed order, they could rain death on slower and more heavily armed and armored hoplites. But caught out in the open against highly mobile and fast cavalry, light infantry stood almost no chance. This is probably why around 700 of the Greeks formed into a "*close-gathered crowd*" (that they did not form a phalanx is another indication they were light infantry) in the slim hope of repelling the cavalry attack, rather than spreading out and being ridden down one by one. But a mass of unarmored infantry was the scythed chariot's sweet-spot, and the charioteers drove them into the mass, scattering those Greeks who weren't cut down by the blades. About 100 were killed before the rest fled back to Agesilaus' camp, and he was able to bring his hoplite heavy infantry up, presumably running Pharnabazus' troops off.

Herippidas' raid on Pharnabazus' camp

Xenophon reports a later strike by Herippidas, one of the 30 Peers who advised Agesilaus, on Pharnabazus' camp. In an interesting contradiction to the notion of Spartan military discipline, Xenophon notes that Agesilaus allocated 2,000 hoplites and 2,000 peltasts to Herippidas, and that the Peer recruited cavalry from allied troops and "*as many other Greeks as could be convinced to join him.*"

However, when the force assembled for the nighttime muster, less than half the troops showed up. Since we don't know how many other Greeks Herippidas convinced to sign on for the mission, it is possible that all the Spartan-led troops allocated arrived, but that's also unlikely. We could be seeing a contradiction to the notion of Spartan discipline and organization in this period. Some of the troops, for reasons we can't know, elected not to turn out for muster.

Herippidas, despite this setback, launched the dawn raid anyway with stunning success. He captured the camp, the baggage and treasure, scattered Pharnabazus' army and killed several of his sentries. Pharnabazus himself, however, escaped.

Herippidas refused to share the plunder with his Paphlagonian and Hellespontine Phrygian allies, turning it over to *laphyropouloi* (Spartan officials in charge of selling war booty) to be sold instead. The profits from this sale were necessary to maintain the army, so this is one case where I am not ready to fault Spartan greed. However, it was a massive diplomatic blunder, since Herippidas was confiscating and selling not only the booty seized by his own troops, but that of his allies. That this was *atypical* for the Spartans *does* poke another hole in the Bronze Lie – because it indicates that the Spartans were *usually* quite diplomatic and expert at coalition-building and made use of soft power, rather than being the brute superwarriors they are always portrayed to be.

The allies whose booty was confiscated promptly deserted the Spartan cause and joined Ariaeus, Artaxerxes' man at Sardis. Xenophon is clear that Agesilaus felt the loss of these allies keenly. This is perhaps what motivated Agesilaus to negotiate with Pharnabazus in 394 BC, but the conference changed nothing and the spring saw Agesilaus mustering a new army to march east. However strong this army was, it certainly wasn't strong enough to threaten any major Persian centers of power (recall Sparta's horrendous record at sieges), and would have been more of a ravaging exercise like the ineffective strategy we saw in Attica during the Peloponnesian Wars.

The Corinthian War

But during this time Tithraustes had come to the conclusion that his best bet to hold onto his newly won domains wasn't using the Persian army, which had at best a checkered record facing Greek hoplites in the field, but Persian gold, which had consistently altered the course of events with Greece for a century.

He sent as his agent Timocrates of Rhodes with currency valued at 50 talents of silver to spread liberally among Sparta's enemies back in Greece. The idea was simple – a fight back home would force Agesilaus to take his army out of Asia. Timocrates bribed representatives at Thebes, Corinth and Argos. Xenophon claims he didn't have to pay the Athenians because "*the Athenians, even though they did not receive a share of this gold, were nevertheless eager for the war, thinking that theirs was the right to rule.*" We should take Xenophon's description here with a grain of salt, however. The Athenians almost certainly took Persian gold, even if not the payment Xenophon specifically references here.

The Oxyrhynchus historian tells a slightly different version of these events – that it was Pharnabazus who sent the gold. The historian also tells us the Athenians did take the gold, and that all the cities which were bribed wanted to act against Sparta anyway, making the money a catalyst, not a cause.

According to Xenophon, Thebes met the terms of its bribe by intervening in a struggle between Phocis and Locris on the Locrian side. As they hoped (if you believe Xenophon, and many don't), the Phocians appealed to Sparta for help. There were no doubt many factors influencing Sparta's decision to take on Thebes, but it's important to remember the boeotarchs' interference in Agesilaus' sacrifice before his departure to Asia Minor. The time for vengeance was clearly at hand.

Haliartus

Sparta promptly ordered Thebes to stand down and submit to arbitration, very likely expecting the Theban response – refusal and ravaging of Phocian land. The Thebans immediately sent to Athens to secure an anti-Spartan alliance (as the Persians surely hoped). Athens agreed. Lysander was duly placed in command of the Phocians and other allies, while Pausanias mustered the Peers, *perioikoi* and other allies at Tegea (the Corinthians, unsurprisingly, refused to join him), then marched north to meet him. The two armies converged on the Boeotian city of Haliartus on the southern shore of Lake Copais in central Boeotia. Lysander followed the now-familiar Brasidian model of inducing cities to revolt against their League, storming those towns which resisted.

Xenophon hints that Pausanias might have been delayed, once again, by unfavorable sacrifices at the border. It's also possible that Lysander, eager for glory as always, deliberately outpaced his king, who was supposed to have the overall command. Lysander surely remembered and was still furious about Pausanias usurping his command during Thrasybulus' insurgency at Athens in 403 BC.

Some scholars believe Plutarch's story that Lysander, enraged that Agesilaus had put him aside during the campaign in Asia, was seeking to manipulate the Delphic oracle to have himself declared king – chosen in accordance with a divine pronouncement that it *"was more for the honor and interest of the Spartans to choose their kings from the best citizens."* Some think that Lysander's rash moves at Haliartus were a result of him desperately attempting to prove himself Sparta's best citizen through a heroic feat of arms. Still others argue that the appointment of Lysander was an insult to Pausanias, and that may have impacted the king's willingness to coordinate.

What's clear is that Lysander marched his army (reinforced now by the cities who had surrendered) to the walls of Haliartus to try to induce it to revolt against the Boeotian League and open its gates to him. The Theban garrison stopped this and Lysander, who refused to wait for Pausanias' army to catch up with him, assaulted the walls.

Sparta's horrendous record in both sieges and assaults was not to be broken that day. Xenophon is unclear about whether a Theban sally took Lysander by surprise or if the Spartan decided to accept a field battle when it was offered, but one thing is clear – the Thebans fought the Spartans and defeated them beside the walls of Haliartus, killing Lysander. That the battle happened close to the walls is an indicator that Lysander was either surprised or made a foolish and prideful tactical choice. Fighting close to city walls, as we've already seen, allowed the city garrison to shower the enemy with missiles (as was underscored when Pausanias tried to recover Lysander's body). The Thebans got their noses bloodied too, chasing Lysander's fleeing troops beyond the safety of the missile cover on the walls and then being mauled when the Spartans and their allies turned to fight. That said, Haliartus was an embarrassing defeat for Spartan arms.

Pausanias arrived too late. Athenian troops reinforced Thebes, preventing him from assaulting the main city of the Boeotian League. More importantly, Lysander's army was shattered and dispersed and the morale of his own troops already precarious. Pausanias negotiated humiliating terms for the recovery of the Spartan dead (including Lysander's corpse) – agreeing to take his troops back to Sparta and leave the Boeotians alone. In a development that won't surprise anyone who has paid any attention to the treatment of Spartan kings, he was put on trial for failing to fight (a hint that maybe Pausanias' failure to reinforce Lysander was deliberate), and went into exile rather than being convicted and executed.

Sparta had now lost both Lysander and Pausanias, two of its most able commanders, in the same instant. Pausanias' son Agesipolis, now officially the Agiad king, was still underage. Not surprisingly, the following year Sparta recalled Agesilaus, once again abandoning the Asian Greeks to their fate. With war now flaring between Sparta, Thebes and Athens, Tithraustes could now absolutely claim his scheme an unmitigated success. He'd lit a fire in his enemy's backfield and they had recalled their expeditionary army to stamp it out. Plutarch gives Agesilaus a wonderful quote as he departed for home – that he had been driven out of Asia by "10,000 archers." He was referring to the symbolic archer stamped on the obverse of Persian gold coins. He left a token force behind – Peisander still acting as admiral, and the Peer Euxenus to command just 4,000 troops on land.

Agesilaus arrived to find the anti-Spartan coalition of Thebes, Athens, Argos and Corinth voting to invade Spartan territory. The much later invasion by Epaminondas of Thebes after the disastrous (for the Spartans) Battle of Leuctra is usually cited by scholars as a dramatic example of the first time Spartan weakness had resulted in an invasion of its territory. But the fact that this vote happened at all, and that this motion was carried, is a significant indicator of how far Sparta's reputation had fallen. If it had ever been, Spartan military might was no longer something that struck terror into the hearts of its enemies.

There was another very interesting tactical development here – Xenophon mentions that the anti-Spartan coalition voted to deploy their phalanx 16 ranks deep (hoplite phalanxes usually deployed around eight ranks deep), so long as it would provide them with enough frontage not to be outflanked. This is significant for two reasons: first, it meant that the Greeks were discovering that a deeper phalanx had more punching power (the added weight of the ranks pushing from behind could help break the enemy line). Secondly, it was a harbinger of the later Hellenistic phalanx to come, for which 16 ranks would be standard (Hellenistic phalanxes wouldn't use the additional ranks for added pushing power, but rather to provide depth to deploy their much longer pikes both offensively and as a defensive canopy against missiles).

The Spartan regent Aristodemus gathered allies and marched north through Tegea to meet the coalition army. Agesilaus was marching overland from the north through Thessaly and the two armies hoped to link up somewhere in central Greece. The coalition army moved south, hoping to crush Aristodemus and possibly cause chaos (maybe in the form of a helot rebellion) before the more experienced commander could arrive. Further, the coalition realized that Aristodemus' northward march took him through allied lands, and in each one he gathered more troops to his banner. The sooner he was intercepted, the sooner this reinforcement could be stopped.

The Nemea

The two armies met just south of Corinth, close to the Nemea river, near the site where myth had it that King Eurystheus had commanded the demigod Heracles to slay the invincible Nemean lion. The Spartans ravaged the countryside and came under fire from coalition light troops (Xenophon doesn't give casualty counts, but he does note that the coalition troops "*did them* [the Spartans] *a great deal of harm by throwing missiles and discharging arrows upon them from the heights*"). The two forces maneuvered against one another until they finally settled into their opposing lines, with the coalition taking cover behind a stream.

The armies were large even by ancient standards – around 19,000 hoplites on the Spartan side (6,000 being actual Spartans, and the rest allies). The Spartans were, as usual, deficient in cavalry and light troops, fielding just 600 horsemen and another 700 specialist light infantry – Cretan archers and slingers from other allied states. The anti-Spartan coalition outnumbered them in heavy infantry, around 24,000 hoplites, and they dominated the field in cavalry – some 1,550 horse (the majority of them Boeotian, with an almost equal number of Athenians). Xenophon doesn't give a specific count of their light troops, but given the comparative sizes, I believe they outnumbered the Spartan contingent as well. Diodorus gives different numbers, but I prefer Xenophon's.

For two days, the Spartans stayed put. Agesilaus' army was marching south, so time was clearly on their side. The pressure was on the coalition to get the fight done so they could regroup and pick the ground of their choice to face the army descending on them from the north. Xenophon tells us that the battle was sparked by fear of engaging the Spartans in direct combat, hoplite to hoplite – the Spartans held the right wing of their army, opposite the coalition left. The command of the coalition army rotated daily, with the contingent in charge for the day holding that army's right wing, which put them opposite the Spartan left, held by their allied troops. Xenophon claims that once the Boeotians were in command and opposite the allied troops, they sounded the advance, happy to condemn the Athenians (on the coalition left) to face the Spartan hoplites.

This story doesn't pass muster with me. For one thing, we know Xenophon was enormously pro-Spartan, and this story of course compliments the Spartans and gives the impression that the Boeotians feared taking them on in the field. But after the debacle of Sphacteria, after the far more recent defeat outside Haliartus, I find it hard to believe that the coalition commanders were shaking in their proverbial boots at the thought of facing Spartan hoplites in battle. I believe that a combination of the pressure to engage before Agesilaus' arrival and the belief that superior numbers, and in particular cavalry dominance, would win them the day helped push the coalition to sound the advance.

But at any rate, that was the formation when the advance was sounded and the coalition crossed the stream and attacked, apparently swiftly and unexpectedly enough that they nearly caught the Spartans by surprise (Xenophon tells us the Spartans were alerted when the enemy started singing their war paean), underscoring yet another Spartan failure to adequately scout or put out pickets to provide early warning. What followed was another set-piece phalanx-on-phalanx battle, as had happened at Mantinea in 418 BC, an ideal and nearly equal test that is often used as an example of Greek warfare even though, as we've seen, it was fairly rare.

The Boeotians apparently operated as an independent unit, failing to work in tandem with the rest of the coalition army. First, they deployed deeper than the agreed 16 ranks. We don't know how deep they deployed exactly, but Xenophon tells us they "*made their phalanx exceedingly deep, and, besides, they also veered to the right in leading the advance, in order to outflank the enemy with their wing.*" This maneuver effectively forced the entire coalition army to slide right, in an effort to prevent gaps from forming in the line. The Spartans, seeing their opportunity, slid to their right, resulting in the left wings of both armies being outflanked and enveloped.

The deeper Boeotian phalanx drove in like a hammer. The weight of all those men, throwing themselves behind their shields and bulling forward, was unstoppable. They immediately punched a hole in the Spartan allies, who collapsed (except for some troops from Pellene in Achaea who held against the Thespians). The undisciplined coalition troops took off in pursuit after the routing Spartan allies.

On the Spartan right, however, the opposite happened. The Spartans flanked and utterly crushed the Athenian troops, and showed what many historians say is typical Spartan discipline and organization, but which we now know was *inconsistent* Spartan discipline and organization. The Spartans did not pursue the fleeing enemy. Instead, they re-formed, dressed their line, and wheeled 90 degrees to face the enemy again. This put them on the flank of the anti-Spartan coalition right wing, which was now returning from the pursuit of the routed Spartan-allied left. The Spartans even patiently let the first ranks of the returning enemy pass them by before charging, taking the anti-Spartan coalition right wing squarely in its flank, out of order, and apparently by surprise.

Xenophon describes this as an incredibly precise and disciplined wheeling maneuver. The Spartans charged across the battlefield, flattening each enemy element one by one. First, they crushed those Athenians who had faced them (ignoring those Athenians still pursuing the fleeing Tegeans). They then engaged and routed the other contingents returning from the pursuit in order – the Argives, Corinthians and last of all the Thebans. The maneuver was devastating. The remainder of the anti-Spartan coalition army was caught out on its flank, staved in and routed. They fled for the safety of Corinth, only to find that the city would not admit them.

The Spartans, once again in an inconsistent show of discipline and organization (or perhaps greed, if we believe they wished to loot the dead) did not pursue, but rather stayed behind to set up a trophy to commemorate their victory. Around 2,800 coalition troops lay dead. The Spartan army had lost less than half that many, nearly all of them allies. Just six actual Spartans were killed in the clash.

The victory was no less significant than Mantinea – in a pitched, hoplite-on-hoplite battle, the Spartans had shown that they had the strength, discipline and courage to win the day against a more numerous enemy, even one with superior cavalry. But even in spite of this, the battle was hardly the end of what would come to be called the "Corinthian War " (because of the fighting's proximity to Corinth). The coalition army was defeated, but it regrouped at its camp outside Corinth, and finally took up position within Corinth's long walls. The Spartan army had taken a significant mauling of its own. The Spartans, however, had the advantage of a second army under Agesilaus, drawing ever closer from the north. For now, Aristodemus commanded his troops to dig in and wait for relief.

Here, we have to pause to note that following this battle, Sparta established two garrisons of around a *mora* each – one at Orchomenus in Boeotia, and another near Corinth. Both of these garrisons were maintained throughout the Corinthian War until 387 BC. These were much larger garrisons than those that had been established at Decelea and was by far the largest deployment of Spartan troops abroad.

These garrisons poke a massive hole in the Bronze Lie – for Xenophon cites them as the primary reason why the Spartans "grew tired of war." This strongly suggests that Spartan Peers did *not* expect military service to occupy the majority of their time, and indicates that while they were certainly the most disciplined and organized troops in Greece, they were *not* full-time professional soldiers, but rather aristocratic dandies for whom war was only a part-time occupation.

Agesilaus, meanwhile, raced through Thessaly to reach Aristodemus' position. Xenophon reports that he was badly harassed by the Boeotian-allied Thessalians, but they don't seem to have seriously impeded his progress. Xenophon reports one notable scene, showing Agesilaus beginning to learn the intricacies of cavalry warfare and adapting to them as a commander, a rare insight into the development of Spartan military doctrine:

> *Agesilaus, however, perceiving the mistakes which each side was making, sent the very stalwart horsemen who were about his person and ordered them not only to give word to the others to pursue with all speed, but to do likewise themselves, and not to give the Thessalians a chance to face round again. And when the Thessalians saw them rushing upon them unexpectedly, some of them fled, others turned about, and others, in trying to do this, were captured while their horses were turned half around.*

Agesilaus punched through Thessaly and entered Boeotia, where he was substantially reinforced. The coalition army had no choice but to march to meet him, though we can't be sure who or how many were sent. In the meantime, however, disaster struck the Spartans many miles to the east.

Cnidus

Agesilaus' recall had left his inexperienced brother-in-law Peisander in command of the Spartan fleet off the coast of Asia. Peisander was signally unqualified for the post (Plutarch is plain that Agesilaus gave Peisander the job "*not out of regard for the public good, but in recognition of the claims of relationship and to gratify his wife, who was a sister of Peisander*").

The best Spartan troops had returned with Agesilaus. Xenophon tells us that the Persian fleet, meanwhile, was commanded by the satrap Pharnabazus and composed largely of crack Phoenician sailors. The veteran Athenian Conon served under the satrap and was in command of the partly Cypriot Greek ships. The Persian fleet also likely outnumbered the Spartan fleet, though only slightly.

The sources are confused and conflicting in their description of the naval battle that occurred off Cnidus in 394 BC. It seems Peisander successfully smashed through Conon's front line of ships, only to be destroyed by the Persian reserve line led by Pharnabazus, which killed Peisander and captured 50 Spartan ships with barely a scratch on them. It's also worth noting that without Persian money, Sparta was unable to put a strong fleet in the water. At Cnidus, the Spartan triremes would have been older and in a worse state of repair, inadequately rowed by those crew who would take lower wages.

The news of the defeat reached Agesilaus outside Orchomenus as Pharnabazus and Conon's fleet did a victory tour along the modern Turkish coast, liberating every Spartan-allied Greek city and isle they came across. Conon convinced Pharnabazus not to garrison them, and to leave them independent, a move that solidified pro-Persian sentiment in the region.

Agesilaus himself, when he received news of the disaster, flat-out lied to his troops. Plutarch tells us:

> ... *that his soldiers might not be visited with dejection and fear as they were going into battle, he ordered the messengers from the sea to reverse*

their tidings and say that the Spartans were victorious in the naval battle. He himself also came forth publicly with a garland on his head, offered sacrifices for glad tidings, and sent portions of the sacrificial victims to his friends.

I can understand the move. The lie would help shore up morale for his entire army, but some of Agesilaus' troops would have been Asian Greeks whom he had taken with him from Asia Minor when he was recalled. With this defeat, their homes and families lay exposed to Persian retribution. It didn't help that the message of the defeat arrived during a solar eclipse, which no doubt would have been perceived as a bad omen by the superstitious ancients.

Coronea

Agesilaus' lie worked for the moment and his army's morale was maintained well enough that he could continue south along the shore of Lake Copais, until he reached the foothills of Mount Helicon near the city of Coronea. He was just west of the walls of Haliartus where Lysander had so rashly spent his life the previous year. Here, the coalition army mustered to block his path south.

The Spartans were outnumbered once again, about 15,000 hoplites (Peers, *neodamōdeis*, Asian Greeks and allies) facing around 20,000 (mostly Thebans and Argives, but with a sizable contingent of Corinthians and Athenians and other allies). Both sides had light infantry and cavalry, but they are not mentioned, and it seems the battle was largely fought by the heavy infantry. It was another set-piece, roughly even infantry battle on relatively flat ground. The coalition troops were still fresh from their whipping at the Nemea, and their morale had to have been shaky, especially given that they were now facing Agesilaus and his more veteran army. The Thebans took the coalition right, closest to the lake, and the Lacedaemonian troops (probably about 1,000 of mostly *perioikoi* under Peer officers) and freed helots (maybe 2,000) took the Spartan right. Just as at the Nemea, it seemed that the stronger contingents of both armies would face the weaker contingents of their respective enemies.

The battle played out very similarly. The armies advanced in near silence until the Thebans (probably deployed extremely deep to give them extra punch and also to shore up the morale of the men in the phalanx) gave a cry and charged, smashing through the Spartan-allied troops on their left. Meanwhile the Argives on the coalition left turned and ran without a fight at the approach of the Spartan Peers. Lest we think this was due to the Spartans' fearsome reputation, Xenophon points out that the coalition's center also turned and fled as soon as the Spartan center (composed not of Spartans but of Asian Greeks) *"came within spear thrust."* The issue was not fear of Spartan Peers, but weak morale overall. Dr Konijnendijk also makes the argument that deeper phalanxes were in part an effort to shore up weak morale in the leading ranks, which could be an additional clue to why they were employed at Coronea.

But the victorious Thebans were looting Agesilaus' baggage train, and so he pushed off the victor's garlands his troops were trying to crown him with, re-formed his men, and advanced. The Thebans, seeing him coming, re-formed and met him. Xenophon is clear that Agesilaus' move was a mistake:

> *At this point one may unquestionably call Agesilaus brave; at least he certainly did not choose the safest course. For while he might have let the men pass by who were trying to break through and then have followed them and overcome those in the rear, he did not do this, but crashed against the Thebans front to front; and setting shields against shields they shoved, fought, killed and were killed.*

The Thebans in their almost certainly extremely deep phalanx took losses, but they broke through the Spartans and made it through to Mount Helicon to join the remains of their routed allies. That it was a hard fight is attested to by the fact that Agesilaus himself was wounded and many of his bodyguards killed. Some later commentators state that the Spartans opened their ranks and let the Thebans pass, then attacked them from behind, but this makes no sense to me. Such a maneuver would be insanely risky, as the Thebans could have attacked either of the halves and defeated them in detail and the Spartans were surely not so stupid (remember the Law of Competence) as to expose their own flanks this way. Further, this directly contradicts Xenophon's narration that specifically says they did not do this. I believe that the Spartans met them and that the Thebans punched through, driving hard at the king and nearly killing him, and burst out the far side to safety.

The coalition troops had taken 600 casualties and the Spartans just over half that number, probably mostly among their allies on the left who had initially been routed by the Theban phalanx.

Coronea was the second indisputable heavy infantry victory for Sparta in as many years. But like the Nemea, it did little. The coalition army, though twice defeated, was still big enough to fight on, and they now held a strong defensive position on Mount Helicon. Agesilaus was wounded and his troops had taken a beating in the final stage of the battle.

Locrian attack on the Spartan rearguard

Agesilaus could not follow up his victory and instead headed to Delphi to dedicate the spoils he'd won in Asia, and also likely to give himself a chance to recover from his wounds.

Meanwhile, one of his generals, Gylis, took the army to ravage Locris, which had joined the anti-Spartan coalition. As the troops marched back with their plunder, Locrian light troops chased them down, peppering them with missile fire. It was a slightly less successful repeat of Sphacteria, but the Locrians still killed 18 Peers that the Spartans, in the depths of their manpower crisis, could ill afford to lose. Among the dead was Gylis himself. While the rest of the Spartans got away, Xenophon is clear how close the expedition came to disaster: "*if some of those who were in the camp at dinner had not come to their aid, all of them would have been in danger of perishing.*"

Agesilaus returned to Sparta and the war ground on. In 393 BC, Conon and Pharnabazus' victorious fleet crossed the Aegean to raid the Messenian coast. Not since Xerxes' invasion roughly 90 years before had a Persian fleet dared to show up in Greek waters.

Naval action, and the fight inside Corinth's long walls

The Persians set up a raiding base under an Athenian governor on Cythera just off the Laconian coast, and aided Athens in improving its defenses. Recall Chilon's earlier statement of how he wished the island would sink beneath the waves. This was Sparta's worst nightmare come true.

Pharnabazus also funded the Corinthian navy, which Xenophon says defeated the Spartans under an admiral named Podanemus in a naval battle somewhere "*in the gulf around Achaea and Lecheum.*" Podanemus was killed and his second in command Pollis wounded. Command of the fleet passed now to Herippidas who seems to have clawed control of the Gulf of Corinth back to Sparta.

In Corinth, the anti-Spartan faction massacred its pro-Spartan enemies and merged its city-state with Argos, forming a joint government. The few pro-Spartan exiles who managed to escape fled to Sicyon and convinced Praxitas, the polemarch of the *mora* stationed there, to attack Corinth, assuring him they could betray its long walls that connected the city to its port at Lecheum. Praxitas took the exiles up on the offer and mustered his *mora,* which included an unspecified (but probably small) number of cavalry, and a large levy of Sicyonian hoplites. The 150-odd Corinthian exiles added their numbers.

He then launched a night attack on Corinth's long walls. The exiles admitted Praxitas' army and the Spartans dug in, building a stockade and digging a trench between the long walls. Argive troops attacked the next day, accompanied by the Athenian general Iphicrates, who would prove a major innovator in ancient warfare, helping not only to defeat Sparta, but to reform and improve the very nature of the phalanx.

The Argives shattered the Sicyonian allies in the Spartan center, routing them and opening up a gap in the Spartan line. The Spartan cavalry commander, Pasimachus, gave orders for the horsemen to tie up their horses and dismount. They then picked up the dropped shields from the fleeing Sicyonians (the hoplite shield was heavy and large and therefore usually the first thing to be thrown away in a rout), and advanced as infantry. Xenophon tells the story that the sigmas painted on the shields deceived the Argives into thinking they faced Sicyonians and not Spartans (sigma is the Greek letter that gives the "s" sound in English – the first letter in Sicyon. At this point in history, the Spartans used the lambda, the Greek letter that gives the "l" sound in English – the first letter in Lacedaemon). It made no difference either way – both Pasimachus and his dismounted cavalry were slaughtered by the more numerous Argives.

Iphicrates and his soon-to-be famous peltasts would enjoy great victories in the future, but not this day. They were beaten soundly by the Corinthian exiles and driven off. The Spartan troops meanwhile wheeled and ran along the stockade to close the gap left by the fleeing Sicyonians. The Argives, seeing that the Spartans were about to cut them off, tried to run back through the breached stockade. This panicked and foolish maneuver earned its just rewards – the Spartans hit the Argives in the flank and broke them. In the end, it was a total Spartan victory with around 1,000 coalition troops killed.

Praxitas cemented his victory by massacring the Boeotian garrison of Lecheum, and knocking holes in each of Corinth's long walls. He then went on to take Sidus and Crommyon and fortified Epieicia before finally withdrawing his troops and heading home. But Sparta was unable to capitalize further on this unexpected and stunning coup. Corinth was still strongly held, and the Spartans had learned from the Peloponnesian Wars how ineffective ravaging the countryside around it could be.

Instead, they sent the envoy Antalcidas to the Persian satrap Tiribazus to beg for peace. I believe this was due at least in part to the establishment of the hostile raiding base at Cythera. I will again repeat that the famous ephor Chilon was quoted that he wished the entire island would sink to the bottom of the sea, a good example of just how frightened the Spartans were of it being used precisely as Pharnabazus and Conon were using it now.

Antalcidas convinced the satrap to have Conon arrested (or else Conon fell victim to political rivalries inside the Persian court), removing a major thorn from Sparta's side. In exchange, Tiribazus offered to formalize what the Spartans had already effectively done when they recalled Agesilaus – abandon the Asian Greeks to Persian control. Tiribazus sent the offer on to his lord Artaxerxes, who refused to end hostilities.

Raiding went on, and here the Athenian Iphicrates excelled, developing a powerful body of mercenary peltasts. His various methods of training and fighting are covered in some detail by the 2nd century AD Macedonian writer Polyaenus, but he is so flattering of Iphicrates that it becomes hard to take what he writes completely seriously. One thing is clear – Iphicrates was an extraordinary general and a great military innovator. In addition to his reforms in training, he is credited with the development of a new military boot known as the Iphicratid.

A "peltast" is anyone who bears the *peltē*, a smaller round shield than the larger and heavier hoplite *aspis*. Many peltasts were skirmishers, wearing little to no armor and carrying either a round or a crescent-shaped *peltē*. However, some scholars believe that later in his career (around the 370s BC) Iphicrates further innovated peltasts that fought as heavy infantry, trained to fight with the *peltē* slung over one arm and hung from the neck, allowing the heavy infantryman to wield a much longer pike in two hands, which would give him a big range advantage over a hoplite with an 8-foot thrusting spear. This style of fighting with a two-handed pike would come to dominate battlefields in Hellenistic phalanxes of later years, and scholars debate whether or not Iphicrates can be credited as one of the original innovators. I believe he can.

Iphicrates' peltasts in these early battles were likely skirmishers. Their successful raids built them a fearsome reputation, though Xenophon points out that some of the younger and faster Spartan hoplites acting as *ekdromoi* (runners-out) had been able to leap out of the phalanx, chase them down and kill some of them. Athens came and rebuilt Corinth's western long wall, which Agesilaus and his half-brother Teleutias recaptured, along with Lecheum.

Lecheum

In 390 BC, Agesilaus campaigned extensively in the area, mostly ravaging and capturing a few strongpoints. He then detached the men in his army from Amyclae to permit them to march home to celebrate the Hyacinthia festival while he attacked the peninsula of Piraeum (modern Perachora) far to the north of Corinth.

These men were escorted by the Spartan hoplites and cavalry garrisoning Lecheum, around 600 hoplites and an unspecified number of horsemen. After escorting the Amyclaean men past the walls of Corinth, the escort turned around and marched back to Lecheum, again past Corinth's walls. Sure, Corinth was garrisoned by a sizable anti-Spartan coalition force, but with Agesilaus having ravaged so successfully and the region taking such a beating at Spartan hands in the past few years, the returning escort didn't believe the enemy would have the guts to attack them.

They were wrong.

Iphicrates and his fellow Athenian general Callias saw that the Spartan escort had no missile troops and made the decision to attack. They were likely encouraged by the fact that Agesilaus was many miles away and wouldn't be able to march to his countrymen's aid. We don't know how many Athenians there were in total, but we know that Callias led a force of hoplites that he stationed near the city wall while Iphicrates led a troop of peltasts in pursuit of the Spartans. These fell on the Spartans, showering them with javelins and killing several.

The Spartan commander (whose name is lost) ordered his youngest and fastest troops to run out in pursuit, but with their heavier weapons and shields they were unable to catch the light, faster peltasts. As soon as these runners-out tried to return to the Spartan phalanx, the peltasts doubled back and hit them with javelins again, in a grim echo of the fights at Ithome and Sphacteria and at the Bithynian camp. This happened a second time, with even younger troops being sent out, but with the same results.

At this point, the Spartan cavalry arrived to assist (according to Xenophon, the best of the hoplites were already dead), but made the bizarre tactical decision not to ride the peltasts down. We can't know why they made this choice, and Xenophon gives us only the vague description that "*the horsemen managed their attack badly; for they did not chase the enemy until they had killed some of them, but both in the pursuit and in the turning backward kept an even front with the hoplites.*"

At last, exhausted and worn down by casualties, the Spartans retreated to a hill just outside Lecheum. Seeing the moment for the *coup de grace* had come, Callias finally led up his hoplites, at which point all Spartan discipline evaporated, and the Spartans ran for their lives, some of them racing into the sea. The Athenians gave chase, slaughtering the routing enemy. In all, 250 were killed.

Agesilaus continued to ravage after news of the defeat reached him, but was finally forced to withdraw, at which point Iphicrates set to work recapturing the strongholds the Spartans had taken and generally reversing their gains in the region.

The Spartans held onto Lecheum, but it was their last battle in the region as part of the Corinthian War. Sparta had ended its operations outside Corinth in defeat.

Methymna

Thibron, recalled from exile, was sent back to Asia in answer to Artaxerxes' refusal to end hostilities. After recapturing the original Spartan base at Ephesus, he began to mount raids, which were "*in every case carried out in a disorderly and disdainful fashion,*" according to Xenophon, and was ambushed by Persian cavalry while practicing throwing the discus, and killed. He was replaced by Diphridas, who was more successful; his achievements included capturing and ransoming a powerful Persian official.

Teleutias, acting as admiral for coastal operations in Asia, also managed to ambush and capture ten Athenian ships bound to aid a king in revolt against Persia. The Athenian general Thrasybulus led an amphibious force in alliance with the Thracians, winning over several pro-Spartan Hellespontine cities, including Byzantium. He then met the Spartan governor of Lesbos, Therimachus, who commanded an allied army of Methymnaeans in a land battle, and killed him.

Thrasybulus would later be killed plundering in Persian territory. This, coupled with the Athenian aid to an anti-Persian revolt, would eventually force Artaxerxes to switch sides and ally with Sparta.

Ambush outside Abydus

Sparta sent Anaxibius as governor of Abydus with three ships and enough money to recruit 1,000 mercenaries to conduct land operations in the Hellespont and undo the damage done by Thrasybulus. Anaxibius hired the troops and commenced operations in the area. Iphicrates was sent to oppose him with 1,200 peltasts. Iphicrates first maneuvered his own ships to make it seem that he was engaged in tax collection elsewhere, then set up an ambush to catch Anaxibius while he was marching back from Abydus after garrisoning another city.

Xenophon tells us that Iphicrates waited until the Spartans were descending a rise (implying that Iphicrates attacked from high ground) and then launched his attack.

Anaxibius immediately saw that matters were hopeless and fought a brave rearguard action beside his young lover. The two of them, along with 12 other Spartan governors, were killed trying to buy time for the rest of the army to escape. Iphicrates still pursued the rest of the fleeing Spartan column, killing around 250.

Agesilaus in Acarnania, and the ambush of Gorgopas

In 389 BC Agesilaus campaigned in Acarnania at the request of Sparta's Achaean allies. The mission appeared to be mostly ravaging, save one battle, which Xenophon describes: "*when the Acarnanians attacked him in a mountain pass he seized the heights above their heads with his light infantry, fought an engagement and, after inflicting severe losses on them, set up a trophy.*" It's a thin description, but it's clearly a battle and one that the Spartans won. It further illustrates Agesilaus' worth as a commander and an adaptable one at that – Spartans weren't known for their good use of light infantry. The Acarnanians sued for peace shortly after. The following year, Agesipolis (now old enough to command) staged a successful ravaging campaign into the Argolid, though there were no battles to speak of.

When Aegina began raiding Athens, Athens sent a fleet to punish it, only to have Teleutias' navy drive it off. The Athenian fleet attempted to harass the Spartan governor Gorgopas, who turned the tables on them in a night attack, capturing four ships. However, Gorgopas met his end when the Athenian Chabrias set up an ambush on Aegina, following Iphicrates' model of baiting the Spartans into a trap and then attacking them with light-armed missile troops. Among the dead were Gorgopas, eight precious Peers, and another 150 Aeginetans and 200 other Spartan allies. But Teleutias made certain the Athenians didn't get to enjoy their victory, immediately making a bold raid on Athens' harbor at Piraeus, sinking triremes and towing off merchant ships, then engaging in a series of coastal raids that underscored that Athens' days of commanding at sea were long over.

Meanwhile, Antalcidas had finally secured Artaxerxes' agreement to end hostilities with the Spartans and bring about peace. Even with Iphicrates' victory over the Spartan escort four years earlier, the Corinthians had had enough. Thebes had learned its lesson at Coronea and Agesipolis had just shown the Argives what they could expect if they kept up hostilities. All that remained was the Athenian fleet, currently blockading Abydus. Antalcidas broke the blockade, and staged a naval ambush that took eight Athenian ships. He was immediately reinforced by both Persian and Syracusan ships. Athens took one look at the odds and decided they were too steep:

The Athenians, therefore, seeing that the enemy's ships were many, fearing that they might be completely subdued, as they had been before, now that the King [of Persia] *had become an ally of the Spartans, and being beset by the raiding parties from Aegina, for these reasons were exceedingly desirous of peace.*

Also remember my earlier mention of the extended deployments of Spartan *morai* as garrisons abroad after the Nemea and how Xenophon hints that the Spartan Peers were sick of having to actually serve full time.

Some called the peace "The Peace of Antalcidas" after the Spartan envoy, but it was more commonly known as "The King's Peace" after Artaxerxes, whose power had clearly made it possible. He was also the chief beneficiary of the peace, which formally ratified the complete abandonment of the Asian Greeks to Persian control. The Spartans, the supposed great antagonists of Persia, the heroes of Thermopylae, had first again and again accepted Persian gold and support, and finally turned their backs on the legacy of the ambassadors who warned Cyrus the Great to leave the Asian Greeks alone. Agesilaus followed it up with additional saber rattling that convinced the Boeotian League to break up, and Argos and Corinth to sever their union.

It was 387 BC and the Corinthian War was over at the cost of thousands of lives, the further tarnishing of Sparta's reputation, and the end of any kind of notion of Spartan hegemony over Greece. The only winner was Persia, now firmly and formally in control of its empire all the way to modern Turkey's western shores. Sparta maintained a strong position in mainland Greece, despite numerous defeats, and would hold onto it for roughly nine years. But as we'll soon see, Sparta continued to campaign with only mixed success over the next few years in an effort to consolidate its hold on mainland Greece.

In less than a decade, the Spartans would embark on their next great war, the one that would snap Sparta's spine and end the city-state as a real military power for all time.

Sparta's record in the Corinthian War

Sparta's record in the Corinthian War is still mixed, but a bit better than the previous campaigns we've examined thus far. Of the 12 battles we discussed, Sparta lost seven and won five (though keep in mind we are mixing small and large fights here as I attempt to give as broad a view of Sparta's performance as possible).

There were some bright spots for Spartan arms in this period – Praxitas' seizing the initiative in his daring attack on the Corinthian long walls, Agesilaus' adaptability in Acarnania, Teleutias' naval campaign of vengeance that showed that Sparta finally equaled Athens on the water. Even Agesilaus' decision to lie after Peisander's death during the naval disaster at Cnidus showed some military genius, holding his army's morale together long enough to get the job done at Coronea.

However, Coronea, though a Spartan victory, was an object lesson. The Theban "extremely deep" phalanx that had punched through the Spartan line and nearly killed Agesilaus was just getting warmed up. Sparta would meet this new tactic again, and though the Spartans clearly tried to account for it, their efforts wouldn't be enough.

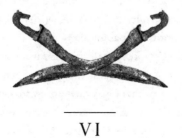

VI

THE BOEOTIAN WAR: WHAT CANNOT BEND MUST BREAK

This has come from my counsel,
Sparta has cut the hair of its glory,
Messene takes its children in,
A wreath of Theban spears,
Crowns Megalopolis,
Greece is free.

Epitaph of Epaminondas Pausanias, *Description of Greece*

The years immediately following the King's Peace saw Sparta embroiled in further military adventures without a moment's rest, as other city-states clearly felt safe enough challenging Sparta's authority to risk military conflict. Further, Sparta's repeated willingness to abandon the Asian Greeks to their fate, surrendering them to Persian authority until the coming of Alexander the Great more than 50 years later, is in stark contrast to its claims to stand for the freedom of the Greeks. That said, I don't want to oversell the oppressiveness of Persian rule. It is very likely that plenty of Asian Greeks preferred Persian overlords to Spartan ones.

There is the very likely apocryphal story that the Spartans preferred not to fight the same enemy repeatedly, lest they learn Sparta's tactics. They had signally failed in this, and there was now an entire generation of Theban, Athenian, Argive and Corinthian veterans with long experience facing Spartans in the field and even beating them. These were wages that Spartans would have to pay very soon.

But for now, Sparta was back in the field by 385 BC, laying siege to Mantinea to dismantle its democratic government and reduce its threat as a center of anti-Spartan opposition in the heart of the Peloponnese. The city performed admirably in resisting the siege (more evidence that Sparta's siege-warfare capability hadn't significantly evolved), though it did surrender when Agesipolis diverted a stream to flood the city.

Diodorus tells us of a renegade Persian admiral named Glos who concluded a military alliance with Sparta against Artaxerxes in 383 BC. This story is strongly attacked by many scholars, but if we believe it, then Sparta apparently felt such shame at betraying the Asian Greeks that it was willing to violate the King's Peace less than five years after it had been enacted. But if it did anything more than make agreements with Glos, this isn't reported (giving credence to the argument that Diodorus made up the story, or perhaps got his timeline wrong).

Next, the anti-Spartan faction in Phlius expelled several partisans from that city who were personally connected to King Agesilaus. The king responded by attacking the city, and Xenophon reports that, in an act totally out of character for a Spartan leader of any kind, let alone a king, Agesilaus refused a bribe to try to get him to wave off. When considering this story, we need to keep in mind that Xenophon was a dear friend of Agesilaus' and wrote the king's biography. Xenophon also reports that the Spartans disliked what appeared to be a mission of personal vengeance by Agesilaus on behalf of his friends and complained that *"merely for the sake of a few individuals they were making themselves hated by a state of more than five thousand men."*

Agesilaus laid siege to the city, which held out twice as long as he'd expected due to good rationing, before it was finally starved into submission, its leaders escaping.

In 382 BC, messengers arrived from the region of Thrace and Macedonia. The city of Olynthus was flexing its muscles, attempting to build a league in the north with itself at its head. Neighboring cities asked for Sparta's intervention and Sparta agreed, levying an army of 10,000, but sending an advance force out immediately under the command of Eudamidas – 2,000 men, a mix of freed helots, *perioikoi* and Sciritae. This force immediately recovered the city of Potidaea and used it as a base from which to begin raiding while it awaited the rest of the army.

This larger army was commanded by Eudamidas' brother Phoebidas and on his march north he wound up making a fateful decision that Sparta would double down on, committing it to a new war that would see Sparta's end as a real military power in Greece.

Thebes, like many cities in Greece at this time, had both an anti-Spartan pro-democracy faction and a pro-Spartan pro-oligarchy faction. The anti-Spartan faction was led by Ismenias and the pro-Spartan faction by Leontiades. As Phoebidas marched past Thebes, Leontiades met with him and asked him to enter Thebes and occupy the city. This would ensure not only that Thebes would act entirely according to Spartan will, but also that the city would provide troops to aid in the coming campaign against Olynthus, for these would surely be withheld if Ismenias' faction should prevail. This was a powerful incentive for Phoebidas to act, but Xenophon is also clear as to Phoebidas' motivations *"for he was a man with a far greater passion for performing some brilliant achievement than for life itself, although, on the other hand, he was not regarded as one who weighed his acts or had much practical wisdom."* In short, Phoebidas didn't agree to Leontiades' offer for the good of Sparta, but rather out of a desire for personal glory and a lack of intelligence. From what we've seen of other leading Spartans, this is entirely believable. Phoebidas did as he was bid, entered Thebes and occupied the Cadmea (Thebes' version of the Acropolis).

It was an act of utter disregard for laws and norms even by the ambiguous standards of the ancient world. The King's Peace had been in place for barely five years. Thebes had offered no provocation against

Sparta. The outrage rippled across Greece, and forced Sparta to at least make a fig leaf of an attempt to punish Phoebidas for his crime (he was fined, but suffered no other punishment). Agesilaus doubled down on this position, arguing in Phoebidas' defense saying that because he had acted in Sparta's best interests, he couldn't be blamed. It was a position that wouldn't be missed by the rest of Greece, who already had come to see Sparta as a high-handed power that talked out of both sides of its mouth. Sparta, great enemy of tyrannies, had taken control of a peaceful city for no reason other than the desire of one of its Peers to win himself glory, and then held onto it out of naked self-interest.

It's important to consider the sources as we contemplate this story. Xenophon was a dear friend of Agesilaus and extremely pro-Spartan, and both Xenophon and Plutarch write Agesilaus' story as a kind of tragedy – the man who was so loyal to Sparta and his friend that it ultimately wound up being the downfall of everything he ever loved. It's important to take it with a grain of salt. However, we don't have a contrary narrative here, so I am presenting the majority view.

A Spartan garrison was stationed on the Cadmea, now backing Leontiades as a strongman ruler on Sparta's behalf. He lost no time in seizing Ismenias at the behest of the Spartan authorities, who sent judges from Sparta and Spartan-allied city-states to convene a kangaroo court. Xenophon even points out that no charges were laid until after the court was in session, so Ismenias had no time to prepare a defense or assemble witnesses.

Unsurprisingly, Ismenias was convicted and executed for accepting Persian gold to start the Corinthian War. While these charges were true, they ignored the fact that Sparta had accepted rivers of Persian gold to win the Peloponnesian Wars and had even joined with the Persian fleet to break the Athenian blockade of Abydus that ended the Corinthian War. This hypocrisy was not lost on the rest of Greece. Xenophon reminds us that around 300 leading Theban anti-Spartan partisans escaped to Athens in a foreshadowing of what was to come.

Phoebidas was replaced by Agesilaus' half-brother Teleutias as the commander of the army, and he marched north to join Eudamidas' force. Leontiades was as good as his word, and Xenophon reminds us that Thebes, now firmly in Sparta's grip, *"eagerly sent with him both hoplites and horsemen."*

Teleutias sent ahead to King Amyntas of Macedon and to Derdas, the strongman in charge of the region of Elymia in southern Macedon. Both sent cavalry to assist as Eudamidas marched on Olynthus.

First and Second Olynthus

Arriving at Olynthus and attacking the city, Teleutias took the left wing, keeping Derdas' cavalry close by partly as a rapid reaction force and partly to honor Derdas by stationing him with the commander of the Spartan army. He posted the Laconian, Theban and other Macedonian cavalry on the right wing.

The Olynthian cavalry charged this right wing, unhorsing and wounding Polycharmus, the Spartan cavalry commander. The cavalry squadron on the Spartan right was routed and the panic spread to the allied infantry, who also began to flee. Xenophon is clear that the battle might have been lost, save for Derdas' cavalry, who charged Olynthus' gates while Teleutias advanced with the left in good order. This forced the Olynthian cavalry to abandon the pursuit of the routing Spartan right for fear they would lose their city gates. Derdas' horsemen got the best of the subsequent cavalry duel, and the Olynthian infantry retreated inside the city. It was a Spartan victory, but the credit was due to the speed and bravery of Derdas' cavalry.

Teleutias withdrew and a stalemate of raids and counterraids ensued. The only real victory against the Olynthians that Xenophon mentions in this period is due entirely to Derdas' Macedonian horsemen once again, and can't be credited to the Spartans.

The one Spartan action we hear of is when Teleutias, "*irritated at their* [the Olynthians'] *audacity*," ordered Tlemondias, who commanded the Spartan peltasts, to attack an Olynthian raiding party. The Olynthian horsemen feigned flight, led the peltasts away from the rest of the army, then turned around and slaughtered them. Tlemondias was among the hundred dead by the time the Olynthians were done.

If the Olynthians had intended to bait Teleutias into a general engagement, they succeeded brilliantly. Furious, he sounded the advance, leading the hoplites forward and directing the remaining peltasts and cavalry to pursue the fleeing Olynthian horsemen and not break off their attack until they were caught. Teleutias had apparently learned nothing from Lysander's rash decision to put himself in range of Haliartus' walls. Teleutias did that now, his rushing troops losing all cohesion in the mad chase, and then suddenly coming under fire from the city. They fell back, still without any of the critical cohesion on which a phalanx's safety depended.

The Olynthians, no fools, saw their chance and took it. The fleeing horsemen wheeled and charged, the Olynthian peltasts and hoplites rushing out from the city to fall on the disordered Spartan phalanx.

It was an utter disaster. Without unit cohesion, a hoplite was intensely vulnerable as an individual fighter. The properly formed Olynthians mowed down the Spartans, killing Teleutias. With the death of the Spartan king's half-brother, all will to fight vanished. The rout was total, with the Olynthians pursuing until (according to Diodorus) 1,200 were dead on the Spartan side. Xenophon is clear on the reason for the defeat: "*to attack under the influence of anger and not with judgment is an absolute mistake. For anger is a thing which does not look ahead, while judgment aims no less to escape harm than to inflict it upon the enemy.*"

Sparta had to have been knocked back on its heels by the disaster. Its response shows how seriously it took the defeat. A half-brother of the Eurypontid king had been slain, and it was the reigning Agiad king, Agesipolis, who led the army that would avenge the insult and restore Sparta's reputation. However, as with Agesilaus in Asia, the ephors made sure the king had a council of 30 Peers to advise (and very likely supervise) him. Recall how one of the ten Peers sent to supervise Agis II kept him from nearly throwing away the Battle of Mantinea in 418 BC before it was even fought.

Xenophon gives us another view of the Spartan manpower crisis, as Agesipolis drew to his banner not Peers, but upper-class *perioikoi*, and the bastard children of male Peers with helot women (note that when the tables were turned much earlier in Sparta's history and Spartan women had children by helots it resulted in the exile of those children). The makeup of the Spartan force was typical for this period, further underscoring both the dwindling number of Peers, and their unwillingness, in complete contradiction to the Bronze Lie, to engage in expeditionary warfare.

Agesipolis only briefly ravaged Olynthian territory before dying of a fever on campaign in 380 BC. He was replaced by Polybiades who through a combination of ravaging and siege caused a famine that forced the Olynthians to finally submit that same year.

Sparta had successfully put an end to Olynthus' attempts to create a league, but at the cost of a king, the half-brother of a king, and thousands of lives. The protracted campaign, with so many embarrassing losses, could not have helped Sparta's reputation but we cannot deny that Sparta's power in Greece was still not seriously challenged. The Spartans had broken Mantinea, prevented Olynthus from forming a league, and taken Thebes without any action from their rivals, even after the setbacks they encountered fighting at Olynthus.

Theban Wages Come Due

But in 379 BC, the chickens sent scattering by Phoebidas came home to roost. Theban exiles, including the general Pelopidas, who would go on to be one of the nails in Sparta's coffin, returned from Athens, slipped into Thebes and butchered the ruling oligarchs.

Pelopidas himself killed Leontiades. Prisoners were released and armed, and the victorious exiles now sent for Athenian troops who were waiting at the border to assist with the liberation. The Spartan garrison sent a panicked message for help to Plataea and Thespiae, but this help was scattered by a charge of Theban anti-Spartan cavalry, who now joined the combined Athenian–Theban force assaulting the Cadmea. The Spartan garrison (according to Xenophon; other sources tell the story differently) realized they were hopelessly outnumbered, and that the public sentiment was against them. They begged to be allowed to depart the city under truce. This was permitted, but Xenophon captures the fury of the Thebans at the injustice they'd suffered, noting that they picked political rivals out of the departing column and murdered them, including their children.

The Athenians also took hostages that might prove valuable for ransom or as political bargaining tools.

Sparta's reaction was disappointing, but not at all surprising. It put the Spartan governor to death for abandoning his post and immediately mustered an army to take Thebes back. It tried to give the command to Agesilaus, but he pleaded old age (he was past 60, the age when a Spartan could be exempt from military service).

Xenophon, who we must remember was a client and dear friend of Agesilaus, says this was simply a cover for the real reason – that Agesilaus knew that if he agreed to the campaign, leading Spartans would criticize him for coming to the aid of tyrants. This can be interpreted in many ways, but I personally align with those scholars who believe Xenophon is for once criticizing Agesilaus' cynicism – that he refused the campaign only because he was worried about his reputation, and not because he truly believed it was wrong.

The simplest answer is also possibly true – that Agesilaus, an old man who had spent his entire life at war, wanted a break.

Command was therefore given to Cleombrotus, the new Agiad king after his brother Agesipolis' death. He avoided the road guarded by Athenian troops (peltasts under Chabrias, whose previous ambush had killed Gorgopas – could Cleombrotus have been frightened to face Athenian peltasts given Chabrias' reputation? Could he have feared Athenian peltasts who may have been trained in the tactics used so successfully by Iphicrates?) and instead took another road guarded by freed Theban prisoners.

In a distinctly un-Spartan show of cunning and adaptability, Cleombrotus deployed his own peltasts on high ground, raining missiles down on the Thebans, killed 150 of them (one or two escaped to bring word to Thebes) and then marched on unhindered to friendly Plataea.

Cleombrotus installed the Spartan Sphodrias at Thespiae as governor, leaving him a third of his army, funding him and directing him to hire mercenaries before marching back home with nothing else accomplished. Xenophon is clear that this was perplexing behavior, and notes that the Spartan troops were "*vastly puzzled to know whether there was really war between them and the Thebans or peace, for he led his army into the country of the Thebans and then left after doing as little damage as possible*." Taken in concert with his avoidance of the Athenian peltasts, a picture emerges of Cleombrotus as a cautious commander, if not a timid one. To be fair to Cleombrotus, it is also possible he shared his father and brother's moderate views and preferred a more peaceful course, but his later actions don't support this argument in my opinion.

But Cleombrotus' show of force worked, panicking the Athenians, who executed one and exiled the other of the two generals who had assisted the Theban exiles in liberating Thebes in the hopes that it would forestall Spartan reprisal. This might have been the end of the war right there – Thebes was isolated, surrounded by enemies, and their chief ally in Athens had gotten cold feet the moment Sparta hinted at flexing its muscles.

The pride of Spartan leaders, their unquenchable thirst for personal glory, a complete contradiction to the Bronze Lie of Spartan tendencies to prioritize the good of the state over the individual, asserted itself once again, ensuring that defeat would be snatched from the jaws of victory.

Sphodrias, as hungry for glory as Phoebidas, took it upon himself to march out at the head of his army for Athens. Xenophon claims he was bribed by the Thebans to do so, and given the Spartan penchant for taking bribes this may well be true, but I believe he was inspired by Phoebidas' example. He had seen that a Spartan Peer could take a city without permission from the government or real provocation, and that leadership would ultimately back him, with glory being his end reward.

Sphodrias unfortunately matched ambition with incompetence. He planned a night march to take the Athenian port of Piraeus ... a march from Thespiae that takes two days.

The sun rose to find his army only halfway there, but clearly revealed his intentions to Athens, which he then confirmed by plundering the area before heading back.

Even now, Athens was too frightened of renewed hostilities with Sparta to do anything. The Athenians kept their peace, confident that this time the perpetrator would be punished. Surely Sparta wouldn't repeat the spectacle of letting off Phoebidas.

This is, of course, exactly what Sparta did.

It turned out that Sphodrias' teenaged son Cleonymus was the beloved of Agesilaus' son Archidamus. Archidamus now lobbied fiercely for Sphodrias' acquittal (despite Sphodrias' refusal to answer the summons of the ephors to come to Sparta to stand trial for his crime) and finally achieved it. Agesilaus admitted Sphodrias' wrongdoing, but said that since he had always "performed the duty of a Spartan, it is a hard thing to put such a man to death; for Sparta has need of such warriors."

The Boeotian War

The shock in Athens must have been total. Sphodrias' acquittal gave legs to the anti-Spartan faction which pointed out correctly that not only had Sphodrias escaped punishment, but he had even been commended for his actions. Athens now threw in its lot with Thebes, creating an effective and powerful alliance to oppose Sparta in what was clearly a full-blown war – called the Boeotian War for the region of Greece where it would be fought ... at its beginning. It would end in Laconia, right on the doorstep of Sparta itself, the first time in the city-state's history that its own lands had been so ravaged.

Theban cavalry attack

Agesilaus was brought out of retirement to clean up Sphodrias' mess, clearly an indication that Cleombrotus' lackluster campaign had eroded Spartan confidence in his leadership. He led the army into Boeotia, screened constantly by the Theban army working from behind a stockade. This army launched a surprise cavalry attack on Agesilaus' troops which he withstood, though not without losses among his light troops and the deaths of two of the dwindling Peers. Agesilaus counterattacked, killed 12 of the enemy and drove them off. He crossed the stockade, ravaged the countryside and installed Phoebidas as governor in Thespiae, from where he carried out successful raids that put the Thebans on their back foot.

Agesilaus found his advance against Thebes blocked by the Theban army, with two units in particular that would continue to spell trouble for Sparta in the years to come. The first was Chabrias' mercenary peltasts, trained in the Iphicratean mode (it is difficult to tell if this means they were skirmishers, or the new heavy infantry peltasts fighting with a longer spear held in two hands and the shield slung from the neck). The second was the famous Theban Sacred Band. Plutarch tells us the Sacred Band was a unit of 300 paired homosexual lovers, originally assigned to guard the Cadmea. Plutarch explains why the lovers' bond made them such a powerful fighting force: "*a band that is held together by the friendship between lovers cannot be broken, since the lovers are ashamed to play the coward before their beloved, and the beloved before their lovers, and both stand firm in danger to protect each other.*" Plutarch credits the Theban general Gorgidas with the unit's creation, and tells us they were initially posted as *promachoi* (the first rank in a phalanx) that they might lead by example. Later, under Pelopidas, they were formed together into a separate unit functioning independently and to stunning success.

Witnessing Chabrias' peltasts and the Sacred Band executing maneuvers, Agesilaus realized he was facing seriously disciplined troops and lost his stomach for the fight. He withdrew and dispersed his army. The fact that Xenophon, who we know was Agesilaus' dear friend, makes no mention of this, tells us how significant it was. The man who was arguably Sparta's most significant king and commander was either too old or too weak, or else not sure enough of his troops to confidently advance against the enemy before him.

Thespiae

It was for Phoebidas to carry on the contest, and he did so with disastrous incompetence. Phoebidas had been successful in a war of ravaging and raiding since being placed at Thespiae, until he reacted to a cavalry raid under the command of Gorgidas. Initially, Phoebidas showed he'd learned the lesson of Teleutias' disastrous overreach, ordering his peltasts to keep tight with the hoplite phalanx, lest they be detached and ridden down. The maneuver was successful "*so that the Thebans in great vexation proceeded to retreat more rapidly than they had advanced, and their muledrivers also threw away the produce which they had seized and pushed for home; so dreadful a panic had fallen upon the army.*"

But Phoebidas mistook the Theban withdrawal for a rout and personally led the peltasts in pursuing them, ordering the slower-moving hoplites to catch up as soon as they could. We can't know that Phoebidas made this fatal mistake out of pride and overconfidence, but judging from his successful taking of the Cadmea and escaping real punishment, it is certainly in character. Unfortunately for Phoebidas, the retreating Thebans reached a ravine which gave them no choice but to turn and fight. This they did, and the countercharge killed Phoebidas and a few of the peltasts, sending the others running. The peltasts' panic infected the hoplites who also turned and ran. There would likely have been a terrific slaughter, but the fleeing Thespians were saved by the gathering dark *"For by this time it was too late in the day for a pursuit."*

It was a minor defeat, but Xenophon is clear on the impact on morale – stiffening Theban spines and encouraging broad resistance to Sparta. Sparta failed to react, very likely because it lacked the manpower and allied support to do so:

> *As a result of this affair the spirits of the Thebans were kindled again, and they made expeditions to Thespiae and to the other cities around them. The democratic factions, however, withdrew from these cities to Thebes. For in all of them oligarchies had been established, just as in Thebes; the result was that the friends of the Spartans in these cities were in need of aid. But after the death of Phoebidas the Spartans merely sent over by sea a polemarch and one regiment, and thus kept Thespiae garrisoned.*

But Diodorus shows us another side of the story that indicates that the Spartans were desperately trying to pivot to deal with their manpower crisis and to shore up allied support in the face of their rock-bottom-and-still-digging reputation and its impact on their allies' willingness to supply them with troops:

> *The Spartans, perceiving that the impulse of their allies to secede was not to be checked, put an end to their former severity and began to treat the cities humanely. By this sort of treatment and by benefactions they rendered all their allies more loyal. And now that they saw that the war was becoming more serious and required strict attention, they set ambitiously*

to work on their various preparations for it, and in particular brought to greater perfection the organization and distribution of their soldiers and the services. In fact they divided the cities and the soldiers that were levied for the war into ten parts. The first part included the Lacedaemonians, the second and third the Arcadians, the fourth the Eleans, the fifth the Achaeans. Corinthians and Megarians supplied the sixth, the seventh the Sicyonians and Phliasians and the inhabitants of the promontory called Acte, the eighth the Acarnanians, the ninth the Phocians and Locrians, and the last of all the Olynthians and the allies who lived in Thrace. They reckoned one hoplite to two light-armed, and one horseman as equivalent to four hoplites.

That last line shows the adaptability of the new system – Sparta allowed their allied cities to play to their strengths, substituting manpower for expensive gear. Too poor to properly equip a hoplite with all that bronze armor? No problem, just send two peltasts who need only javelins and small shields. Doing fine for money, but have a lower population? No problem, equip one cavalryman and keep three able-bodied men at home. It's a rare note of Spartan adaptability and pivoting to meet difficult circumstances.

Capture of the Theban fleet and Cleombrotus' second attempt to enter Boeotia

Another rare note of Spartan cunning made itself apparent in 377 BC, when the Thebans, starving due to constant ravaging of the countryside, sent a fleet to Thessaly with ten talents to buy corn. The Spartan governor Alcetas in Oreus on Euboea's north coast had three triremes, which he carefully kept hidden to encourage the Thebans to sail back in range. This they did, and Alcetas struck, capturing the fleet, its crew and the corn. He imprisoned the crew in the acropolis, but they managed to escape, raise the town in revolt, and then recapture their ships and the cargo of food, which they took on to Thebes. Oreus apparently remained in Theban hands, as Xenophon notes that *"thereafter the Thebans brought in supplies of corn easily."*

Cleombrotus led the next campaign in 376 BC as Agesilaus was bedridden with a ruptured vein in his leg. He attempted the same maneuver with his peltasts that had worked for him three years earlier (taking the heights), but the Thebans and Athenians had learned their lesson and didn't let him repeat it. They'd already taken the high ground and "*allowed the peltasts to pursue their ascent for a time, but when they were close upon them, rose from their concealment, pursued them, and killed about forty.*"

Naxos

Cleombrotus, disheartened and defeated, gave up attempting to enter Theban territory and disbanded his army. Unsurprisingly, Sparta's allies were furious to have been dragged into a war that Sparta's own kings seemed not terribly bothered to try and win. They demanded action, and Sparta responded by manning 60 triremes under the command of the admiral Pollis, presumably the same man who had been wounded as second in command of the Spartan fleet in 393 BC. Stationed off Aegina, this fleet was able to interdict food shipments to Athens and force the Athenians to act.

They did, and in 376 BC an Athenian fleet under Chabrias that significantly outnumbered the Spartans met them in a naval battle off Naxos. While Pollis broke the Athenian left, killing its commander, Chabrias deployed reserves to save the day and squeak out a victory with both sides losing nearly equivalent numbers of ships. Still, it was certainly an Athenian victory at sea over Sparta, the first truly significant one since the Corinthian War.

Alyzeia

The defeat, coming on the heels of Phoebidas' death and Cleombrotus' withdrawal, boosted Theban and Athenian confidence even higher and they worked hard to coerce or convince more and more cities to revolt against Sparta, which even lost Thespiae, its main foothold in Boeotia. The Athenian fleet, a real sea power for the first time since the Peloponnesian Wars, successfully raided the Laconian coast under the command of the admiral Timotheus. In 375 BC, the Spartans dispatched a fleet under Nicholochus to put a stop to the raids, which were bringing over Spartan allies like Corcyra. The two fleets clashed off Alyzeia and Sparta was once again defeated, though we have almost no details on how the battle went.

Tegyra

The next battle of the Boeotian War is one of its most famous and dramatic. Fought in 375 BC, Tegyra foreshadowed Thebes' ascendancy.

Pelopidas made a daring march on Orchomenus with only the 300 hoplites of the Sacred Band and 200 cavalry, probably hoping to win the city over to Thebes while the Spartan garrison of two *morai* (around 1,200 men) was away campaigning in Locris. As he circled around Lake Copais, he discovered that Sparta had sent another garrison to reinforce the city. With only 300 infantry and 200 horsemen, Pelopidas knew better than to assault a walled city with a strong garrison, and wisely turned back ... only to run smack into the original Spartan garrison outside Tegyra on Copais' north shore, returning from its mission in Locris.

We can't be sure of the exact numbers, but we know the Spartans outnumbered the Thebans at least 3-to-1. Worse, Pelopidas' rear was now covered by the Orchomenus relief garrison, allowing him no line of retreat. The commander was literally trapped. Plutarch gives Pelopidas one of the most badass quotes in ancient history – told by his scouts that he'd blundered into the enemy, Pelopidas reportedly replied, "No, it is they who have blundered into us." Whether or not he actually said this, Pelopidas certainly delivered on the spirit of the words.

The Theban commander ordered his cavalry to charge the Spartan line, forming his infantry into a tight phalanx. While we can't be sure, this evokes the densely packed, extra-deep formation we saw the Thebans use successfully before at Coronea. It seems this was becoming something of a doctrine for the Thebans, who had realized that extra phalanx depth allowed the additional punch and push they needed to hammer their way through broader but shallower formations, as well as shoring up morale in the front ranks. Plutarch indeed says that this was Pelopidas' thinking, and that the Theban formed his hoplites *"expecting that wherever they charged he would be most likely to cut his way through the enemy, who outnumbered him."*

The Spartan generals, Gorgoleon and Theopompus, were probably overjoyed. Not only did they outnumber the enemy, but Pelopidas was going on the offensive, playing right into their line where their superior numbers could envelop him and crush his flanks.

But they got more than they bargained for – the Sacred Band hit the Spartan line like a runaway truck with Pelopidas in the lead, barreling straight for the Spartan commanders, both of whom were killed instantly. Pelopidas had clearly bet that if he cut the head off the snake, the body wouldn't be much of a threat.

It was a good bet.

With its leaders dead, the Spartan army broke into confusion, allowing the formed Thebans to smash through the ranks, who were parting in the hope that Pelopidas merely wanted to break through and escape.

He didn't.

Instead, he "*used the path thus opened to lead his men against those of the enemy who still held together, and slew them as he went along, so that finally all turned and fled*" according to Plutarch, who is equally clear about what the upset victory meant for the military reputation of both Sparta and Thebes:

> ... *this battle first taught the other Greeks also that it was not the Eurotas, nor the region between Babyce and Cnacion, which alone produced warlike fighting men, but that wheresoever young men are prone to be ashamed of baseness and courageous in a noble cause, shunning disgrace more than danger, these are most formidable to their foes.*

The Eurotas is the river on which Sparta is built, and the Babyce and Cnacion were likely the names of tributaries to it. In other words, Tegyra showed the world that the Spartans weren't the only badasses in Greece. There were brave men born in Boeotia, too.

The defeat was the writing on the wall – Sparta's grip on Greece, to the extent it had ever been cemented by its short-lived victory in 404 BC, was faltering. The north flared up again, with the Thessalian Jason of Pherae expanding his power in Thessaly. Unlike with Olynthus, Sparta was now helpless to respond, and no army was sent north to challenge him despite a desperate appeal in 375 BC from one of Sparta's Thessalian allies, Polydamas of Pharsalus. Xenophon describes the Spartans tallying up the available manpower, reckoning the number of troops they had abroad to those they would need for use closer to home and straight up deciding they didn't have the manpower to send.

Jason's army was built around peltasts trained in the Iphicratean-style, and now I believe these were not the skirmishing peltasts, but rather pike-armed heavy infantry, using a smaller shield to allow them both hands to wield their longer weapons. These were similar to the troops Alexander the Great would use to conquer Persia in roughly 50 years.

As a result, Sparta agreed to a renewal of the King's Peace – with Sparta dominant on land and Athens on the sea, both with the Persian king's approval (it's not clear whether or not Thebes agreed to this peace. Sparta was likely hoping the end of the Boeotian War would free it up to face Jason if need be.

Second Corcyra

The peace was over before it even started. Almost immediately, Athens and Sparta were backing rival pro-democratic and pro-oligarchic factions in cities. By 374 BC, a Spartan fleet was off Corcyra and the Spartan admiral Mnasippus was ravaging the island to rip it from Athenian rule. The Athenians botched manning a relief fleet and replaced the admiral with Iphicrates, which delayed its setting out.

In the meantime the starving Corcyreans sallied against Mnasippus, who had cut pay to his troops thinking the campaign was nearing its end. This combination of cut pay and his using force to beat complainers into line damaged morale among his men. Still, Mnasippus defeated the initial sally and chased the Corcyreans to the funeral monuments outside the city, where the fleeing troops found their courage and climbed the monuments, throwing rocks and javelins down on their pursuers. At the same time, more Corcyrean hoplites sallied from the city and attacked the flank of Mnasippus' phalanx where the Spartan troops (likely the only Peers were officers, and the rank and file were allies and lower classes) were stationed.

These troops attempted to countermarch to form a double-depth phalanx (the Spartans had clearly learned their lesson from Coronea and Tegyra and realized they had to fear a double-depth punch-through more than being outflanked). But this maneuver was new to the Spartans, who normally deployed only eight ranks deep, and the countermarch was either bungled or too slow, leading the Corcyreans to think the Spartan-led troops were fleeing. Overjoyed, they charged, catching the Spartan-led troops in mid-countermarch, with the phalanx completely out of order. The Spartan-led troops broke immediately, panic spread from the wing to the rest of the line, and the entire formation broke apart. Mnasippus was killed and Hypermenes, his second in command, didn't even bother to try to salvage the situation. Worried about Iphicrates approaching with the Athenian fleet, the Spartan took as much loot as he could carry and fled, narrowly escaping the arrival of the Athenians.

Discord and jealousy between Thebes and Athens forced both parties to sue for peace once again in 371 BC. Sparta agreed (probably counting itself lucky), but came into conflict with Thebes when the latter in effect refused to make the cities it had captured independent, attempting to swear to the peace on behalf of the Boeotian League that Sparta had forced to disband, and that Thebes had been rebuilding throughout the Boeotian War. The Spartans in turn ordered Cleombrotus not to demobilize his army at Phocis, and instead to invade Thebes.

Once again, Sparta had been offered an off-ramp to open war, and once again, it had failed to take it.

It would not get another chance.

FOCUS BATTLE: LEUCTRA (371 BC) – SPARTA BREAKS

Leuctra, more than any other battle in Sparta's long history, can be said to have determined the city's fate.

Thermopylae, despite being an arguably disastrous defeat, had been an incredible propaganda victory, one that had cemented the Spartans' reputation (undeservedly) as the bravest and strongest warriors in all of Greece. Sphacteria had opened a crack in that reputation, exposing the Bronze Lie briefly for all of Greece to see, but Sparta had managed hoplite-on-hoplite victories at First Mantinea, the Nemea and Coronea which helped to patch up that reputation somewhat, though it still teetered.

Leuctra snapped Sparta's spine. The defeat shattered the city-state's reputation and self-confidence with a finality that ensured neither would recover.

The run-up to the battle initially went well for Sparta. Cleombrotus stole a march on the Thebans, leading 2,000 hoplites and a thousand cavalry into Boeotia according to Plutarch. This doesn't match other reports of the ultimate sizes of the armies at Leuctra, so it's possible that Plutarch is either wrong or describing an advance force that Cleombrotus used to clear the way to Thebes while the main army caught up. Xenophon reports that this force surprised the Theban fort at Creusis (possibly modern-day Paralia Livadostratas), capturing its wall and 12 triremes anchored there. Pausanias also reports that the Spartans massacred a Theban force under Chaereas which was guarding a pass, though it isn't clear precisely when and how this happened.

Cleombrotus now led his troops to the plain of Leuctra outside Thespiae and camped on high ground with a force of around 10,000–11,000 hoplites and an additional 1,000 cavalry. Xenophon lets us know that 700 of these were the precious and dwindling Spartan Peers. While we don't know the exact number of Peers, we can estimate this represented as many as 60 percent of the entire population, a serious risk of Sparta's elite military manpower. The Thebans camped on a hill opposite, challenging the Spartan advance with a smaller force, probably around 6,000 or maybe 7,000 hoplites with a cavalry squadron probably a little larger than the Spartan horse.

Plutarch gives a lot of superstitious omens about why the ground was spiritually bad for the Spartans to fight on, but we won't consider that (again, this is a book of history, not mythology). Plutarch also gives Pelopidas another incredible and Hollywood-worthy quote as he armed and prepared to deploy. His wife, weeping, begged him not to lose his life in the coming fight. "Wife," Pelopidas supposedly said, "you can give this advice to a private soldier, but I command, and commanders should be begged not to lose the lives of others."

While this line is very likely untrue, what Plutarch reports next probably is true – that the Thebans were terrified of facing the larger army of the Spartans, and that a heated debate arose between the six boeotarchs as to whether they should accept Cleombrotus' offer of battle. Initially, Epaminondas, one of the boeotarchs and the architect of the Theban victory at Leuctra, was in favor of giving battle, but was opposed by the other five.

Pelopidas threw his weight behind Epaminondas and Plutarch notes that *"although he had not been appointed boeotarch, he was captain of the sacred band, and highly trusted, as it was right that a man should be who had given his country such tokens of his devotion to freedom."* Xenophon adds to the motivations behind the boeotarchs' decision to take the Spartans on:

> *The Theban commanders ... calculated that if they did not fight, the cities round about would revolt from them and they would themselves be besieged; further, that if the people of Thebes were thus cut off from provisions, the city itself would be in danger of turning against them. And since many of them had been in exile before, they thought that it was better to die fighting than to be exiled again.*

Still, it was clearly a near thing, and if we believe Pausanias, it took the arrival of a seventh boeotarch to swing the vote in favor of fighting.

DRIVEN BY SHAME AND DRINK

Meanwhile, back in the Spartan camp, Xenophon reports that Cleombrotus' advisors were reminding him about his inaction in 379 BC, and how if he backed down from a fight with Thebes again:

> *... you will be in danger of suffering the utmost penalty at the hands of your state. For they will remember against you not only the time when you reached Cynoscephalae and laid waste no part of the country of the Thebans, but also the time when, on your later expedition, you were beaten back from making your entrance.*

Once again, pride and fear of reprisal motivated a Spartan king to make a bad decision, just as Agis had almost thrown his army away at Mantinea in 418 BC. At Leuctra, Cleombrotus had no body of supervising Peers to hold him back.

Xenophon also talks about superstitious omens, which we'll ignore, but he adds that Cleombrotus and his advisors drank wine with their morning meal and this perhaps made them a bit more aggressive than they would otherwise have been. Another contradiction to Sparta's legend – that the Spartans supposedly never drank to excess.

Xenophon reports that the Theban camp followers and presumably their more cowardly troops who decided to quit the field before the battle were attacked by Spartan mercenaries – Phocian peltasts, and Phliasian cavalry, who drove them back into the Theban camp. This inadvertently made the Theban army stronger, Xenophon reports, since these troops now had no choice but to fight. Xenophon's assessment doesn't sound right to me. Troops with poor morale who have already suffered a defeat aren't going to add to an army's strength, and camp followers aren't fighters at all, but prostitutes, merchants, artisans and servants without real fighting skill.

Both phalanxes drew up on the plain opposite one another. We don't have a good breakdown of the order of battle, save that the Thebans posted the Sacred Band on their left opposite Cleombrotus and his *hippeis* guard on the Spartan right. Both armies posted their cavalry squadrons out in front of their phalanxes, but although these units were more or less matched in terms of numbers (with a slight advantage to the Thebans), they were horribly mismatched in training. While the Spartans had certainly made great advances in their command of the sea, they had hadn't made similar strides in developing their skill as horsemen. In fact, the one example we have of Sparta advancing in cavalry warfare is Agesilaus' cavalry fight near Dascylium in 395 BC, a lesson that the Spartans proved they'd failed to learn at Lecheum just four years later. So we shouldn't be surprised to read Xenophon's report that "*Now the cavalry of the Thebans was in good training as a result of the war with the Orchomenians and the war with the Thespians, while the cavalry of the Spartans was exceedingly poor at that time.*"

Xenophon also notes that the Spartan cavalry was supplied by the richest men (another possible indicator of bad wealth inequality in Sparta at this point in history, though it is possible that these horsemen were largely allied troops and not Spartans at all) and the untrained underlings actually in the saddles were the "*least strong of body and the least ambitious.*"

The deployment of cavalry out in front of the armies is curious. While this wasn't unheard of (recall that the Thebans at Tegyra led with a cavalry charge), in ancient battles, cavalry more frequently operated on the flanks and attempted to either envelop the enemy or to threaten enemy flanks once an

Leuctra – 371 BC

Spartans

Thebans

Heavy infantry

Cavalry

1. The battle opens with a cavalry engagement where the Spartans get the worst of it.
2. The routing Spartan cavalry flee through the lines, disordering the infantry.
3. The Spartan line continues to advance, but the Theban flank is "refused" (deployed in echelon away from the Spartans), and the Spartans cannot reach it in time.
4. The Theban "living spear" (author's term) – an extra-deep phalanx – charges the Spartan right and breaks it, killing King Cleombrotus.
5. The Spartans break and rout.

infantry unit was pinned by its opposite party (and to defend against the same being done to their own side). It's possible that what we're seeing here is the advance parties of the armies engaging one another as the hoplites drew up behind them, a tactic we've seen in multiple battles, often to disastrous effect. It's also possible that the Spartan cavalry commander simply didn't know what the heck he was doing, judging from Xenophon's description of the condition of the Spartan cavalry, and that the Theban commander of horse decided to take advantage of the error.

Xenophon now turns to a description of the infantry, telling us specifically that the Spartan sworn bands deployed at a depth of no more than 12 ranks. This is actually deeper than was typical for the period, and possibly an effort by the Spartans to increase depth at the cost of frontage based on their experience fighting deeper Theban formations at battles such as Coronea and Tegyra. We certainly saw Mnasippus disastrously attempt to address this on Corcyra.

A LIVING SPEAR POINTED AT SPARTA'S HEART

But the Thebans one-upped them, deploying the Sacred Band and their other best troops in a unit *50* ranks deep. This sacrificed frontage to a large degree, increasing the risk of being outflanked, but in effect created a living spear aimed at Cleombrotus' unit on the Spartan right, a formation that would have the momentum and push power of 50 young, strong men, all bulling irresistibly forward. At their head stood Pelopidas, the hero of Tegyra, who knew first hand just how to employ this living weapon against the Spartans. Xenophon is clear as to the motive for this gamble: the Thebans figured that "*if they conquered that part of the army which was around the king, all the rest of it would be easy to defeat.*"

The gamble was exacerbated by the Theban army being outnumbered by some 2,000–3,000 men. This meant that the Spartan phalanx would easily envelop the Thebans on both sides. If they couldn't deliver the knockout blow they'd planned quickly enough, they'd be outflanked and destroyed.

Which meant the battle had become a race – the Thebans trying to destroy Cleombrotus and his bodyguard (with the anticipated impact on Spartan morale) and the Spartans trying to swamp the Theban line before they could accomplish this.

But there's another point to consider. Leuctra is a flat field between two hills. The Spartan command element was on foot. We have little information on scouting, reconnaissance and intelligence efforts on either side, but we have seen repeated Spartan failures to conduct necessary advance reconnaissance in anticipation of a battle. So, it stands to reason that the Spartans did *not* have a good notion of the Theban deployment, and since the command was on foot, they would be able to see only the first rank of the Theban hoplites. My point here is that the *massive* depth of the Sacred Band on the Theban left – a long, narrow column running straight back – may have been hidden. The Spartans may have had no idea about what the Thebans had planned for them.

We have a much later example of the same maneuver – the Battle of Cannae in 216 BC, where the Carthaginian general Hannibal crushed Rome in what's considered one of the worst disasters in the history of warfare. Hannibal accomplished this signal achievement by hiding his own long, narrow columns of elite African veteran infantry in plain sight, using the flat battlefield and the Romans' relatively low vantage point to conceal them behind the men in front of them.

Another thing to note – elite troops in ancient Greece were usually stationed on the army's right, as the Spartans had done (some scholars dispute this, claiming there was more flexibility in where the best troops were placed). By placing his best troops on the left, Epaminondas was innovating, taking the initiative, and throwing the Spartans further into confusion.

If the Spartans didn't understand the battle they were fighting, Epaminondas surely did. He knew that the Spartans' greater numbers were bound to swamp, envelop and quickly overwhelm his own force. He had to buy his battle line as much time as he possibly could to deliver the knockout blow with the Sacred Band. To accomplish this, he used a simple yet ingenious maneuver – he deployed his line "in echelon," "refusing" his right flank to the enemy. These terms mean that the units to the right of the Sacred Band were deployed in a diagonal line leaning toward the Theban rear and away from the Spartans. This meant that the Spartans would have more ground to cover to reach the Theban right – it would take them *longer*, buying the Thebans precious minutes they would need for the Sacred Band to do its job. Diodorus adds that the Theban right was ordered to give ground when finally engaged (also a tactic Hannibal used at Cannae, ordering his center to slowly yield to the Romans to draw them in). Finally, it's possible that Epaminondas understood that Sparta's allies (who would be deployed on the Spartan left) were reluctant to fight and might advance more slowly than the Spartan right, which would buy even more precious time.

All the sources agree that the battle unfolded quickly. The cavalry engaged even as the hoplites were deploying with predictable results. The outmatched and possibly outnumbered Spartan horsemen were broken, routed, and driven back on their own lines. Here the decision to deploy out front of the infantry paid dividends to the Thebans and set the Spartans up for defeat – the Spartan horsemen fled straight through the hoplite lines, whose ranks had to break apart to let them pass or else risk being trampled.

This would have had two immediate consequences – first, disorder. The Spartans would now have to close the gaps in their line, dress their ranks and regroup, all while closing with the advancing Thebans opposite them.

This may seem simple, but it wasn't. Keep in mind that you're talking about approximately 10,000 men, all of whom are amped up on adrenaline, frightened and laser-focused on the rapidly closing enemy. Most of them would have been wearing helmets (probably mostly the *pilos* cap which would have left their ears clear, though some might have covered the ears, depending on how they were worn), and this was a period before radios, loudspeakers or any real way to significantly amplify the human voice. Also keep in mind that a crowd that large kicks up a huge amount of dust, even on grass-covered ground, obscuring vision.

Finally, the army would have been *loud* as individual men would have called encouragement to one another, whispered prayers to the gods or sung the paean. My point is that issuing orders to such a mass and ensuring they dressed the line and got the gaps closed would have been enormously challenging, and even if the more disciplined Spartan Peers (who we have seen over and over again were probably less consistently disciplined and organized than they are reputed to have been) could do this instinctively, their allied troops very likely could not. It is quite possible that the Spartan phalanx at Leuctra was still recovering from its disorder when it finally met the enemy.

The second consequence was an impact to the most critical factor in an ancient battle – morale. Seeing your own troops wounded and killed, watching them flee past you, throwing down their weapons, stripping off their helmets or casting aside their shields in their eagerness to save their own lives, does not make you optimistic about your side's chances in a coming battle. It is an intensely demoralizing sight, and we have seen again and again how panic was infectious, and demoralization of troops was one of the most fatal blows an ancient army could sustain. The Spartan army engaging the Thebans at Leuctra may have been grappling with disorder *and* panic simultaneously when the lines finally engaged. One of these alone would have been difficult to overcome. Both together would have been fatal to even the greatest army in the world.

The infantry battle unfolded exactly as Epaminondas hoped it would – the Spartan left certainly had the greater frontage necessary to envelop the Theban right, but it had more ground to cross to reach the refused flank, and it would have progressed more slowly as the men wrestled with the disorder and panic induced by the fleeing cavalry. Worse, it now had to deal with the victorious Theban cavalry, who were free to harass the Spartan phalanx unimpeded, either throwing javelins and then wheeling away, or attacking the flanks with spears, depending on how they were armed (we don't have details, unfortunately).

Meanwhile, the Sacred Band led the 50-rank-deep Theban living spear and charged directly for Cleombrotus. Plutarch claims that Epaminondas slid the killing column to the left, forcing Cleombrotus' unit to separate from the rest of the army and leaving it isolated for Pelopidas and his lightning charge. I doubt this because of the disparity of numbers. The Spartan line likely outstretched the Thebans on both flanks, and so the Spartans would have had no need to shift no matter what the Sacred Band did. And even if they didn't have the numerical superiority, such a detachment would have left a suicidal gap in the Spartan line. It would be for Pelopidas to come to Cleombrotus, no matter where he was.

Pelopidas was more than happy to oblige.

The *hippeis* around their king were the best of Sparta's best, likely fit, athletic, young, well-trained and convinced of their own superiority, which would contribute to high morale. But no sooner did the dust raised by their fleeing horsemen clear than the Theban column was on them, slamming into their front rank like a freight train, rank after rank of men throwing their weight behind their shields, pushing on the back of the man in front, creating an unstoppable mass of pressure that the shallower depth of the Spartan phalanx couldn't hope to resist. The *hippeis* would have been driven helplessly back, staved in, the line breaking apart. The Spartans would have fought like lions to protect their king, but they would have been unable to keep themselves from being shoved back, thrust aside, until they found themselves fighting for their lives around Cleombrotus.

Sound familiar? It should. This is precisely what happened at Tegyra, and also at Coronea where Agesilaus was wounded when the Theban column drove straight through to him. But at Coronea, the Thebans were bent on breaking through the Spartans to escape to the remains of their routed army.

At Leuctra, their mission was clear – kill the king.

Xenophon tells us that the king's guard fought well, but couldn't hold back the tide. He names the Spartans who fell – Deinon, the Spartan general and Cleonymus, Cleombrotus' tent-mate. He also names Sphodrias, the man responsible for driving Athens into Thebes' arms and ensuring that Sparta would face two major city-states in the Boeotian War. These deaths, along with those of other members of the royal bodyguard, caused the Spartan right to collapse. A total of 400 of the 700 Peers present on the field, probably around 33 percent of all the Peers left in Sparta, were cut down in a single strike.

Those who remained broke and quit the field.

They carried with them King Cleombrotus, mortally wounded.

Xenophon, a pro-Spartan partisan to the last, does his best to put a brave face on what was clearly a disaster. He claims the Spartan right fell back, when it is plain they at the very least retreated and may have routed. The evidence for this is that the Spartan left also gave way, despite the fact that it had either not yet come to grips with the Theban right, or had only just made contact, given the Theban refused right flank and the presence of the Theban cavalry. This actually makes sense, as the Spartan left would have seen the right crack, and realized it would be outflanked and that it was useless to stay in the fight.

He also claims that the ability of the Spartans to carry their king's corpse off the field is evidence that the Spartan right fought well. This does match the defeated Spartans at Thermopylae, who also fought well enough to successfully carry off the body of their king to the Colonus where they made their final stand.

Epaminondas' plan had been executed to perfection and the results were exactly as expected. Cleombrotus was, as far as the rest of the army knew, dead – the first Spartan king to fall in battle since Leonidas at Thermopylae more than a century earlier. The bravest and noblest of the Peers were retreating to their camp, the ground littered with hundreds of corpses of Sparta's elite, trampled under the feet of the pursuing Theban Sacred Band. The word spread through the ranks of the remaining Spartan troops like wildfire and the panic was total. The army's spirit failed wholesale and the disorder begun by the fleeing Spartan cavalry escalated – organization collapsed, the rout went systemic.

The Thebans, who had marched to Leuctra outnumbered and by no means sure of their victory, were masters of the field. Xenophon credits the routing troops with reorganizing and establishing a defense once they reached the trench surrounding their fortified camp, which was on defensible high ground. The Spartans, humiliated, refused to accept their defeat. Some wanted to violate the usual custom of battle and attack the Thebans while they set up their victory trophy. However, either cooler heads prevailed, or else it became apparent that this would only exacerbate the slaughter beyond the 1,000 casualties the Spartans had already suffered, for the polemarchs called a meeting and it was decided to agree to a truce.

The Spartans made a formal submission and acknowledgment of defeat by requesting permission to collect their dead. The Thebans granted this and erected their victory trophy as they warily watched the Spartan burial detail. This trophy was different from others in that it was permanent. The surviving base was restored and still stands on the battlefield to this day.

Epaminondas and Pelopidas likely surveyed the field with their hearts alight, realizing the enormity of what they'd accomplished. They had faced the Spartans in a pitched battle, outnumbered, on flat ground, phalanx to phalanx.

And they had won, completely and decisively, killing the Spartan king and driving the enemy from the field.

It was the nail in the coffin of Sparta's military reputation and the end of its purported dominance of Greece. From this day forward, Sparta would be on its heels, backpedaling in the face of enemies who not only no longer feared it, but were confident in their ability to face and defeat its armies under any conditions.

The aftermath of the battle shows just how badly rattled the defeat left Sparta. Xenophon tells us (in what is likely another bit of pro-Spartan propaganda) that the families of the survivors wept and went about silently, while the families of the slain rejoiced for their relatives who had sold their lives bravely. A new army was immediately called up and placed under the command of Agesilaus' son Archidamus (for Agesilaus was apparently not recovered from some new illness. Maybe the same vein acting up) and marched north to rescue the shattered remains of Cleombrotus' army and avenge the loss.

But the Thebans weren't idle. They sent to Athens for help and probably weren't surprised not to receive it, since Athens was concerned about Thebes' rising power and hoping it would have lost at Leuctra. However, Jason of Pherae jumped at the chance to get involved, marching south with reinforcements and blitzing through Phocis (with which he was at war) before his enemies even realized he was on the march. That he arrived well in advance of Archidamus shows that the Spartans were proceeding cautiously, or else slowed trying to rally allied troops who might be justifiably hesitant as news of the Spartan defeat was surely spreading.

The Thebans wanted to crush the remains of the Spartan army in a pincer movement, with Jason's troops attacking from the heights above the Spartan camp while the Thebans advanced from below. Jason wisely warned against this. Not only would the Thebans be fighting uphill, but the Spartans would be fighting like a cornered bear, desperate for their lives.

Instead, Jason persuaded the Spartans to depart under a truce. Some scholars have also suggested that Jason argued for the truce in an effort to keep a weakened Sparta in play against the rising power of Thebes, which he was worried might become a threat to him. The remains of Cleombrotus' army marched away, linking up with Archidamus' relief force, which, strengthened with an additional 9,000-odd troops, was in a good position to continue its advance into Boeotia and challenge the Thebans and Jason's troops if Archidamus wished.

Instead, the prince marched home.

There are many ways to interpret Archidamus' actions. Some may view his decision not to fight as sensible and prudent, but it is also possible that low Spartan morale was a factor – that Prince Archidamus and the Spartans he led were absolutely terrified. Leuctra had shown them that the best Sparta had to offer simply wasn't up to the task of beating Thebes in a fair fight.

But whether motivated by prudence or by fear, Archidamus' march home was a withdrawal in the face of an enemy the Spartans knew they could not defeat.

The Bronze Lie revealed in its full finality, at long last.

VII

THE END OF SPARTA: IRREFORMABLE AND IRRELEVANT

After Eucleidas and his forces had in this way been cut to pieces, and the enemy, after their victory there, were coming on against the other wing, Cleomenes, seeing that his soldiers were in disorder and no longer had courage to stand their ground, took measures for his own safety. Many of his mercenaries fell, as we are told, and all the Spartans, six thousand in number, except two hundred.

Plutarch, *Life of Cleomenes*

This glaring contradiction between Sparta's self-image and its reality convulsed the government. Plutarch is clear that much of the blame fell on Agesilaus, with some reverting to the old argument that his ascendancy, backed by the long dead Lysander, had offended the gods by defying the Delphic oracle's warning about a "lame king."

Agesilaus also bowed to expediency in regard to the surviving Peers who lived through Leuctra. By Spartan custom, they should have been labeled "tremblers" whose cowardice allowed them to survive when their braver comrades died, but as with the return of the surviving Peers from Sphacteria, their large numbers (and possibly the backing of their powerful families), coupled with Sparta's now desperate need for fighting men, combined to move Agesilaus to mercy. Agesilaus reportedly suspended the laws for a day, declaring them not in force when the tremblers were to be judged, which Plutarch regards as a wise move that somehow enabled both men and laws to escape with their reputation intact. Plutarch's insane mental gymnastics aside, he gives the actual reason for Agesilaus' decision in an earlier passage, saying the Spartan government – "*hesitated to inflict the penalties required by the laws, since the men were numerous and powerful, for fear that they might stir up a revolution.*"

Sparta probably feared two things most as a result of the defeat – a helot revolt and being opposed by its neighboring states in the Peloponnese. The former didn't happen, but the latter did. Elis, Mantinea, Tegea and Argos all made decidedly anti-Spartan moves, any one of which would have provoked a military response. Eventually Sparta found itself facing an Arcadian League backed by Theban power on its very own doorstep.

The Boeotian War Continues

Sparta finally mustered an army in 370 BC to try to put all this right, though it had to have been dogged by faltering morale and worry at the bewildering array of enemies amassed against it. Agesilaus, though an old man, had recovered enough to take command. Xenophon reports that Agesilaus, after occupying the city of Eutaea on the border with Arcadia, ordered all the plunder his men had taken to be given back, an indicator of Sparta's weak position and desire not to offend its few remaining allies. Recall that Agesilaus had shown willingness to champion Sparta's interests even when it savaged its reputation, including backing Phoebidas' taking of the Theban Cadmea and Sphodrias' unprovoked march on Athens. Contrast this with Herippidas' handling of plunder after sacking Pharnabazus' camp.

Orchomenus

Meanwhile, the Spartan Polytropus raised a force of mercenaries to defend Orchomenus against the Mantineans. He successfully helped with the defense but then repeated the mistake of several Spartan commanders in pursuing the enemy too closely and out of order, so that he was killed when the Mantineans counterattacked and his leaderless troops fled.

Agesilaus absorbed the mercenary force and ravaged Mantinea. Tracked by an allied army of Arcadians, he was forced to maneuver and then escape without giving battle. Xenophon is clear about his real goal – to boost Spartan morale after Leuctra, without risking further losses:

> ... he continued his march as rapidly as possible to Eutaea, even though it was very late, with the desire of getting his hoplites away before they even saw the enemy's fires, so that no one could say that he had withdrawn in flight. For he seemed to have brought the state some relief from its former despondency, inasmuch as he had invaded Arcadia and, though he laid waste the land, none had been willing to fight with him.

Returning to Laconia, he disbanded his army.

But while this near bloodless campaign may have helped Spartan morale, it did the same for Thebes, whose opinion of Spartan arms as toothless and easily beaten was confirmed. Pelopidas' and Epaminondas' stars had risen high after Leuctra and they now contemplated an invasion of Laconia, spurred on by the Arcadian anti-Spartan coalition. The Thebans had been fighting the Spartans for a generation now and had a good measure of the enemy they faced, a fact Plutarch alludes to when he puts the (again, probably apocryphal) quote in the mouth of the Spartan Antalcidas addressing Agesilaus after his wounding at Coronea "*Indeed, this is a fine tuition-fee which you are getting from the Thebans, for teaching them how to war and fight when they did not wish to do it.*" Comic book writer Kieron Gillen puts it even better in his outstanding comic book *Three*, intended to be the historical answer to Miller's *300*, in which he has Spartans bemoan their inadvertent training of the Thebans in how to defeat them (by fighting them repeatedly) "we forged the spear that struck us down."

The Thebans had some hesitations about fighting the Spartans on their home territory, but were ultimately convinced by Sparta's own subjects turning traitor as they saw the writing on the wall. Xenophon tells us:

> ... *when people had come from Caryae* [in Sciritis, which had always been a loyal Spartan satellite] *telling of the dearth of men, promising that they would themselves act as guides ... and when, further, some of the perioikoi appeared, asking the Thebans to come to their aid, engaging to revolt if only they would show themselves in the land, and saying also that even now the perioikoi when summoned by the Peers were refusing to go and help them – as a result, then, of hearing all these reports, in which all agreed, the Thebans were won over ...*

Xenophon is clear, Sparta's manpower's crisis was exacerbated by the peeling off of some manpower from formerly loyal sources of troops – the *perioikoi* and the Sciritae.

Diodorus tells us that the Spartans were so worried about the pending invasion that they appealed to their old enemy Athens for aid. Diodorus certainly appreciated the irony of this move: "*nothing is stronger than necessity and fate, which compelled the Spartans to request the aid of their bitterest enemies.*" The Athenians, wary of Thebes' growing power, voted to assist Sparta, deploying Iphicrates at the head of 12,000 troops to go to their old enemy's rescue.

Defense of the pass against the Arcadians, and Tegeatis

And so Laconia was, at long last, invaded. Four major forces entered by four different routes – Thebans, Arcadians, Argives and Eleans. Xenophon tells us of the Spartan Ischolaus, who tried to hold a pass against the Arcadians, and met with initial success, but was finally killed when the Arcadians fell back and showered the Spartans with missiles.

Diodorus tells us that the Argives overwhelmed and defeated the Spartan blocking force at Tegeatis under the command of the Spartan Alexander, who fell in the fighting.

With the entry open, the anti-Spartan coalition pillaged the region, burned the town of Sellasia and advanced into Laconia. Xenophon describes the shock of Sparta's women, who were finally experiencing first hand what Sparta had visited on others so many times – the sight of an invader burning family estates close to the city's border:

> ... the women could not even endure the sight of the smoke, since they had never seen an enemy; but the Peers, their city being without walls, were posted at intervals, one here, another there, and so kept guard, though they were, and were seen to be, very few in number. It was also determined by the authorities to make proclamation to the helots that if any wished to take up arms and be assigned to a place in the ranks, they should be given a promise that all should be free who took part in the war.

This effort raised 6,000 troops, to which were added the mercenaries who'd fought at Orchomenus, as well as other allied troops. The Thebans finally crossed the Eurotas and came close to the city, but were driven back by an ambush. The Thebans seemed happy to leave the city alone (where defenses would be most firm) and contented themselves raiding south, joined by deserting *perioikoi* – that is, if you believe Xenophon's story. Xenophon tells us they burned every unfortified settlement they could find, but failed to take any walled towns and were unable to take Sparta's dockyards at Gythium.

But when we keep in mind Xenophon's intensely pro-Spartan bias, it makes more sense to credit Diodorus, who tells us that Epaminondas indeed assaulted Sparta itself, and that there was a desperate fight for the city:

> ... the Spartans with the aid of their strong natural defenses killed many of those who pressed rashly forward, but finally the besiegers applied great pressure and thought at first they had overcome Sparta by force; but as those who tried to force their way were some slain, some wounded, Epaminondas recalled the soldiers with the trumpet, but the men of their own accord would approach the city, and would challenge the Spartans to a pitched battle, bidding them otherwise admit their inferiority to the enemy. When the Spartans replied to the effect that when they found a suitable occasion they would stake everything on one battle, they departed from the city. And when they had devastated all Laconia and amassed countless spoils, they withdrew to Arcadia.

It's important to note that such devastation wouldn't have been necessary if the *perioikoi* had all gone over to Thebes. Clearly, many of them remained loyal to Sparta.

Plutarch credits two people in particular with Sparta's defense, but the far more interesting story is that of Isidas, the son of the same Phoebidas who started the Boeotian War. According to Plutarch, Isidas burst from his house naked with a spear in one hand and a sword in the other and fought the enemy off. The Spartan response was typical (if you believe Plutarch): "*For this exploit it is said that the ephors put a garland on his head, and then fined him a thousand drachmas, because he had dared to risk his life in battle without armor.*"

But having completed their ravaging of Laconia, the Thebans had a final indignity to inflict on Sparta. Epaminondas founded a new city of Messene on the slopes of Mount Ithome, where the Messenians had held out against Sparta centuries ago. The anti-Spartan coalition set up something similar to Israel's "right of return" system for modern Jews, with all claiming Messenian ancestry welcome to come and take up residence. They were joined by rebel helots and *perioikoi* as well as other Greeks seeking their fortune. This hostile city just off Sparta's flank was surely a tactical concern, but the moral impact of the founding cannot be overstated. So much of Sparta's military history can be described as an effort to prevent this very thing from coming to pass – a free and independent Messenia with its own city as a rallying point.

When the Thebans and their allies finally left, Sparta found itself returned in just the space of a few months more or less to its original borders in the archaic era. Laconia was a smoking ruin. Messenia was free and hostile. The states to the north that had for so many centuries been reliable Spartan allies were armed and taking the field in opposition.

In the blink of an eye, Sparta had shed nearly every vestige of its former glory. It would never again dominate even the Peloponnese, much less Greece.

Pallene and Asine

The following years confirmed this. According to Diodorus, the Arcadians captured the Laconian city of Pallene, killing the Spartan governor and garrison there. They repeated this success after evading an Athenian blocking force, taking the Laconian city of Asine, killing the Spartan garrison and their commander, the Spartan Peer Geranor.

Xenophon also describes the Thebans surprising and defeating the Spartan garrison at Pallene during this period, and it isn't clear if this is another angle on the attack on Pallene described by Diodorus or a separate attack. The Thebans later intervened in Achaea to install anti-Spartan democracies there, but the plan appears to have backfired according to Xenophon:

> ... those who had been thus exiled speedily banded themselves together, proceeded against each one of the cities singly, and as they were not few in number, accomplished their restoration and gained possession of the cities. Then, since after their restoration they no longer followed a neutral course, but fought zealously in support of the Spartans, the Arcadians were hard pressed by the Spartans on the one side and by the Achaeans on the other.

Persia inserted itself once again into this chaos, the satrap Artabazus sending Philiscus with the usual endless stream of gold to try to negotiate a peace. When this failed, he threw this money behind Sparta, hiring likely Greek mercenaries for their war effort. These were joined by supporting troops sent by Dionysius I of Syracuse (including Celtic warbands) and Spartan troops under the command of Prince Archidamus in a counteroffensive. Archidamus stormed Caryae, and showed no mercy, putting "*to the sword all whom he took prisoner.*" He then marched into Arcadia and set to ravaging its lands.

It's worth noting that Sparta, once again, worked hand-in-glove with *both* Persian-hired troops and troops supplied by a tyrant, yet another glaring contradiction to Sparta's reputation for opposing both.

The Tearless Battle

During this expedition, the troops sent by Dionysius' remit expired, and they headed home. On the way, they were cut off and attacked by the newly independent Messenians, and sent to Archidamus for help. A combined Arcadian–Argive force sought to intercept the Spartan prince, and Archidamus deployed his troops for battle. Archidamus' pre-battle speech to his troops is a painfully clear look at just how far the Spartans had fallen, and how keenly they felt the shame of their new status:

> *Fellow citizens, let us now prove ourselves brave men and thus be able to look people in the face; let us hand on to those who come after us the fatherland as it was when we received it from our fathers; let us cease to feel shame before wives and children and elders and strangers, in whose eyes we used once to be the most highly honored of all the Greeks.*

Xenophon gives no details of the battle that followed, save that the Spartans were victorious and that the Celts and cavalry (presumably Dionysius' troops) killed many among the fleeing enemy. The Spartans dubbed this "the Tearless Battle" on account of the fact that not a single Peer was killed. Though, at least according to Xenophon, there were tears of joy and gratitude at Sparta for it finally had a victory that restored some shred of honor. Diodorus is less flattering: "*Indeed since the defeat at Leuctra this was their first stroke of good fortune, and it was a surprising one ...*"

But if the Tearless Battle boosted Sparta's morale, it did not have a practical benefit. Diodorus reports that the Arcadians went on in 368 BC to found the city of Megalopolis, which would prove an independent and anti-Spartan bulwark to the north, hemming Spartan ambitions in just as the newly founded Messene did to the west.

First Sellasia and intervention in the Arcadian–Elean War

On his father's death, Dionysius II sent 12 triremes packed with troops who aided the Spartans in recapturing Sellasia. In 366 BC, Sparta's allies finally broke off, making peace with Thebes and Arcadia, leaving the Spartans (who would make no peace that left Messenia independent) to fight on alone. Isolated, Sparta still achieved a military victory, seizing Gythium through a trick if Polyaenus is to be believed.

He relates a short story about the same Isidas who was both honored and fined for his defense of Sparta, saying he:

> *... formed a group of a hundred youths of his acquaintance, who oiled themselves and bound wreaths of olive around their heads. Then they*

concealed daggers under their arms, and ran naked across the plain, with Isidas in the lead and the others following. The Thebans, who were deceived by their appearance, supposed that they were just exercising themselves. But the Laconians took out their daggers and fell upon them. After killing some of the Thebans, and driving out the others, they regained possession of Gythium.

In 365 BC, the Spartans intervened on behalf of Elis, which had apparently become a Spartan ally in the intervening years, in a war between Ellis and the Arcadians. In an initial engagement, the Spartan Peer Socleides was killed, which prompted Archidamus to take the field at the head of as full a levy as Sparta could muster.

Cromnus

Archidamus seized the city of Cromnus, then departed, only to have it come under siege by the Arcadians. Archidamus responded by ravaging the region, and when this failed to draw the Arcadians off, marched to seize a hill overlooking the besiegers' position.

He never made it. His peltasts and cavalry, scouting ahead, came into contact with the Arcadian *eparitoi*, 5,000 picked Arcadian hoplites kept as a standing force. Either there was a breakdown in discipline or else the two forces came upon one another unexpectedly and the Spartan troops couldn't break off contact. They attacked instead, drawing in the heavy infantry of both sides. The Spartans got the worst of the clash:

... at this juncture the Spartans were no longer able to hold out against the superior weight of the Arcadians, but Archidamus quickly received a wound straight through his thigh and speedily those who fought in front of him kept falling, among them Polyaenidas and Chilon, who was married to the sister of Archidamus; and the whole number of them who fell at that time was not less than thirty.

Falling back, the Spartans regrouped and while Xenophon puts a kind face on it, begged for a truce as the Arcadians advanced to finish the job. Fortunately for the Spartans, the Arcadians granted it and set up a victory trophy as the

Spartans collected their dead and retreated. The Spartans tried to make good on this defeat with a night attack on the besiegers' stockade, but despite capturing a portion of it, they were cut off by the enemy, who captured over a hundred Peers and *perioikoi*.

Arcadia now made a critical misstep. In an effort to keep paying the *eparitoi*, a faction of Arcadians seized the treasures dedicated at Elis. The sacrilege caused huge divisions in the anti-Spartan coalition, fracturing it. Mantinea quit the League and declared independence. Sparta seized the opportunity to form a Spartan–Elean–Mantinean coalition. Athens, still concerned with Theban ascendency, threw its lot in with Sparta once again. In 362 BC, this division finally forced Epaminondas to march the Theban army south to deal with the new axis of enemies.

Defense of Sparta

Learning that Agesilaus had marched the Spartan army to Pallene and that Sparta lay virtually undefended, Epaminondas decided to try his luck once again, and made a lightning attack on the city. The strike would surely have succeeded had not a Cretan deserter warned the Spartans of the attack, giving Agesilaus the chance to double time back home.

Per Xenophon, Agesilaus arrived with a small force just ahead of the enemy, having been forced to leave most of the army behind either for purposes of speed or to counter Theban troops near Mantinea. Epaminondas approached the city from high ground, and Archidamus counterattacked with a smaller force fighting uphill. Xenophon is clearly at a loss to explain how the prince carried the day and offers only this:

> *Archidamus led the advance with not so much as a hundred men and, after crossing the very thing which seemed to present an obstacle, marched uphill against the adversary; at that moment the fire-breathers, the men who had defeated the Spartans, the men who were altogether superior in numbers and were occupying higher ground besides, did not withstand the attack of the troops under Archidamus, but gave way.*

It may be that, fighting in defense of their city, the Spartans found the will to actually perform the heroics with which they are so often credited.

Second Mantinea

Epaminondas withdrew to Tegea. Already stinging from his defeat at Sparta, and getting news that the horsemen that he'd sent on to Mantinea had been worsted by a party of Athenian cavalry, he decided he had to give battle to remove the stain from his honor (and also to prevent consequences when he returned home). The opportunity came against an allied Spartan–Athenian–Elean–Mantinean army outside Mantinea. This battle was the Second Battle of Mantinea, and it played out nearly identically to Leuctra.

Epaminondas marched his troops as if they were going to encamp, even going so far as to order them to ground their shields once the line was fully stretched out. Apparently the Spartans and their allies bought this like it was on sale, and were caught completely by surprise when Epaminondas suddenly ordered the troops to take up their weapons and charge: *"Epaminondas led forward his army prow on, like a trireme."* The deployment was identical to Leuctra – a deeply packed mass of Theban hoplites on the left, the weaker troops advancing in echelon with the right flank refused. Once again, the Theban cavalry easily routed their weaker Peloponnesian counterparts, and once again the Spartans couldn't hope to stand against the deep mass of Theban hoplites.

The battle plan worked, but Epaminondas received a mortal wound in the process. Bereft of leadership, the Thebans were unable to capitalize on the victory, and were badly mauled by the Athenians as they attempted to withdraw. In the end, both sides claimed victory.

The result was a final peace, signed by all except the Spartans, who still petulantly (and unrealistically) refused to sign onto any truce that did not grant them control of Messenia. Agesilaus, ancient now, lived out his days as a mercenary in Egyptian service, desperately trying to raise the money Sparta would need to hire mercenaries to take Messenia back. He died in 360 BC, not in battle, but from natural causes on his way home. His son would also die in mercenary service in an even more ironic turn – serving at the behest of Taras, that city founded by the disgraced sons of faithless Spartan wives while their husbands were away at war. The money they earned was not enough to restore Sparta to glory – the rule of Greece would fall to another power, one that no one could have predicted.

Sparta's record in the Boeotian War

Of the 22 engagements we examined in the Boeotian War, Sparta was clearly victorious in 13, a fairly good record compared to previous wars. That said, the Boeotian War saw the undeniable breaking of Spartan power at Leuctra. There were some heroic fights afterward, most notably Sparta's outstanding defense of its home city, but the fact that this defense was necessary at all (very likely for the first time in Sparta's history) was the writing on the wall for the city-state's future.

There were also some notable moments of adaptability, including Cleombrotus' use of peltasts as he marched into Boeotia, and Mnasippus' (failed) effort to double the depth of his phalanx at Corcyra. But ultimately, Sparta failed to learn the lesson of Leuctra, as shown by its being defeated by an identical deployment at Second Mantinea. Lastly, we saw that once the propaganda value of Sparta's vaunted reputation was finally destroyed, it was unable to keep the loyalty not just of its Peloponnesian allies, but the subordinate *perioikoi* populations as well, costing it the manpower it needed to hang on to its dominant position in the Peloponnese.

And finally this – with the deaths of both Agesilaus II and his son campaigning abroad as mercenaries, we see the terrible price exacted by Sparta's failure to establish itself as a commercial power. Since the Peloponnesian Wars, Persian gold had funded its military adventures. When access to this was cut off, Sparta didn't have the funds to keep its war machine running.

Enter Macedon

Macedon, a bit-player in these struggles to date, had sent Philip II as a hostage to Thebes years earlier, where the young prince had been influenced by the great Theban military minds of Epaminondas and Pelopidas, as well as possibly Iphicrates. Returning to Macedon, he greatly expanded the kingdom's power, took on Athens, and then intervened in Greece's Third Sacred War, which ended with Macedonian domination of central Greece.

This Third Sacred War was essentially a conflict between Thebes and Phocis, though Thebes was acting as the principal member of an "Amphictyonic League" (a kind of religious league of Greek tribes that was dedicated to administering the sacred site of Delphi and the oracle there). The league had, under Thebes' influence, levied an extremely harsh fine in 357 BC against both Phocis (for cultivating land sacred to Apollo) and Sparta (for Phoebidas' unprovoked occupation of Thebes).

The Phocians couldn't pay, and secured the backing of Sparta (because it wished its own fine to be canceled) and Athens (because it wanted to check Thebes' power) to march on Delphi – the city the Amphictyonic League was charged with defending. The Phocians captured Delphi, but, more importantly, they captured the temple of Apollo's incredibly rich treasury, which provided them with more than enough money to fund an very long and drawn-out war that ground on for a decade and wound up sucking in a large part of Greece.

Meanwhile, Philip had been slowly expanding Macedonian territory in the north, and had captured the Athenian-allied cities of Pydna and Potidaea, putting him at war with Athens. When Thessaly was dragged into the Sacred War against Phocis, Philip intervened on the Amphictyonic League's side, resulting in a crushing victory at Crocus Field in 353 BC against Phocis and Athens. This was followed by Philip's first gaining mastery over Thessaly, and finally occupying Thermopylae and holding all of Greece at his mercy. Peace terms were arranged in 346 BC which solely benefited Philip and Macedon, making him a member of the Amphictyonic League and thus giving him the excuse he would need to intervene in any future Sacred Wars.

Just seven years later (in 339 BC), Philip had his excuse. Another charge of cultivating sacred land (this time against the city-state of Amphissa) invoked the punishment of the Amphictyonic League, and Philip launched a campaign against it. Athens and Thebes, rather than honor their commitment to the league (they were both members) instead allied against Macedon and a Fourth Sacred War was ignited.

This Fourth Sacred War was decided when Philip defeated a united Greek army at Chaeronea in 338 BC, his 18-year old son Alexander the Great leading the famous companion cavalry to annihilate the Theban Sacred Band to a man, all of them dying where they stood, in ordered ranks. Philip, who had fond memories of his rearing in Thebes, wept at the sight of their corpses. But I suspect these were at least in part crocodile tears, as they were shed by a man standing victorious astride a battlefield that had made him the undisputed master of Greece.

We only really have one good source for this battle (Diodorus), but his brief account is worth reading:

The armies deployed at dawn, and the king [Philip] stationed his son Alexander, young in age but noted for his valor and swiftness of action, on one wing, placing beside him his most seasoned generals, while he himself at the head of picked men exercised the command over the other; individual units were stationed where the occasion required. On the other side, dividing the line according to nationality, the Athenians assigned one wing to the Boeotians and kept command of the other themselves. Once joined, the battle was hotly contested for a long time and many fell on both sides, so that for a while the struggle permitted hopes of victory to both.

Then Alexander, his heart set on showing his father his prowess and yielding to none in will to win, ably seconded by his men, first succeeded in rupturing the solid front of the enemy line and striking down many he bore heavily on the troops opposite him. As the same success was won by his companions, gaps in the front were constantly opened. Corpses piled up, until finally Alexander forced his way through the line and put his opponents to flight. Then the king also in person advanced, well in front and not conceding credit for the victory even to Alexander; he first forced back the troops stationed before him and then by compelling them to flee became the man responsible for the victory. More than a thousand Athenians fell in the battle and no less than two thousand were captured. Likewise, many of the Boeotians were killed and not a few taken prisoner. After the battle Philip raised a trophy of victory, yielded the dead for burial, gave sacrifices to the gods for victory, and rewarded according to their deserts those of his men who had distinguished themselves.

The pan-Greek coalition opposing Macedon at Chaeronea included Athens, Thebes, Corinth, Megara, Achaea, Chalcis, Epidaurus and Troezen. That Sparta did not participate in the battle is telling – the great xenophobic defenders of Greece were unwilling to muster to its defense. They were also clearly unable to do so. They still held out against Philip's efforts to bring them to terms, leading to one of the more famous Laconic quips in history. When

Philip warned them that if the Spartans forced him to defeat them in war, he would devastate their farms and homes, they replied with a single word: "If."

Philip responded by laying waste to Laconia, though he left Sparta untouched. This was certainly not out of fear or a lack of ability to crush the city if he so wished, but much more likely out of a desire to leave the Spartans in place as a regional power to check other possible enemies in the Peloponnese. Philip finished by forming the League of Corinth – a massive political entity that incorporated nearly every Greek city-state for the first time in the region's history. The sole exception was Sparta, which would certainly have nothing to do with any League that had a free and independent Messenia as a member.

After his father's assassination in 336 BC, Alexander the Great went on to complete his now famous conquest of Persia, winning the greatest empire in the history of the world to that date. With the backing of the Corinthian League (*sans* Thebes, which had tried to rebel, compelling Alexander to completely destroy the city and sell all its surviving occupants into slavery), Alexander could truly claim to be leading the Greek world on a final mission of vengeance to repay the Persians once and for all for their incursions of the 5th century BC.

Except the Spartans. That their absence was keenly felt was underscored by Alexander's sending of 300 (note the number) suits of armor to Athens after his victory at the Battle of the Granicus in 334 BC, including the inscription: "*Alexander, son of Philip, and all the Greeks **except the Spartans**, give these offerings taken from the foreigners who live in Asia.*"

In fact, Agis III, Agesilaus' grandson, attempted to form yet another Spartan–Persian alliance to attack the Macedonians in their rear, though the Persians were too hard pressed to be able to take advantage of the opportunity (he intrigued with Pharnabazus III, the grandson of the Pharnabazus who had been such a thorn in Agesilaus' side). It's worth noting that many Athenians served with the Persian army opposing Alexander. It is also worth noting that the Macedonians were arguably Greek (indeed, the Macedonian Argead royal house had won this very designation earlier regarding their efforts to compete in the Olympics), and finally avenging Greece against Persia.

The Spartans – great defenders of Thermopylae, the people who had produced the famous 300 who would be lionized by the movie of the same name, who gave their lives to keep the Persians out of Greece, were now the sole Greeks attempting to keep the Persian Empire alive at the expense of other Greeks. The Persians did provide the Spartans with money for mercenaries, which Agis used to hire a corps of 8,000 Greek veterans who had served under Persian command at the Battle of Issus in 333 BC.

Megalopolis

In 331 BC, Alexander the Great defeated Darius III at the Battle of Gaugamela. It was a stunning victory, fought against heavy odds, with most scholars agreeing that a combination of tactical brilliance and daring bravery won the Macedonians a decisive victory – culminating with a dramatic cavalry charge led personally by Alexander which broke the Persian center, slaughtered Darius' royal guard and his Greek mercenaries, and sent the Persian king running for his life. While Gaugamela wasn't the final battle in Alexander's Persian campaign, it is widely considered the decisive blow that toppled the Achaemenid Persian empire once and for all.

Diodorus reports that after news reached the Greeks of Alexander's stunning victory, Agis III saw his chance. If he struck now, with Alexander's army far afield and busy in Persia, he could possibly win Greece back from Macedonian power. Even better, Alexander's governor in Thrace, Memnon, had revolted, forcing Alexander's regent in Macedonia, Antipater, to march against him.

Agis tried to unite Greece behind him in a war of liberation, but Athens stayed loyal to Alexander (this was probably at least partially due to fear and horror at the annihilation of Thebes). However, the Peloponnesians threw in their lot with Sparta and Agis led out an army of some 20,000 infantry and 2,000 cavalry to besiege Megalopolis. Antipater abandoned operations in Thrace, pardoned Memnon, and marched south, amassing allies until his force doubled the size of Agis'.

The two armies met outside Megalopolis in 331 BC. Diodorus gives us next to no details about the battle, other than telling us that the Spartans *"fought furiously and maintained their position for a long time"* and that the Greek allies eventually broke and fell back. Agis was struck down and, if we believe Diodorus, insisted on remaining behind to fight a rearguard action to buy time for the rest of the fleeing Greek troops to escape. In the end, 5,000 Spartan and allied troops were killed to 3,500 Macedonians. Plutarch tells us that Alexander, hearing of the victory, is said to have joked, "Well, it seems while we were busy in Persia, there was a battle of mice in Arcadia." This is usually interpreted as jealousy over Antipater's upstaging of Alexander, but it can also be read as a dismissal of Spartan military might.

Sparta was forced to sue for peace, the terms of which forced its entry into the Corinthian League. Sparta was now for the first time in its history a subordinate member of an alliance, and with an equal and independent Messenia as an ally. When Alexander's death in 323 BC sparked the Greek rebellion known as the Lamian War, Sparta was noticeably absent from the largely Athenian and Aetolian army that tried to throw off the Macedonian yoke. They lost, resulting in Athens' democracy being replaced by a pro-Macedonian junta, but Sparta's absence was surely a sign that Sparta had recovered neither the will nor the ability to carry on the contest after the defeat at Megalopolis. In the years that followed, the successor kings that ruled Greece after Alexander's death largely left Sparta alone, not out of any particular fear or respect, but because it was a backwater with little of value that posed no real threat.

Sparta in the Hellenistic Age

Though ancient folk certainly didn't use the term, modern scholars mark Alexander's death in 323 BC as the beginning of the Hellenistic Age – a period that most agree lasts until the Roman Emperor Octavian's defeat of Mark Anthony in the naval Battle of Actium in 31 BC. The term is rooted in the Greek *helas* (the Greek word for Greece) and is meant to indicate that period of time when Greek language and culture ("Greekness," if you will) reached its absolute height, in terms of both geographical expansion and influence. In the Hellenistic Age, more of the world was "Greekified" than at any other time.

The Spartans almost certainly did not notice. They had far bigger fish to fry.

Third Mantinea, and the second defense of Sparta

Plutarch tells us that the successor king Demetrius I Poliorcetes (the besieger) nearly captured Sparta in 294 BC:

Near Mantinea, where Archidamus the king [Archidamus IV] *confronted him, he conquered and routed his foe, and then invaded Laconia. And after he had fought a second pitched battle hard by Sparta itself, where he*

captured five hundred men and slew two hundred, it was thought that he
as good as had the city in his power, although up to this time it had never
been taken.

But Sparta was saved by his rivals Lysimachus and Ptolemy drawing his attention (and his army) away.

In 272 BC, Pyrrhus of Epirus, his efforts to conquer Rome frustrated, was invited to conquer Sparta by the Spartan prince Cleonymus (then serving in Pyrrhus' army), who had been passed over for the Agiad throne in favor of his nephew Areus I. Sparta's army was away at the time of Pyrrhus' attack on the city, and Plutarch tells us that Archidamia, the widow of the Spartan king Eudamidas (who succeeded Agis III after his death in the Battle of Megalopolis) refused to send Sparta's women to safety and instead put them to work in defense of Sparta, building fortifications and helping the few defenders (bringing them fresh missiles, food and water, and dressing wounds) hold on until the Macedonians sent help (they liked Pyrrhus even less than the Spartans, it seemed). These reinforcements helped the city hold until the Spartan army could return and force Pyrrhus to abandon his attack.

Corinth and Second Megalopolis

Sparta joined Athens in again trying to throw off Macedonian rule during the Chremonidean War, allying with Ptolemaic Egypt. The Spartan king Areus, who had chased Pyrrhus off from his city, was defeated in a pitched battle outside Corinth in 265 BC and killed. Athens held out alone for another three years before being starved into surrender.

Pausanias tells us that Areus' son Acrotatus II made an attempt to conquer Megalopolis again in 262 BC, but he was met by the Macedonian-installed tyrant Aristodemus the Good and defeated, losing his life in the battle.

Sparta experienced a brief last-gasp of relevancy, resulting from an extraordinary pair of reformer kings. The first, Agis IV, began to reverse Sparta's love of wealth and luxury and "restore" it to the mythic old Lycurgan mode. Since we know this old mode was inconsistently applied at best, it's very possible that Agis' "reforms" were actually an attempt to force the Spartans to adhere to their own mythic conception of themselves as wealth-hating egalitarians. Plutarch tells us he set the example by giving up expensive luxuries and seeking to restore Sparta's ancient laws. The younger Peers were galvanized by his example, and embraced this largely legendary view of themselves, trying to remake themselves in the image of the idea of Leonidas and his 300, if not the reality. Agis seems to have been motivated by a genuine desire to restore Sparta to its former glory.

Possibly as a move to garner support, Agis IV proposed a cancellation of debts (a sign that these were a problem among Sparta's decidedly luxury-loving elite) as well as a land redistribution program. He further proposed Sparta's first real social enfranchisement – offering to open the ranks of the Peers to badly needed new blood drawn from "*the provincials and foreigners who had received the rearing of freemen and were, besides, of vigorous bodies and in the prime of life.*" (This included some of the *perioikoi.*) These measures, which very well might have reversed Sparta's decline, were vigorously opposed by Agis' Agiad co-king Leonidas II, who worked with the *gerousia* to defeat the measures. Agis responded by deposing Leonidas and even dismissing and replacing the ephors. But Agis was undercut by his uncle Agesilaus (not the same Agesilaus we've been reading about in this book so far), who supported cancellation of debts to get his own debts wiped away, and then deliberately blocked the proposed land reforms to avoid having to give up his vast estates. This eroded public confidence in Agis' commitment to enact reform and sparked a counter-revolution and a restoration of Leonidas to the throne.

Agis and his co-king Cleombrotus II were deposed, but whereas Cleombrotus was exiled, Agis was executed without trial, along with his mother and grandmother – the same Archidamia who had so heroically marshaled to Sparta's defense against Pyrrhus. While many Spartan kings had been deposed and exiled, only Cleomenes I had ever died in a manner that could be argued as akin to execution.

Agis' widow Agiatis was forced to marry Leonidas' son, Cleomenes III, who became the Agiad king on his father's death. Plutarch tells the story as if Agiatis' influence moved Cleomenes to embrace the reformist spirit of her late husband and to be disgusted by Sparta's embrace of luxury. Whether or not this is true, what can't be denied is that this new Cleomenes presided over Sparta's last gasp of military expansion and aggression. In the seven years of what some historians call the Cleomenean War, we catch a glimpse of the old Sparta – confident and forceful.

At the time of Cleomenes' ascension in 235 BC, the northern and central Peloponnese was dominated by the Achaean League which was seeking to extend its power over the entire region under its leader Aratus. Per Plutarch, Sparta, Elis and much of Arcadia held out, and Achaean harassment of Spartan-allied Arcadian towns gave Cleomenes the *casus belli* he needed to march out at the head of the Spartan army. The ephors sent that army to occupy Belbina near Megalopolis. Aratus responded by trying to capture Spartan-allied Tegea and Orchomenus, but the traitors he was relying on to open the city gates lost their nerve, and he marched his army home empty-handed.

Plutarch tells a great story that Cleomenes sent him a letter asking him what his army had been doing in the region. Aratus wrote back stating he'd been deploying to prevent Cleomenes from taking Belbina, upon which Cleomenes replied, "Huh, that's funny. Because your torches and ladders seem to have marched off on their own." The two leaders maneuvered against one another, with Aratus refusing a pitched battle at Pallantium – "*in fear of this boldness,* [he] *would not suffer his general to hazard the issue*" – according to Plutarch – despite vastly outnumbering the Spartan army. This moral victory greatly improved Sparta's spirit, and Plutarch invokes in praise of Cleomenes the very likely apocryphal saying, "*the Spartans do not ask how many of the enemy there are, only where they are.*" It was perhaps partly due to Cleomenes' surging reputation that the successor king Ptolemy III (previously allied with the Achaeans in their efforts to resist Macedon) began funding Cleomenes, per Polybius.

Mount Lycaeum and a different Leuctra

The Achaean League now invaded Spartan-allied Elis, which sent for Spartan help. As Aratus' army was withdrawing near Mount Lycaeum, Cleomenes caught it out of formation and "*put their entire army to panicked flight, slew great numbers of them, and took many prisoners*" per Plutarch. Unfortunately, we have no real details of the battle. Plutarch then tells us that Aratus seized Mantinea, a victory that so disheartened the Spartans that they refused to let Cleomenes campaign further until he bribed them to do so.

This expedition captured Leuctra outside Megalopolis (not the same site of Sparta's greatest defeat) and forced the Achaeans to come out to fight. They did so, and initially defeated Cleomenes' army, forcing him to withdraw across a series of ravines, which he managed to accomplish in good order.

However, Plutarch tells us that one of Aratus' Megalopolitan commanders, Lydiadas, disobeyed orders not to pursue, and gave chase with cavalry who became disordered on the broken ground. Plutarch tells us that Cleomenes responded with *"Cretans and Tarantines"* (probably mercenary troops from Crete and Taras – most likely Cretan archers and Tarantine light horsemen wielding javelins). Lydiadas was killed, the cavalry routed and *"At this the Spartans took courage and with a shout fell upon the Achaeans and routed their entire army. Great numbers of them were slain, and their bodies Cleomenes restored at the enemy's request,"* save the body of Lydiadas. Cleomenes *"arrayed it in a purple robe and put a crown upon the head, and then sent it back to the gates of Megalopolis."* This uncommonly vicious act underscores how deeply Sparta resented the presence of Megalopolis on its northern frontier, a constant reminder of the cost of its defeat at Leuctra and its inability to reassert its dominance over the Peloponnese.

With this victory, Cleomenes' star had risen to the point where he felt confident enacting a similar coup to Agis IV, save that where Agis had deposed and replaced the ephors, Cleomenes massacred them. Now, effectively sole ruler of Sparta, he implemented the reforms Agis IV had envisioned, leading the way by donating his own lands and those of his supporters to the state.

Plutarch tells an interesting story in which Cleomenes justified his own massacre of the ephors, replacing an oligarchy with an effective dictatorship, by comparing his coup to that of Lycurgus and stating that, like Lycurgus, Cleomenes did so for the good of the Spartans, who had become weak, lazy and addicted to luxury. Here, we may have evidence for the likely mythical Lycurgan coup and founding legend, and for his reputed (and clearly not consistently enforced) austerity. This mythical tale of Lycurgus, who was so disgusted by Sparta's chaos and fondness for the luxury that corrupts men's souls that he took matters into his own hands and reformed the state by force, may have been a backward-looking justification – a myth created or at least inflated by Cleomenes III to justify his own and very real coup.

Cleomenes, per Plutarch, made good on his reforms. He redistributed the land in equal plots, opened the citizen rolls to the *"most promising of the perioikoi, and thus raised a body of four thousand men-at-arms ..."* He also modernized the Spartan phalanx, retraining and equipping it in the new

Macedonian style – not as hoplites, but as foot companions whom "*he taught to use a long pike, held in both hands, instead of a short spear, and to carry their shields by a strap instead of by a fixed handle.*" This new phalanx would likely have deployed in 16 ranks as opposed to just eight, mirroring the Antigonid (Macedonians, named for the dynasty founded by Antigonus I Monopthalmus) armies they would face in the field. He also resumed the Upbringing and the public messing system, which is a strong indicator that they had fallen out of use, or had become slack, if they were ever practiced per the model originally laid out in Plutarch's *Life of Lycurgus*. It is also possible that Cleomenes was creating systems out of whole cloth based on a mythic ideal of Sparta's past.

Cleomenes was absolute monarch of Sparta, and Plutarch is clear that he shared that power in name only, and only for appearances' sake: "*desiring to give the name of absolute power a less offensive sound, he associated with himself in royal power his brother Eucleidas.*"

Dyme

Cleomenes marched his newly reinforced and retrained army out to ravage the territory around Megalopolis. With this army, he liberated Mantinea from its Achaean garrison (which is to say gave the citizens the courage to drive the garrison out); he then threatened the Achaean city of Pherae, forcing the Achaeans to face him at Dyme. The two armies fought a battle here, for which we have no details. Plutarch offers this inadequate description: "*He [Cleomenes] was completely victorious, routed their phalanx, slew many of them in the battle, and took many prisoners also. Then he went up against Langon, drove out the Achaean garrison, and restored the city to the Eleans.*"

After this battle, Plutarch tells us that the Achaeans were even willing to surrender leadership of the League to Cleomenes, but illness prevented him from taking up the post. Plutarch's obvious pro-Cleomenes bias has to be taken into account as his narrative describes Aratus' dastardly scheming against the will of the Achaeans who all suddenly seem happy to hand command of their lives over to Cleomenes. Aratus would have none of it:

> ... to avoid the Spartan barley-bread and short-cloak, and the most dreadful of the evils for which he denounced Cleomenes, namely, abolition of wealth and restoration of poverty, he cast himself and all Achaea down

before a diadem, a purple robe, Macedonians, and oriental behests. And that he might not be thought to obey Cleomenes, he offered sacrifices to Antigonus and sang paeans himself, with a garland on his head, in praise of a man who was far gone with consumption.

If you believe Plutarch (and you should not), Aratus would rather have invited the "oriental" Antigonid king Antigonus III Doson (Doson means "intending to give") into Greece than surrender power to a true Greek like Cleomenes, who would have forced him to abandon luxury as he had done for the Spartans. That Aratus invited Antigonus to relieve the Achaeans is surely true, but his motives were likely just a desire to stop losing battles to the Spartans.

Cleomenes, meanwhile, invaded Achaea, taking the city of Pellene by storm, and bringing over two more without a fight. He then threatened Argos, securing that city's alliance – to include giving hostages and accepting a Spartan garrison. This was a signal achievement for Sparta. For all the years it had warred with Argos, no Spartan had ever succeeded in forcing the Argives to accept a Spartan garrison or to give hostages. Even Cleomenes' namesake, in his successful war against Argos, had only ever succeeded in burning its sacred grove, and not taking the city itself.

In 226 BC, Cleomenes III's star burned so brightly it was hard to look at it. Sparta truly seemed to have found its footing and to be on the verge of a return to its old glory. Cities began to flock to Cleomenes' cause. Phlius and Colonae came over. Aratus fled Corinth and Cleomenes occupied the city and besieged the Achaean garrison shut up in its citadel. Cleomenes then took three more cities, all the while trying to get Aratus to surrender the Corinthian citadel, even offering a large sum of money and the promise of a joint garrison. Aratus, in desperation, turned to Antigonus for help, sending his own son as a hostage to secure the alliance. While Cleomenes laid siege to Sicyon in an effort to capture Aratus, Antigonus marched for the Peloponnese at the head of 20,000 infantry and 1,300 cavalry.

Cleomenes abandoned his siege of Sicyon and fortified the Oneian hills, there to defend the Peloponnese from the advancing Antigonid army. Plutarch is clear that Cleomenes did not have confidence in his ability to take the Antigonid phalanx head on. Instead, the Spartans sought *"to wear out the Macedonians by a war of posts and positions, rather*

than to engage in formal battle with their disciplined phalanx." While
Cleomenes met with initial success in holding off the Antigonid army,
Antigonus succeeded in causing Argos to revolt from Sparta, forcing
Cleomenes to withdraw from Corinth and fall back to prevent Argos from
falling. He assaulted Argos as Antigonus took and garrisoned Corinth.
Again, he met with initial success, but fled once he saw Antigonus' army
descending on the city.

What followed was a succession of Antigonid advances and Spartan losses.
Plutarch provides a good summary:

> He [Cleomenes III] *had made the greatest possible conquests in the*
> *briefest possible time, and had come within a little of making himself*
> *master of all of the Peloponnese by a single march through it, but had*
> *quickly lost everything again. For some of his allies left him at once, and*
> *others after a little while handed their cities over to Antigonus.*

Cleomenes was clearly frightened of the Antigonid army and unwilling to
face it in battle, even as he lost all the gains he'd made for Sparta one after the
other.

At this point, Ptolemy cut off funding to Sparta, likely due to pressure
from Antigonus, despite the fact that Cleomenes had given Ptolemy his
mother and children as hostages. Desperate, and with Antigonus capturing
Tegea and Mantinea, Cleomenes freed all the helots who could pay a fee of
five Attic minai. A mina was weight of silver worth around 100 drachmas.
This allowed him to raise 500 talents, which he used to pay mercenaries,
and also to equip 2,000 helots in the "Macedonian manner" (with two-
handed pikes, and smaller shields slung from the neck and worn on the left
arm, leaving both hands free to handle the long pike). These helots were
meant to counter the *leukaspides* (White Shields), a division in Hellenistic
phalanxes that I theorized in *Legion Versus Phalanx* was probably an inferior
corps to the more elite *chalkaspides* (Bronze Shields). Using this newly
raised force, Cleomenes feinted toward Sellasia, then marched on his true
objective – Megalopolis, which he succeeded in capturing, forcing the
defenders to flee. He plundered the city, burning it to the ground, at
long last avenging Sparta against the thorn put in its side after Leuctra.

Polybius tells us that he managed to net 300 talents from his sacking, which no doubt went a long way to make up for the shortfall from the loss of Ptolemy's support.

Cleomenes then proceeded to plunder around Argos, trying to convince that city to return to the Spartan fold, but he succeeded only in convincing Antigonus that the Spartans wouldn't go down without a fight. In the summer of 222 BC Antigonus assembled his army and marched south into Laconia, threatening Sparta itself. Cleomenes had no choice but to bar his way at Sellasia.

FOCUS BATTLE: SECOND SELLASIA (222 BC) – LOSING IN THE "MACEDONIAN MANNER"

Plutarch's account of the battle that followed in both his *Life of Cleomenes* and *Life of Philopoemen* is cursory at best. Fortunately, Polybius gives a detailed account, complete with order of battle, description of terrain and battle narrative.

Antigonus' army consisted of some 29,200 troops, of whom 1,200 were mounted. The infantry was made up of 10,000 Macedonian phalangites (men formed into the Hellenistic phalanx, wielding a two-handed pike some 21 feet long, with the small shield slung around their necks and strapped to the left arm, leaving the left hand free to hold the pike). This phalanx was likely divided into two corps – Bronze Shields and White Shields, as we've mentioned, with the Bronze Shields being the better of the two. From Macedon, Antigonus also fielded 3,000 peltasts and 300 cavalry. He brought another 1,000 Agrianians (probably wielding javelins, for which they were known), 1,600 Illyrians under Demetrius of Pharos (a famous figure in the Illyrian Wars against Rome), 1,000 Gauls (Celts – possibly fighting in a loosely organized warband) and another 3,000 mercenary infantry and 300 mercenary cavalry. The Achaeans who had invited their former enemy in to help fielded 3,000 infantry and 300 cavalry. Commanding the cavalry arm of the Achaeans was a 31-year-old man named Philopoemen. He would acquit himself well in the battle to come, and would go on to fight Sparta again, and to be a principal agent in its final subjugation. Other Greeks included the Boeotians supplying 2,000 infantry and 200 cavalry, the Acarnanians' 1,000 infantry and 50 cavalry, the Epirotes' 1,000 infantry and 50 cavalry and the Megalopolitans' 1,000 infantry under Cercidas (Polybius points out these were "armed in the Macedonian manner" as phalangites. From this we can assume that the other Greeks fought as hoplites or possibly as *thureophoroi*, a term used to describe troops using the *thureos* – a heavy shield with a horizontal center-grip inside of a metal boss, and a reinforced spine that ran vertically across the shield's surface – very similar to the *scutum* which would gain fame as the shield of the Roman legionary).

Against this, the cash-strapped Cleomenes (Plutarch is very particular in pointing out that without Ptolemy's money, he simply couldn't afford to raise a big enough army to properly face Antigonus, who had all the wealth of Macedon behind him) raised a decent, but smaller force – just under 21,000 men. We have much less detailed information on the Spartan army, save that several thousand of them were the newly raised Spartan citizens fighting as Hellenistic phalangites. These were augmented by a large corps of mercenaries (though how they were armed, we don't know) and the *perioikoi*. Cleomenes probably had under 1,000 horsemen.

Cleomenes intended to make up for the shortfall in troops by picking his ground well, and there's some evidence in Polybius that he effectively used reconnaissance and scouting (or possibly intelligence) to determine Antigonus' route (something Sparta had a poor record of, as we have seen). He stationed his army to block the main route into Laconia and to Sparta, at a pass carved by the Oenus river as it wended its way between two mountains – Evas on his left and Olympus on his right. He then built a palisade (probably a log wall) and dug a trench in front of it. It was an excellent defensive position, and Cleomenes deployed to make the most of it.

He packed the pass with his most mobile troops – his small force of horsemen, surrounded by his skirmishers: mercenary light infantry and probably helots armed with javelins, slings and rocks. This might seem like a weak force to hold a pass, and it was ... if your objective was to hold a pass (for which you'd want a phalanx). But I don't think that was Cleomenes' objective. We've already seen that he was a skilled and able commander, so he stationed his most mobile troops in the pass for a reason.

That reason was to tempt the Antigonids to force it. The Spartan mobile force could then retire, drawing the Antigonids in, exposing their flanks to the rest of the Spartan army who were deployed on the heights of the two mountains. On Mount Evas, on the Spartan left, Cleomenes' brother and co-king Eucleidas commanded the *perioikoi* and allied heavy infantry. On Mount Olympus on the Spartan right, Cleomenes commanded the Spartan phalanx (armed in the "Macedonian manner") and the mercenary heavy infantry. If the Antigonids decided to force the pass, either or both of these wings could attack them on their flank from high ground. If they didn't take the bait and decided to assault the heights, they'd be fighting uphill, and Cleomenes would have a mobile force in his center either to harass their flanks or to pursue routing troops. It was a smart, even clever deployment, and it should have won him the battle.

But Antigonus was also a canny and veteran commander. He immediately recognized the strength of Cleomenes' position and knew that a direct assault would be suicide despite his advantage in numbers. He camped behind a stream and observed the enemy position for several days, weighing his options. Polybius' narrative implies that Antigonus both scouted Cleomenes' lines and probably used light troops to harass the Spartans into making a mistake and engaging on some portion of the battlefield, creating an opening the Antigonids could exploit. But Cleomenes didn't take the bait, and at last Antigonus realized he had to risk a general engagement.

This decision was very likely driven by morale considerations. Ancient armies considered it cowardly to shrink from a fight, and holding tens of thousands of troops idle would strain morale as men got into trouble, deserted or went hungry on tighter rations as the area was picked clean and foragers were forced to range farther and farther afield for supplies. As Antigonus had the larger army, these concerns would have weighed more heavily on him.

Polybius gives us a detailed layout of Antigonus' army. Opposite Eucleidas' position on Mount Evas, he positioned his Bronze Shields corps of phalangites. These men would have been the stronger of the two corps in the Antigonid phalanx. Behind them, he positioned Greek allied troops, backed up by a reserve force of 2,000 Achaeans. While we can be reasonably sure the Bronze Shields were a pike-armed Hellenistic phalanx, we can't be certain how the other Greeks were armed. It's possible they were also equipped as phalangites,

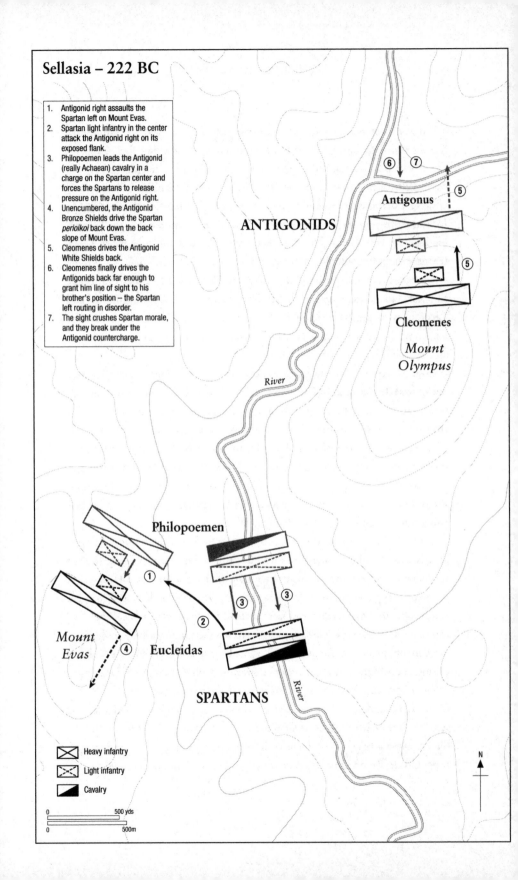

Sellasia – 222 BC

1. Antigonid right assaults the Spartan left on Mount Evas.
2. Spartan light infantry in the center attack the Antigonid right on its exposed flank.
3. Philopoemen leads the Antigonid (really Achaean) cavalry in a charge on the Spartan center and forces the Spartans to release pressure on the Antigonid right.
4. Unencumbered, the Antigonid Bronze Shields drive the Spartan *perioikoi* back down the back slope of Mount Evas.
5. Cleomenes drives the Antigonid White Shields back.
6. Cleomenes finally drives the Antigonids back far enough to grant him line of sight to his brother's position -- the Spartan left routing in disorder.
7. The sight crushes Spartan morale, and they break under the Antigonid countercharge.

ANTIGONIDS

Antigonus

Cleomenes

Mount Olympus

River

Philopoemen

Mount Evas

Eucleidas

SPARTANS

River

Heavy infantry

Light infantry

Cavalry

N

0   500 yds

0   500m

as hoplites, or even as *thureophoroi*. Also stationed here were the Illyrian troops under Demetrius of Pharos. Again, we don't know how the Illyrians were armed and deployed, but it's possible they fought in looser order, maybe as a warband. Illyria is intensely mountainous country, and it's also possible that Antigonus was taking advantage of the Illyrians' mountaineering capabilities.

The Antigonid cavalry, under the command of Alexander, were posted opposite the pass facing the Spartan cavalry. Beside these he posted 1,000 Achaean and Megalopolitan infantry (again, no details about how they were armed, but it's possible they were light troops if Antigonus was seeking to mirror the Spartan force). Antigonus personally commanded the Antigonid left opposite Cleomenes on Mount Olympus. Polybius doesn't specifically state which troops he commanded, but by process of elimination we know it had to include the White Shields and probably also the Gauls, Agrianians and other troops. Polybius also notes that the Antigonid phalanxes were deployed at double depth owing to the narrowness of the ground. This would mean the phalanxes were likely deployed in 32, rather than 16 ranks, which would give them enormous pushing power, as we've previously seen with earlier Theban formations.

Once the army was in position, Polybius reports that Antigonus signaled with a linen flag for the Illyrian contingent to begin the assault. The Illyrians set off and began their march up the face of Mount Evas toward the Spartan troops above them. As the armies closed, skirmishers on both sides would have begun throwing javelins, slinging stones, shooting arrows. Here and there you would have heard a bellow of pain, a muffled curse as a man went down with his helmet staved in by a sling bullet. Any Spartan skirmishers would have enjoyed greater range as they were attacking from high ground, whereas the Illyrian troops would have had to get much closer to deploy their own missile weapons effectively.

It's unlikely that the Illyrians came on alone, as Polybius later reports on "*Illyrians, Macedonians, and the rest who were advancing with them.*" It is likely that the more lightly armed Illyrians went first, attempting to clear the way for the Bronze Shields and allied Greek troops coming behind them. These troops would have lurched forward amid a huge plume of dust, the bronze and iron of their weapons and armor clattering. Officers would have bellowed to their men to keep the lines dressed, knowing all too well how lethal a gap in the phalanx would be. The noise must have been deafening.

We can tell from Polybius' description that there were no troops behind the Achaeans, so it's possible the Greek allied infantry were billeted in the phalanx line alongside the Bronze Shields (an indicator that they were also equipped as pike-armed phalangites). It's also likely that the line was spread too narrow, and the Achaean reserve pressed too closely behind the phalanx, because Polybius reports that the light troops in the Spartan center saw "*that the Achaean lines were not covered by any other troops behind them*" and rushed out from the pass, flooded around the base of Evas, and attacked the Antigonid right on its flank. Eucleidas, secure on high ground, held position. As the Illyrians reached them, the Spartan *perioikoi* under his command attacked down the slope.

Polybius severely criticizes Eucleidas' decision to hold position. Again, we don't know how the *perioikoi* were armed, but fighting down a slope grants an advantage even if they were using shorter hoplite spears. Charges downhill have greater momentum and move at greater speed, and the impact against defending troops is greater as they are knocked back into the men behind them. The downhill charge might have given Spartans with shorter weapons the advantage of letting them close rapidly inside the killing range of the enormous pikes of the Bronze Shields, which were little more than giant broomsticks once an enemy was within a few feet of the wielder. A phalangite faced with an enemy up close would have no choice but to drop his pike and draw his sword, but this was a backup weapon and the phalangites were not expert in its use, and the smaller round *peltē* of the phalangite wasn't a great shield for individual fencing, especially not compared to the larger and heavier hoplite *aspis*. Polybius doesn't give much in the way of detailed description, but despite Eucleidas' decision to hold his ground, Polybius does note that the Antigonid right found itself in "*a state of great peril*" attacked from front and flank, and with the frontal attack coming from high ground.

Polybius and Plutarch now tell an interesting story about the "young" (31) Philopoemen, who had already proven himself fighting against Cleomenes at Megalopolis (continuing to fight despite a wound), begging the more senior Antigonid officers for permission to charge with his cavalry to rescue the flagging Illyrians. Both Polybius and Plutarch claim that he was ignored due to his youth and inexperience, and that he finally took matters into his own hands and charged. I don't believe this narrative. It would be incredibly stupid to send the Illyrian contingent in unsupported, and then leave them to be cut to pieces when the Spartan light infantry surrounded them. Worse, this same Spartan light infantry, in their eagerness to outflank the Illyrians, had shown their own flank to the Antigonids and it would have been foolish not to take advantage of it.

I think Polybius (an Achaean himself who revered Philopoemen and even carried his ashes at his funeral) and Plutarch (who was using Polybius as a source) were doing their best to polish the man's memory. I think the truth is that either that the Illyrians were sent in the hope of drawing the Spartans out, or else that Philopoemen's plan to charge the light troops was immediately approved, or even ordered by senior leaders in the Antigonid army.

However it happened, Philopoemen did charge, sending his cavalry into the light troops assailing the Illyrian flank. The Spartan light troops were themselves probably keenly aware of how exposed they were on their own flank, and so it's not surprising that Polybius describes them breaking off their attack and returning to their original position in the center of the pass where the Spartan horsemen could provide assistance. Plutarch makes the story even bigger, turning Philopoemen into something of an action hero.

According to Plutarch, after the Spartan light troops were driven off, Philopoemen dismounted and waded into the fighting on foot. He had both thighs pierced by a javelin, yet somehow managed to break the weapon in half, pull it out of the wound, and carry on fighting. This is almost impossible to swallow. At its widest point, an ancient javelin would have been over an inch in diameter, and Plutarch specifically mentions that it was tied with a leather thong. I cannot imagine that a man with a fresh hole in both thighs more than an inch across was going to be able to fight effectively in hand-to-hand combat (Plutarch specifies that Philopoemen used his sword). Purportedly, after Antigonus was told that the "youngster" Philopoemen had charged without orders, the king responded that Philopoemen was a good general who had seized the initiative, and that the generals who complained about him were the youngsters. All of this sounds like myth-making, but it's a good story. Polybius tells the story slightly differently, having Philopoemen lead the Greek cavalry to engage the Spartan cavalry in the center after having relieved the Antigonid right, and had his horse killed under him, which forced him to fight on foot, at which point he received this unlikely javelin wound.

However it happened, Philopoemen's charge had freed up the Antigonid right to continue its assault on Evas, leaving Eucleidas to hold the heights against the advancing Illyrians, Bronze Shields and allied Greek heavy infantry. Polybius explains that Eucleidas' decision to hold the heights instead of charging down the slope with his full force was driven by the goal of "*catching the enemy at as great an elevation as possible, that their flight might be all the longer over steep and precipitous ground.*" The problem with this plan is that it assumes that victory is assured, which wasn't the case. Instead, the enormous weight of the Bronze Shields formation drove the Spartans back. Plutarch and Polybius both note the greater weight of the Antigonid troops' armor, an indication that the trend of shedding heavy armor that we saw in the Peloponnesian Wars was reversed under the demands of the new pike-armed Hellenistic-style phalanx. Fighting with a 21-foot pike in 16 ranks makes it impossible to run or even turn easily, and so speed and maneuverability had become much less of a factor in heavy infantry combat. More importantly, the smaller *peltē* shield provided less cover and was less maneuverable as the bearer's hand projected past the rim to hold the pike, rather than gripping the *antilabē*. This would make the phalangite much more vulnerable to missiles – heavier armor was the answer to this.

More complete armor (greaves, cuirass, helmet) made a phalangite fatigued more quickly, but it also made him heavier, giving him more forward momentum and pushing-power, especially with 31 ranks of similarly equipped comrades behind him (remember that the Antigonid phalanxes were deployed at double depth at Sellasia) pushing him forward. So it's not surprising that the Spartan *perioikoi* and their allies found themselves driven back. Since they were already at the highest point on Evas, they quickly found themselves first fighting on the more or less level summit and then pushed down the far slope, surrendering the high ground advantage to the Antigonids and taking on the disadvantage of fighting uphill. Eucleidas' troops began to lose ground rapidly, their order breaking apart as the Spartan phalanx stumbled and skidded backwards down Evas' slope with the Antigonids pressing them hard from above.

Plutarch tells another story here, and this one a bit more believable. As Eucleidas' position came apart, Cleomenes sent for Damoteles, the commander of the Spartan crypteia, to provide a report on how the Spartan left was holding up. According to Plutarch, the Antigonids had bribed Damoteles to give a false report and he told Cleomenes that Eucleidas was fine and the Spartan left was holding. We have no way to know if this was true, but it certainly matches the trend of Spartans being highly susceptible to bribes. Whether or not he was inspired by Damoteles' false report, Cleomenes sounded his own advance and brought his phalanx charging down the slope to clash with the White Shields under Antigonus himself. Here, the Spartans were victorious, very likely due to their attacking down a slope, but also possibly due to the inferior training and equipment of the White Shields.

But this narrative comes from Plutarch, who has Cleomenes' phalanx driving the Macedonians back some thousand yards. Polybius has both Cleomenes and Antigonus holding their heavy infantry in position and fighting with their light troops.

Both Polybius and Plutarch agree that, at some point, Cleomenes finally saw his brother's troops breaking and routing down the reverse slope of Evas, with the Antigonid right in pursuit. Polybius also has Cleomenes seeing the Spartan cavalry in the center being beaten by the Achaean and allied cavalry under Philopoemen. Plutarch puts a theatrical quote in Cleomenes' mouth: "*I have lost thee, my dearest brother, I have lost thee, thou noble heart, thou great example to Spartan boys, thou theme for a song to Spartan wives!*" before realizing that all was lost and giving up hope. Polybius has Cleomenes demolishing the defensive palisade, sounding the recall for his light troops, and charging with his phalanx. Polybius describes the fight as evenly matched, with both sides advancing and giving way, until at last Antigonus ordered a countercharge and the double depth of the White Shields phalanx proved impossible to bear up against.

The Spartans broke and fled, with the Antigonids in pursuit. With both sides of the Spartan line in total rout, the Antigonid victory was complete and decisive. It had broken not only Cleomenes' power, but all hope of a resurgent Sparta. Cleomenes' reformist ambitions were shattered. If we believe Plutarch, of the 6,000 Peers (most of them newly made under Cleomenes' reforms), only 200 survived. The king fled back to Sparta only long enough to move on to the Spartan port at Gythium, there to board a ship for Alexandria and his mother at the court of Ptolemy. He would remain there as a refugee until his death three years later.

Antigonus occupied Sparta without resistance, the first time in the city's history it had been taken. Plutarch reports that he stayed only three days, "restored" law and order, forbade his troops from plundering, then departed. While Plutarch implies that this act was a sign of respect for Sparta's dignity, it is more likely a sign of Sparta's irrelevance – not a city of great wealth, not necessary as an important defensive position, not of great cultural significance to the Antigonid king.

The ironic gut punch came later – a messenger arrived reporting an Illyrian uprising that required Antigonus' immediate attention. If the messenger had arrived just a few days earlier, per Plutarch, Antigonus would have had to withdraw his army and march back north without fighting at Sellasia at all.

Fourth Mantinea

Cleomenes had turned Sparta into an effective sole monarchy and with his exit, Sparta's government was in a complete state of flux. While the sources do not specifically say it, most scholars assume that Eucleidas was killed at Sellasia, which meant that even that fig leaf of a co-king was gone. The result was a power vacuum and Sparta struggled under a succession of doubtful kings and tyrants. During this period the ephors were restored, possibly at the direction of Antigonus during his occupation. We hear of a Lycurgus ruling as the Eurypontid king in 219 BC (who ascended to the throne, per Polybius, by bribing the ephors), succeeded by his son Pelops, who was too young to reign. Lycurgus was eventually either expelled or murdered by the tyrant Machanidas, a Tarentine mercenary leader who led Sparta to defeat in a fourth battle of Mantinea against the Achaean League led by Philopoemen in 207 BC.

With Machanidas' death, Nabis became the regent for Pelops. Every source we have is in agreement that Nabis was an absolute tyrant, but again that doesn't mean much. Polybius was pro-Achaean (he was an Achaean in Roman service) and therefore wanted to justify the Achaeans' anti-Spartan stance, Livy was a Roman and wanted to justify Rome's war with Nabis. Diodorus is a little more reliable, and he also comes out swinging against Nabis. All three writers describe him as a brutal ruler who delighted in torturing people with an iron maiden built to resemble his equally cruel wife. He reportedly ruled through terror, at the head of a band of pirates, cutthroats and bandits. He certainly seems to have ruled as a single king, with no real check on his power.

But when we read between the lines, we can see Nabis aggressively pursuing the same reforms that Agis IV launched and Cleomenes III advanced – he redistributed land (though the sources claim it was to his supporters) and expanded the citizen rolls once again to enroll more Peers in the phalanx. He sold helots their freedom, which can be seen as either reformist or greedy depending on where you stand. This looks a lot like Cleomenes III's reign, which was spoken of in glowing terms by Plutarch, and like Cleomenes, Nabis was able to build a powerful army. He also built Sparta's first city wall, an act that is clearly viewed by the sources as a sign of weakness – Sparta had historically relied on the strength of its men, not a wall, to protect the city. It seemed that the Spartan phalanx wasn't the only aspect of the Spartan military machine that modernized in the Hellenistic age.

Nabis used his new army to attack Messene around 202 BC, in violation of Sparta's alliance with the Messenians (Polybius calls the attempt "*treacherous*," though given Nabis' commitment to a reformist program which attempted to hearken back to the good old days under Lycurgus, he may have also hearkened back to Sparta's former mastery over the Messenians). Philopoemen led a Megalopolitan army to drive him out again, though Plutarch describes it as a series of maneuvers, not a battle. When Rome and the Antigonids came into conflict during the Second Macedonian War, Nabis' alliance with the Aetolians drew Sparta into the conflict on the Antigonid side. As an inducement to fight, the Antigonid king Philip V gave Nabis the city of Argos, which the Antigonids had captured.

Nabis allied with Crete and gave it use of the Spartan port at Gythium as a base to raid Roman and allied (Achaean) shipping. I'd call that effective military strategy, but Polybius called it piracy. Nabis realized that Philip V was going to lose the war and switched sides to Rome on the condition that he could keep the territory he now controlled. However, under substantial Achaean influence, Rome demanded that Nabis surrender Argos after it finally defeated Philip V and broke Antigonid power forever at the Battle of Cynoscephalae in 197 BC. The Roman excuse was that pirates were still operating out of Gythium.

In 195 BC, the Roman consul Titus Quinctius Flamininus, the victor of Cynoscephalae, marched into Laconia at the head of a full consular army of 40,000 men. He was joined by 10,000 troops of the Achaean League. There are precious few details on the campaign that followed, but what is clear is that the Spartan army fought heroically and successfully, grinding a better trained and equipped, and more numerous enemy to a stalemate. Gythium surrendered, but only after a brutal fight where the Romans reluctantly gave the defenders terms to leave under truce and return to Sparta.

Flamininus placed Sparta itself under siege (proving the utility of the new wall), and assaulted it successively until Nabis finally agreed to terms. Sparta lost Argos and the cities of the Laconian coast, which Nabis began trying to regain almost as soon as Flamininus had marched the Romans away.

The Achaeans responded immediately, routing the Spartans and shutting them up inside the city. Nabis appealed to the Aetolians, who were now allied with the Seleucids (another successor dynasty founded by one of Alexander the Great's generals) and fighting Rome, for help. Livy reports that the Aetolians sent 1,000 infantry and 300 horsemen to assist the Spartans. Among these was Alexamenus, who was secretly charged with assassinating the tyrant. This he did in 192 BC, striking Nabis down with a lance. The Aetolians tried to occupy Sparta, only to be repulsed by the furious Spartans. The Achaeans, no fools, stepped in and took the city.

The Achaeans tore down the city walls and forced Sparta to join the League. Sparta continued as a Greek city until Rome absorbed all of Greece into its expanding empire in 146 BC, but the city was never again truly independent. Sparta's long history as a military power in the Mediterranean world was, at long last, over.

Sparta's record in the Hellenistic age

Of the ten battles we've examined in the Hellenistic age, Sparta won just four. It's important to remember that three of those were part of the Cleomenean

War sparked by the ambition and energy of Sparta's great reformer Cleomenes III. Apart from some truly notable victories brought about partly by a modernization campaign that saw the Spartan phalanx taking on the more advanced pike-armed Hellenistic form, Sparta's record is almost exclusively one of being whipped from field to field, with no fewer than three kings killed in combat, more than every other period of Spartan history combined. Sparta's record in this period reinforces my earlier position – that Leuctra in 371 BC snapped Sparta's spine, damaging its self-confidence, reputation abroad, financial wherewithal and manpower reserves to the point where it could no longer effectively project power in the Peloponnese, let alone beyond the peninsula's borders. Sparta ended its days as a military nonentity, an also-ran in the evolving geo-politics of the Greek world, dominated first by the successor dynasties founded by Alexander the Great's generals, and finally by a relentlessly expanding Rome.

VIII

CONCLUSION: THE BRONZE LIE

For if Sparta were now desolate and nothing of it left but the temples and floors of the buildings, I think it would breed much disbelief in posterity long hence of their power in comparison of the fame. For although of five parts of the Peloponnese it possesses two and has the leading of the rest and also of many confederates without, yet the city being not close built and the temples and other edifices not costly, and because it is but scatteringly inhabited after the ancient manner of Greece, their power would seem inferior to the report. Again, the same things happening to Athens, one would conjecture by the sight of their city that their power were double to what it is.

Thucydides, *History of the Peloponnesian War*

We have now given a fairly comprehensive, though by no means exhaustive, reckoning of Sparta's combat record on land and sea, in sieges and assaults, in set-piece battles and raids, in victory and defeat. We have seen Spartans display glorious bravery, suicidal idiocy, nobility and greed. At every step, we have seen Spartans contrasted with their legend – the self-effacing superwarriors, preferring death to surrender, denying themselves luxury, refusing to make common cause with the enemies of Greece.

CONCLUSION

We have seen, again and again, that absolutely none of the myths about Sparta are true, that the towering edifice of laconophilia that so pervades American and European (and to a lesser extent global) culture is a bronze lie, built on wishful thinking, a deep-rooted sense of inadequacy and a burning desire for a symbol that can compel striving for greatness.

The Spartans were not who we say they were.

Which of course begs the question, who were they?

Before I tackle that question, I want to be clear once again about something else we have *not* seen in the pages of this book. We have *not* seen *evil* people. We have seen a flawed society, not a failed one. We have seen a mixed record, not a damning one. We have seen failures, but we have also seen greatness. We have seen rigidity, but also adaptability.

In short, we have seen *human beings* – flawed and flailing, just as we all are.

And for me, that makes the Spartans much more inspiring than the superwarrior mythology that currently cloaks their past. As I said in the introduction, I am inspired by other humans who are as flawed as I am. Because it is in our striving to overcome failures that we connect with other people, not in lionizing mythical triumphs that real humans can never achieve. The Spartans we've met in these pages *were* extraordinary. They *did* do extraordinary things. And they managed to do them in spite of the human flaws of cowardice, greed, self-aggrandizement and poor judgment that we *all* fall victim to. The Spartans we've seen were no better than their Athenian, Theban, Corinthian and Persian rivals. But they were also no worse. If this book has done its job, it is the *humanity* of a Sparta at war that has surfaced in the recounting.

But we set out specifically to analyze Sparta's military record, so let's review what we've seen overall. We examined 126 military engagements (battles, skirmishes, raids, sieges, assaults and other fights) involving Spartan arms. Sparta can truly be said to have won just 50 of them. Five were stalemates, leaving us with 71 defeats. That is a mixed record that looks generally bad for Sparta. In fact, Sparta's wins exceeded its losses in just two of its wars (the Greco-Persian and Cleomenean), and these two wars had the fewest recorded engagements. Sparta's very first recorded battle (the Battle of the Ravine – 739 BC) must be judged a defeat. Sparta's second recorded battle (the Battle of the Kings – 738 BC) was a stalemate, but one in which the Spartan king Theopompus was routed and fled the battlefield. Sparta's first recorded victory was actually its fifth recorded battle (the Last Battle – 724 BC).

However, we can't just consider Sparta's military performance strictly based on a win/loss count. Rather, we must also note that Sparta had an outsized impact on not only Greece, but Asia Minor as well, and on the policy and borders of the Persian Empire.

Sparta absolutely dominated the Peloponnese for much of the city-state's history and can lay claim (briefly) to mastery of Greece as well. This implies that Sparta's wins were more impactful than its losses in some cases, and goes some way toward evening up the ledger when we ask ourselves how "good" was the Spartan military? Taken holistically, the answer must be this – they did all right. Certainly they were a force to be reckoned with, and certainly they were nothing like the unbeatable gods-of-the-battlefield that is their reputation.

Let's dive into the specifics of how Sparta performed, where it triumphed and where it fell down.

The Lycurgan Ideal and the Spartan Mirage

We've seen fairly conclusively that the details of the Lycurgan model for Spartan excellency – rigid self-denial, hatred of wealth, prioritization of the state over the individual, preferring death to surrender, hatred of foreigners, prohibition of gold and silver money and the practice of infanticide – are all either outright falsehoods, or else greatly exaggerated.

We've seen, in the reforms of Cleomenes III, the possibility that some of this was a Hellenistic era invention – a "return" to a mythic past that may have been partially invented out of whole cloth to justify later attempts at "reform."

We've also seen that most of how modern people view Sparta comes from Plutarch's *Life of Lycurgus*, which has been roundly disproven under scrutiny. It's possible that the Lycurgan myth had a grain of truth in an effort to deal with land accruing to the wealthy that caused major civil unrest around the time of the First Messenian War, but we cannot know for sure. Archaic Sparta transitioned from the *aristoi*-led warbands (the *promachoi* in the Homeric sense) to the phalanx. This may have been tied to a revolution or reform around an imbalance in land/wealth holdings. It may have even necessitated a coup. Some form of the mythical Lycurgan system may have been the thing that replaced Sparta's warbands, a form of professionalization that gave Sparta something other Greeks perceived as a military edge.

The Spartans' reputation as champions of "freedom" who liberated subject populations from tyranny is not supported by the evidence. Leaving aside that Sparta was an apartheid society supported by a slave caste, we see example after example of Spartans supporting tyrants. Especially notable were Spartan attempts both to set up the Spartan agent Isagoras as a tyrant in Athens and later to restore the tyrant Hippias when it suited them. Their victory at Caryae (369 BC) was partly due to the support they received from the Syracusan tyrant Dionysius I.

At every point of the Spartan myth, we have seen repeated examples of Spartans behaving completely contrary to their legend to the point where we're left with little choice but to disbelieve Plutarch's narrative almost in its entirety. If anything, Plutarch is hinting at aspects of Spartan culture, but the extent to which grains of truth underpin them can never be fully known.

Cults of Personality

One of the most important pillars of the Bronze Lie is the notion that Spartans were entirely selfless, happily subordinating individual interests to the primacy of the state. The individual was supposedly erased and the group identity imposed on all to the benefit of all.

The evidence shatters this idea with example after example of individual self-aggrandizement and the pursuit of personal objectives often to the detriment of the good of Sparta as a whole.

When Cleomenes I's tattered reputation forced him into exile, he promptly traveled to Arcadia and began to raise an army that I have no doubt he would have used to march on Sparta had he not been recalled, very likely by a government who feared that very thing. His co-king Demaratus, deposed with the help of a well-placed bribe, fled to Persia, there to advise Greece's greatest enemy on how best to destroy his countrymen. In these two kings, it was abundantly clear that loyalty to Sparta extended only as far as Sparta's advancing their personal interests.

After Plataea (479 BC), Pausanias attempted to name himself as the sole victor in a self-aggrandizing inscription on the famous serpent column dedicated at Delphi to celebrate the victory. The egomania on display was so offensive that the Spartans had the inscription erased and replaced with a list of 31 city-states under the heading "those who fought in the war." The Spartan regent went on to possibly conspire first with Persia and then with the helots to overthrow the Spartan state, actions that eventually led to him being deliberately imprisoned and starved to death by the Spartan government.

Lysander, arguably the architect of Sparta's final victory in the Peloponnesian Wars, worked relentlessly to build up leadership in Spartan-allied cities that were personally loyal to him. He also relied on his personal magnetism to cultivate relationships that benefited Sparta incidentally, but were really dependent on him. The best example of this is the fact that the Persian prince Cyrus closed his purse to the Spartan navy once Lysander was no longer admiral. It was Lysander's person that kept the gold flowing in, not the state's authority. Lysander later took to the life of a celebrity. He had bronze statues made to honor himself, famously gave a cap full of silver to Antilochus for writing a poem praising him, and made no objection when Samos remade a festival in his honor. Lysander's death at Haliartus may have been due to his refusal to share glory with Pausanias, prompting him to attack the city without the critical support that the second Spartan army would have provided. It also displayed Spartan lack of savvy for operations near fortified positions, since he clearly put his army (just as Agis II had done at Athens) in range of missiles shot or thrown from the city walls.

Clearchus' rebellion against Spartan authority resulted in something very akin to Spartan civil war when Spartans fought against another Spartan outside Selymbria in 403 BC. Clearchus' willingness to act on his own initiative and to seek personal glory, even when doing so might be considered to run counter to the interests of the Spartan state, was something we witnessed in Pausanias, and would witness again in the actions of Lysander, Phoebidas and later Sphodrias.

CONCLUSION

Discipline and Military Organization

Sparta's legend rests strongly on the idea that its army was the only truly professional army in all of Greece. This is not true in the modern sense of the word "professional." The Spartan Peers were aristocrats who lived lives of leisure, and that leisurely life gave them time to train *somewhat* for war.

But even this partial training yielded an enormous advantage over the completely amateur armies of the rest of ancient Greece, and it certainly yielded advantages to Sparta in several battles. However, we should remember Aristotle's point from chapter II – that the Spartans were only "professional" in comparison to the other epically unprofessional Greek city-states. It wasn't that Spartans trained particularly hard or well, it was that they trained *at all*. Further, the price of this training was an apartheid system that meant Sparta was perpetually impaired by the very real threat of a slave revolt, a development that greatly inhibited its military freedom of action and resulted in multiple and very real military setbacks.

We have seen on multiple occasions that Sparta's celebrated military discipline was at best highly inconsistent.

In the Battle of the Kings (738 BC) we see some evidence of Spartan discipline exceeding that of its enemies. This might be an early indicator of professionalism, but could also be that Pausanias was deceived by Hellenistic myth-making sources. The Spartan king Theopompus' decision to engage in single combat with Euphaes might be an indication that maybe Pausanias was misled, or that the transition to an organized, disciplined army was gradual. Either way – Theopompus broke ranks, and was beaten and routed. You can call his action brave or foolhardy, but you cannot call it disciplined.

In Sparta's assault on Samos (520 BC), the Peers Archias' and Lycopas' outpacing their comrades to pursue the fleeing Samians into the sally port (at the cost of their lives) displayed a lack of discipline and organization well after the age of the warband had ended. That they acted on their own counter to orders is underscored by the fact that they found themselves inside the enemy fortification alone. None of their comrades kept up with them, suggesting that the rest of the army adhered to orders to hold position.

During Cleomenes' march on Athens to punish them for his humiliating ejection (507 BC), his co-king Demaratus refused to fight. Demaratus' objections were supposedly moral, but it is far more likely that he was seeking to undermine his rival co-king, or otherwise felt that the battle would not go well for Sparta. But regardless of his reasoning, it was an unforgivable lapse of discipline and organization that had the unsurprising effect of completely savaging Spartan morale and causing the army to break up as allies could justifiably say they were meeting their obligations and obeying the orders of a Spartan king. That the incident was embarrassing to Sparta is evidenced by the ephors enacting the law that the two kings should never take the field together again.

At Plataea (479 BC), we saw Amompharetus defy his commander's orders and refuse to move his *lochos* (possibly as many as 1,000 men), likely in reaction to Pausanias' cowardly switching of the Spartan position to avoid facing the Persians, and his later refusal to accept Mardonius' offer of a mass duel. This total breakdown of discipline nearly cost the Greeks the battle and caused both the Spartans and Athenians to be caught out of position, utterly bungling the planned withdrawal. Amompharetus' breach of discipline was matched by Pausanias' willingness to simply abandon Amompharetus and his *lochos* and withdraw without them. That this move spurred Amompharetus to action is irrelevant; it was a signal lapse of discipline and military professionalization at every level of the Spartan command.

That withdrawal was necessitated by another unprofessional lapse – failure to protect supply lines and in particular the sole water source that was available to the Greeks.

The next evidence of lapsed Spartan discipline comes at the First Battle of Mantinea (418 BC) when the Spartan commanders Aristocles and Hipponoidas defied their king's orders and did not move their units to plug the gap that resulted when he was forced to shift some of his units left to prevent his line from being enveloped. We can't be certain of their reasoning, but it's possible they mirrored Amompharetus' sentiments about Pausanias at Plataea – disgusted by Agis' tarnished reputation for having made the unauthorized peace with the Argives that forced him to lead the Spartans to Mantinea under supervision.

Whatever their reasoning, their failure to plug the gap permitted the Mantinean and Argive picked troops to exploit it, shattering the Spartan left. That would have been the end of the battle for Sparta except that the

Mantineans and Argives were equally undisciplined, and went on to loot the baggage instead of rolling up the enemy line. This provided a critical respite that the Spartans were able to seize to achieve ultimate victory, but certainly not a victory owed to their reputed discipline and organization. It should also be noted that the Spartans' disciplined restraint in declining to pursue their beaten enemy was possibly only the result of Pharax (the same man who restrained Agis from throwing away the Spartan army in the first place in an effort to redeem his reputation) forbidding it.

Spartan discipline was apparently just as inconsistent at sea. At the Battle of Cynossema (411 BC), discipline broke down in the Spartans' pursuit of the fleeing Athenian ships, which wound up costing them the victory when Thrasybulus counterattacked unexpectedly, catching the Spartan fleet out of order and sending panic through them. At Abydus that same year, the Spartans broke formation in their retreat, turning the rush to escape into an ocean-going rout that permitted the Athenians to defeat them in detail.

Less than half the agreed troops appeared for the appointed muster when the Spartan Herippidas prepared to raid Pharnabazus' camp in 395 BC, indicating either a lack of commitment among Spartan troops or a lack of control over Spartan allies. This may have played into Herippidas' later decision to sell the booty looted from the camp rather than distribute it, with the effect of alienating important Spartan allies.

After this long catalog of lapses of discipline, we get a rare glimpse of Sparta living up to its reputation at the Battle of the Nemea (394 BC), when the Spartans held formation and declined to pursue the routing Athenians on the coalition left. This put them in the position to make a flank attack on the returning Boeotian troops, who themselves had been in pursuit of the routed Spartan left. It was a rare instance of disciplined action directly resulting in a Spartan victory.

Both Olynthian battles were disasters for Sparta, but while Derdas' cavalry managed to salvage things in the first of them, in the second, a collapse of Spartan discipline resulted in a catastrophe that claimed the life of Agesilaus' half-brother Teleutias. Xenophon, very much a pro-Spartan partisan, is clearly damning in his description of the reason for the defeat – Teleutias gave in to anger and allowed himself to be baited into shooting distance of the city walls, forgetting the lessons of Haliartus and Agis' defeat outside Athens.

Phoebidas in 378 BC committed a similar sin at Thespiae, overstretching the pursuit and failing to maintain pacing with his hoplite corps. The unsurprising result was his own death in the counterattack and the subsequent panic that caused his army to rout. It may have been a kind of justice for his underhanded taking of the Theban Cadmea, but it certainly didn't speak well of Spartan discipline.

Leuctra was a long string of failures to live up to the Spartan reputation for coolheaded military bearing. Cleombrotus' decision to give battle in the first place was at least partly prompted by his humiliation over his long record of inaction and his concern about political fallout should he fail to show progress. He then proceeded, quite contrary to Sparta's legendary disdain for drunkenness, to drink wine in an effort to get his courage up, with the implication being its corresponding impact on his decision-making capabilities. His poorly trained cavalry failed to hold up against the Thebans, and their disordered rout had a significant impact on the Spartan line.

Manpower Crisis, Slavery and Spartan "Strength"

Although it is rarely considered as part of Sparta's reputation, the city-state's relationship to its slave caste, the helots, and its efforts to grapple with its slowly declining population of Peers were principal factors in Sparta's military record.

The evidence shows that Sparta both relied on and reacted to the military potential of its *perioikoi* and its helot population, and that this relationship grew more and more pronounced as the core population of Spartan Peers shrank. This manpower crisis and Sparta's necessary focus on preventing a helot revolt greatly inhibited its ability to project military force outside the Peloponnese and limited its ability to project Spartan policy abroad.

Further, Sparta frequently did not display confidence in its military superiority, nor did it act from a position of strength. Spartan military history is rife with concessions, declining battle when it was offered, retreats, withdrawals and seeking truce or a negotiated settlement.

Pausanias, questionable though his report is, describes helot participation in battle in both the First and Second Messenian Wars. Although they are almost never credited for their impact on the outcome of Spartan battles, their relevance is clear from the earliest days of Spartan warfare.

Sparta's victory over Tegea and creation of the Peloponnesian League shows weakness, not strength. Sparta's policy in both the Messenian Wars clearly demonstrated a preference for subjugation and dominance rather than alliance and influence. While the Peloponnesian League was a system of unequal alliance, it was also *not* subjugation and reduction of a subordinate population to helotage. The evidence suggests that the Spartan defeats at the battles of Hysiae and the Fetters (669 and 550 BC) undermined Spartan confidence in their ability to subjugate their neighbors, forcing them to adopt a different policy – relying on negotiation, diplomacy and soft power, rather than brute force.

The long and costly Messenian Wars and the learned experience of managing both their Laconian and Messenian helot populations may have also contributed to this change in policy.

We can also see Spartan insecurity regarding their ability to project military power and win battles in their failure to respond to Croesus', Maeandrius' or Aristagoras' pleas for help against Persia. This failure to march to the aid of friendly Greeks can also be interpreted as a fear of moving the army out of position to respond to a helot revolt. If we accept the argument that Cleomenes I's expedition against Athens was a pet project and not a broader Spartan effort (I do not), then the decision to march on Athens after Cleomenes' ejection from the city by an angry mob in 510 BC indicates that Sparta felt they *had to* respond with military force, despite Cleomenes' acting on his own. This would make the most sense if Sparta feared that the loss of face and appearing weak by allowing Athens to escape unpunished might spark a helot revolt or embolden Sparta's subject allies in the Peloponnesian League. In fact, Sparta's attack on Athens after Cleomenes' ejection can be accurately called one of the root causes of the Greco-Persian War, as it forced Athens into an alliance with Persia, which in turn caused Darius I to view Athens as a rebellious subject-state that required a Persian response after Athens' involvement in the Ionian revolt.

When Cleomenes returned to punish Athens for humiliating him, his Corinthian allies refused to fight at the 11th hour, leading to the complete disintegration of the army. While Corinth's ostensible reason for leaving was moral, this doesn't hold water by the incredibly opportunistic standards of ancient Greece. Far more likely is that Corinth lacked confidence in Sparta's ability to win the coming contest and came up with an excuse to avoid what it was sure would be a losing battle.

After his victory at Sepeia (494 BC), Cleomenes was reluctant to pursue the defeated Argives into their sacred grove, opting instead to use a ruse (lying to them that their ransoms had been paid) to coax them out. When this was discovered, he opted to burn the grove down rather than send his troops into it to finish off an already demoralized and defeated force. It is possible that these choices reflect fear and a lack of confidence in his army. Sepeia came on the heels of the Battle of the Champions, where we know Sparta's 300 best warriors were slaughtered to a man. Sparta had defeated Argos' army in the field following that duel in what I assume was a phalanx-on-phalanx battle. However, in the presumably wooded terrain of the sacred grove, it would have been impossible to properly deploy a phalanx, resulting in a series of individual combats ... much like the Battle of the Champions that Sparta lost. If this thinking is occurring to me in AD 2021, then it's entirely possible that it occurred to Cleomenes in 494 BC and that he felt that deploying troops into the wooded terrain of the grove meant he might lose (or at least take unacceptable casualties), and so opted first for trickery, then later for firing the grove.

The Spartans' reputation as lords of the battlefield was built almost at a single stroke at Thermopylae (480 BC) and grew possibly from Themistocles' relentless propaganda about the heroic suicide of 300 bold Spartans in the face of an army more than 100 times their number.

But the evidence destroys this myth at every turn. Thermopylae was never a suicide mission. Leonidas had every hope of being reinforced by a larger army, and the army he had was quite large to begin with when you consider how tiny the pass was. This is because he very likely didn't march to Thermopylae with 300 men, but something more like 1,000, and that's not even counting the helots, who we know would have fought alongside their masters. There were at least one for every Peer, but it could have been many more (at Plataea, there were seven helots for each Peer). They joined a sizable force made up of 7,000 Greeks overall, including the much more impressive contribution of 700 Thespians (massive compared to Sparta's relatively tiny contribution of Peers). Herodotus was clear in saying that each contingent of Greeks took its turn in the pass, and based on Sparta's reputation as "professionals" and their later relationships with foreign troops, we have to consider the possibility that the Peers functioned as *xenagoi* (officers in charge of non-Spartan troops). We also see Leonidas sending for help, and why would he do that if Thermopylae was a suicide mission?

We must assume that Leonidas knew he had enough troops to hold the pass. He was likewise confident that his sizable contingent of 1,000 Phocians fighting on their home territory and possibly under the command of a Spartan *xenagos* officer would be sufficient to hold the Anopaia Path. The Spartans had seen the aftermath of Marathon. They knew what a Greek hoplite could do to lightly armored Persian infantryman.

Further evidence of lack of confidence in Spartan prowess came later in the same battle. Herodotus tells the unbelievable story that Leonidas selflessly dismissed his Greek allies who he decided wouldn't fight effectively. This also supports the suicide-mission narrative that Herodotus works hard to sell. The far more likely story is that these same allies, hearing of the Phocian failure to hold position on the Anopaia Path, refused Leonidas' orders and marched home while he cursed them for cowards. The Greek allies voted with their feet, and it was a vote of no confidence in Sparta's ability to hold the pass until help arrived.

Prior to the naval Battle of Salamis (480 BC) the Spartan Eurybiades agreed to move the Greek fleet to the Saronic Gulf. This disastrous decision was very likely motivated by fear of meeting the Persian fleet without a ready means of escape. If the Greeks had gone through with it, it was very likely that the fleet would have broken up, with each contingent sailing to defend its home waters, and that the remainder would have been annihilated in the open water of the Saronic Gulf which would have given the Persian fleet room to bring its superior numbers to bear. It was only Themistocles' threat to take the Athenian ships and leave that stiffened Sparta's spine enough to stand and fight, a move that surely saved the day for Greece.

At the Battle of Plataea (479 BC), Sparta brought the staggering number of seven helots per Peer, for a total of 35,000 slave-infantry. While this corps certainly provided a marked combat advantage to the Spartan contingent, it is also possible the Spartans wanted to take such a large helot contingent to reduce the population back in Laconia and Messenia, particularly the military-aged males who would be critical to any helot revolt. This may have been a sign of Spartan insecurity at being able to keep the helots intimidated with such a large number of Spartan Peers away from home.

Later in the battle, we saw Pausanias switching positions with the Athenians twice in an effort to keep his troops from facing the Persians, matching them instead with more familiar Persian-allied Greek troops. The fig leaf of an excuse given was that the Athenians were more experienced in fighting Persians, but I think it's pretty clear that Pausanias was frightened to face them. The only Spartans ever to face Persians were dead in a heap at Thermopylae, and that surely had left an impression on the Spartan regent. Pausanias' decision to decline Mardonius' invitation to a mass duel supports the view that Pausanias was afraid and lacked confidence in Sparta's ability to triumph. He had to know how these decisions would look to the rest of the Greeks and the impact it would have on his army's morale.

Pausanias reinforced the perception of cowardice in his later refusal to advance even when his phalanx came under a withering storm of Persian arrows. Herodotus excuses this as the Spartan king desperately seeking favorable omens, but we have repeatedly seen the Spartans' convenient relationship with religious restrictions. Also possible was that Pausanias feared to commit his troops and used the omen-taking as an excuse to delay until support could arrive. The Tegeans, far less eager to hide behind their shields until enough lucky shots made their contingent combat-ineffective, finally moved to the attack on their own, embarrassing the Spartans into fighting. The omens (surprise, surprise) suddenly became favorable the moment the Tegeans charged the enemy.

At the Battle of Mycale (479 BC) Sparta was suspiciously slow to join the attack. Herodotus excuses this by noting that it had to cross difficult terrain, but when we consider earlier evidence (failure to appear at Marathon, the reluctance to march for Plataea), a picture begins to emerge of a possible Spartan preference of letting their allies do the hard fighting. That was certainly the case at Mycale, where by the time Sparta joined in the battle, it was against an enemy already mauled and demoralized by its allies.

Sparta surely seemed ascendant in the wake of its victory in the Greco-Persian War. But both Pausanias and Leotychides disgraced themselves in public fashion immediately following the war, and Sparta's refusal to live up to the expectation that it would continue to lead the Hellenic League, effectively ceding the pole position to Athens, clearly resulted in a Greece that was considerably less impressed than it otherwise might have been. The best evidence of this is that Sparta found itself fighting two major battles right on the heels of chasing the Persians out of Greece – Tegea and Dipaea – both against other Greek city-states and within a decade of its celebrated role in saving Greece from foreign domination.

Archidamus' first action following the great earthquake of 464 BC was to muster the Spartan army. This act underscored how fragile Sparta's hold was over its slave caste and followed the pattern of Spartan fear following any major setback or commitment of its army. That the helot revolt which we now term the Third Messenian War immediately followed proved Archidamus was not overreacting.

Sparta's signing of a generational peace with Argos in 451 BC was certainly not an indication of military confidence in the wake of Spartan victory over Persia, and even if it was an indication of prudence, it still pokes a hole in the Bronze Lie – the Spartans were reliant on diplomacy and careful use of soft power, rather than victory on the battlefield.

Samos' appeal for Spartan help in its revolt against Athens in 440 BC resulted not in the confident declaration of a military mission, but in a cautious polling of Sparta's allies in the Peloponnesian League, a poll that raised Corinthian objections that ultimately waved Sparta off from going to war. Corinth's objections were overcome not by Sparta, but by Athens' aggression against Potidaea. Even then, Sparta still sent for an oracle, possibly indicating that it was preparing yet another religious excuse not to go to war. This oracle was followed by multiple embassies to Athens ostensibly seeking a peaceful solution.

King Archidamus argued passionately for peace and against Sparta's plan of ravaging the Attic countryside. While this reflects positively on Archidamus, it is not evidence of a bold Sparta confident in its military superiority. Even after being overruled and directed to lead the army into Attica, Archidamus still sent a final embassy to Athens, and then laid siege to Oenoe (despite what he must have known was his army's poor record in sieges) in the hopes that the move would frighten Athens into a peace overture and avoid what he knew would be a long and costly war. While this gambit ultimately failed, it contributes to the impression of a Sparta not confident in its ability to bring Athens to heel.

The twin naval defeats at Rhium and Naupactus cemented Athens' domination on the water and did lasting damage to Sparta's impression of its own naval strength and its confidence it could beat Athens at sea. We see immediate evidence of this in Sparta's failure to assist Mytilene in its attempt to throw off the Delian yoke. Alcidas' fig leaf of an attempt, followed by his immediate flight, underscores this lack of faith in Spartan naval strength. Even following the Battle of Corcyra (427 BC), Sparta's first recorded naval victory, the Spartan fleet fled the moment Athenian naval reinforcements arrived.

With the Spartan admiral Thrasymelidas, the apple clearly didn't fall far from Alcidas' tree. Bringing his fleet down from Corcyra to respond to Demosthenes' establishment of a fortified position at Pylos (425 BC), the Spartan deliberately avoided the Athenian fleet, dragging his ships over the isthmus at Leucas – it's very likely that Thrasymelidas understood he was outmatched on the water, and lacked the confidence to take on the superior Athenian navy. This concern was proved all too correct in the subsequent battle inside the bay.

Sparta's treacherous ploy of pretending to reward, and later executing the 2,000 strongest helots is possible evidence of Spartan terror of yet another helot revolt in the wake of the humiliating loss at Pylos and Sphacteria. Fear of a helot uprising may also have been a motivating factor in the use of the 700 *brasideioi* in Brasidas' campaign in the north, possibly an attempt either to further denude the helot population at home, or to provide an incentive to the helots to keep the peace in the hope of future rewards. It also shows the strain of Sparta's growing manpower crisis, as did Brasidas' reliance on mercenaries in addition to slave troops.

Sparta's legendary punishment of those who survived battles as "tremblers" proved to be inconsistently applied when those tremblers were present in large enough numbers. The survivors of Sphacteria were well-connected members of wealthy families, and their influence proved the custom of punishing those who survived defeat in battle either entirely mythic, or at the very least pliable. The decision to go easy on the survivors of Sphacteria may also have been connected to Sparta's accelerating manpower crisis. Tremblers they may have been, but the 120 Peers recovered from Sphacteria were fighters too, who had given a strong accounting of themselves before they'd finally been utterly outflanked. These were men who'd graduated the Upbringing, Sparta's most important military asset. With its accelerating manpower crisis, Sparta couldn't afford to simply throw them away.

Spartan self-confidence may have still been at a low ebb six years after Sphacteria, when Agis II confronted the Argives outside their own city. Agis' surprise truce, made without consulting the Spartan government, was clearly interpreted as cowardice at home, as evidenced by Sparta's stern reaction once Argos broke the truce. This appearance of cowardice dogged Agis for the rest of his career and spurred overcompensation that nearly resulted in him throwing away the entire Spartan army by attacking at a disadvantage at the First Battle of Mantinea in 418 BC.

The army that Agis took to Mantinea was bolstered by a contingent of 2,000 *neodamōdeis*, the freed helots who would play a larger and larger role in Spartan armies. Spartan reliance on these troops provided simultaneous evidence of concern over helot obedience (both by denuding the population of those who were capable of fighting, and by dangling the potential reward of freedom in exchange for loyalty to the Spartan state) and the exacerbation of Sparta's manpower crisis as their rigid citizen franchise not only kept them from creating new Peers, but also forced them to cast Peers out of the ranks if they experienced a financial setback that made them no longer able to pay their mess dues. We also saw a decision to send the oldest and youngest hoplites back to Sparta, possibly out of concern over the helots.

In 411 BC, the Spartan admiral Astyochus refused to engage the Athenians on the water despite Persian gold and Syracusan naval aid, evidence of a Sparta that still lacked confidence in its naval capability, and likely a prisoner of Athens' reputation for naval supremacy (probably no longer justified at this point).

But this wasn't Astyochus' worst blunder. In a move that very likely cost Sparta the chance to end the war in a single stroke, he refused the offer of Athens to betray its own fleet, opting instead to run to his Persian purse-masters with a report. It didn't help, and the needed funds were not forthcoming. We saw a similar failure to capitalize on a position of strength after Praxitas' victory inside Corinth's long walls (392 BC), which the Spartans used simply as an opportunity to beg the Persians for peace. This move was likely motivated partly by the pressure placed on them by the raiding base on Cythera, but it is also another data point in a record of Sparta's low self-confidence in its ability to project military power.

Perhaps the most damning account of Spartan confidence in the wake of defeat is the famous intercepted message home following the loss at Cyzicus (410 BC) – "Fleet destroyed. Mindarus dead. The men starve. We don't know what to do." This message was followed by a Spartan peace overture that was rejected by an Athens which saw no reason to come to terms with an enemy so clearly on its back foot.

Spartan self-confidence was apparently low enough to concern Eteonicus, causing him to lie to avoid revealing the Spartan defeat at Arginusae in 406 BC. This may very well have sustained Spartan morale, but the fact that the morale was weak enough to necessitate the measure is telling. Sparta *again* sued for peace after Arginusae and Athens *again* refused to grant the truce, once again making a move to throw away a chance at an off-ramp that might have preserved its independence.

Even in the wake of the final Spartan victory at Aegospotami the following year, Sparta ceded domination of the Greeks living in Asia Minor (along modern Turkey's west coast) to Persia, showing that the Spartans clearly understood that Persian support was responsible for their ultimate victory.

Sparta's handling of the Athenian insurgency of 403 BC did not evidence military self-confidence or bold freedom of action. Thrasybulus' speech to his men before the Battle of Munichia (403 BC) clearly displays a commander who was not cowed by the reputation of his enemy. The Spartans were simply men the Athenians had beaten before and could be confident of beating again. The extremely light Spartan casualties at Munichia may indicate that the pro-Spartan (and possibly Spartan-led) force broke *before* contact with the enemy.

Corinth's and Thebes' refusal to join the Spartan reaction force marching to deal with Thrasybulus at the Battle of Piraeus (403 BC) displayed city-states not overly concerned with offending the victor of the Peloponnesian Wars. Pausanias' move to make concessions with the Athenians, eventually resulting in the restoration of Athens' democracy, was to my mind shrewd and very likely nipped what would have otherwise been a much wider insurgency in the bud. It spoke well of Pausanias, but it certainly didn't speak well of Sparta's supposed mastery of Greece. Just a year after Aegospotami, it was unable to dictate policy to anyone, to rely on its allies for military aid, or to even quell a challenge to its military power without making concessions to the enemy.

Pausanias' conciliatory moves toward Athens paid dividends when the city-state sent troops to assist with his campaigning in Elis. However, Thebes and Corinth once again refused to help, showing real fissures in Sparta's supposed mastery of Greece.

When Thibron campaigned in Ionia in 399 BC, Sparta sent him with a force almost entirely of *neodamōdeis* indicating the extent of the manpower crisis at the time. We also saw the campaign relying heavily on "native" (Ionian) troops to support the war effort in Asia Minor.

Cinadon's conspiracy roughly the following year underscored the fragility of Sparta's grip on its helot population, but also showed growing unease among other population classes resulting from the refusal to extend the franchise of the Peers. As that population continued to dwindle, it's unsurprising that others would seek to challenge it. Underscoring this point was Agesilaus' arrival on the coast of Asia Minor with an army largely made up of *neodamōdeis* and just 30 Peers. Again, we may see in the large complement of freed helot hoplites an effort to denude the population of its best fighters or the dangling of freedom in exchange for loyalty. Once again, Thebes and Corinth refused to send troops to assist the Spartan king, and now Thebes went further in interrupting Agesilaus' sacrifice, an insult he never forgot. Athens too, refrained from joining the expedition. Sparta was clearly inspiring neither loyalty nor fear in its supposed allies.

We can also see a lack of confidence in morale in Agesilaus' decision to lie about the Spartan defeat at Cnidus in 394 BC (a defeat that was partly brought about by Agesilaus putting his incompetent brother-in-law in charge of the Spartan navy), though this was more likely done out of concern for the Asian Greek troops accompanying Agesilaus' army, whose homes now lay open to Persian retribution.

Agesilaus' own morale seems to have failed after witnessing the disciplined maneuvers of Chabrias' peltasts and the Theban Sacred Band prior to the Battle of Thespiae in 378 BC. Xenophon's silence on this is as loud as a shout, especially when we consider what a close friend he was to the Spartan king. Agesilaus' confidence in his army, or in his ability to lead it, appears to have failed in the face of a committed and disciplined enemy.

Perhaps the most famous example of what can charitably be described as caution on the part of a Spartan commander was the actions of the relief army sent to answer for the defeat at Leuctra in 371 BC. Archidamus withdrew after negotiations with Jason of Pherae, quite likely frightened of facing the army that had just inflicted a crushing defeat that had seen a Spartan king killed and 1,000 casualties besides.

Agesilaus, whose record of championing Sparta's interests at all times, even when it blackened its reputation (as evidenced by his defense of both Phoebidas' and Sphodrias' actions), made the very out-of-character decision to return the plunder taken during the capture of Eutaea, a possible indication of Sparta's weakened position *vis-à-vis* the rest of Greece. He later maneuvered extensively in Arcadia but avoided battle, and Xenophon confirmed that his goal was to bolster Spartan morale, savaged after the loss at Leuctra, without further loss of Spartan lives. It didn't work, and we begin to see the inevitable defections of the Sciritae and *perioikoi* to Thebes.

One could see this weakness as a driver in the Spartan decision to accept assistance from both Persia and a foreign tyrant simultaneously to engineer their victory at Caryae in 369 BC, but the truth is that Sparta already had a long record of accepting foreign support. We must absolutely credit Sparta in living up to its reputation in defense of the city when Epaminondas attempted to take it in 362 BC, able to wrest a victory from what appeared to be the jaws of certain defeat – outnumbered and fighting uphill besides.

But a Sparta stripped of its prime agricultural wealth and its subject Messenian population could no longer generate the money necessary to pay its increasingly mercenary army. Agesilaus' death while returning from mercenary duty was a sad comment on Sparta's desperate need to generate the wealth that its legend claimed it hated.

Sparta slid into military irrelevance, as evidenced by its failure to participate at Chaeronea, perhaps one of the most significant battles in determining the future of Greece. Philip of Macedon ravaged Laconia at will, but didn't bother taking Sparta not because he couldn't, but because it better served his purposes as a regional power checking other enemies. That honor would be left to the Antigonid king Antigonus III Doson after his victory at the Second Battle of Sellasia in 222 BC. Alexander the Great's description of the Battle of Megalopolis as a "battle of mice" was a stinging indication of the contempt the Macedonian leader held for Spartan arms.

Scouting and Reconnaissance

Scouting and reconnaissance were absolutely fundamental to ancient warfare and were in practice at the time we've examined in this book. Scouting featured prominently in the Battle of Kadesh between Egypt and the Hittites (1274 BC), one of the earliest battles recorded, and there's no evidence that scouting fell out of fashion in the years that followed.

The evidence shows that Sparta had a poor record of effectively scouting before, during and after battles, or during critical battle-related operations, such as establishing a camp.

At the Battle of Ithome (728 BC), we saw Sparta ambushed in the midst of the battle by Aristodemus' mobile rapid-reaction force, an indication that it failed to gather sufficient intelligence on the Messenian troop counts, deployment and armament.

The disastrous outcome of Sparta's first expedition to subjugate Athens (511 BC), which included the death of the Spartan commander Archimolius, was due to Sparta's failure to detect and react to the fact that the battlefield had been carefully groomed to give a decisive advantage to the Thessalian cavalry (obstacles removed, holes filled). Basic battlefield reconnaissance would very probably have prevented this defeat.

Sparta evidenced multiple and disastrous failures to scout at the Battle of Pylos and Sphacteria (425 BC). The first of these was the Spartans failing to oppose the Athenian entry into the bay, allowing themselves to be caught napping with their ships still beached, having missed the opportunity to take on the Athenian fleet in the tight confines of the straits where their superior numbers would have counted for little and where the lack of room to maneuver would have neutralized much of their superior seamanship. The consequences for this failure to spot the Athenian fleet farther out were immediate and terrible – Sparta lost its entire fleet at a single stroke, and saw its 420 hoplites deployed to the island of Sphacteria cut off, a development that would shape the course not only of this battle, but of the entire Archidamian phase of the wars.

The second reconnaissance failure was the Spartans at the "first position" on Sphacteria allowing themselves to be taken completely by surprise. Per Thucydides, the surprise was total despite the ground cover being burned off, which likely meant they would have had a clear view of the assault force. It's also worth noting that they were probably aware the assault was coming, as Demosthenes' and Cleon's demand for their surrender had announced the Athenian intention to storm the island.

The final reconnaissance failure came at the end of the battle, where the remaining Spartans discovered that the unscalable heights of Mount Elias to their rear were scalable after all. This would only have been possible if the Spartans had failed to properly review their fallback positions, something they would have had plenty of time to do while they were cut off on the island and awaiting relief. It was this final failure to adequately scout that resulted in the Spartans' position being made utterly hopeless, and forcing them to make a Thermopylae-style choice to live up to Demaratus' description of them as men who would "abide at their posts and there conquer or die." But while the Spartans at Thermopylae lived up to that description, the Spartans at Sphacteria most decidedly did not, and their subsequent surrender was a turning point in Sparta's military reputation that would dog it for the rest of its history.

After Agis II completed his flooding operation at the First Battle of Mantinea (418 BC), he failed to deploy scouts ahead of his column on his march back out to meet the Argive alliance and wound up blundering smack into the enemy. The battle was a Spartan victory, but clearly not due to careful reconnaissance of the enemy's position.

Thrasybulus' successful dawn raid on the Spartan camp in 403 BC would not have been possible had the Spartans properly posted scouts or pickets to alert them of enemy presence in the area. When you consider that the Spartans were camping within striking range of an enemy position, it's a puzzling lapse.

At the Battle of the Nemea (394 BC), we are told the Spartans were alerted to the enemy's advance by the sound of their war cry and not by scouts, pickets or any other reconnaissance. Likewise, Iphicrates' successful ambush on the Spartan column outside Abydus in 390 BC indicates yet another costly failure to adequately scout. Cleombrotus suffered a similar ambush in his second march into Boeotia in 376 BC, another possible indicator of failing to scout. This ambush resulted in Cleombrotus quitting his campaign altogether, infuriating Sparta's allies and providing impetus to the disastrous naval engagement at Naxos that same year.

Siegecraft and Assaults on Fortified Positions

The evidence shows that Sparta struggled with sieges and assaulting fortified positions, and showed little substantive improvement over its entire military history. If we believe Pausanias' narrative of the First Messenian War, Sparta was unable to take a single fortified position despite three years of trial and error, and Sparta's first recorded battle (the Battle of the Ravine – 739 BC) resulted in a defeat as soon as the Messenians fortified their position.

The Spartans again demonstrated weakness in the face of fortifications later in the First Messenian War when they bottled the Messenians up in their fortress on Mount Ithome. Again, Pausanias is a questionable source, but if we believe him, then Sparta didn't assault the Messenian position for five years. This may have been due to a war with Argos at the same time, but this isn't proven, and so we have to at least consider the possibility that Sparta's failure to take the fortress for such a long period was due to its being unable to overcome the defenses.

Sparta's unsuccessful attempt to take Samos by siege (520 BC) shows little improvement in its siegecraft. After investing the fortress for 40 days, it finally gave up and returned home, having accomplished nothing.

Though he was able to enter Athens in 510 BC, Cleomenes I was powerless to take its fortified Acropolis and had to resort to capturing members of the tyrant Hippias' family in order to get the defenders to quit their fortified position.

After the Persian defeat at Plataea (479 BC), the Spartans pursued the routing troops to their fortified camp, but were unable to storm it, relying on Athenian assistance to make a breach that could be exploited. The evidence shows that even with a way in, the Spartans were hesitant to make an assault, leaving the honor of first-into-the-breach to the Tegeans, who also went on to sack Mardonius' tent.

Sparta's lack of confidence in its ability to take fortified positions was reflected in its opposition to Athens' rebuilding of its walls, destroyed when the city was taken by the Persians in 480 BC. Sparta used the veiled threat of promising to protect Athens from its enemy (the obverse of that coin being the same army that would protect it could also destroy it) to try to convince it to leave the walls leveled, on the flimsy premise that should the Persians ever retake the city, they would be able to make use of its defenses. Themistocles cleverly found a way to subvert this effort and Athens' walls were rebuilt, but the fact that Sparta spent political capital in an effort to prevent the walls from being reconstructed is evidence of its concern about the challenge they would later present. As evidenced by Athens' successful defenses against Agis during the Decelean phase of the Peloponnesian Wars, those concerns were well justified.

At the Second Battle of Ithome (464 BC), Sparta was once again unable to make headway against the Messenian fortifications and appealed to the Athenians for help specifically based on their skill at taking fortified positions. When Sparta later sent the Athenians away (sowing the seeds that would become the Peloponnesian Wars), it remained unable to crack the Messenian nut, and finally had to resort to a negotiated settlement to get the Messenians to quit their position.

King Pleistoanax's ravaging of Attica in support of the 446 BC Euboean revolt was so signally unable to capture even a single fortified position that the king was accused of accepting bribes to stay his hand and driven into exile on his return home.

King Archidamus opened the phase of the Peloponnesian Wars that bore his name with a futile siege of Oenoe (431 BC), hoping it would frighten the Athenians into suing for peace. This effort failed either to take Oenoe or to frighten the Athenians.

In 411 BC after Alcibiades' successful gambit resulted in an Athenian oligarchy, Agis sallied forth from Decelea to take advantage of the situation. However, the Athenian oligarchs were not as pro-Spartan as he perhaps supposed and the sight of the manned walls forced him to withdraw once again. It would not be the last time. In 407 BC, he would again be defeated and forced to quit Athens, foiled by the city's fortifications, manned by old men and boys. That defeat was exacerbated by Agis' mistake of bringing his troops within missile range of the defenders on the walls, an error that would be repeated by Lysander outside Haliartus in 395 BC and Teleutias at the Second Battle of Olynthus in 381 BC.

The Spartan capture of Cyzicus (410 BC) was a joint land operation with the same Persians they'd fought at Thermopylae. The Persians were well known for their talents as siege engineers and they very likely provided the engines and expertise that made the capture of the city possible.

When Spartan heavy-handedness finally sparked Athenian insurgency in 403 BC, Thrasybulus was able to use the fortress at Phyle as a base of operations. Sparta proved unable to effectively assault or besiege the position. Sparta was again unsuccessful in its siege of Larissa just four years later. With the close of the Corinthian War, Sparta was still showing difficulty prosecuting sieges, this time against Mantinea and Phlius – both ultimately successful, but only after an intense struggle. The necessity for the sieges in the first place underscored that Sparta's reputation was certainly no longer cowing other Greek city-states.

Giving and Accepting Bribes

Sparta's reputation as a culture that shunned wealth and luxury is one of the foundational elements of the Bronze Lie. Not only does the evidence show that this wasn't true, but Spartan greed was a driving factor in some of their military outcomes, especially in that most telling indication of the pursuit of wealth – taking bribes. The Spartans also appear to have been rather adept at *giving* bribes as well, a further indication that they well understood the power of money and its effectiveness in advancing military objectives.

Sparta's first recorded victory of the Second Messenian War (and Sparta's second recorded victory in battle – the Battle of the Great Trench in 682 BC) was won with a bribe, the first in Greek history according to Pausanias, when the Spartans paid Aristocrates to withdraw the Arcadian allied contingent through the Messenian lines. This shows great cunning, but not battlefield prowess. The resulting victory was certainly a compliment to Sparta, just not the kind of compliment they built their reputation on.

Croesus' "gift" of gold for the statue of Apollo could also be considered as Sparta's taking a bribe to enter into an alliance, but the opposite argument (that gifts are routinely part of establishing diplomatic relations) also holds true here. But even if we don't consider Croesus' gift to be a bribe, we can't ignore Herodotus' story that the Spartan emissaries bearing the expensive mixing bowl to Sardis sold it and pocketed the money when they found the intended recipient was gone.

Scholars dispute the story that Sparta quit its siege of Samos (520 BC) due to being bribed to leave, but the story is more believable when you consider that coins similar to the ones purportedly used to bribe them (electrum-plated lead) have been found.

Cleomenes' failure to capture the city of Argos despite defeating the Argive army at Sepeia (494 BC) resulted in charges that he'd been bribed to leave the city in peace. While we can't know the truth of this, it fits nicely with later charges that he bribed the Delphic oracle to help him depose his co-king Demaratus.

Sparta's celebrated victory at Plataea (479 BC) was almost immediately tarnished by the actions of its leaders moving to punish those who had cooperated with the Persians. Leotychides' disastrous punitive campaign to chastise Thessaly was cut short when he accepted a bribe from the pro-Persian Aleuad clan to wave off. The glove packed with silver was discovered in his tent, forcing the king into exile rather than face charges back home.

When, just 25 years after the Persians had been driven from Greece, they sent their envoy Megabazus to bribe the Spartans into an invasion of Attica, Sparta did not comply, but it certainly took the money, effectively both conspiring with and ripping off its hated enemy at the same time.

The Spartan king Pleistoanax was driven into exile after being accused of accepting a bribe to ineffectually ravage Attica around 446 BC. This, of course, could simply have been the king's inability to take fortified positions and the pursuit of the wrongheaded ravaging strategy that served Sparta so poorly throughout all phases of the Peloponnesian Wars, but given the history of bribes in Sparta, we have to at least consider there may have been some truth to it.

Despite Gylippus' brilliant leadership during the Spartan expedition to Sicily, he joined the ranks of the many Spartan leaders whose careers were cut short by accusations of bribery, condemned to death in absentia after fleeing the charges.

Following the defeat of Athens' disastrous Sicilian expedition, Sparta eagerly accepted the gold proffered by the Persian satraps Tissaphernes and Pharnabazus.

This policy would prove to be both consistent and wise moving forward, but it certainly ran counter to Sparta's reputation both as a champion of Greek liberty against "oriental" despotism and its purported hatred of wealth.

At the Second Battle of Sellasia, if we believe Plutarch, the Spartan Damoteles was bribed to give a false report. This would indicate that the Spartan susceptibility to bribery persisted past the supposed return to the Lycurgan mode after the reforms of Cleomenes III. Speaking of Lycurgus, his namesake supposedly gained the Eurypontid throne by bribing the ephors, per Polybius.

Winning by Trickery and Diplomacy

Meeting military objectives using deception, coercion or diplomacy is not a thing to be ashamed of. The legendary Chinese general Sun Tzu's famous quote bears repeating here: "For to win one hundred victories in one hundred battles is not the height of skill. To subdue the enemy without fighting is the height of skill. Hence to fight and conquer in all your battles is not supreme excellence; supreme excellence consists in breaking the enemy's resistance without fighting."

But the use of trickery and diplomacy to achieve military objectives is the opposite of the Bronze Lie. Sparta's reputation was built on victory in battle, not on espionage or diplomatic speeches. But the evidence we've examined shows that the Spartans were incredibly able spymasters, made extensive use of information and clandestine operations, and relied on diplomatic overtures nearly as often as they did on armed force to achieve their military objectives.

Our first recorded Spartan capture of an enemy position was the capture of the Messenian town of Ampheia using a night ambush when the town's gates were still open. In the aftermath of the Spartan defeat at the Battle of Ithome (728 BC), they attempted to infiltrate the Messenian position with 100 spies pretending to be deserters. Pausanias' quote in Aristodemus' mouth – "*The crimes of the Spartans are new, but their tricks are old*" – certainly implies that Sparta had a reputation for deception. When this failed, Sparta attempted to pry Messenia away from its allies with a series of diplomatic embassies to Arcadia. If we believe Pausanias, Sparta's final victory in the First Messenian War came partly from a trick that caused the Messenians to interpret a Delphic oracle unfavorably, with corresponding damage to Messenian morale.

The Battle of Eira (669 BC), which won the Second Messenian War for Sparta, was secured through a betrayal – the Spartan deserter who deserted back to alert the Spartans to a vulnerability in the Messenian watch. The betrayal was so significant that some might suspect this man was never really a deserter at all, but rather a clandestine agent planted by Sparta for this very purpose. It certainly matched the prior plan to infiltrate 100 Spartan "deserters" into the Messenian camp.

It's possible that Sparta "won" the mass duel described as Battle of the Champions (546 BC) by lying about Othryades' survival, though its victory in the field battle that followed was a genuine combat victory.

Cleomenes I won the Battle of Sepeia (494 BC) through trickery, though the precise nature of the trick depends on which source you believe. Herodotus gives the hard-to-swallow (for it is based on the assumption that the Argives were fools) story that the Argives mimicked every Spartan action, allowing Cleomenes to pretend to stand down and then launch a surprise attack after the Argives likewise stood down. The more believable story comes from Plutarch, who tells us that Cleomenes violated a truce to attack the Argives while they were unawares. After the Spartan victory, Cleomenes used deception again to coax the Argives out of their hiding spot in the sacred grove, lying to them that their ransoms had been paid and murdering them as they exited.

At Thermopylae (480 BC), we saw the Spartans engaging in a feigned retreat in order to trick the Persians into breaking ranks and moving out of bow range into the killing zone where the Spartans excelled.

Brasidas can be truly said to be one of Sparta's heroes of the Peloponnesian Wars, helping to swing the balance of the Archidamian phase significantly back toward Sparta's advantage due to his enormously successful campaign in the north. But while we absolutely must give Brasidas credit for his brilliant campaign, we must also acknowledge that the majority of his gains were won *without* fighting – via diplomacy, coercion or the cunning employment of fifth columns inside hostile cities. Brasidas' signal taking of Torone was due to traitors who opened the gates to the Spartans. One of Brasidas' rare defeats came when he tried to take a city by main force (Eion – 424 BC).

Thucydides is clear that cities wanted to come over to the Spartan cause because of Brasidas' reputation for "gentleness."

It's fascinating to wonder if the wounds Brasidas took storming the beach at Pylos taught him a valuable lesson in the dangers of rushing in and made him a more sober and careful commander. Perhaps he considered those scars, remembered the sting of the Athenian javelins, and thought better of fighting unless he absolutely had to. We can never know for sure, but one thing is certain – the Brasidas who marched north into Thrace was surely a different man than the one who lost his shield at Pylos.

This is not to say that Brasidas wasn't a gifted battlefield commander. Even his defeat at Lyncestis (423 BC) showed real brilliance and he very clearly kept a mere loss from turning into a complete disaster. His battle plan at Amphipolis was well executed, and though it cost him his life, yielded a victory for Sparta that saw Amphipolis in its camp for a long time to come.

Sparta's crushing victory in the Battle of Eretria in 411 BC was won largely with the help of pro-Spartan Eretrians willing to betray their purported Athenian allies. Sparta still managed to squander the victory when Agesandridas failed to follow up with an attack on Athens or its ports.

Religious Observance

It's difficult for a modern person to grapple with ancient Greek religious beliefs. For the ancients, the experience of the divine was real and immediate in a way that can be hard to empathize with in AD 2021.

We have to keep this in mind when we consider Sparta's approach to religion, but we also cannot deny that there is at least the suspicion of some degree of cynicism, that Sparta, or at least some Spartans, used religion much like modern televangelists, a convenient excuse for whatever self-interested action they wished to take, or to avoid taking.

An early example is their murder of the sacrosanct Persian heralds who came to demand earth and water as tokens of submission to Darius. That Sparta felt this to be a violation of sacred law is shown by its effort to balance the ledger by sending Spartans to Darius to kill as recompense. The Great King refused, as the Spartans must have known he would.

After the Spartan victory at Sepeia (494 BC), Cleomenes happily committed twin sacrileges – he burned the Argive sacred grove (using the fig leaf of delegating the task to his helots, so they would fall victim to the religious pollution, and not the vaunted Peers), and then sacrificed at the temple of Hera despite being specifically forbidden to do so.

There are two ways to consider these sacrileges – some may wish to excuse Sparta, since these acts were committed by one man (Cleomenes). However, it may also be argued that, as king, Cleomenes was in an unusual position and his actions reflected on and couldn't be separated from the city-state he represented.

When Athens and Plataea mustered to resist the Persian army at Marathon (490 BC) Sparta invoked the Carneia as a religious excuse. Whether or not this was genuine, we cannot deny that it advanced a likely foreign policy goal – for Athens to attrit itself against Persia so that Sparta could mop up the weakened victors. Apart from the policy objectives, there is the possibility that it simply feared the Persians and was not confident in its ability to defeat them, or that it was in the midst of another helot revolt that kept its army pinned in place.

But even if all three of these things were true, it at least raises the suspicion that the Carneia may have been a convenient excuse to arrive at Marathon *after* the battle had been fought. That this religious observance may have been at least partially an excuse is supported by the Spartans' second invocation of it at Thermopylae (480 BC). Whereas the Carneia meant that *no* Spartan could march to battle at Marathon, for unknown reasons the same festival meant that suddenly 300 Spartans and a king marching was acceptable.

The Spartans later invoked the festival of the Hyacinthia as a reason not to march to Plataea (479 BC) and it was only the Athenian threat of giving its fleet over to Persia that convinced them to do so. Fear was one possible motive, another would have been advancing a similar policy goal to Marathon – allowing Sparta to shelter behind the fortified isthmus of Corinth while Persia wasted its army conquering central Greece, losing troops to battle, hunger and desertion. Then, Sparta would be in a position to mop up the survivors and project its will on a weakened Greece.

While Sparta's dragging of the helots out of the temple of Poseidon where they were seeking sanctuary surely did not cause the great earthquake of

464 BC (contrary to the legend), I certainly believe that the incident occurred and that the Spartan authorities were all too willing to violate the sacred laws of a temple sanctuary in the case of slaves (whereas they scrupulously observed them in the case of the royal Pausanias).

Agis II's muster to aid Epidaurus in 419 BC was delayed by a number of religious conflicts – the Carneia once again, followed by numerous unfavorable sacrifices at the border. Both Thucydides and Diodorus believe these religious concerns to be genuine, but we have to consider the possibility that they masked worry about Sparta's ability to prevail. This is supported by Agis' surprise peace deal with Argos shortly after this, which speaks to the possibility of the Spartan king experiencing a crisis of confidence. That is certainly how the Spartan government interpreted his actions once Argos broke the truce, as evidenced by its threat of levying a stern fine and demolishing his home.

After the Spartan victory after the First Battle of Mantinea (418 BC), Argive democrats overthrew the pro-Spartan oligarchic faction in their city. Sparta, despite being in the midst of a religious festival, was willing to march to its supporters' aid. Religious reasons were suddenly valid in preventing a later expedition against Argos just prior to Athens' disastrous decision to invade Sicily.

Agis conveniently interpreted an earthquake as a reason to wave off his campaigning in Elis, and we saw King Pausanias all too happy to plunder sacred soil after being driven away from the Elean gymnasium in 401 BC.

At Cebren, Dercylidas likely used unfavorable sacrifices as an excuse to delay attack while his agents worked to betray the city from the inside. This reflects positively on him as a commander, possibly following Brasidas' example of taking positions without fighting.

Again, it is absolutely possible that Sparta did indeed act out of genuine religious conviction, but we cannot deny the inconsistent application of religious restrictions on Sparta's military actions.

Bravery Unto Death

No single quote better sums up the Bronze Lie than Demaratus' words to Xerxes, that Spartans *"must abide at their post and there conquer or die."*

For this to be true, every Spartan defeat would necessarily mean a 100 percent casualty rate, which would have had an absolutely devastating impact on Spartan manpower (far above and beyond the actual manpower crisis Sparta faced). And yet this specific aspect of Sparta's reputation, immortalized by the defeat at Thermopylae (480 BC), has persisted into modern times more than anything else we know about Spartan warriors.

The evidence shows that this reputation is entirely unearned. Thermopylae was the exception, not the rule, of Spartan conduct in battle. The sources show us Spartans fleeing, surrendering and retreating every bit as often as any other Greek city-state.

In Sparta's second recorded battle (the Battle of the Kings – 738 BC), we see King Theopompus routed and put to flight. We see another Spartan king fleeing battle just 55 years later (King Anaxander at the Battle of the Boar's Tomb – 683 BC). Incidentally, Anaxander's flight gives us some of our possible first evidence of the transition from the old "heroic" style of combat to the new phalanx warfare (as evidenced by the description of the battle, which looks like a clash of lines with the Spartan king's unit breaking and fleeing, allowing Aristomenes to roll up the Spartan line). King Anaxander seems to have made running from a fight something of a habit, and we saw him fleeing yet again during Aristomenes' cattle raid near Pharae.

Cleomenes I is reported to have invaded Athens (510 BC) as a personal project. I don't believe this. Given the expedition's disastrous outcome and Sparta's record of lying to cover up defeats (such as at the Battle of the Champions), I think it's probable the Spartan government spread the story that it was a personal effort of Cleomenes rather than have the blame for the failure fall on Sparta. But whether it was Cleomenes' pet project or not, it is one of the earliest examples of a Spartan surrender. Cleomenes was shut up and besieged on the Athenian Acropolis not by a professional army, but by an angry mob – one of the earliest examples of "people power." Cleomenes' reaction was not to dig in and conquer or die, but rather to negotiate a truce so he could safely flee the city, leaving his Athenian allies to be put to death.

We will likely never know what caused the Spartan Cnemus' army to advance out of order in his ill-fated attempt to take Acarnanian Stratus in 429 BC, allowing his troops to be defeated in detail. But we do know that

Cnemus wisely withdrew, harassed all the way by Acarnanian slingers, before arranging for a truce to collect his dead.

The Spartan Menedaeus' behavior after the Spartan defeat at Olpae (426 BC) is a particularly devastating blow to Sparta's conquer-or-die reputation. Not only did the Spartan accept a deal that would allow him to escape with his own skin intact, he deliberately sold out his allies to accomplish it. It is interesting that this particularly egregious example of cowardice receives a fraction of the attention of the more famous (and in my opinion, more dignified) Spartan surrender at Sphacteria.

Spartans did show bravery at Pylos (425 BC), deliberately wrecking their ships on rocky shores in an effort to get at Demosthenes' fortified position. But while this was certainly brave, it was also tactically unsound, as it allowed the grossly outnumbered Athenians to surround the gangplanks at the very few sandy spots where they could be put down, forcing each Spartan marine to confront three to five enemies on the shore. This foolhardy tactical choice cost the Spartans dearly, forcing them to abandon the assault without taking the fortified position or the beach.

Perhaps the bravest action of the entire assault was Brasidas' heroic charge down his own gangplank, leading his men by example, and attempting to be the first to set foot on the occupied beach. Of course, this same bravery exposed him to withering missile fire, which wounded him so badly that he barely made it a few steps before collapsing back into his ship, his shield slipping off his arm to be lost in the sea.

When the 420 Spartan hoplites were cut off on Sphacteria, Sparta did not shrug its collective shoulders and expect its stranded warriors to conquer or die. Rather, the Spartans pulled out all the stops to save them and ensure their safe return, including agreeing to serious concessions (such as the surrender of their fleet) that meant real setbacks to Sparta's position in the war. The Spartan speech to the Athenians during the brief armistice is not a proud demand for the return of their effectively captured men; rather, it is a desperate plea for mercy. Whatever value was placed on the lives of the 300 at Thermopylae, Sparta clearly valued the lives of the men on Sphacteria very highly indeed.

Sphacteria is arguably the most famous incident of Spartan surrender in the city-state's history. A total of 120 of the celebrated Peers, the beating heart of Sparta's reputation for warrior supremacy, displayed the all too human compunction to value life over legacy. Thucydides was clear that this action shocked all of Greece and resulted in a sea change in the perception of Sparta's prowess. Sparta's relationship with the world beyond its borders would be different moving forward.

Rigidity and Adaptability

There's a lot of evidence of cultural rigidity and a failure to adapt as one of Sparta's greatest military shortcomings. There's a tendency to think of the ancient battlefield as static, but nothing could be further from the truth. The ancients were military innovators, and ancient warfare was in a constant state of flux throughout the period we've examined. Think of all the changes we've seen thus far: the evolution of the archaic period *aristoi*-led warband into the hoplite phalanx, with all the social change that egalitarian formation required. The development of the Argive-grip, which gave rise to the *aspis*, which changed the face of warfare in ancient Greece and around the world. We saw the lightening of armor throughout most of the period under study, until it began to be reintroduced in concert with the new Hellenistic, pike-armed phalanx. We saw refinements in tactics by the Thebans – the increased depth of phalanx ranks to provide additional punching power, and the echelon deployment to buy that deeper phalanx time to act. We saw Iphicrates' reforms to equipment. We saw an increasing reliability on missile-armed light troops and cavalry. We saw the growing importance of naval warfare.

What we didn't see, by and large, was a Sparta eager to embrace these changes. While much of Sparta's past is shrouded in myth, one thing the evidence supports is that Sparta was a sclerotic and conservative society. The Spartans were slow to change, and in the heat of battle, this clearly cost them.

I don't want to overstate the case. Sparta could and did adapt in every arena, including in the field of arms, but in the end, it remained overly dependent on its heavy infantry capability, didn't adequately embrace the importance of combined arms, didn't expand the Peer franchise and didn't develop strong native capabilities in siege engineering, cavalry, light infantry or naval warfare.

The first example of a failure to adapt is in siegecraft. We clearly see Sparta challenged by fortified positions again and again, in war after war, with no marked improvement in its record despite numerous opportunities to learn "on the job."

Cleomenes I clearly learned from the defeat of Sparta's first anti-Athenian expedition (511 BC), noting the preparation of the ground to benefit the Thessalian cavalry. His response, to do the opposite and *add* obstacles to the battlefield, worked, and is a clear example (though also a rare one) of a Spartan commander learning from past mistakes and adapting to battlefield realities.

King Archidamus' ineffectual raiding into Attica in the Archidamian phase of the Peloponnesian Wars relied on cavalry patrols to protect the Spartan infantry from mobile and well-trained Athenian cavalry. However, these patrols were provided not by Spartans, but by Boeotians. While this may be seen as evidence of Spartan failure to sufficiently invest in cavalry during this period, it may also indicate that the Spartans realized the need for mounted support while operating on the Attic plain, and coordinated with their allies to make sure it was provided.

Archidamus showed greater adaptability in his prosecution of the siege of Plataea (430 BC). Thucydides describes Spartan ingenuity and flexibility as they engaged in a kind of leapfrog with the city's defenders, coming up with new and innovative ways to defeat each new defense as soon as the Plataeans developed it. Unfortunately for Archidamus, the defenders also showed great ingenuity and, in the end, Sparta was unable to take the city without a long siege. It accomplished it, but only after half the defenders had escaped.

At Sphacteria (425 BC), Sparta's failure to adequately invest in light troops resulted in a repeat of the defeat it had suffered at the Battle of Ithome centuries earlier. The Athenian light troops were able to shower the Spartans with missiles, then outrun the more heavily armed and armored Spartan hoplites, racing back to resume their attack the moment the Spartans gave up the chase. Spartan *ekdromoi* (runners-out) were not a sufficient answer. The Spartans would fall victim to the very same tactics at the Battle of Lecheum in 391 BC.

However, Nicias' capture of Cythera and subsequent raids on the Laconian coast forced Sparta to raise a mobile rapid reaction force of cavalry and archers which could respond quickly to the Athenian near complete freedom of movement. While this showed adaptability, Thucydides was careful to point out that the use of such a force was contrary "to their custom," which perhaps makes Sparta's willingness to do it a sign of its desperation in the face of lightning raids they were powerless to prevent.

Gylippus' leadership of the Spartan expedition to Syracuse shows both Spartan rigidity and flexibility in equal measure. Examples include his failure to appreciate the critical role of the Syracusan cavalry (like most Spartans, he likely considered mounted combat an inferior military role), which cost the Spartans dearly in the Battle Between the Walls (414 BC). However, he accepted personal responsibility for the failure, which appears to have staved off a potential morale crisis among his troops. This kind of personal reckoning was highly unusual for Spartan leaders.

Sparta's failure to grasp the criticality of combined arms in warfare and its continued viewing of cavalry as a subordinate and inferior military arm stung it yet again at the Battle of Chalcedon in 408 BC, where Alcibiades' cavalry superiority resulted in a Spartan rout, including the death of the Spartan commander Hippocrates.

Sparta's ultimate victory in the Peloponnesian Wars was certainly a result of its superiority at sea. However, the evidence doesn't show a Sparta eagerly embracing naval warfare as an equivalent arm to its land army and fostering a native capability. Rather, we see a Sparta reliant on Persian gold to fund the construction of ships and the payment of crews. Most notably toward the end of the Peloponnesian Wars, we see Spartan gold sufficient to lure rowers away from the Athenian fleet, rather than fielding Spartan crews. While this is arguably a form of adaptation, we should note that Sparta appears to have largely outsourced its naval capability, much as it outsourced its cavalry needs during the earliest campaigns into Attica. This resulted in a navy so powerful that Callicratidas felt confident enough to leave 50 ships behind to blockade Mytilene while he sailed to meet the Athenian fleet at Arginusae in 406 BC. It's worth noting that at Arginusae Callicratidas showed similar suicidal bravery to Brasidas at Pylos, with very similar results.

Agesilaus displayed some resourcefulness and ingenuity during his Asian campaign. After the cavalry skirmish near Dascylium in 395 BC, Agesilaus clearly learned from the defeat and made moves to shore up Sparta's deficiency in cavalry. He assigned rich men the obligation to provide cavalry, but allowed them to substitute an underling. He staged competitive contests in his army to improve overall fitness, with specific prizes for missile troops, and prepared markets to provide for his army on the march. He again displayed the ability to learn from his enemy during his march through Thessaly to meet up with Aristodemus' army in 394 BC, ordering his cavalry to pursue the Thessalians relentlessly, not giving them a chance to engage in harassment tactics. The tactic worked and doubtless smoothed his passage through Thessaly with fewer casualties.

The Battle of the Nemea and the Battle of Coronea that same year both displayed a significant innovation, but not by Sparta. Thebes was beginning to discover that increasing the depth of its phalanx provided enough forward momentum to break through the Spartan line. It was an innovation that Sparta would struggle and largely fail to counter in the years to come. We saw this at Coronea (394 BC), where the deeper Theban phalanx was able to penetrate the Spartan line to escape, nearly killing King Agesilaus in the process. We saw it again at Tegyra (375 BC), where the extra depth enabled Pelopidas to win a resounding victory despite being vastly outnumbered. We saw it perhaps at its most pronounced at Leuctra (371 BC), where the living spear of the Theban 50-rank phalanx punched through the defense of the Spartan royal bodyguard and claimed Cleombrotus' life as well as the Spartans' reputation as masters of hoplite battle. Cleombrotus was the first Spartan king to die in battle since Leonidas at Thermopylae, more than a century earlier.

At the Second Battle of Corcyra (373 BC), we saw the Spartans at least make an attempt to come to grips with this tactic, when the Spartan commander Mnasippus attempted a countermarch to increase the depth of his own phalanx. That this effort was bungled doesn't detract from the fact that it was made, and is a possible indicator of Spartan commanders reacting to their defeats fighting the Thebans in previous battles.

Clearly this lesson didn't stick, and we see Sparta defeated at the Second Battle of Mantinea (362 BC) by nearly identical tactics and against the same opponent it had fought at Leuctra.

As I mentioned earlier, the Battle of Lecheum (391 BC) was the fourth example of Spartan heavy infantry being defeated by the same tactic – missile-armed light infantry attacking, outrunning their more heavily armed (and thus slower) enemies, then immediately doubling back to resume their attack. We saw this same tactic used to great success at Ithome (728 BC), Sphacteria (425 BC) and the Bithynian camp (399 BC). At Lecheum, the results are even more puzzling as the Spartan cavalry elected to keep pace with the hoplites, rather than ride down the enemy light infantry. We can't know the reasons for this inexplicable decision, but we do know it signed the Spartan force's death warrant, and the resulting rout was another blow to the Spartans' reputation as disciplined military professionals, as they fled pell-mell and utterly out of order.

Sparta clearly had not developed a solid answer to the problem of dealing with an enemy with a strong missile-armed component, but we did see some examples of improvement later in its military history. Agesilaus possibly learned from Iphicrates' successful use of missile-armed light infantry occupying high ground in his ambush outside Abydus (390 BC), and repeated the same tactics against the Acarnanians the following year. Cleombrotus used similar tactics to good effect during his march to Plataea in 379 BC, though he failed to capitalize on the victory, installing Sphodrias as governor in Thespiae and marching home with so little accomplished that his own men were confused about whether or not Sparta was at war.

In the wake of Phoebidas' death and the defeat at Thespiae in 378 BC, we see a remarkable burst of Spartan adaptability – a complete reformation of the recruiting system intended not only to address the manpower crisis, but to provide troops in a range of roles, as well as reversing the current trend of deteriorating alliances by making it easier for allies to contribute according to their means.

The evidence paints a picture at odds with Sparta's legend; not superwarriors, but reasonably competent warfighters dogged by norms in their military culture that held them back. These included failure to adequately appreciate the importance of scouting and intelligence gathering, poor siegecraft and an insistence on the primacy of their hoplite corps that prevented them from adequately investing in a native cavalry, light infantry or naval capability. They were certainly badly limited by their insistence on keeping the helot population in a state of servitude, and by their refusal to extend the franchise of the Peers to a larger number of people. Finally, they were held back by the same things that hold back people in every military endeavor – greed and a desire for self-interested glory. Their celebrated military professionalism was at best inconsistent, and very likely an overblown reaction by other Greeks who weren't professional at all. Spartans surrendered, fled and negotiated like everyone else, sometimes to their advantage, and sometimes to their shame.

PART III

TANGLING MYTH
AND REALITY

IX

THE "MORON LABEL": THE SPARTANS AND THE POLITICAL FAR RIGHT

In the popular imagination, Sparta embodies the ideal of strength and tenacity for many – particularly those on the right – concerned with defense of the second amendment. One need only glance at Neville Morley's superb "Thucydides and Contemporary Politics" syllabus to see how this romance with Sparta and with Thucydides has influenced the political climate today. Within NRA groups in particular, historical figures like King Leonidas are valorized for their bellicosity and patriotic dedication.

Professor Sarah Bond, *This is Not Sparta: Why the Modern Romance with Sparta is a Bad One*

So, now we have examined Sparta's military record not comprehensively, but certainly fully enough to understand that they were not the superwarriors they are reputed to be, and not all that different from any other fallible society.

It's interesting, sure, but why does it matter? What's so bad about mythologizing the Spartans? Surely a little hero-worship never hurt anybody, right?

Wrong.

To truly understand the toxicity of the modern love-affair with the myth and not the reality of ancient Sparta, we need to examine laconophilia's long history, rooted almost as far back as Thermopylae itself.

There are at least 39 towns named Sparta in America alone, and I gave up counting the number of American and Canadian high school sports teams named "The Spartans" once I hit 100. Two National Collegiate Athletic Association (NCAA) division I teams are named "the Spartans" (Michigan State and San Jose State), a notable pop-culture marker in sports-obsessed America. But that's just scratching the surface of Sparta's grip on the popular imagination. Browse any online bookstore using the search term "Spartans" and you will be surprised (or not surprised, in my case) to find that the vast majority of the results are not works of history, but of self-help – *The Spartan Way: Eat Better, Train Better, Think Better, Be Better* crowds the listings alongside *Self Discipline: The Spartan and Special Operations Way to Mastering Yourself* and *Mental Toughness Mastery*, a book which lacks the word "Spartan" in the main title, but features the stylized Corinthian helmet made famous by *300*. Alongside these self-help tomes are inspirational volumes that at least make a nod to history, like *The Spartans – 300 Quotes, Facts, and Sayings of History's Greatest Warriors.*

The fact that these are not works of history underscores that modern audiences want the myth, not the reality, of ancient Sparta. The common theme is plain – if you want to be victorious at an athletic contest, if you want to win a fight, if you want the grit, discipline and sheer toughness to be victorious at life, you would do well to emulate the Spartans. More importantly, it's apparent that our passion for the myth of Spartan warrior supremacy is based on deeply rooted insecurity. We want to be shown the path to toughness, self-denial and combat excellence precisely because we are so intensely certain that we are lacking in these virtues.

This reverence for Sparta unfortunately does not limit itself to people looking to get in shape or make their alma mater proud. The myth of Sparta's military prowess has become a sacred symbol of the far right, embraced by groups like Greece's neo-fascist Golden Dawn, Europe's burgeoning Identitarian movement and hard-right organizations in the United States like the National Rifle Association (NRA). I was "on the job," as we say, with the New York City Police Department (NYPD) at the time I wrote *Legion Versus Phalanx*, and we received regular bulletins warning of terrorism threats inside the United States. In the wake of Charlottesville, Virginia's terrifying August 2017 "Unite the Right" rally, where Heather Heyer was run down and murdered by white supremacist James Fields and more than two dozen other people were seriously injured, hate crime watchdog group the Southern Poverty Law Center sent us a bulletin detailing the logos and symbols used by the hate groups involved.

The ancient symbology on display was impossible to miss. It included the vexillum of the Roman Republic (SPQR for *Senātus Populusque Rōmānus*, "The Senate and the People of Rome"), the ancient sun wheels of Germanic tribes, and of course the Greek lambda ("L" or "L" for "*Lacedaemōn*," as the Spartans called themselves "Lacedaemonians") falsely believed to have been painted on the Spartan shields at Thermopylae. In August of 2018, Stewart Rhodes, the founder of the right-wing anti-government and anti-immigration American militia group Oath Keepers appeared on right-wing conspiracy media outlet *Infowars* to announce the launching of "Spartan training groups" that would prepare people to defend the country against the "violent left." The group's website invoked 19th-century American philosopher Ralph Waldo Emerson's essay "Self Reliance," which exhorts readers to "*hear the whistle of a Spartan fife*" (a nod to references in both Thucydides and Plutarch that Spartans used the double-reeded oboe-like *aulos* to keep in step while marching to battle).

Rhodes' announcement is a dark spin on the Spartan symbolism that fuels the cottage industry of self-help books encouraging self-discipline. These books are benign, seeking to draw on the Spartan myth to galvanize people to self-improvement. But Rhodes' call seeks to use the myth to galvanize people to violence, and specifically to anti-immigrant violence.

The bedrock of this is also the foundation stone of Sparta's legend – the near-mythic Battle of Thermopylae in 480 BC. We've reviewed the facts of the battle in the pages of this book, but we'll put them aside for now, and look solely at the myth to see how it is put to use by groups like the Oath Keepers. The myth of Thermopylae, told in countless books and essays, and again in the 1962 hit Rudolph Maté film *The 300 Spartans*, was already in the pop-culture canon when comic book legend Frank Miller was a little boy. In a later interview, Miller admitted that watching the film *"changed the course of my creative life,"* and inspired him to write the 1998 graphic novel *300*. A smash hit, the comic won three coveted Eisner awards and caught the attention of Zack Snyder, who went on to direct a film adaptation which was released in 2006. The movie was intensely controversial, drawing a huge outcry from the Iranian government and activist community, enraged by its portrayal of their Persian ancestors. Western critics lambasted the film as well, with the *New York Post* implying that the film would have pleased Hitler, and the *Orlando Sentinel* comparing it to fascist art. Unsurprisingly, the right-wing *National Review* magazine ranked the film number 5 on its 25 Best Conservative Movies of the Last 25 Years list.

Like it or hate it, one thing couldn't be argued – *300* was a smash hit, searing the myth of Spartan prowess on the popular consciousness, where it still dominates today.

Here is the myth – Xerxes I, King of Kings, led an army of a thousand nations to conquer Greece. His army was so vast that resistance seemed futile. Yet 300 brave Spartans, professional killers who knew nothing but war, boldly sallied forth under their king Leonidas to make a stand at Thermopylae, where a mountain peak and the water's edge forced the massive Persian horde to funnel into a tight space where their numbers would count for little. Weak and effeminate, the Persians could not hope to dislodge the Spartans, who slaughtered them like cattle despite the enormous disparity in numbers. They surely would have held the pass indefinitely if not for the actions of a scurrilous traitor – Ephialtes (now the Greek word for nightmare), a misshapen hunchback who was too deformed to serve in the Spartan line. Enraged at his rejection, he led the Persians by a hidden path to his countrymen's rear, trapping them in a pincer movement. Seeing that all was lost, the Spartans refused to surrender and bravely died fighting to the last man. Their heroic example inspired the rest of Greece to resist, and was directly responsible for the eventual defeat of Persia at the Battle of Plataea the following year.

Both the comic and the 2006 film portray this myth with clearly racist and anti-immigrant overtones. *300* makes no effort to beg off its message – an inspirational paean to 300 brave, muscular, beleaguered white men valiantly holding the entry into western Europe against an invading, brown-skinned horde.

The Persians are uniformly dark-skinned and effeminate, faces painted with thick makeup, clothing and armor dripping with gold. Xerxes is depicted as an androgynous hedonist, his brooding eyes rimmed with kohl, his lips, nose and ears all pierced with gold rings linked by delicate golden chains. The scene where Ephialtes is seduced into helping the Persians takes place in Xerxes' tent, where an orgy is underway the likes of which crosses the line for carnal lust into satanism (complete with a cameo by a goatheaded man). The Spartans by contrast are uniformly white Europeans (Leonidas is played by Gerard Butler, who makes no effort to hide his Scottish accent). Hollywood puts makeup on everyone, but Snyder was at pains to conceal it on the Spartans every bit as much as he played it up on the Persians. They appear bare-chested and bare-legged, fighting in what can be charitably described as booty shorts, their bodies so chiseled that it comes as no surprise that the film launched a fitness craze bearing the Spartan name.

The year after *300* aired, Joe de Sena founded the wildly popular "Spartan" race, a series of obstacle races that have been franchised in 30 countries. Celebrated for their toughness, Spartan races are colloquially called "mud runs" as they frequently end with competitors covered in mud that they've run or crawled through while tackling varied obstacles, with activities ranging from climbing under barbed wire to throwing spears. The race's emblem, which is seen nearly everywhere the Spartans are invoked since *300* first showed in theaters, is the stylized Corinthian helmet worn by Leonidas in the film. The symbol has become a visual byword for warrior prowess, often in the face of hopeless odds. When I visited Sparta in 2019 the city was clearly still, 13 years after *300*, shamelessly cashing in on the popularity of the film. The stylized helmet was visible everywhere, most often on trinkets and t-shirts marketed for sale to foreign tourists.

That helmet is most often seen above the Greek words "ΜΟΛΩΝ ΛΑΒΕ" (*molōn labe*), which translates (roughly) to "come and take them," Leonidas' supposed words of defiance in response to Xerxes' demand that the Spartans surrender their arms.

In the 21st century, the term has become a rallying cry for "gun rights" advocates in the United States and around the world, a bellow of defiance directed at government overreach, the purported grasp of the violent left that galvanized Rhodes to found his Spartan training groups.

But long before today the phrase had already captured the imagination of would-be warriors holding what they believed were hopeless positions. We cannot be certain that Colonel John McIntosh was channeling Leonidas when the British demanded the surrender of Fort Morris on November 25, 1778, but we do know that his famous reply was "*come and take it!*" The same cry was taken up by Texian settlers 57 years later in response to the Mexican army's demand that they return a cannon they had been loaned to protect themselves from Comanche raids. The words were blazoned beneath an image of the cannon on a battle flag flown at the Battle of Gonzalez where Mexican dragoons skirmished unsuccessfully with the Texian rebels to decide the matter. That same cannon and that same phrase are blazoned above crossed meat cleavers on the flag of the American Guard – a hard right white supremacist group that evolved from the Indiana chapter of a group called the Soldiers of Odin USA, a branch of an extreme anti-immigrant and anti-refugee group that originated in Finland in 2015. Texas senator Ted Cruz has repeatedly invoked the same phrase, though whether he is invoking Gonzalez or Thermopylae, it's hard to tell. Probably, it doesn't matter. It is the motto of multiple military units, most notably the United States Special Operations Command Central (SOCCENT).

But the phrase has special currency with the National Rifle Association (NRA) and the gun-advocacy community in the United States, where it is a byword for the commitment to upholding the right to bear arms and a warning growl of the willingness to use violence to resist government overreach.

A quick search on social media will reveal the words in both English and Greek, almost always blazoned beneath the stylized Corinthian helmet, on t-shirts, key-chains, pens, bumper stickers, inlaid into gun handles, tattooed on skin, and on patch after patch after patch, usually velcroed onto tactical packs carried by military and civilian alike.

The term is so synonymous with right-wing gun-fetishism that political opponents have coined a mocking term to counter it – the "Moron Label."

But Thermopylae looms larger than just Leonidas' single (and very likely apocryphal) quote. The Greek neo-fascist party Golden Dawn gathers each year at the site of the battle, lighting torches and chanting nationalist and anti-immigrant slogans. Their spokesman Ilias Kasidiaris stated in 2012, "Those millions of illegal immigrants, racially, are the descendants of the first waves of Xerxes' army. Those wretched people, with no military value, were smashed by the wall of Spartan fighters. Now their descendants, bloodlessly, have taken over an entire country and an entire people." The invocation of the myth so clearly on display in Snyder's 2007 film – the stalwart European defenders holding back the horde of immigrant invaders – is on full display.

But Golden Dawn is far from the only hard right movement trading on the Thermopylae myth. Alleanza Nazionale, a rebranding of the fascist party Movimento Sociale Italiano after its 1995 dissolution, used images from the film in posters captioned "Defend your values, your civilization, your district." An article in March 31, 2019's Sunday edition of the UK's *Daily Mail* was titled "LAST STAND OF THE SPARTANS," depicting the heads of pro-Brexit ministers Anne-Marie Trevelyan, Steve Baker and Mark Francois superimposed onto the chiseled, armored torsos of three supposedly Spartan warriors. Thermopylae imagery was rife in the campaign imagery supporting candidate Donald Trump in his bid for the American presidency. Writing for the *Washington Post* in 2016, reporter Ishaan Tharoor pointed out that a YouTube video posted by a user under the handle "Aryan Wisdom" depicted then-candidate Trump as Leonidas, holding back an invading tide that included Soros and Obama. At the time of this writing, the video has been viewed roughly five million times. When Trump was finally elected, his advisor Steve Bannon logged into his computer with the password "Sparta" in a respectful nod to the mythic warrior legacy. In multiple violent clashes at rallies and protests, right-wing activist John Turano, the "Berserker of Berkeley," also known as "Based Spartan," famously wore a muscled cuirass and crested Corinthian helmet intended to represent the panoply worn by Spartan hoplites at Thermopylae (Turano later recanted his positions and departed right-wing activism). The French far-right white nationalist movement *Génération Identitaire* expanded into Europe, the US and Australia, where it is more commonly known as Identitarianism. Its symbol, blazoned in gold against a black background, is the circle of a hoplite's *aspis*, the round 3-foot diameter shield that was his principal piece of equipment. It is divided by the upside-down V of the Greek lambda I mentioned earlier.

Hitler himself repeatedly expressed admiration for the Spartans, though his focus was on another disputed piece of their legend – the belief that

Spartan infants were inspected by the *gerousia*, the council of Spartan elders, and if found to be deformed or sickly either exposed or flung into a chasm in the foothills of Mount Taygetus which runs to the west of the city. Eugenics were of great interest to a man obsessed with creating an ethnostate under the rulership of a master race, and he praised their *"exposure of the sick, weak, deformed children."* Hitler is also quoted as saying: *"The Spartans were once capable of such a wise measure ..."* and *"The subjugation of 350,000 Helots by 6,000 Spartans was only possible because of the racial superiority of the Spartans."* Hitler's admiration for Spartan eugenics and purported racial purity has much older roots, tracing all the way back to 19th century German scholar Karl Müller, whose *Geschichten hellenischer Stämme und Städte* includes *Die Dorier*, a history of the Dorian race believed responsible for founding the Spartan state. Müller's work lionized the invaders from the north and dovetailed first into Teutonicism, and then into the early evolution of Nordicism, the pseudo-anthropological notion of a Nordic master race, which would become the cornerstone of Nazi ideology.

To be fair to Müller, he had no control over how later thinkers would use his ideas, and he died before completing his full work, which might have presented a more even view of Greek history. Besides, Müller was hardly alone. European thinking about inherent inequality and the superiority of the Nordic race was already maturing in the fevered minds of thinkers like the French aristocrat Joseph de Gobineau, whose writings influenced the famous composer (and anti-Semite) Richard Wagner.

Some would be surprised to learn that Nordicism sprouted first in the United States before it was parroted by Nazi eugenicists like Alfred Rosenberg and Hans Günther. Most famous among these is the early 20th century writer Madison Grant, whose *The Passing of the Great Race* depicted an America strengthened by northern and western European stock, and weakened by the southern and eastern European immigration. Wildly popular in the United States, the book was instrumental in positioning Grant to influence the development of American law, including the federal Immigration Act of 1924 that prevented immigration from Asia and set quotas on immigrants from the eastern hemisphere, and Virginia's odious Racial Integrity Act of 1924 designed to prevent interracial mixing.

Grant's writings and philosophy were embraced wholesale by Nazi nordicists, and it is not the least bit surprising to see Hitler's admiration for the legend of Spartan eugenics or that he saw in their origin story of a settlement by a northern invader, the familiar tones of Nordic superiority. It's highly likely that Müller's thinking about the Dorians factored into the perspectives of all of these racial theorists and scientific racists, Nazis or otherwise.

Müller's dark spin on laconophilia was only the latest in a long tradition of Sparta-worship, nearly as old as Sparta itself. What's stunning about the Thermopylae myth and the assignment of mythic status to the Spartan warrior is how quickly it took hold. Looking at the sources, we can clearly see the myth gaining currency almost as soon as Leonidas' severed head was fixed to a pole on Xerxes' orders. As I mentioned before, historian Tom Holland has theorized that some of this was a deliberate propaganda effort by the Athenian general and politician Themistocles, known to be a master of spin, in an effort to keep up the spirits of the Hellenic League facing overwhelming odds in defying the invading Achaemenid Persians. This can't be conclusively proven with the source material available to us, but from what I know of Themistocles and Greece's position right after Thermopylae, it makes a lot of sense.

Sparta-worship expressed in fashion evokes the current "tacticool" obsession in modern culture – the worship of US Navy SEALs and other special warfare operators imitated in casual street wear. The wildly popular apparel companies Grunt Style and 5.11 Tactical have huge followings among civilians who have never served and will never serve in the military, gleefully sporting tactical gear or t-shirts invoking military catchphrases (frequently praising the Spartans). Veterans derisively refer to the trend as "Holster Kissers" or "Airsoft People," remarking on the tendency of these types to engage in Airsoft simulations, as opposed to the far less forgiving world of real combat.

I don't know that the ancient Greeks felt the same way about laconophilia, but I do know that as early as the 5th century BC, Xenophon reported the famous Athenian philosopher Socrates as wearing only a single, filthy, thin cloak, which some scholars interpret to mean he was aping the supposed Spartan fashion of wearing only their single, thin *tribōn*, left unwashed, all year round. A 1st century BC bronze from Pompeii depicting Socrates and 5th century BC philosopher Diotima shows Socrates clad in a thin cloak and leaning on a staff that some scholars say is a Spartan *bakteurion* – the T-shaped

Spartan staff carried by Spartan leaders and officials. It is, however, important to note that this artifact was produced several centuries after Socrates' death.

The 4th century BC Athenian orator Demosthenes criticized "*men who by day put on sour expressions and pretend to play the Spartan, wearing short cloaks and single-soled shoes, but when they get together and alone leave no kind of wickedness or indecency untried.*" Plato, writing his *Republic* at the turn of the 4th century BC, quotes his teacher Socrates noting that most prefer the Spartan style of government. Even the famous Aristotle, also in the 4th century BC, more critical of Sparta, admitted that its constitution produced virtuous citizens obedient to law.

In the 5th century BC Athenian comic playwright Aristophanes' *The Birds*, he notes that men "*were mad for Sparta; they wore their hair long and honored fasting, they went filthy as Socrates and carried staves.*" Xenophon, from whom we have most of the very little we know of how the Spartans governed themselves, made no secret of his intense Spartan sympathies. He opens his *Constitution of the Spartans* with these famous lines: "*One day I realized that Sparta, though among the least populated of states, was evidently the most powerful and most celebrated city in Greece; and I started wondering how this could have been. But when I considered the institutions of the Spartans, I wondered no longer.*" In addition to soldiering alongside Spartans as a mercenary in Cyrus the Younger's failed bid to take the Persian throne, Xenophon was friends with the Spartan king Agesilaus II, and wrote his biography. His sons may have been educated in the brutal Spartan *agōgē*, the "Upbringing" of Spartan youths that supposedly trained them from the age of seven for a life at war.

Sparta's legend clearly carried on despite the many loses it suffered on land and sea. Sparta declined and slid into irrelevance after its defeat by Thebes in the early 4th century BC, until it was outright mocked by Alexander the Great at the dawn of the Hellenistic age. And yet its legend clearly persisted. The turn of the 2nd century BC historian Polybius was an Achaean, the league that would eventually dominate Sparta as an ally of the Romans, and Sparta had long been in decline before he was born. Yet even Polybius wrote that if safety and security was what you were after "*there is not now nor has there ever been government better than Sparta's.*"

Long after its fall from power, Sparta remained a tourist attraction for the ancients. The famous 1st century BC Roman senator and philosopher Cicero described visiting Sparta to witness the *diamastigōsis*, a supposed ancient ritual where Spartan boys were flogged bloody, and sometimes to death, before the altar of Artemis Orthia. Supposedly in the days of Thermopylae, the ritual had been part of the regimen of the *agōgē*, toughening up the boys for their careers as Spartan hoplites, but many scholars believe that in Cicero's day it was made even more brutal to satisfy the crowds of tourists. I align with those scholars who believe the ritual was invented entirely in Roman times as a means to make money off tourists.

In the 3rd century AD, the Spartans (on behalf of the Romans) added an amphitheater to better accommodate the crowds who came to watch. Xenophon and the 2nd century AD Greek geographer Pausanias give different accounts of the ritual, with Xenophon stating that the Spartan boys had to run a gauntlet of whips to steal cheese off the altar, and Pausanias simply having them whipped there while a priestess of Artemis considered whether the weight of a wooden statue of the goddess she held indicated that the goddess demanded more blood. Some scholars (with whom I agree) believe the two writers are describing *different* rituals, with the static whipping of Pausanias' story being a Roman invention designed to appeal to paying crowds.

Throughout the Roman period, the supposedly wealth-hating and xenophobic Spartans engaged in the usual methods that tourist economies employ to attract foreigners and separate them from their money – hosting fairs, creating tax-exemptions to attract foreign merchants, encouraging commerce however they could. As I noted earlier, they still do today.

Laconophilia marched on throughout western arts and letters, and always on the same theme – worshipping at the altar of the Spartans' legendary self-denial, restraint and devotion to duty. The turn of the 3rd century AD Egyptian Christian apologist Origen Adamantius compared Leonidas' self-sacrifice at Thermopylae to Christ's passion. Synesius of Cyrene, a Christian bishop in the 5th century AD, proudly (and falsely) traced his lineage to the Spartan royal houses, hardly a sign of being ashamed of Sparta.

The turn of the 15th century Italian travel writer Ciriaco de' Pizzicolli rhapsodized about Leonidas in his travelogue. Even the famous Machiavelli got in on the act, praising Sparta in his *Discourses on Livy*. While critical at times, the father of modern political science notes with admiration that

"That republic, indeed, may be called happy, whose lot has been to have a founder so prudent as to provide for it laws under which it can continue to live securely, without need to amend them; as we find Sparta preserving hers for eight hundred years, without deterioration and without any dangerous disturbance." Machiavelli's Scottish contemporary George Buchanan favorably compared the self-restraint of Spartan kings to the hedonism of the monarchs of his own time. John Alymer, the Bishop of London in Buchanan's time, wrote that *"Lacedaemonia [meaning Sparta], [was] the noblest and best city governed that ever was."*

But perhaps the greatest summary of western Renaissance attitudes toward Sparta is captured in Michel de Montaigne's *Of Cannibals*, which performs the astonishing mental gymnastics necessary to hold the defeat of Thermopylae higher than the victories that actually pushed the Persians out of Greece: *"There are defeats more triumphant than victories. Never could those four sister victories, the fairest the sun ever beheld, of Salamis, Plataea, Mycale, and Sicily, venture to oppose all their united glories, to the single glory of the discomfiture of King Leonidas and his men, at the pass of Thermopylae."*

Fast-forwarding to the 18th century AD, we see laconophilia (or, at least, Leonidasophilia) alive and well in the lengthy and overblown poetry of English politician Richard Glover, whose poem *Leonidas* goes on and on:

> *All on the great Leonidas unite,*
> *Long known his country's refuge. He alone*
> *Remains unshaken. Rising, he displays*
> *His godlike presence. Dignity and grace*
> *Adorn his frame, and manly beauty join'd*
> *With strength Herculean. On his aspect shines*
> *Sublimest virtue, and desire of fame,*
> *Where justice gives the laurel; in his eye*
> *The inextinguishable spark, which fires*
> *The souls of patriots: while his brow supports*
> *Undaunted valour, and contempt of death.*

No less than the American founding father Samuel Adams lamented that his native Boston would never be the "Christian Sparta" he had hoped it would.

Fellow founding father John Dickenson described the Spartans as "*as brave and free a people as ever existed.*"

Other founding fathers were less enamored. John Adams wrote "*The institution of Lycurgus was well calculated to preserve the independence of his country, but had no regard to its happiness, and very little to its liberty ... civil liberty of it was little better than that of a man chained in a dungeon; ... The influence of this boasted legislation ... was to produce warriors and politicians, and nothing else.*" Alexander Hamilton described Sparta a "*little better than a well regulated camp,*" and George Washington lambasted "*the rule of military monks.*"

Samuel Adams' contemporary, the legendary Swiss thinker Jean Jacques Rousseau, practically drooled over Sparta's myth, praising "*that city as famous for its happy ignorance as for the wisdom of its laws, whose virtues seemed so much greater than those of men that it was a Republic of demi-gods rather than of men.*"

This just skims the surface, miles wide and fathoms deep, of the legions of historical thinkers and writers in love, not with the *history* of Sparta, which is based on a lack of good sources and is difficult to grasp, but on the *legend* of Sparta, which is clearly a fundamental element of modern European and American culture. Most people have never heard of laconophilia, even as they live in a world so dramatically shaped by it, as is so often the way with root-level cultural mores. When something is as common as the grass, it's easy to forget it's there. Belief in Sparta's legend has shaped everything from the French Revolution to the British educational system to the Ivy League colleges of America to the Israeli Kibbutz movement. The *idea* of who the Spartans were, and most importantly how they fought, is at the core of so much of who we are in America and Europe.

This isn't surprising, for the Spartans left no written record of what they thought of themselves, or anyone else for that matter. For the perspective of native Spartans, we have only a few scattered fragments of poetry (and one of those poets, Sparta's cultural cornerstone Tyrtaeus, may have been Athenian. Another, Alcman, may have been born in Lydia on the coast of what is now Turkey). Plutarch tells us that one of the Spartan "Rhetras" (the Spartan charter or foundation documents, purportedly handed down to the state's founding father Lycurgus from the Delphic oracle) specifically forbade writing down any of the laws, so that the citizens would be forced to know them by heart. The Spartans were at their core secretive about their government and xenophobic, so much so that the 5th century BC Athenian general and historian Thucydides judged it impossible to reckon the size of Spartan armies *"due to the secrecy of their government."* Plutarch notes that Spartans were forbidden from traveling outside Sparta in the time of Lycurgus to prevent them from being corrupted by foreign influence. Further, Lycurgus *"drove away from the city the many which poured in for no useful purpose, not because he worried they might imitate his form of government and learn useful lessons in virtue, as Thucydides says, but rather that they might not become in any way teachers of evil."*

Reading this, it's not surprising to see anti-immigrant political movements lionizing the Spartans. Herodotus tells us the story of Gorgo, the daughter of the Spartan king Cleomenes I (and the eventual wife of the famous Leonidas) warning her father not to listen to the words of the Ionian Aristagoras when the latter came to Sparta to plead for help in the Ionian people's efforts to throw off the yoke of Persian rule: "Father, take care. The foreigner will corrupt you." Spartan custom even supposedly forbade fighting the same enemy too many times, lest they learn to imitate Spartan tactics.

So it is not surprising to find so many outsiders worshipping the *myth* of Sparta, rather than the reality of a people who clearly wanted above all to be mysterious. This leaves us with the daunting task of trying to penetrate the Spartan Mirage, to try to see through the propaganda and enormous gaps in the literary and material record and try to answer the question, who *were* the Spartans, really?

But as we've seen in the preceding pages, the Spartans were people – like the Persians, like the Athenians, like the Thebans, like all of us. To appreciate their warrior legacy, to honor it and be inspired by it, we are so much better served by trying to see it clearly. In honestly embracing a fallible people in their effort to be extraordinary, we can defuse the toxic image that political extremists hold up – superwarriors too perfect for any one of us to identify with. It is a myth proven not just misleading, but dangerous, and one that robs us of the chance to truly connect with one of the most fascinating military endeavors in human history.

We do not need a bronze lie to be enthralled by Sparta.

The beating, human heart of the truth is more than enough.

APPENDIX A: HISTORIOGRAPHY AND OBJECTIVITY

Historiography

Historiography is the study of the study of history. It examines how we research, analyze and write history. This is a book about ancient warfare, and not historiography, so I won't delve too deeply into this topic, but there are some points that need to be made if we're going to understand how we use primary sources and how they affect the stories we tell.

If we're going to learn how to drive a car, we need to know at least some basics about how the engine runs. This is important because it helps us diagnose cause and effect while we drive. Car dragging to the left after a big boom? We probably blew out a tire. We don't just trust our senses (the boom, the dragging). We rely on our knowledge of how the mechanism works.

The same is true with history. It's critical to take time to study the discipline itself, to understand who the sources are and what their agendas are. Where are they getting their information? What cultural influences and personal goals are affecting the stories they tell?

In today's politically volatile environment, the charge of "fake news" is constantly hurled. We have started to read even the most reputable news sources with a critical eye. What is this TV anchor's agenda? Why are they telling the story they are? This is unsettling, because it makes it difficult to trust, but it is good training for the historian. We must also be on a constant lookout for "fake news" when we examine the sources. We must be skeptical of what the ancient writers say, and what the ancient artists portray.

Objectivity

Because ancient writers and artists *did* have agendas. History in the ancient world was designed to entertain as much as it was designed to educate, and many writers were more than happy to fudge or even invent facts in an effort to make a better dramatic narrative. The turn of the 1st century AD Roman historian Titus Livius, better known as "Livy," is a great example of this tendency to dramatize.

Much art and literature in the ancient world was patronized in some way, which is to say that it was made to please a specific client. In many cases the writer had a cultural or historical perspective they wanted to advance, or had to advance, if they wanted to keep their head attached to their body.

Livy wrote during the reign of Augustus, who had ascended to power after a vicious civil war and was in the process of a delicate dance wherein he established himself as an emperor in fact but not in name. Would publishing a history of Rome praising the old republican system offend the new master of Rome? Would Livy be punished for taking this view? How might this affect his writing? Polybius was a Greek kept as a hostage in Rome. He probably had fierce pride in his Greek heritage, but also knew he had to please his Roman captors. Unlike Livy, he was a soldier who had experienced battle first hand. This also gave him a stake in how military legacy is portrayed. He was a client of the Aemilii family, who had a prominent role in the historical events he wrote about. How did these complicated and diverse elements affect Polybius' view of the same events?

The idea that historians should write what is true above all else, that they should be impartial, certainly existed in the ancient world (we see contemporary sources talk about this very thing), but it has been refined and gained greater acceptance in the modern day. As we study history, we have to remember that many ancient sources weren't trying to be objective. It's up to us to interpret their stories carefully, checking sources against one another, checking written sources against material sources, and applying our own experiences to what we read. In examining sources, historians have to be skeptical detectives.

The Importance of "I Don't Know"

Ancient history is either a really tough field, or a really easy one, depending on how you look at it. The further back you go in time, the less survives, particularly writing. At the time this book is published, we'll be going back nearly 3,000 years at the most. This is good if you're a completist. Ancient history sometimes appeals to collector-types (I freely admit to being one), because it's possible to read literally all the primary source material we know of on a particular topic. On the other hand, when you're done, you're done. You can supplement this with material records from archaeology, such as pottery, masonry, paintings, and arms and armor. You can also consider other scientific evidence, like geography, weather, physics and psychology, but, once again, a period of 3,000 years puts a lot of wear and tear on even the toughest materials, including the ground itself. So you run out of historical source material more quickly than you'd like. I'd wager that everyone studying ancient history has felt the scholarly equivalent of Oliver Twist asking for more food. Even if you haven't read your Dickens, you probably know that sometimes there just isn't any more.

And after that, it's all analysis. This is the historian's job, to take this meager record and bang it around in our heads until meaning falls out of it. But the truth is that there are many questions that we will never be able to conclusively answer. We can get close, to be sure, but not to the level of certainty that we'd like. Because time has marched on, and there is no additional data. We can't interview warriors two millennia in their graves. We can't triple-check our sources' sources, when the sources they were referencing are lost. We're ready to be pleasantly surprised if new material should be discovered, but we're not holding our collective breath.

So we guess. That's right, we are *guessing* at a lot of the details we proclaim so confidently in the pages of books like these. There are heated and ongoing debates surrounding every aspect of ancient warfare. Did hoplites appear suddenly or evolve gradually? Is there a distinctly "western" way of warfare that originated with the phalanx? How did the Roman battle line deploy exactly? Could the *quincunx* (checkerboard) formation really have worked, as more than one contemporary source attests?

The only correct answer is, "I don't know." We often engage in passionate scholarly debates with an air of certainty that makes little sense. Educated guesses remain just that, guesses. I have done my best here to make liberal use of the words "probably" and "possibly" as I make my case. I enjoy the freedom to let my imagination run wild, and I love the detective work of history, which is the act of taming that imagination and securing it as tightly to the few facts we have as possible.

But it remains critical that we are just as careful to admit what we don't know as often as we present what we do. It sets an honest backdrop for the story to come, because the truth is that the little we *do* know about warfare in the ancient world is amazing.

APPENDIX B: THE FUNDAMENTALS OF ANCIENT BATTLE

There are some basic concepts that are almost universal across all ancient battles, and begin to solidify during the classical period (in the 5th century BC) as warfare became more organized. In order to properly understand the breakdowns of the battles in this book, it's important to understand these fundamentals. Any officer, commissioned or noncommissioned, will have learned these basics in academy, and most wargamers pick them up as they simulate battles and see them play out on the tabletop. But for those of you who are neither wargamers, nor prior service members, we'll review them here. Please keep in mind that this is grossly oversimplified, and deliberately so, as I'm trying to convey basic ideas to the reader as efficiently and simply as possible.

Before we launch into this, I want to make sure that readers understand the terms "rank" and "file," as they're used frequently throughout the book. Most readers are probably familiar with the terms but, just to be sure, files refer to lines of soldiers arranged from front to back of a formation. Ranks refers to the lines from side to side. So a single line of eight men standing one behind the other would be a single file with eight ranks. A line of the same men standing shoulder to shoulder would be eight files and only one rank.

The Battle Line, Frontage and Flanking Maneuvers

Ancient battles usually revolved around battle lines. A battle line is exactly what it sounds like – a bunch of soldiers or warriors all lined up, more or less shoulder to shoulder, usually laterally, providing as much "frontage," or left-to-right distance, as possible.

More frontage is good, because this increases the chance of an "envelopment" or preferably a "double-envelopment." An envelopment occurs when a battle line overlaps the enemy's, allowing your line to curl around it and attack your opponent's line from both the front and the side, which is commonly called the "flank" by both modern militaries and military historians. This envelopment, and the striking of the enemy's battle line from the flank, is commonly called "outflanking" or "turning a flank." A double-envelopment occurs when your line overlaps the enemy on both flanks, allowing you to curl in around both sides of the enemy line at once, as the famous Carthaginian general Hannibal Barca did at the Battle of Cannae in 216 BC.

Troop Types – Heavy Infantry, Light Infantry and Cavalry

Battle lines are almost always composed of "heavy infantry." This term is used to mean different things, sometimes referring to the weight of the soldiers' weapons and armor, and sometimes referring to the tightness of their formation. A Greek or Hellenistic (Hellenistic refers to the cultural descendants of the Greeks, such as the Macedonians and the successors of Alexander the Great) phalanx, a Roman legion, a Celtic warband, a line of Persian levy spearmen, are all examples of heavy infantry in a battle line. The heavy infantryman's primary job was close or "shock" combat, fighting with hand weapons like swords or spears, toe to toe with the enemy.

The battle lines would line up facing one another, and then close to clash together. The opposing forces usually had one of three goals:

1. To break through the enemy line, causing it to collapse.
2. To outflank the enemy line and attack the enemy from two directions at once.

3. To get units *behind* the enemy's battle line, said to be in the enemy's rear or "backfield," and attack the enemy units from the rear.

The benefits of flanking and rear attacks are plain. If you only have to worry about the enemy in front of you, you can focus your full attention on that enemy. This is why battle lines are so strong everywhere but the flanks. If you have a friendly soldier to either side of you, your flanks are covered, and all you have to do is deal with the enemy straight ahead. If you have a shield, you only have to cover your front, and all your attacks will be in one direction. If you have an enemy on your front *and* your flank, you're in trouble. Now, you have to fight in two directions at once. You move your shield to defend against a spear thrust coming from the enemy in front of you, and the enemy to your flank has an open shot at your ribs. You shift your shield to cover your ribs, and the enemy in front of you puts his sword through your face. Being attacked from the *rear* is a veritable death sentence, since you can't defend at all, and turning to face the enemy to your rear necessarily exposes your rear to the enemy who was previously to your front. In this instance, the only hope you have is your armor.

So covering the flanks, and therefore the rear, of the battle line was critical. Many generals used terrain, anchoring the flanks of their battle lines on marsh, or mountains, or deep rivers. The idea was that the enemy couldn't turn a flank, because he couldn't pass the terrain to do it. But, assuming that terrain wasn't available, ancient generals usually stationed troops on the flanks who had the double role of both protecting their battle line from envelopment, and also turning the enemy battle line's flank if they could.

This job was most often performed by cavalry, whose speed made them ideally suited for the task. Let's say you defeat your enemy's flank guard and now have an opportunity to get into their backfield to attack their units from the rear. You want to be able to get there as quickly as possible, to put your enemy in the pinch where they are attacked from both front and rear before they can do the same to you. Mounted troops are ideal for this work. Because they are the fastest troops on the field, they can also take the lead in running down "routing" troops. Routing troops are running away with no effort to keep fighting, as opposed to "retreating," which means you are leaving the battle in good order, fighting as you go.

Another troop type was commonly seen in ancient battles – light infantry, sometimes referred to as "skirmishers." These troops usually fought in dispersed order. Think of a cloud of gnats or a school of minnows. This formation is very different from the shoulder-to-shoulder ordered ranks of the heavy infantry described above. Skirmishers were usually lightly armored, and in many cases had no armor at all. They were often armed with missile weapons, such as the javelin, the sling or the bow. Heavy infantry moved more slowly, both on account of their equipment and because of their need to keep in formation or else risk the flank and rear attacks I just described. More often than not, heavy infantry had no missile weapons of their own, which made them vulnerable to skirmishers, who could run up, shower them with missile fire, then run away before the heavy infantry could charge them. Not all light infantry were skirmishers, and not all heavy infantry lacked missile weapons (most notably, the Roman legionary), but the distinction between heavy and light infantry and their respective shock and missile delivery roles was the general rule on ancient battlefields.

Of course, skirmishers were vulnerable to cavalry, who could easily catch them, and often were armed with missiles themselves (usually javelins), but if the cavalry stopped to fight hand to hand with skirmishers, they in turn would be vulnerable to being charged by the heavy infantry.

Skirmishers usually deployed out in front of the battle line, and their main role was to "soften up" the enemy battle line with missile fire, causing wounds, deaths and damage to equipment that would impair the enemy's ability to fight in the close combat to come when the battle lines clashed. When that clash appeared imminent, the skirmishers would "retire" either by rushing back through the ranks of the heavy infantry (who would open to admit them), or rushing around the flanks of their own battle line to get out of the way.

Unit Cohesion and Morale

Two more things to note here: "cohesion," the ability of military formations to *stay* in formation even when they're moving and fighting, is critical to this sort of combat. Since each soldier in a formation protects the flanks of the soldiers next to them, if the cohesion of a battle line fails, individual soldiers suddenly become susceptible to flank and rear attacks. Keeping cohesion was a constant challenge when you consider that most ancient formations consisted of thousands of people. Everything, from marching straight ahead, to backing up, to inclining or "wheeling" or something as simple as opening up enough to let the retiring skirmishers through risked the spread of disorder, creating gaps in the line as some soldiers marched more slowly than others, or stumbled, or bumped into the men around them. This disorder could lead to exposure to flank and rear attacks, and sow confusion in the ranks. And it was all complicated by the lack of advanced communications technology such as radio or loudspeakers, and with many of the soldiers wearing helmets that made it hard to hear. Relaying commands that might help control disorder was very difficult. Ancient battles were, at their heart, attempts to control chaos. The legion and the phalanx, like all military formations, were an effort to provide this control, ordering soldiers for mutual defense, to make the best use of their particular equipment, and to instill the heart and discipline necessary to keep it together in the midst of the nightmare of battle.

Confusion in the ranks lowered morale, which is the pivotal element in ancient battles. The vast majority of casualties in any ancient battle did not occur during the fighting, but during the rout, when one side's nerve broke and it abandoned any semblance of cohesion for a full-scale flight, with every man for himself, trying to escape with his life.

Bringing the enemy to this panic point was the primary goal of most ancient generals. Many factors play into morale: training, unit pride and *esprit de corps*, quality of equipment, physical health, rest and food, the inspiration of leaders and the belief in a just cause. In tight formations and on battlefields where communication was spotty and difficult and with most of the soldiery deeply superstitious, panic was a constant risk. The sight of one unit fleeing might indicate a tiny setback in one limited portion of the battlefield, or it might mean the defeat of the entire army, and it was up to the individual soldier to judge, moment to moment, whether it was worth it to stay in the fight or to look to his own life.

Even today, the critical importance of standing firm in the face of the enemy is underscored by Article 85 of the Uniform Code of Military Justice, the system of law that governs military members in the United States. Anyone who "... quits his unit, organization, or place of duty with intent to avoid hazardous duty or to shirk important service" may be punished under the article.

The penalty, in time of war, is death.

GLOSSARY

Achaemenid
term used to describe the ancient Iranian empire that spanned from 553 BC to its final conquest by Alexander the Great in 330 BC. Also called the Achaemenid Persians or Achaemenids.

agelai
"packs." Unit of organization for boys enrolled in the Upbringing.

Agiad
one of ancient Sparta's two royal houses.

agōgē
"Upbringing." The purportedly (and almost certainly mythically) brutal system of training Spartan boys for a lifetime at war.

akinakēs
a light, straight-bladed long knife popular with Persian troops.

Apple Bearers
a 1,000-strong elite unit of Achaemenid Persian heavy infantry, who possibly served as a direct bodyguard to the king. So-named because of the golden "apples" counterbalancing their spears. Scholars debate whether this unit was separate from or part of the Immortals.

archōn
"leader." A chief magistrate of an ancient Greek city-state.

antilabē
a loop, sometimes of leather or cloth, on the edge of the *aspis* gripped normally by the left hand.

Argive grip	the dual-point grip system used in the *aspis* and consisting of the *porpax* (holding on the forearm near the elbow), and the *antilabē* (held by the hand).
aristoi	noblemen in ancient Greece.
aspis	one of the hoplite's main pieces of equipment. A deeply convex, round shield roughly three feet in diameter with an offset rim that could be used to hang the weight of it on the hoplite's shoulder. Made of wood and sometimes faced with bronze, and held with an "Argive grip."
aulos	a dual-piped ancient wind instrument. Sounds a bit like an oboe.
barbarian	one who does not speak Greek. Literally means "they don't speak Greek. Everything they say just sounds like 'bar bar bar.'"
boeotarch	a chief officer and general of the Boeotian League.
brasideioi	"Brasidas' people." Seven hundred helots equipped as hoplites and placed under the command of the Spartan hero Brasidas. Freedom was to be their reward for faithful service.
Carneia	a major festival held in honor of Apollo's aspect as god of herds (*Carneus*). The most important of Sparta's religious festivals.
chalkaspides	"Bronze Shields." A corp of heavy infantry within a Hellenistic phalanx.
crypteia	"Secret Squad." An elite training cadre whose role isn't fully known, but purportedly included surveilling and brutalizing the helots.
cuirass	complete body armor (breast and backplates or their equivalent).
diekplous	"rowing through and past." An ancient naval maneuver consisting of moving past an enemy ship (hopefully shearing off their oars in the process), then cutting hard in to ram them in the quarter or stern.

Dorians	a major ethnic group of ancient Greece, distinguished by their Doric dialect.
dory	a roughly 7–9 foot thrusting spear with a leaf-shaped iron head and a bronze butt spike called a *saurōtēr*. Usually made of ash. It is sometimes called a *doru*.
eirēn	prefect. Supervisor and instructor of youths enrolled in the Upbringing.
ekdromoi	"runners out." Younger, fitter hoplites who would exit the phalanx to run down light infantry.
eparitoi	an elite and specially selected body of Arcadian troops.
ephors	collectively referred to as the "Ephorate." "Guardians" – five Spartans elected for a single year and forbidden to hold the office more than once, serving as chief executives of the state, with powers to check the dual kings.
epiteichisma	a fortress in enemy territory.
enōmotarchoi	officers in charge of the *enōmotiai*.
enōmotiai	"sworn bands." While the exact size is uncertain, we're reasonably sure this was the tactical unit of maneuver in the Spartan army.
epistoleus	secretary.
erastēs	the senior partner, usually an adult, in an ancient Greek pederastic relationship.
erōmenos	the junior partner, usually an adolescent boy, in an ancient Greek pederastic relationship.
Eurypontid	one of ancient Sparta's two royal houses.
Great Rhetra	the purported constitution of the ancient Spartans. It was supposedly never written down, and transmitted only orally.
greaves	combination knee and shin armor.
gerōn	elder. A Spartan aged 60 or older and exempt from military service.
gerousia	the Spartan council of elders, which consisted of 28 men over the age of 60, each elected to the office for life.

guest friendship	a formal and ritualized alliance between two individuals in the ancient world that included mutual obligations of hospitality and also material and political support.
harmost	a Spartan military governor.
hēbōn	a Spartan youth of 18–20 years of age enrolled in the Upbringing.
helots	Sparta's slave caste.
Heraclids	the purported descendants of the mythical demigod Heracles.
hippeis	"cavalry." An elite corps of 300 infantry (despite the name) chosen from the the *hebontes*. One of their possible roles was as a royal bodyguard to the kings.
hoplite	pronounced "hop-light." The anglicized version of the Greek *hoplitēs*, which is pronounced "hoplee-tays." Literally "the man with the war gear." The dominant heavy infantryman of ancient Greece. Minimally equipped with the *aspis* shield and the *dory* spear, the full *hopla* (panoply) could include body armor, greaves, a helmet, and a sword.
hippagretai	men appointed by the ephors to select the *hippeis*.
homoioi	"peers" or "similars," the term *Spartiatai* used to refer to one another.
hoplitodromos	"Hoplite's Run." An armored foot race.
Hyacinthia	the second most important of Sparta's festivals, celebrated in the village of Amyclae to commemorate the death of Hyacinthus.
hypomeiones	"Inferiors." A poorly understood status that saw a Spartan as less than a *Spartiate*, but still possibly able to fight in the army.
Immortals	a 10,000-strong elite Achaemenid Persian heavy infantry unit which served as both a tactical unit and a palace guard.
kopis	a short, cleaver-like sword, sharp only on one side.
klēros	a land allotment.

Lacedaemon	ancient Sparta.
laconophilia	a love of all things Spartan.
laphyropouloi	Spartan officials in charge of selling war booty.
leukaspides	"White Shields." A corps of heavy infantry within a Hellenistic phalanx.
lochagoi	officers in charge of the *lochoi*.
lochoi	"ambushes." A unit of organization in the Spartan army.
metics	resident aliens in ancient Greek city-states.
mina	a weight of silver equal to around 100 drachmas.
mora	"division." A unit of the Spartan army, probably counting both infantry and cavalry.
mothax	"stepbrother." A free but impoverished Spartan inferior who was sponsored by the family of a Peer as a path back to that status.
myriad	10,000 troops.
navarchos	admiral.
neodamōdeis	"New People." Helots liberated in exchange for military service.
obol	an ancient Greek coin.
obai	"villages." Units of organization in the Spartan army.
oikos	"household." A broad term that can refer to either a family, the family's domains and properties, or the physical house itself.
oliganthrōpia	Sparta's accelerating manpower crisis, as fewer and fewer Peers degraded the strength of its army.
ōthismos	the mass-shoving match between two phalanxes in shield-to-shield contact. It continued until one of the phalanxes broke and the rout and pursuit began.
paean	a song/hymn of triumph sometimes sung as a war cry.
paideia	"education." Another term used to describe the rearing of Spartan children (as opposed to *agōgē*), used by Xenophon.
paidiskos	an older boy enrolled in the Upbringing.
paidonomos	"boy herder." A supervisor or boys in the Upbringing.

pais	"boy." The rank held when a Spartan child was first enrolled in the Upbringing.
partheniai	"sons of virgins." A caste of ancient Spartan who left the city-state and founded the colony of Taras (modern Tarento) in southern Italy. Their exact status is disputed, but one theory has it that they were the bastard sons of Spartan wives cheating on their husbands away fighting in the Messenian Wars.
peltasts	anglicization of *peltastai* – "Men who bear the small shield." Technically refers to any warrior bearing the *peltē* small shield. However it usually refers to specialist light infantry, often armed with javelins.
peltē	a small shield, sometimes crescent-shaped and sometimes round, made from wicker or wood.
pentēkosty	"band of 50." A unit of the Spartan army whose size we're not sure of (despite the name).
pentēkonter	a ship rowed by a single bank of 50 oars.
pentēkonteres	officers in charge of the *pentēkostyes*.
perioikoi	"people who live around." Second-class but free subjects of Sparta who likely fought in the army and handled much of the artisanal work required by the city-state.
pezhetairoi	"foot companions (of the king)." Armed with long (18–21 foot) pikes wielded in both hands, and with smaller shields slung about the neck.
polemarch	anglicization of *polemarchos*. "War leader." A senior military title in ancient Greece.
phalanx	the dominant heavy infantry formation in ancient Greece across the Classical and Hellenistic ages. It consisted of a line of men, more or less shoulder to shoulder, with shields overlapping, and spears pointing forward. In the Hellenistic age, when pike-armed troops wielded their weapons with both hands, smaller shields were slung from the neck and no longer overlapped.

polis	the ancient Greek city-state.
porpax	a loop, sometimes of bronze, in the center of the *aspis* through which the hoplite would thrust his arm up the elbow.
pilos	a pattern of helmet. Conical and covering only the top and back of the head.
promachoi	"those who fight out in front." In the archaic period, warriors who fought as individual heroes out in front of the warband. In the classical period, the first hoplite in the file.
psiloi	a general term for light infantry, usually missile-capable.
Pythia	the oracle of the god Apollo at Delphi, empowered to speak with the voice of the god to predict the future.
refusing a flank	a military term meaning that a flank/wing of the army is held farther back from the enemy's line, angling toward the rear. Such a flank is said to be "refused."
sally port	a door in a fortification wall that defenders can use to rush out to the attack.
satrap	the Achaemenid title for a provincial governor.
saurōtēr	literally "lizard killer." A bronze butt spike attached to a *dory*. Probably killed more people than lizards. Useful for sticking the weapon straight up in the ground, stabbing down at an opponent, or using as a backup spearhead if the main head snapped off.
spara	a Persian shield, usually rectangular and of wicker construction.
sparabara	"shield bearer." A warrior in Persian service, usually carrying a spear and the *spara* shield.
Spartiate	a fully enfranchised Spartan citizen.
Sciritae	a mountain people subject to Sparta on the northern border with Arcadia. Occupied a special role in the army.
stratēgos	general.

syskēnia	"tent group." Xenophon's term for the communal mess.
syssition	the communal dining mess that purportedly formed the center of Spartan military life and was a key component of the citizenship franchise.
thētes	the lowest social class of free Athenian citizens.
thureophoroi	infantry wielding the *thureos* shield – an oblong shield with a central reinforcing spine and held in the center by a handle behind a metal boss.
tiara	a cloth hood with a drape to cover the face.
triakontēr	a small ship of 30 oars.
trireme	an ancient ship rowed by three banks of oars.
xenagoi	officers in charge or foreign troops.
xiphos	a short, leaf-bladed sword.

BIBLIOGRAPHY

Wargames

Tabletop and computer wargaming isn't just fun, it's a great way to both tactically and strategically model the military thinking and outcomes of ancient battles. Of course, any gaming model is inherently flawed. Sacrifices in historical accuracy are constantly made to improve playability, and all gaming systems turn on mathematical logic that just doesn't exist in the organic and chaotic environment of actual combat. Players should take wargames with a heavy grain of salt, and always accompany them with other source material (preferably reading the ancient sources!), but wargames also shouldn't be ignored. What would have happened if Leonidas and the Greeks hadn't advanced into the wide space of the pass at Thermopylae? What would have happened if Pausanias had taken up the Persian offer of a mass duel at Plataea? These are the kinds of questions that wargames can help us to ask and answer.

I highly recommend that readers examine the online board gaming resource boardgamegeek.com to see the full range of historical wargames available, but my personal favorites (offering a strong balance between historical accuracy and playability) are:

- The Great Battles of History (GBoH) series by GMT Games.
- The Fields of Glory (FoG) series by Osprey Publishing on the tabletop and FOG II on the PC.

- The "little blue book" series of wargames from Osprey. *Men of Bronze* is a great place to start.

Experimental Archaeology (Reenactment)

I am constantly making the argument that it is really impossible to truly grasp the internality of ancient combat unless you actually *do* it. Of course, we can't actually fight and harm one another in AD 2021, but there are reenactment groups all over the world that will allow you to put on the armor, stand in the phalanx, engage in the charges, withdrawals and other maneuvers, and generally experience the intense reality of the events we've described in this book – from the weight of the armor and how/where it rubs and chafes, to the overheating you experience wearing it in the hot sun, to the difficulty seeing and hearing (and thus executing maneuvers in formation).

Unfortunately, Greek hoplite reenactment societies are far fewer and less well funded than Roman legionary ones, but a quick Google search will turn up options (if any) in your area. If there aren't any in your area, many groups are happy to have an online relationship with you, and then invite you out for reenactment events when they occur annually. For those readers who are lucky enough to be able to contact these groups and join them locally, I cannot recommend enough picking up shield and spear and feeling these things for yourself. I guarantee it will deepen your understanding of how the ancient Greeks fought.

Ancient Sources

Primary sources (accounts written by those who lived during or close to the events they are describing) are always your best bet to understanding the reality of what happened. Objectivity and analytical standards differed in the ancient world, and I discussed some of the challenges you'll face in interpreting the ancient sources in Appendix A. That said, I strongly encourage those interested in reading further to always consider primary sources *before* you consider secondary ones (those written by modern scholars). A secondary source is always a modern person's *interpretation* of the source material, and I believe you're much better off reading the original texts and reaching your own conclusions.

Of course not everyone has Latin or Greek, but that's no problem. Pretty much all the ancient sources are available online, free to read, and already translated into modern English. A quick Google search will turn up lots of options, but my favorite is the Perseus Digital Library offered by Tufts University. Not only does it have pretty much all the sources available in translation, it has lots of helpful notes, and you can even load the original Latin and Greek if you have some reading ability in those languages and want to read in the original! The tool even links to the standard lexicon, the Liddell-Scott-Jones (LSJ) for those who need a little extra help. All of it is available free, but I certainly hope you'll consider donating to Tufts to support the project.

Historians and philologists can quibble endlessly about which translations are best, so I will just provide a list of sources below and encourage you to find a translation that works for you.

Aeneas Tacticus – *How to Survive a Siege*
Aeschines – *Speeches*
Aeschylus – *Complete Plays*
Alcaeus of Mytilene – *Fragments*
Alcman – *Fragments*
Andocides – *On Peace with Sparta, On his Return, On the Mysteries, Against Alcibiades*
Anon – P (*Hellenica Oxyrhynchia*)
Archilochus – *Poems*
Aristophanes – *Acharnians, Birds*
Aristotle – *Constitution of the Athenians, Nicomachean Ethics, Politics*
Arrian of Nicomedia – *Anabasis of Alexander, Ars Tactica*
Athenaeus of Naucratis – *Dinner Table Philosophers*
Callinus – *Elegiac Poems*
Claudius Aelianus – *Various History*
Cornelius Nepos – *Lives*
Ctesias of Cnidus – *Persica*
Demosthenes – *Speeches*
Dicaearchus of Messana – *Life of Greece, Description of Greece*

BIBLIOGRAPHY

Dinarchus – *Speeches*

Dio Chrysostom – *Orations*

Diodorus Siculus – *Library of History*

Diogenes Laertius – *Lives of Eminent Philosophers*

Euripides – *Complete Plays*

Heracleides of Lembus – *Epitomes and Excerpts*

Julius Pollux – *Vocabulary*

Lucius Mestrius Plutarchus – *Moralia, Parallel Lives*

Lycurgus of Athens – *Against Leocrites*

Lysias – *Speeches*

Marcus Junianus Justinus Frontinus – *Epitome of Philippic Histories*

Marcus Tullius Cicero – *Tusculan Disputations*

Pausanias – *Description of Greece*

Philo of Byzantium – *Compendium of Mechanics*

Philodemus of Gadara – *On Music*

Photius I – *Lexicon*

Pindar – *Nemean Odes*

Plato – *Crito, Laws, Republic*

Polyaenus – *Strategems*

Polybius – *Histories*

Porphyry of Tyre – *Fragments*

Publius Flavius Vegetius Renatus – *Epitome of Military Science*

Quintus Curtius Rufus – *Histories of Alexander the Great*

Sophocles – *Complete Plays*

Soudas – *Suda*

Strabo – *Geography*

Terpander – *Fragments*

Theophrastus – *On Characters*

Thucydides – *History of the Peloponnesian War*

Titus Livius – *From the Founding of the City*

Tyrtaeus – *The Elegiac Poems*

Valerius Harpocration – *Lexicon of the Ten Orators*

Xenophanes of Colophon – *Fragments*

Xenophon – *Agesilaus, Anabasis, Constitution of the Spartans, Cyropaedia, Hellenica, On Horsemanship*

Modern Sources

I know I just recommended that you always consult ancient sources whenever you can, but that doesn't mean that you can afford to ignore modern ones. Modern scholars often have the benefit of years of full-time study of the ancient world, and their analysis can be based on expertise that a casual student lacks. You absolutely should consider modern scholarship on the ancient world, but I suggest that you always keep in mind that you are reading a modern person's *interpretation* of past events. No matter how expert a person is, they are fallible and prone to the biases, assumptions and omissions we all make. If you are armed with at least a cursory reading of the ancient sources, you will be on much better footing to make up your own mind about whether or not you agree with what modern historians say (including me!).

I am a big fan of historical fiction. Because it is fiction, it can often invoke a degree of drama and wonder that is tougher to tease out of a non-fiction work. But if reading modern non-fiction puts you at risk of accepting a modern scholar's misinformation, the risk in historical fiction is doubly so. That said, there are amazing authors out there writing meticulously researched historical fiction that will transport and educate you.

Here are some of the modern sources I consulted in writing this book.

Osprey books

D'Amato, Raffaele and Salimbeti, Andrea, *Early Iron Age Greek Warrior 1100–700 BC* (Warrior, 2016).

De Souza, Philip, *The Greek and Persian Wars 499–386 BC* (Essential Histories, 2003).

Campbell, Duncan B., *Spartan Warrior 735–331 BC* (Warrior, 2012).

Fields, Nic, *Syracuse 415–413 BC* (Campaign, 2008).

Fields, Nic, *Thermopylae 480 BC* (Campaign, 2007).

Sekunda, Nicholas, *Greek Hoplite 480—23 BC* (Warrior, 2000).

Sekunda, Nicholas, *The Spartan Army* (Elite, 1998).

Sekunda, Nicholas, *The Ancient Greeks* (Elite, 1986).

Shepherd, William, *The Persian War in Herodotus and Other Ancient Voices* (2019).

Shepherd, William, *Pylos and Sphacteria 425 BC* (Campaign, 2013).

Shepherd, William, *Plataea 479 BC* (Campaign, 2012).

Shepherd, William, *Salamis 480 BC* (Campaign, 2010).

Other modern books

Adams, Samuel, *Writings*.

Adkins, Lesley and Adkins, Roy A., *Handbook to Life in Ancient Greece*, Oxford University Press, Oxford (1997).

Alymer, John, *An Harborowe for Faithful and Trewe Subiectes*.

Anderson, J.K., *Military Theory and Practice in the Age of Xenophon*, University of California Press, Berkeley (1970).

Bardunias, Paul M. and Ray, Fred E., *Hoplites at War: A Comprehensive Analysis of Heavy Infantry Combat in the Greek World, 750–100 BCE*, McFarland, Jefferson (2016).

Bennett, Bob and Roberts, Mike, *The Spartan Supremacy 412–371 BC*, Pen & Sword, Barnsley (2014).

Bradford, Ernle, *Thermopylae: The Battle for the West*, Da Capo, Cambridge (1980).

Briant, Pierre, *From Cyrus to Alexander: A History of the Persian Empire*, Eisenbrauns, Winona Lake (2002).

Brouwers, Josho, *Henchmen of Ares: Warriors and Warfare in Early Greece*, Karwansaray, Rotterdam (2013).

Buck, Robert J., *Thrasybulus and the Athenian Democracy: The Life of an Athenian Statesman*, Franz Steiner Verlag, Stuttgart (1998).

Burliga, Bogdan and Sekunda, Nicholas (eds), *Iphicrates, Peltasts and Lechaeum*, Akanthina, Barnsley (2014).

Butera, Jacob C. and Sears, Matthew A., *Battles and Battlefields of Ancient Greece: A Guide to their History, Topography and Archaeology*, Pen & Sword, Barnsley (2019).

Campbell, David A., *Greek Lyric Poetry*, Bristol Classical Press, London (1991).

Cartledge, Paul, *Thermopylae: The Battle that Changed the World*, Overlook Press, Woodstock (2006).

Cartledge, Paul, *The Spartans: the World of the Warrior Heroes of Ancient Greece*, Vintage, New York (2003).

Cartledge, Paul, *Sparta and Lakonia: A Regional History*, Routledge, Abingdon-on-Thames (2002).

Cartledge, Paul, *Agesilaos and the Crisis of Sparta*, Johns Hopkins University Press, Baltimore (1987).

Cavanagh, William, et al., *Continuity and Change in a Greek Rural Landscape: The Laconia Survey (Supplementary Volume 26)*, The British School at Athens, Athens (2002).

Cawkwell, George, *The Greek Wars: The Failure of Persia*, Oxford University Press, Oxford (2005).

Clark, Jessica H., *Triumph in Defeat: Military Loss and the Roman Republic*, Oxford University Press, Oxford (2014).

Clark, Jessica H. and Turner, Brian (eds), *Brill's Companion to Military Defeat in Ancient Mediterranean Society*, Brill, Leiden (2018).

Doran, Timothy, *Spartan Oliganthropia*, Brill, Leiden (2018).

Ducat, Jean, *Spartan Education: Youth and Society in the Classical Period*, Classical Press of Wales, Swansea (2006).

Everitt, Anthony, *The Rise of Athens: The Story of the World's Greatest Civilization*, Random House, New York (2017).

Everson, Tim, *Warfare in Ancient Greece: Arms and Armour from the Heroes of Homer to Alexander the Great*, The History Press, Mount Pleasant (2005).

Fine, John V.A., *The Ancient Greeks: A Critical History*, Harvard University Press, Cambridge (1983).

Finley, M.I., *Economy and Society in Ancient Greece*, Chatto and Windus, London (1981).

Foulis, Andrew and Foulis, Robert (eds), *Spartan Lessons; or, The Praise of Valour: in the Verses of Tyrtaeus, an Ancient Athenian Poet, Adopted by the Republic of Lacedaemon, and Employed to Inspire Their Youth with Warlike Sentiments*, Glasgow (1759).

Grant, Michael, *The Rise of the Greeks*, Charles Scribner's Sons, New York (1988).

Green, Peter, *The Greco-Persian Wars*, University of California Press, Berkeley (1996).

Guimier-Sorbets, Anne-Marie and Morizot, Yvette (eds), *L'enfant et la mort dans l'Antiquité – le signalement des tombes d'enfants: Nouvelles recherches dans les nécropoles grecques*, Maison Archeo, France (2010).

Hamilton, Edith, *The Greek Way*, W.W. Norton, New York (1964).

Hammond, N.G.L., *A History of Greece to 322 BC*, Oxford University Press, New York (1986).

Hignett, Charles, *Xerxes' Invasion of Greece*, Clarendon Press, Oxford (1963).

Hodkinson, Stephen (ed.), *Sparta: Comparative Approaches*, Classical Press of Wales, Swansea (2010).

Hodkinson, Stephen, *Property and Wealth in Classical Sparta*, Classical Press of Wales, Swansea (2000).

Hodkinson, Stephen and Morries, Ian Macgregor (eds) *Sparta in Modern Thought*, Classical Press of Wales, Swansea (2010).

Hodkinson, Stephen and Powell, Anton (eds), *Sparta: The Body Politic*, Classical Press of Wales, Swansea (2009).

Hodkinson, Stephen and Powell, Anton (eds), *Sparta and War*, Classical Press of Wales, Swansea (2006).

Hodkinson, Stephen, and Powell, Anton (eds), *Sparta: New Perspectives*, Classical Press of Wales, Swansea (1999).

Holland, Tom, *Persian Fire – The First World Empire and the Battle for the West*, Anchor Books, New York (2005).

Hornblower, Simon and Spawforth, Anthony (eds), *The Oxford Classical Dictionary*, Oxford University Press, Oxford (2003).

Hunt, Peter, *Slaves, Warfare and Ideology in the Greek Historians*, Cambridge University Press, Cambridge (1998).

Hyland, John O., *Persian Interventions: The Achaemenid Empire, Athens & Sparta, 450–386 BCE*, Johns Hopkins University Press, Baltimore (2018).

Kagan, Donald and Viggiano, Gregory F., (eds), *Men of Bronze: Hoplite Warfare in Ancient Greece*, Princeton University Press, Princeton (2013).

Kennell, Nigel M., *Spartans: A New History*, Wiley-Blackwell, Chichester (2010).

Kennell, Nigel M., *The Gymnasium of Virtue: Education and Culture in Ancient Sparta*, University of North Carolina Press, Chapel Hill (2007).

Konijnendijk R.B., *Classical Greek Tactics: A Cultural History*, Brill, Leiden (2018).

Lacey, James, *The First Clash: The Miraculous Greek Victory at Marathon and its Impact on Western Civilization*, Bantam, New York (2013).

Lazenby, J.F., *The Spartan Army*, Pen & Sword, Barnsley (2012).

Lazenby, J.F., *The Peloponnesian War*, Routledge, Abingdon-on-Thames (2003).

Lazenby, J.F., *The Defence of Greece, 490–79 BC*, Liverpool University Press, Liverpool (1993).

Lee, John W.I., *A Greek Army on the March: Soldiers and Survival in Xenophon's Anabasis*, Cambridge University Press, Cambridge (2007).

Lewis, D.M., *Sparta and Persia: Lectures Delivered at the University of Cincinnati*, Brill, Leiden (1977).

Machiavelli, Niccolo, *Discourses on the First Decade of Titus Livius*

Matthew, Christopher, *An Invincible Beast: Understanding the Hellenistic Pike Phalanx in Action*, Pen & Sword, Barnsley (2015).

Matthew, Christopher, *A Storm of Spears: Understanding the Greek Hoplite at War*, Pen & Sword, Barnsley (2012).

Matthew, Christopher and Trundle, Matthew, *Beyond the Gates of Fire: New Perspectives on the Battle of Thermopylae*, Pen & Sword, Barnsley (2013).

Matyszak, Philip, *Sparta – Fall of a Warrior Nation*, Pen & Sword, Barnsley (2018).

Matyszak, Philip, *Sparta – Rise of a Warrior Nation*, Pen & Sword, Barnsley (2017).

Ollier, François, *Le mirage spartiate: étude sur l'idéalisation de Sparte dans l'antiquité grecque de l'origine jusqu'aux cyniques, et étude sur l'idéalisation de Sparte dans l'antiquité grecque du début de l'école cynique jusqu'à la fin de la cité*, Arno Press, New York (1973).

Olmstead, A.T., *History of the Persian Empire*, University of Chicago Press, Chicago (1948).

Pomeroy, Sarah. B., *Spartan Women*, Oxford University Press, Oxford (2002).

Powell, Anton (ed.), *A Companion to Sparta*, Wiley-Blackwell, Chichester (2017).

Pritchett, Kendrick W., *The Greek State at War* (Vols 1–5), University of California Press, Oakland (1975–91).

Rahe, Paul Anthony, *The Grand Strategy of Classical Sparta. The Persian Challenge*, Yale University Press, New Haven (2015).

Roberts, Jennifer T., *The Plague of War: Athens, Sparta, and the Struggle for Ancient Greece*, Oxford University Press, Oxford (2017).

Rees, Owen, *Great Battles of the Classical World*, Pen & Sword, Barnsley (2016).

Rusch, Scott M., *Sparta at War – Strategy, Tactics, and Campaigns, 550–362 BC*, Frontline, London (2014).

Ruzicka, Stephen, *Trouble in the West: Egypt and the Persian Empire, 525–332 BC*, Oxford University Press, Oxford (2012).

Sabin, Philip, *Lost Battles – Reconstructing the Great Clashes of the Ancient World*, Continuum, London (2007).

Schwartz, Adam, *Reinstating the Hoplite: Arms, Armour and Phalanx Fighting in Archaic and Classical Greece*, Franz Steiner Verlag, Stuttgart (2013).

Sears, Matthew A., *Understanding Greek Warfare*, Routledge, Abingdon-on-Thames (2019).

Simonton, Matthew, *Classical Greek Oligarchy: A Political History*, Princeton University Press, Princeton (2017).

Snodgrass, A.M., *Arms and Armour of the Greeks*, Cornell University Press, Ithaca (1967).

Strauss, Barry, *The Battle of Salamis: The Naval Encounter that Saved Greece – and Western Civilization*, Simon and Schuster, New York (2004).

Tigerstedt, Eugène Napoleon, *The Legend of Sparta in Classical Antiquity*, Almqvist & Wiksell, Stockholm (1965).

Van Wees, Hans, *Greek Warfare – Myths and Realities*, Bristol Classical Press, Bristol (2004).

Van Wees, Hans (ed.), *War and Violence in Ancient Greece*, Classical Press of Wales, Swansea (2000).

Warry, John, *Warfare in the Classical World*, Barnes & Noble, New York (1998).

Weil, Henri, *Études sur l'antiquité grecque*, Hachette, Paris (1900).

West, M.L., *Greek Lyric Poetry*, Oxford University Press, Oxford (2008).

Wrightson, Graham, *Combined Arms Warfare in Ancient Greece: From Homer to Alexander the Great and his Successors*, Routledge, Abingdon-on-Thames (2019).

Modern periodicals

Adkins, A.W.H., "Callinus 1 and Tyrtaeus 10 as Poetry" in *Harvard Studies in Classical Philology* 81 (1977), pp. 59–97.

Africa, Thomas W., "Cleomenes III and the Helots" in *California Studies in Classical Antiquity* 1 (1968), pp. 1–11.

Alcock, Susan E., "The Pseudo-History of Messenia Unplugged" in *Transactions of the American Philological Association* 129 (1999), pp. 333–41.

Andrewes, A., "Two Notes on Lysander" in *Phoenix* 25-3 (1971), pp. 206–26.

Andrewes, A., "Ephoros Book I and the Kings of Argos" in *The Classical Quarterly* 1-1/2 (1951), pp. 39–45.

Burrows, Ronald M., "Pylos and Sphacteria. A Reply to Mr. Grundy" in *The Classical Review* 11-1 (1897), pp. 1–10.

Busolt, Georg, "Spartas Heer Und Leuktra" in *Hermes* 40-3 (1905), pp. 387–449.

Campbell, Duncan B., "Maneuvers at Mantineia: How was the Spartan Army Organized?" in *Ancient Warfare* VI-2 (2012), pp. 47–52.

Cary, M., "The Alleged Achaean Arbitration after Leuctra" in *The Classical Quarterly* 19-3 (1925), pp. 165–166.

Cary, M., "Notes on the Ἀριστεία of Thebes" in *The Journal of Hellenic Studies* 42 (1922), pp. 184–191.

Chambers, James T., "On Messenian and Laconian Helots in the Fifth Century B.C." in *The Historian* 40-2 (1978), pp. 271–285.

Catling, H.W., "The Work of the British School at Athens at Sparta and in Laconia" in *British School at Athens Studies* 4 (1998), pp. 19–27.

Cawkwell, G.L., "Orthodoxy and Hoplites" in *The Classical Quarterly* 39-2 (1989), pp. 375–389.

Cawkwell, G.L., "The Decline of Sparta" in *The Classical Quarterly* 33-2 (1983), pp. 385–400.

Cawkwell, G.L., "Agesilaus and Sparta" in *The Classical Quarterly* 26-1 (1976), pp. 62–84.

Cawkwell, G.L., "Epaminondas and Thebes" in *The Classical Quarterly* 22-2 (1972), pp. 254–278.

Charles, Michael B., "Immortals and Apple Bearers: Towards a Better Understanding of Achaemenid Infantry Units" in *The Classical Quarterly* 61-1 (2011), pp. 114–133.

Christesen, Paul, "Xenophon's 'Cyropaedia' and Military Reform in Sparta" in *The Journal of Hellenic Studies* 126 (2006), pp. 47–65.

Comfort, H., "The Date of Pausanias, Book II" in *American Journal of Archaeology* 35-3 (1931), pp. 310–318.

Crump, M. Marjorie, "Vergil and the Messeniaca of Rhianus" in *The Classical Review* 35-7 (1921), p. 157.

David, Ephraim, "Aristotle and Sparta" in *Ancient Society* 13-14 (1982), pp. 67–103.

Decety, Nathan, "When Valor isn't Always Superior to Numbers: Homoioi Oliganthrôpia Caused by Attrition in Incessant Warfare" in *Klio* 100-3 (2018), pp. 626–666.

Den Boer, W., "Political Propaganda in Greek Chronology" in *Historia: Zeitschrift Für Alte Geschichte* 5-2 (1956), pp. 162–177.

Dezső, Tamás and Vér, Ádám, "Assyrians and Greeks: the Nature of Contacts in the 9th–7th Centuries BC" in *Acta Antiqua Academiae Scientiarum Hungaricae* 53 (2013), pp. 325–359.

Dillery, John, "Reconfiguring the Past: Thyrea, Thermopylae and Narrative Patterns in Herodotus" in *The American Journal of Philology* 117-2 (1996), pp. 217–254.

Dillon, Matthew P.J., "The Lakedaimonian Dedication to Olympian Zeus: The Date of 'Meiggs & Lewis' 22 ('SEG' 11, 1203a)" in *Zeitschrift Für Papyrologie Und Epigraphik* 107 (1995), pp. 60–68.

Echeverría, Fernando, "Hoplite and Phalanx in Archaic and Classical Greece: A Reassessment" in *Classical Philology* 107-4 (2012), pp. 291–318.

Evans, J.A.S., "Tyrtaios, Frag. 8, 1–2" in *Glotta* 40-3/4 (1962), pp. 182–83.

Falkner, Caroline, "Sparta and Lepreon in the Archidamian War (Thuc. 5.31.2-5)" in *Historia: Zeitschrift Für Alte Geschichte* 48-4 (1999), pp. 385–394.

Ferejohn, John and McCall Rosenbluth, Frances, "Warlike Democracies" in *The Journal of Conflict Resolution* 52-1 (2008), pp. 3–38.

Figueira, Thomas J., "Xenelasia and Social Control in Classical Sparta" in *The Classical Quarterly* 53-1 (2003), pp. 44–74.

Figueira, Thomas J., "Population Patterns in Late Archaic and Classical Sparta" in *Transactions of the American Philological Association* 116 (1986), pp. 165–213.

Flower, Michael A., "Simonides, Ephorus, and Herodotus on the Battle of Thermopylae" in *The Classical Quarterly* 48-2 (1998), pp. 365–379.

Forrest, W.G., "The Date of the Lykourgan Reforms in Sparta" in *Phoenix* 17-3 (1963), pp. 157–179.

Fraser, A.D., "The Myth of the Phalanx-Scrimmage" in *The Classical Weekly* 36-2 (1942), pp. 15–16.

Fraser, A.D., "Xenophon and the Boeotian Helmet" in *The Art Bulletin* 4-3 (1922), pp. 99–108.

Gercke, A., "Der Neue Tyrtaios" in *Hermes* 56-4 (1921), pp. 346–354.

Goldsworthy, A.K., "The 'Othismos', Myths and Heresies: The Nature of Hoplite Battle" in *War in History* 4-1 (1997), pp. 1–26.

Hamilton, Charles D., "From Archidamus to Alexander: The Revolution in Greek Warfare" in *Naval War College Review* 48-1 (1995), pp. 84–95.

Hammond, N.G.L., "The Lycurgean Reform at Sparta" in *Journal of Hellenic Studies* 70 (1950), pp. 42–64.

Hanson, Victor, "Epameinondas, the Battle of Leuktra (371 B.C.), and the 'Revolution' in Greek Battle Tactics" in *Classical Antiquity* 7-2 (1988), pp. 190–207.

Hilton, John, "War and Peace in the Ancient Greek Novel" in *Acta Classica* 48 (2005), pp. 57–85.

Hindley, Clifford, "Eros and Military Command in Xenophon" in *The Classical Quarterly* 44-2 (1994), pp. 347–366.

Hinze, Kurt, "Zwei Heimatberaubte Spartanische Dichter" in *Rheinisches Museum Für Philologie* 83-1 (1934), pp. 39–52.

Hodkinson, Stephen, "Une cité pas comme les autres?" in *L'Histoire* 446 (2018), pp. 42–47.

Hodkinson, Stephen, "Patterns of Bronze Dedications at Spartan Sanctuaries, c. 650–350 BC: towards a Quantified Database of Material and Religious Investment" in *British School at Athens Studies* 4 (1998), pp. 55–63.

Hodkinson, Stephen, "Land Tenure and Inheritance in Classical Sparta" in *The Classical Quarterly* 36-2 (1986), pp. 378–406.

Holladay, A.J., "Hoplites and Heresies" in *The Journal of Hellenic Studies* 102 (1982), pp. 94–103.

Hopper, R.J., "A Note on Aristophanes, Lysistrata 665-70" in *The Classical Quarterly* 10-2 (1960), pp. 242–247

Hornblower, Simon, "When Was Megalopolis Founded?" in *The Annual of the British School at Athens* 85 (1990), pp. 71–77.

Hunt, Peter, "Helots at the Battle of Plataea" in *Historia: Zeitschrift Für Alte Geschichte* 46-2 (1997), pp. 129–44.

Huys, Marc, "The Spartan Practice of Selective Infanticide and its Parallels in Ancient Utopian Tradition" in *Ancient Society* 27 (1996), pp. 47–74.

Jacoby, F, "Studien Zu Den Älteren Griechischen Elegikern. I. Zu Tyrtaios" in *Hermes* 53-1 (1918), pp. 1–44.

Jeffery, L.H. and Cartledge, Paul, "Sparta and Samos: A Special Relationship?" in *The Classical Quarterly* 32-2 (1982), pp. 243–265.

Jones, Nicholas, "The Topography and Strategy of the Battle of Amphipolis in 422 B.C" in *California Studies in Classical Antiquity* 10 (1977), pp. 71–104.

Jordan, Borimir, "The Honors for Themistocles after Salamis" in *The American Journal of Philology* 109-4 (1988), pp. 547–571.

Kelly, Amanda, "The Cretan Slinger at War – A Weighty Exchange" in *The Annual of the British School at Athens* 107 (2012), pp. 273–311.

Kelly, D.H., "Thucydides and Herodotus on the Pitanate Lochos" in *Greek, Roman, and Byzantine Studies* 22 (1981), pp. 31–38.

Kelly, Thomas, "The Argive Destruction of Asine" in *Historia: Zeitschrift Für Alte Geschichte* 16-4 (1967), pp. 422–31.

Kõiv, Mait, "The Origins, Development, and Reliability of the Ancient Tradition about the Formation of the Spartan Constitution" in *Historia: Zeitschrift Für Alte Geschichte* 54-3 (2005), pp. 233–264.

Knottnerus, J. David and Berry, Phyllis E., "Spartan Society: Structural Ritualization in an Ancient Social System" in *Humboldt Journal of Social Relations* 27-1 (2002), pp. 1–41.

Konijnendijk R.B., "Mardonius' Senseless Greeks" in *Classical Quarterly* 66 (2016), pp. 1–12.

Konijnendijk, R.B., "Neither the Less Valorous nor the Weaker: Persian Military Might and the Battle of Plataia" in *Historia* 61 (2012), pp. 1–17.

Koursoumis, Socrates, "Revisiting Mount Taygetos: The Sanctuary of Artemis Limnatis" in *The Annual of the British School at Athens* 109 (2014), pp. 191–222.

Krentz, Peter, "Marathon and the Development of the Exclusive Hoplite Phalanx" in *Bulletin of the Institute of Classical Studies*, Supplement 124 (2013), pp. 35–44.

Lazenby, J.F., "The Archaia Moira: A Suggestion" in *The Classical Quarterly* 45-1 (1995), pp. 87–91.

Lazenby, J.F., "Logistics in Classical Greek Warfare" in *War in History* 1-1 (1994), pp. 3–18.

Lazenby, J.F., "The Diekplous" in *Greece & Rome* 34-2 (1987), pp. 169–177.

Lorimer, H.L., "The Hoplite Phalanx with Special Reference to the Poems of Archilochus and Tyrtaeus" in *The Annual of the British School at Athens* 42 (1947), pp. 76–138.

Luginbill, Robert D., "The Battle of Oinoe, the Painting in the Stoa Poikile, and Thucydides' Silence" in *Historia: Zeitschrift Für Alte Geschichte* 63-3 (2014), pp. 278–292.

Luginbill, Robert D., "Othismos: The Importance of the Mass-Shove in Hoplite Warfare" in *Phoenix* 48-1 (1994), pp. 51–61.

Luraghi, Nino, "Becoming Messenian" in *The Journal of Hellenic Studies* 122 (2002), pp. 45–69.

Macan, Reginald W., "A Note of the Date of Tyrtaeus, and the Messenian War" in *The Classical Review* 11-1 (1897), pp. 10–12.

Markle, Minor M., "A Shield Monument from Veria and the Chronology of Macedonian Shield Types." In *Hesperia: The Journal of the American School of Classical Studies at Athens*, 68-2, (1999), pp. 219–254.

Matthew, Christopher A, "When Push Comes to Shove: What Was the 'Othismos' of Hoplite Combat?" in *Historia: Zeitschrift Für Alte Geschichte* 58-4 (2009), pp. 395–415.

Michell, H., "The Iron Money of Sparta" in *Phoenix* 1 (1947), pp. 42–44.

Millender, Ellen G., "Spartan Literacy Revisited" in *Classical Antiquity* 20-1 (2001), pp. 121–164.

Moles, J.L., "Xenophon and Callicratidas" in *The Journal of Hellenic Studies* 114 (1994), pp. 70–84.

Morgan, J.D. "Sellasia Revisited" in *American Journal of Archaeology*, 85-3 (1981), pp. 328–330.

Nielsen, Thomas Heine, "A Note on 'The Hellenic League Against Persia' and the Sanctuary of Zeus at Nemea" in *Classica et mediaevalia* 58 (2007), pp. 165–178.

Parker, V., "The Dates of the Messenian Wars" in *Chiron* 21 (1991), pp. 25–47.

Pearson, Lionel, "The Pseudo-History of Messenia and its Authors" in *Historia: Zeitschrift Für Alte Geschichte* 11-4 (1962), pp. 397–426.

Piper, L.J., "Spartan Helots in the Hellenistic Age" in *Ancient Society* 15-17 (1984), pp. 75–88.

Pomeroy, Sarah B., "Spartan Women among the Romans: Adapting Models, Forging Identities" in *Memoirs of the American Academy in Rome* Supplementary Volume 7 (2008), pp. 221–234.

Pownall, Frances Skoczylas, "Condemnation of the Impious in Xenophon's 'Hellenica'" in *The Harvard Theological Review* 91-3 (1998), pp. 251–277.

Rey, Fernando Echeverría, "'Taktikè Technè' – The Neglected Element in Classical 'Hoplite' Battles" in *Ancient Society* 41 (2011), pp. 45–82.

Rhodes, P.J., "Thucydides on Pausanias and Themistocles" in *Historia: Zeitschrift für Alte Geschichte* 19-4 (1970), pp. 387–400.

Rop, Jeffrey, "The Phocian Betrayal at Thermopylae" in *Historia: Zeitschrift für Alte Geschichte* 68 (2019), pp. 413–435.

Rop, Jeffrey, "The Outbreak of the Rebellion of Cyrus the Younger" in *Greek, Roman, and Byzantine Studies* 59 (2019), pp. 57–85.

Rop, Jeffrey, "The Historical Context of the Reply to the Satraps Inscription (IG IV 556)" in *Journal of Ancient History* 5 (2017), pp. 304–322.

Rop, Jeffrey, "Reconsidering the Origin of the Scythed Chariot" in *Historia: Zeitschrift für Alte Geschichte* 62 (2013), pp. 167–181.

Rubincam, Catherine, "The Topography of Pylos and Sphakteria and Thucydides' Measurements of Distance" in *The Journal of Hellenic Studies* 121 (2001), pp. 77–90.

Salapata, Gina, "Laconian and Messenian Plaques with Seated Figures: The Socio-Political Dimension" in *The Annual of the British School at Athens* 108 (2013), pp. 187–200.

Sansone, David, "Agesilaus and the Case of the Lame Dancer" in *Illinois Classical Studies* 37 (2012), pp. 75–96.

Schmitz, Winfried, "Sklavenaufseher Der Heloten?" in *Historia: Zeitschrift Für Alte Geschichte* 63-3 (2014), pp. 293–300.

Schwinge, Ernst-Richard, "Tyrtaios Über Seine Dichtung (Fr. 9 G.-P. = 12 W)" in *Hermes* 125-4 (1997), pp. 387–395.

Scott, Andrew G., "Plural Marriage And The Spartan State" in *Historia: Zeitschrift Für Alte Geschichte* 60-4 (2011), pp. 413–424.

Shero, L.R., "Aristomenes the Messenian" in *Transactions and Proceedings of the American Philological Association* 69 (1938), pp. 500–531.

Shimron, B., "The Spartan Polity after the Defeat of Cleomenes III" in *The Classical Quarterly* 14-2 (1964), pp. 232–239.

Shipley, Graham, "Sparta and Its Perioikic Neighbours: a Century of Reassessment" in *Hermathena* 181 (2006), pp. 51–82.

Shipley, Graham, "The Extent of Spartan Territory in the Late Classical and Hellenistic Periods" in *The Annual of the British School at Athens* 95 (2000), pp. 367–390.

Talbert, Richard J.A., "The Role of the Helots in the Class Struggle at Sparta" in *Historia: Zeitschrift Für Alte Geschichte* 38-1 (1989), pp. 22–40.

Thommen, Lukas, "Spartas Umgang mit der Vergangenheit" in *Historia: Zeitschrift Für Alte Geschichte* 49-1 (2000), pp. 40–53.

Thommen, Lukas, "Spartanische Frauen," in *Museum Helveticum* 56-3 (1999), pp. 129–149.

Tober, Daniel, "'Politeiai' and Spartan Local History" in *Historia: Zeitschrift Für Alte Geschichte* 59-4 (2010), pp. 412–431.

Toher, Mark, "On The Ειδωλον Of A Spartan King" in *Rheinisches Museum Für Philologie* 142-2 (1999), pp. 113–127.

Toynbee, Arnold J., "The Growth of Sparta" in *The Journal of Hellenic Studies* 33 (1913), pp. 246–275.

Trego, Kristine M., "Agesilaus the Puppet? The Effects of Thematic Development on Plutarch's Story of the Accession" in *Illinois Classical Studies* 39 (2014), pp. 39–62.

Treu, Max, "Der Schlussatz Der Grossen Rhetra" in *Hermes* 76-1 (1941), pp. 22–42.

Von Blumenthal, Albrecht, "Zur 'Lykurgischen' Rhetra" in *Hermes* 77-2 (1942), pp. 212–215.

Wade-Gery, H.T., "The Spartan Rhetra in Plutarch, Lycurgus VI: C. What Is the Rhetra?" In *The Classical Quarterly* 38-3/4 (1944), pp. 115–126.

Wade-Gery, H.T., "The Spartan Rhetra in Plutarch Lycurgus VI: B. The Eynomia of Tyrtaios" in *The Classical Quarterly* 38-1/2 (1944), pp. 1–9.

Walbank, F. W., "Antigonus Doson's Attack on Cytinium (REG 101 (1988), 12-53)" in *Zeitschrift Für Papyrologie Und Epigraphik* 76 (1989), pp. 184–192.

Wallace, Paul W., "The Anopaia Path at Thermopylai" in *American Journal of Archaeology* 84-1 (1980), pp. 15–23.

Wallace, Shane, "Defending the Freedom of the Greeks: Antigonos, Telesphoros, and the Olympic Games of 312 B.C." in *Phoenix*, 68-3/4 (2014), pp. 235–246.

Waters, Matthew W., "Earth, Water, and Friendship with the King: Argos and Persia in the Mid-fifth Century" in *Studies in Ancient Oriental Civilization* 68 (2014), pp. 347–352.

West, William C., "The Trophies of the Persian Wars" in *Classical Philology* 64-1 (1969), pp. 7–19.

Williams, Mary Frances, "Philopoemen's Special Forces: Peltasts and a New Kind of Greek Light-Armed Warfare (Livy 35.27)" in *Historia: Zeitschrift Für Alte Geschichte* 53-3 (2004), pp. 257–277.

Wylie, Graham, "Lysander and the Devil" in *L'Antiquité Classique* 66 (1997), pp. 75–88.

Yates, David C., "The Archaic Treaties between the Spartans and Their Allies" in *The Classical Quarterly* 55-1 (2005), pp. 65–76.

INDEX

References to maps are in **bold**.

INDEX